THE WAY FORWARD

From Early Republic to People's Republic (1912 – 1949)

Jing Liu

UNDERSTANDING

CHINA

THROUGH COMICS

VOLUME 5

A GRAPHIC NOVEL HISTORY FROM STONE BRIDGE PRESS

Berkeley CA

Published by
STONE BRIDGE PRESS
P.O. Box 8208 • Berkeley, California 94707
TEL 510-524-8732 • sbp@stonebridge.com • www.stonebridge.com

Text and illustrations © Jing Liu.

First edition, 2022.

Book layout based on a design by Linda Ronan.

Printed in the United States of America.

LIBRARY OF CONGRESS CATALOGING-IN-PUBLICATION DATA
Names: Liu, Jing (Author of graphic novels), author, illustrator.
Title: Foundations of Chinese civilization / Jing Liu.
Description: First edition. | Berkeley : Stone Bridge Press, 2016. | Series: Understanding China through comics | Includes bibliographical references and index.
Identifiers: LCCN 2016009755 (print) | LCCN 2016012382 (ebook) | ISBN 9781611720273 (alk. paper) | ISBN 9781611729184 (ebook)
Subjects: LCSH: China—History—Comic books, strips, etc. | Graphic novels.
Classification: LCC DS735 .L576 2016 (print) | LCC DS735 (ebook) | DDC 931—dc23
LC record available at http://lccn.loc.gov/2016009755

p-ISBN 978-1-61172-070-9
e-ISBN 978-1-61172-952-8

CONTENTS

TIMELINE

1911 —— Chinese Revolution breaks out in Wuchang
Sun Zhongshan serves as provisional president of Republic of China

1912 —— Qing dynasty falls
Yuan Shikai becomes president of the Republic

1913 —— Parliament clashes with Yuan Shikai over reorganization loans
Yuan dissolves Parliament

1914 —— World War I begins
Japan seizes Shandong and issues Twenty-one Demands

1915 —— Yuan restores the monarchy but dies six months later

1916 —— Warlord Era begins

1917 —— Former Beiyang generals fight over control of Beijing
China joins World War I on the side of the Allied powers

1918 —— Sun Zhongshan forms military government in Guangzhou
WWI ends
1918 Flu Pandemic spreads

1919 —— Treaty of Versailles awards Shandong to Japan
May Fourth Movement begins

1921 —— Comintern aids formation of Chinese Communist Party
Mao Zedong attends first Communist National Congress

1923 —— Soviet Union aids Nationalist Party led by Sun Zhongshan

1924 —— Sun tasks Chiang Kai-shek with forming Huangpu Military Academy

1925 —— Sun Zhongshan dies

1926 —— Chiang Kai-shek consolidates his power and launches Northern
Expedition

1927 —— Nationalist Party splits
Chiang purges Communists

1928 —— Chiang reunifies China under Nationalist government in Nanjing

1929 —— Chiang's military reduction plan leads to Central Plains War
Great Depression begins

1930 —— Chiang directs encirclement campaigns against Communists

Year	Event
1931	Mao Zedong establishes Chinese Soviet Republic in Jiangxi Japan invades northeast China
1932	Chinese and Japanese troops clash in Shanghai
1933	Japanese expansion in north China leads to battle at Great Wall Nationalist army encircles Communists with blockhouses
1934	Communists begin Long March
1936	Communist survivors settle in Yan'an After Xi'an incident, Chiang Kai-shek is forced to agree to a United Front with Communists against Japan
1937	Second Sino-Japanese War enters full swing
1938	Chiang orders breach of Yellow River dikes at Huayuankou to slow down Japanese advance
1939	World War II begins
1940	Japan takes northern French Indochina
1941	United States extends Lend-Lease program to China and stops oil exports to Japan Japan attacks Pearl Harbor
1942	Japan cuts last land connection to China for Lend-Lease supplies Joseph Stilwell comes to China as Chief of Staff to Chiang Kai-shek
1943	Allies hold summits in Cairo and Tehran to coordinate the war effort
1944	Operation Ichigo, Japan's largest offensive, inflicts heavy casualties on Nationalists Tension between Stilwell and Chiang leads to Stilwell's recall
1945	WWII ends with defeat of both Germany and Japan Mao Zedong and Chiang Kai-shek hold peace talks in Chongqing
1946	George Marshall joins talks between Communists and Nationalists
1946	George Marshall comes to China to join negotiations between Communists and Nationalists
1947	Marshall returns to United States after negotiations fail Chinese civil war breaks out
1949	Nationalists under Chiang Kai-shek lose civil war and flee to Taiwan Mao Zedong declares establishment of People's Republic of China

INTRODUCTION

Today, China has the largest population and the second-largest economy on earth. Anyone who wants to understand current world history must study, among other things, the story of this rising power.

It was not always so. In the early twentieth century, China was still a poor agrarian society ruled by a dynasty that had been in power since 1644. Its lack of development allowed invasion on all sides by colonial powers. How, then, did China nationalize and move forward to its current position so quickly? The key lies in the period covered in this book.

Jing Liu's fifth volume on Chinese history helps us to understand modern China by simplifying, as much as can be done, the extremely complex developments that occurred in China between 1912, when it declared itself a republic, and October 1949, when Mao Zedong established the People's Republic of China. During this period, China experienced World Wars I and II and the Great Depression together with the rest of the world. But China also experienced these major events along with a civil war between Nationalists and Communists, with repeated Japanese invasions, and with support from an ever-changing set of allies.

This book is a page-turner, made of dramatic stories only matched by its sweeping art. The actions of various nations weave together in such tangled ways that one can only wonder how things might be different today if alliances or events had evolved differently at any number of pivotal points. But such is the mystery of history. We will never know.

If your prior vantage point is Western, reading this book will open your eyes to new versions of the twentieth century seen through a Chinese lens. If you want to know more, I suggest you also read the author's earlier four histories, which demonstrate how forces of unity vs. chaos have dominated China for 5,000 years, creating a very specific cultural perspective. Luckily for the reader, Liu transforms complicated histories into pleasurable discourse through clever cartoons, graphs, maps, and charts. I hope you enjoy this book as much as I did.

Lorie Hammond, Ph D
Professor Emerita, CSU Sacramento
Founding Director, Peregrine School,
Davis, California

Previously in
Understanding China through Comics

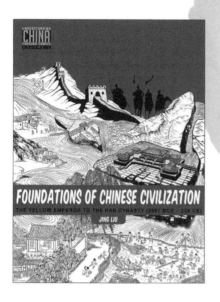

UNDERSTANDING CHINA THROUGH COMICS
FOUNDATIONS OF CHINESE CIVILIZATION
THE YELLOW EMPEROR TO THE HAN DYNASTY (2697 BCE – 220 CE)
JING LIU

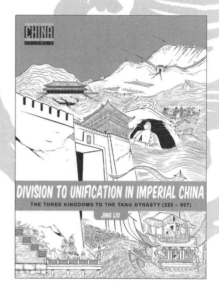

UNDERSTANDING CHINA
DIVISION TO UNIFICATION IN IMPERIAL CHINA
THE THREE KINGDOMS TO THE TANG DYNASTY (220 – 907)
JING LIU

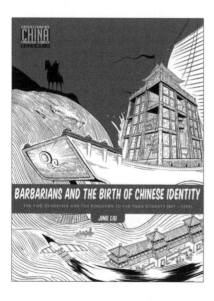

UNDERSTANDING CHINA THROUGH COMICS
BARBARIANS AND THE BIRTH OF CHINESE IDENTITY
JING LIU

UNDERSTANDING CHINA THROUGH COMICS
THE MAKING OF MODERN CHINA
THE MING DYNASTY TO THE QING DYNASTY
JING LIU

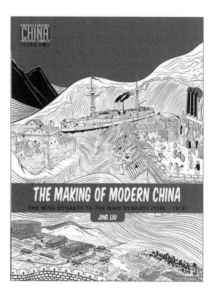

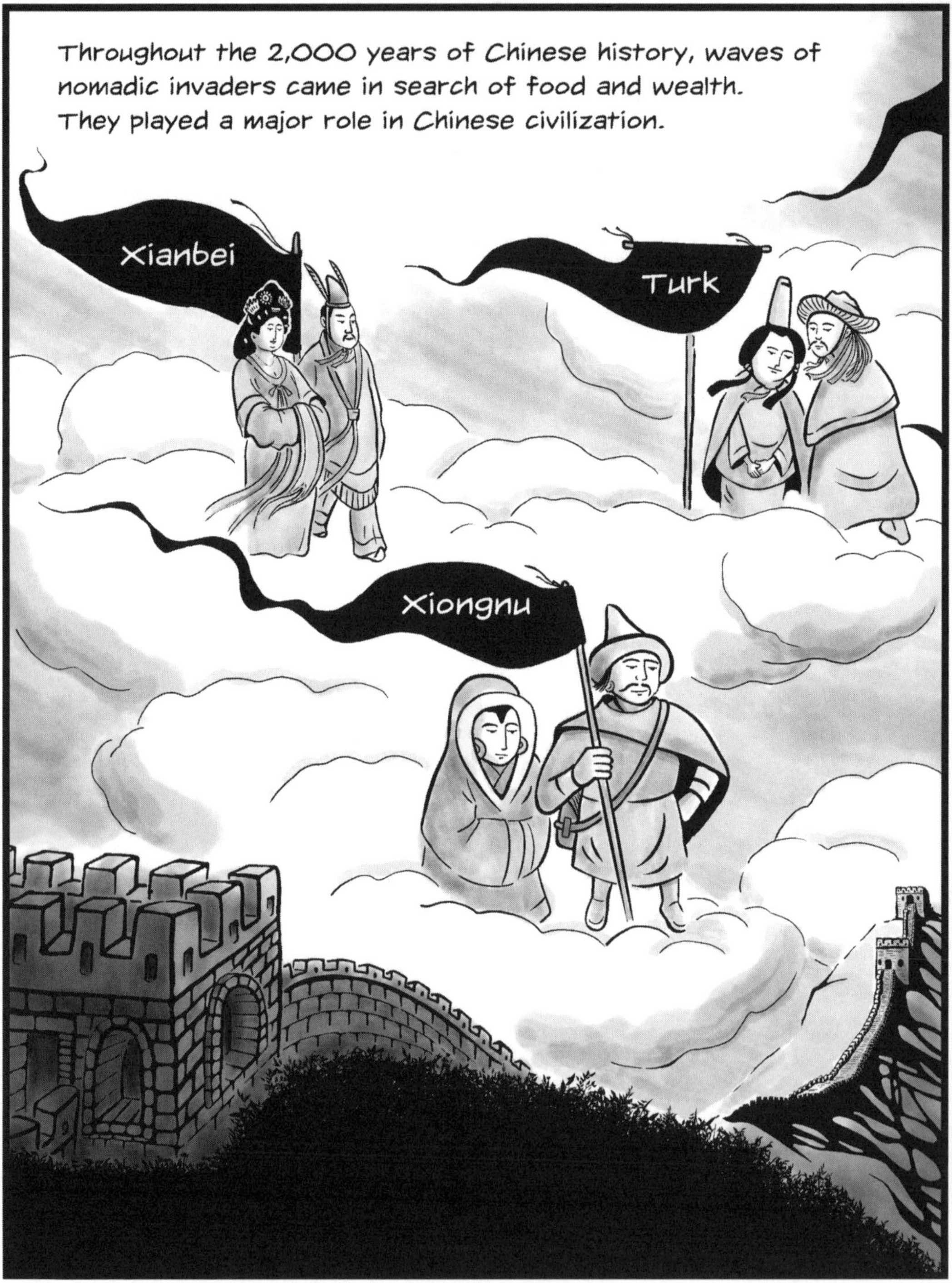
Throughout the 2,000 years of Chinese history, waves of nomadic invaders came in search of food and wealth. They played a major role in Chinese civilization.
Xianbei
Turk
Xiongnu

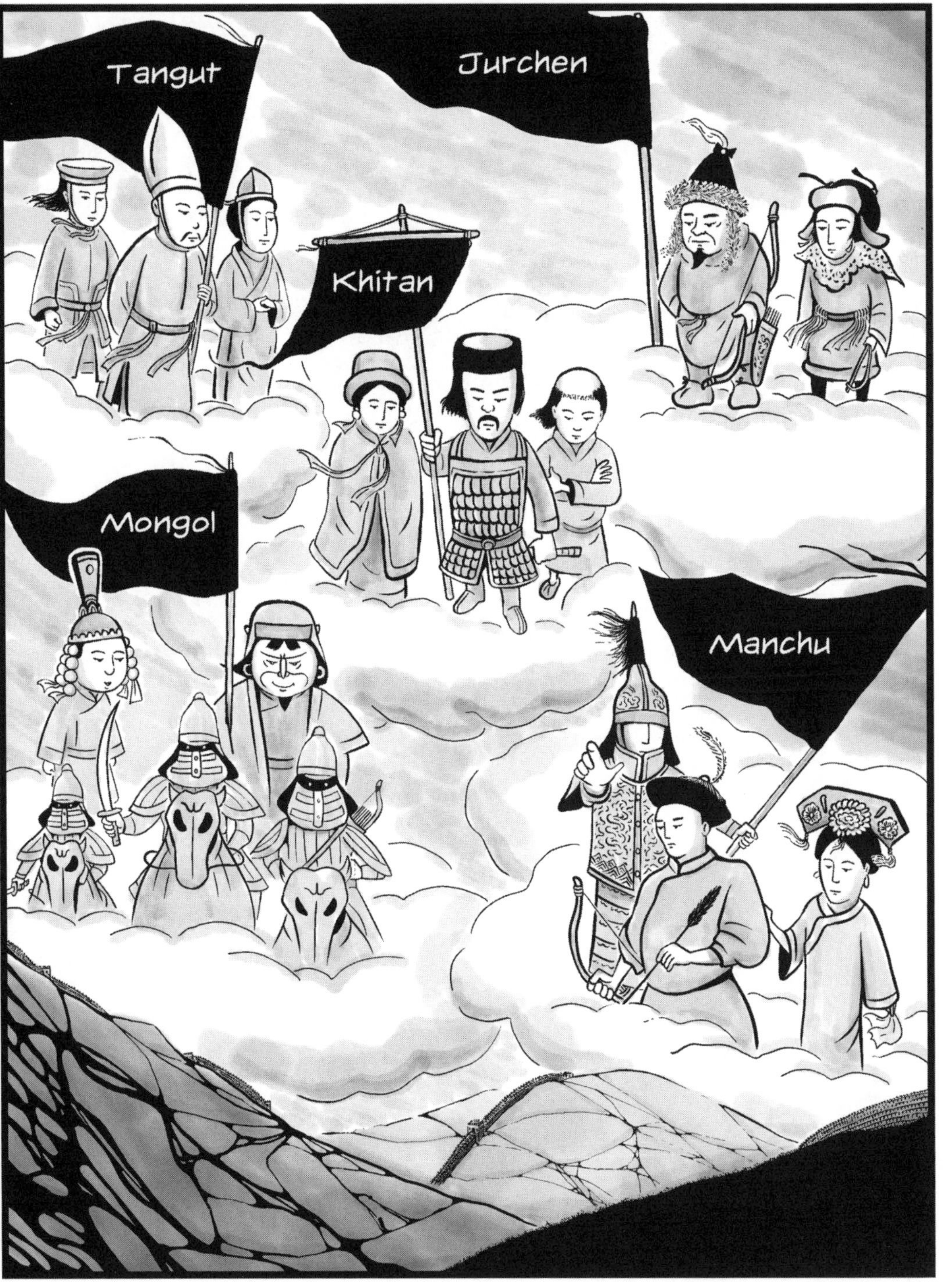
Tangut
Jurchen
Khitan
Mongol
Manchu

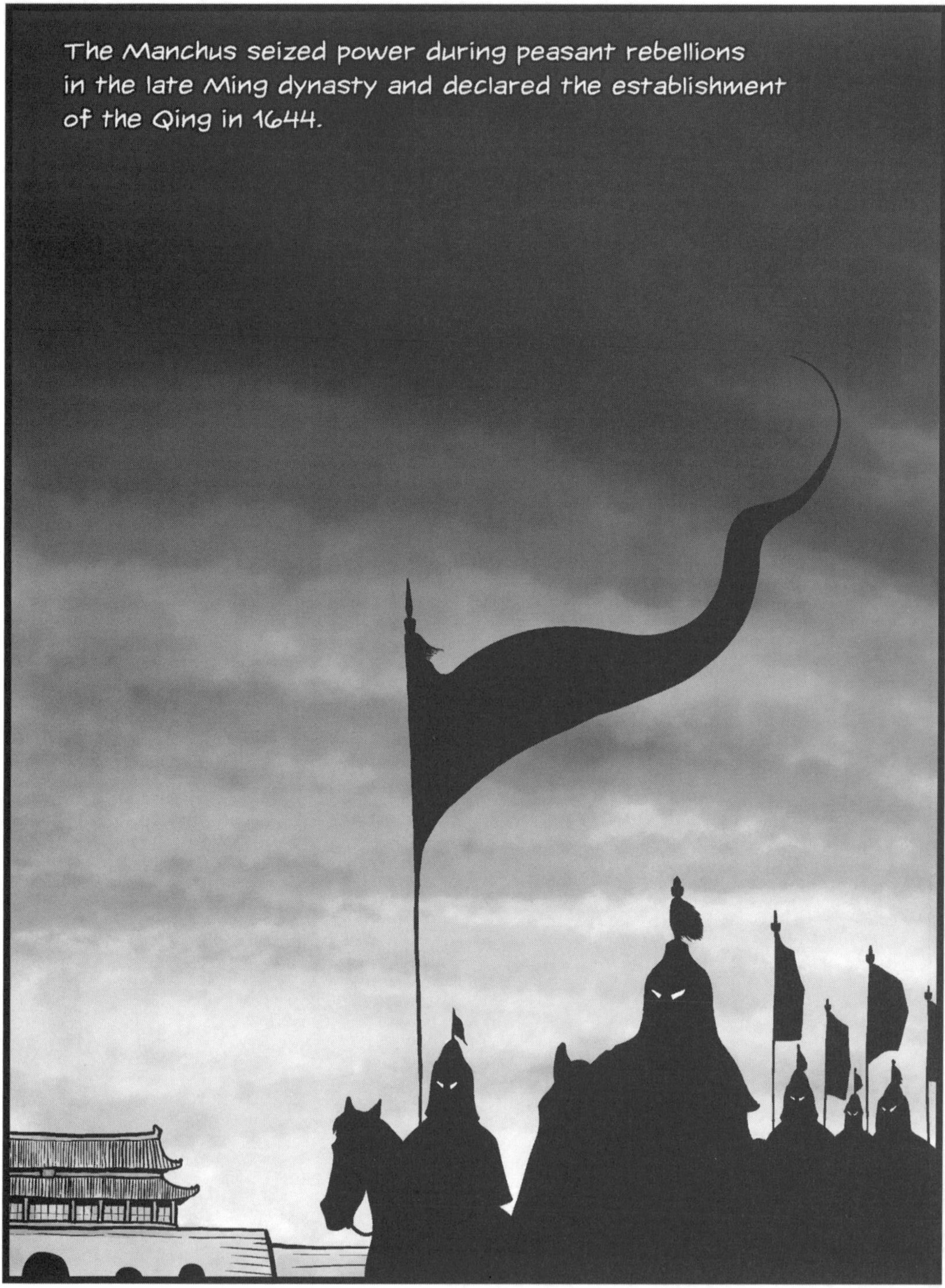
The Manchus seized power during peasant rebellions in the late Ming dynasty and declared the establishment of the Qing in 1644.

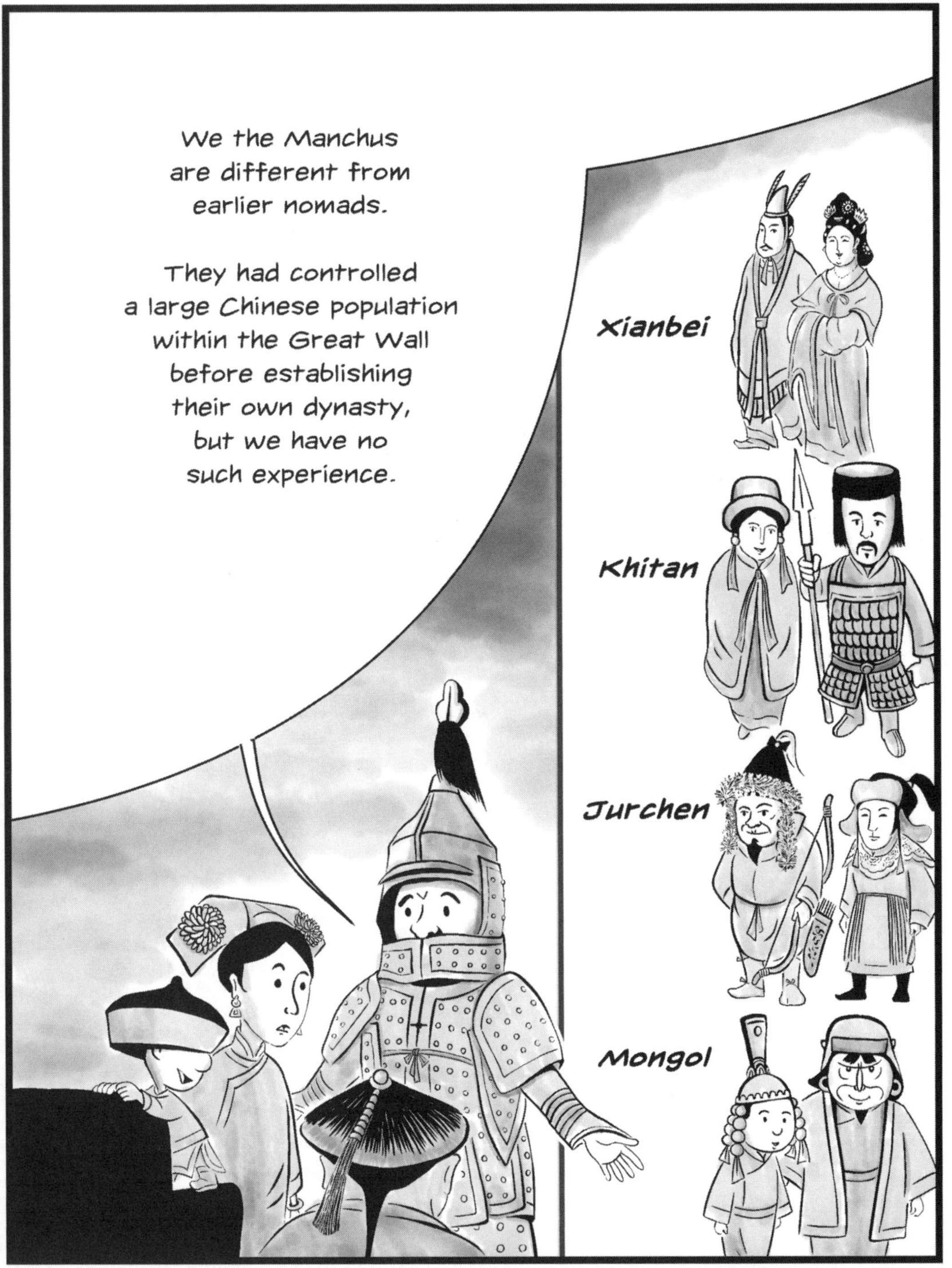
We the Manchus are different from earlier nomads.

They had controlled a large Chinese population within the Great Wall before establishing their own dynasty, but we have no such experience.
Xianbei
Khitan
Jurchen
Mongol

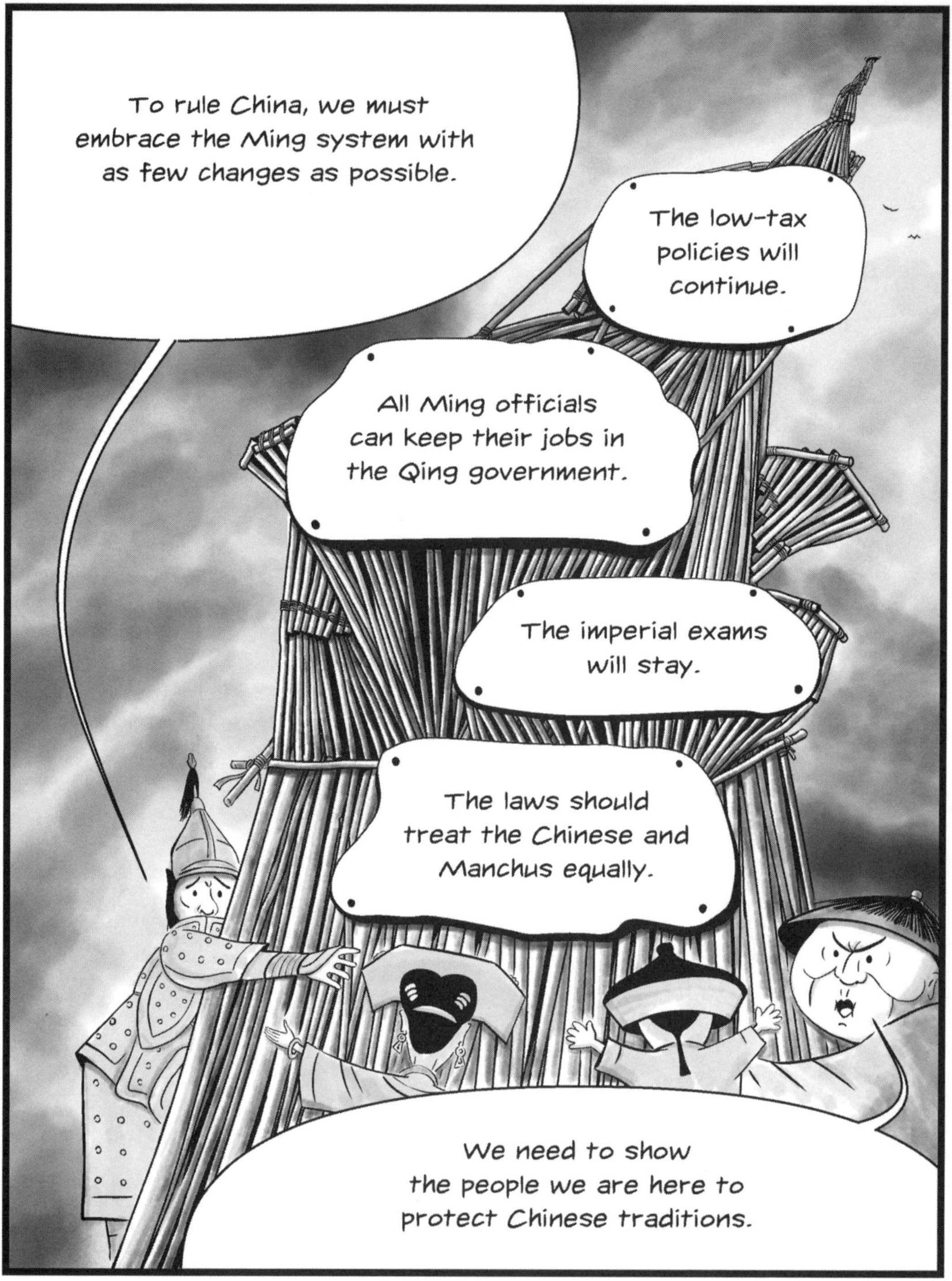
To rule China, we must embrace the Ming system with as few changes as possible.
The low-tax policies will continue.
All Ming officials can keep their jobs in the Qing government.
The imperial exams will stay.
The laws should treat the Chinese and Manchus equally.
We need to show the people we are here to protect Chinese traditions.

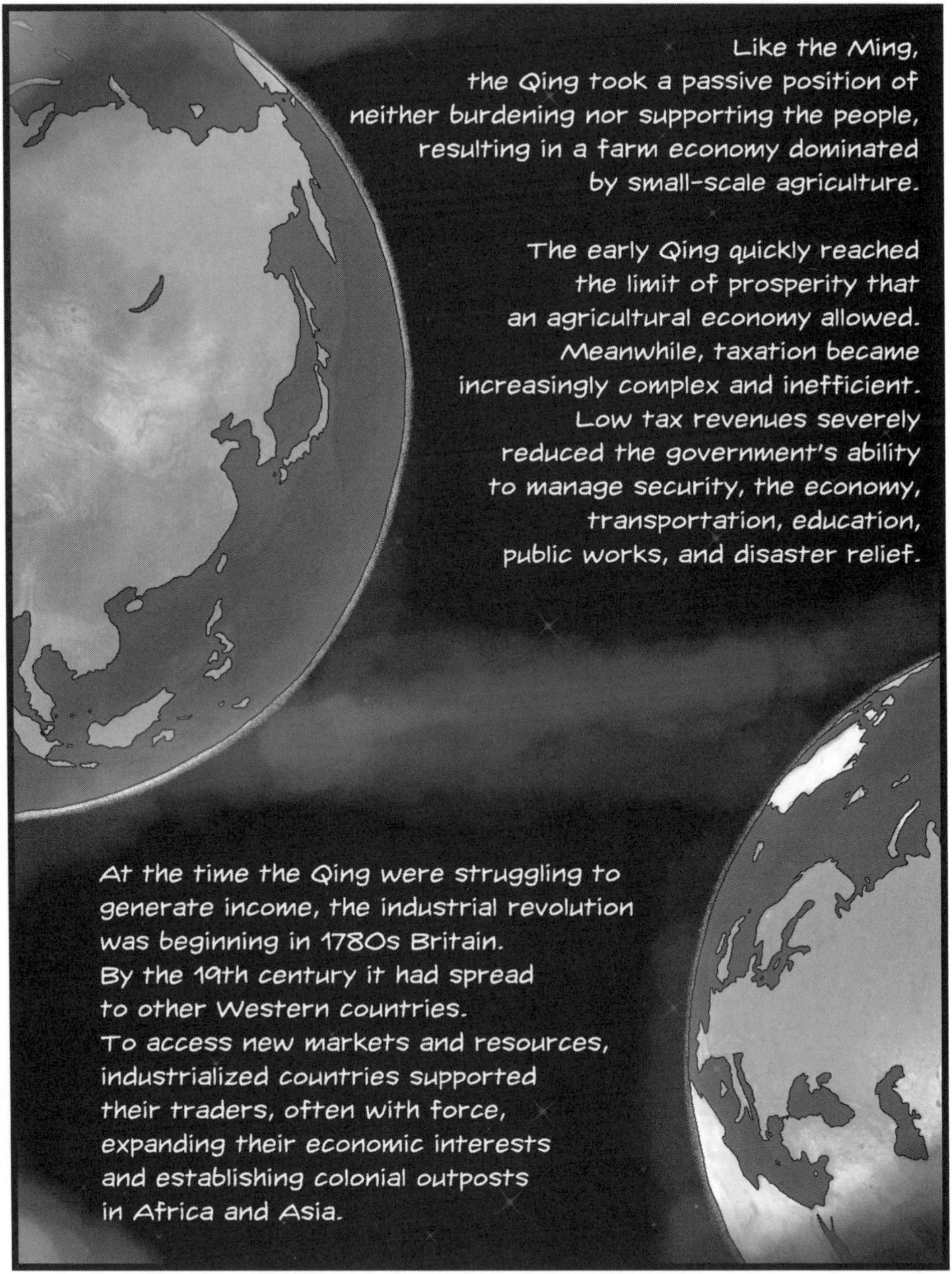
Like the Ming, the Qing took a passive position of neither burdening nor supporting the people, resulting in a farm economy dominated by small-scale agriculture.
The early Qing quickly reached the limit of prosperity that an agricultural economy allowed. Meanwhile, taxation became increasingly complex and inefficient. Low tax revenues severely reduced the government's ability to manage security, the economy, transportation, education, public works, and disaster relief.
At the time the Qing were struggling to generate income, the industrial revolution was beginning in 1780s Britain. By the 19th century it had spread to other Western countries. To access new markets and resources, industrialized countries supported their traders, often with force, expanding their economic interests and establishing colonial outposts in Africa and Asia.

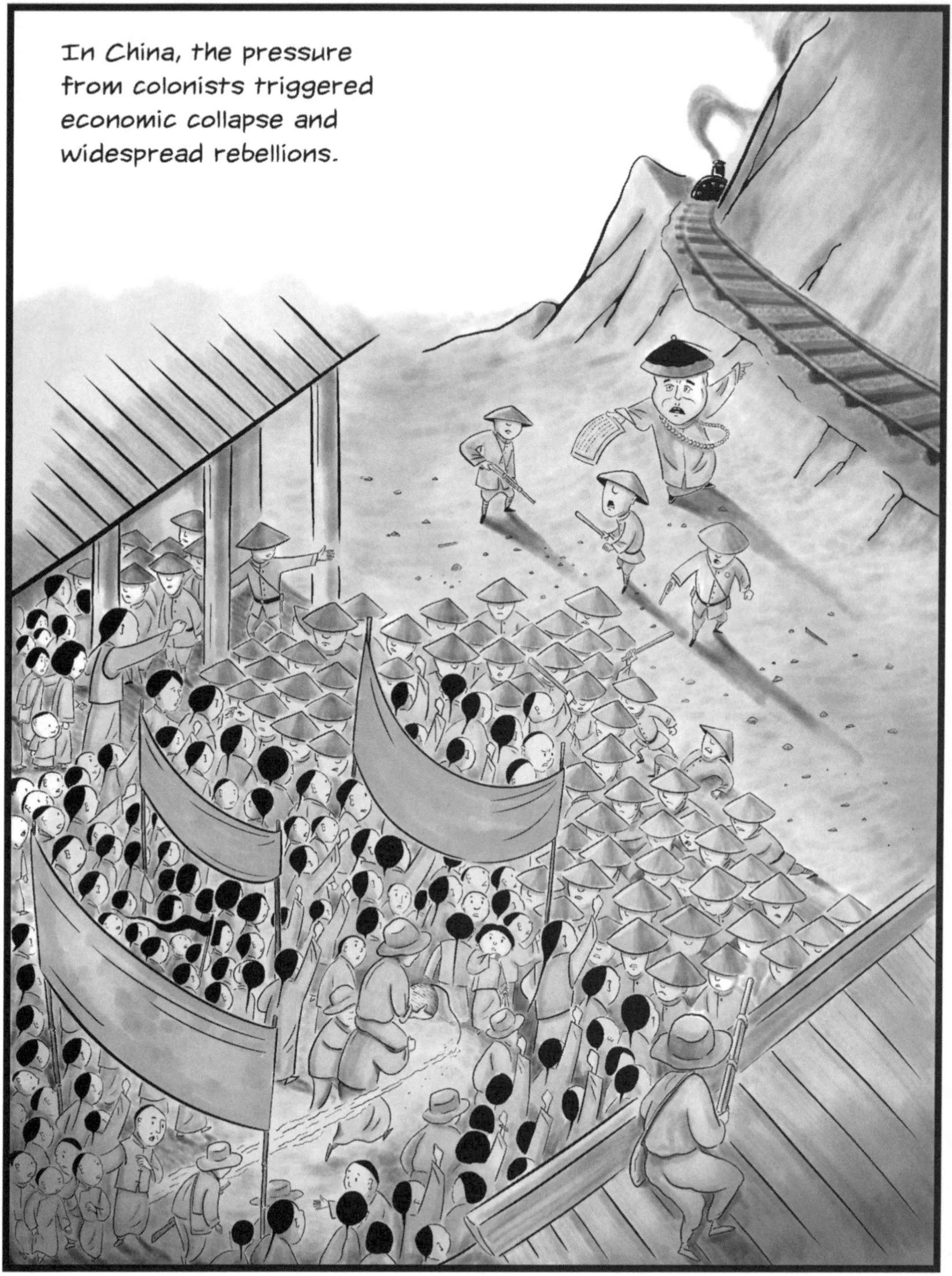
In China, the pressure from colonists triggered economic collapse and widespread rebellions.

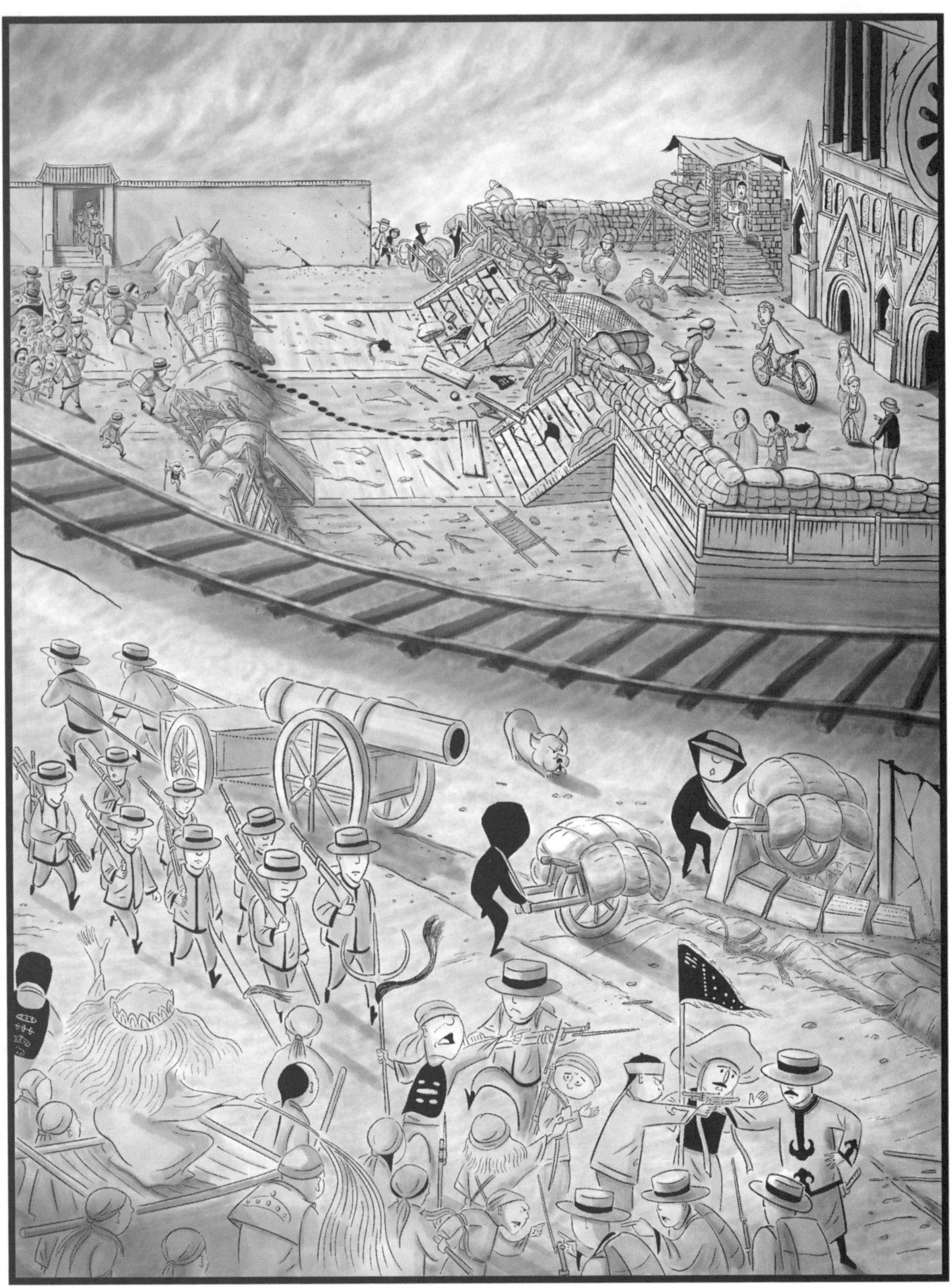

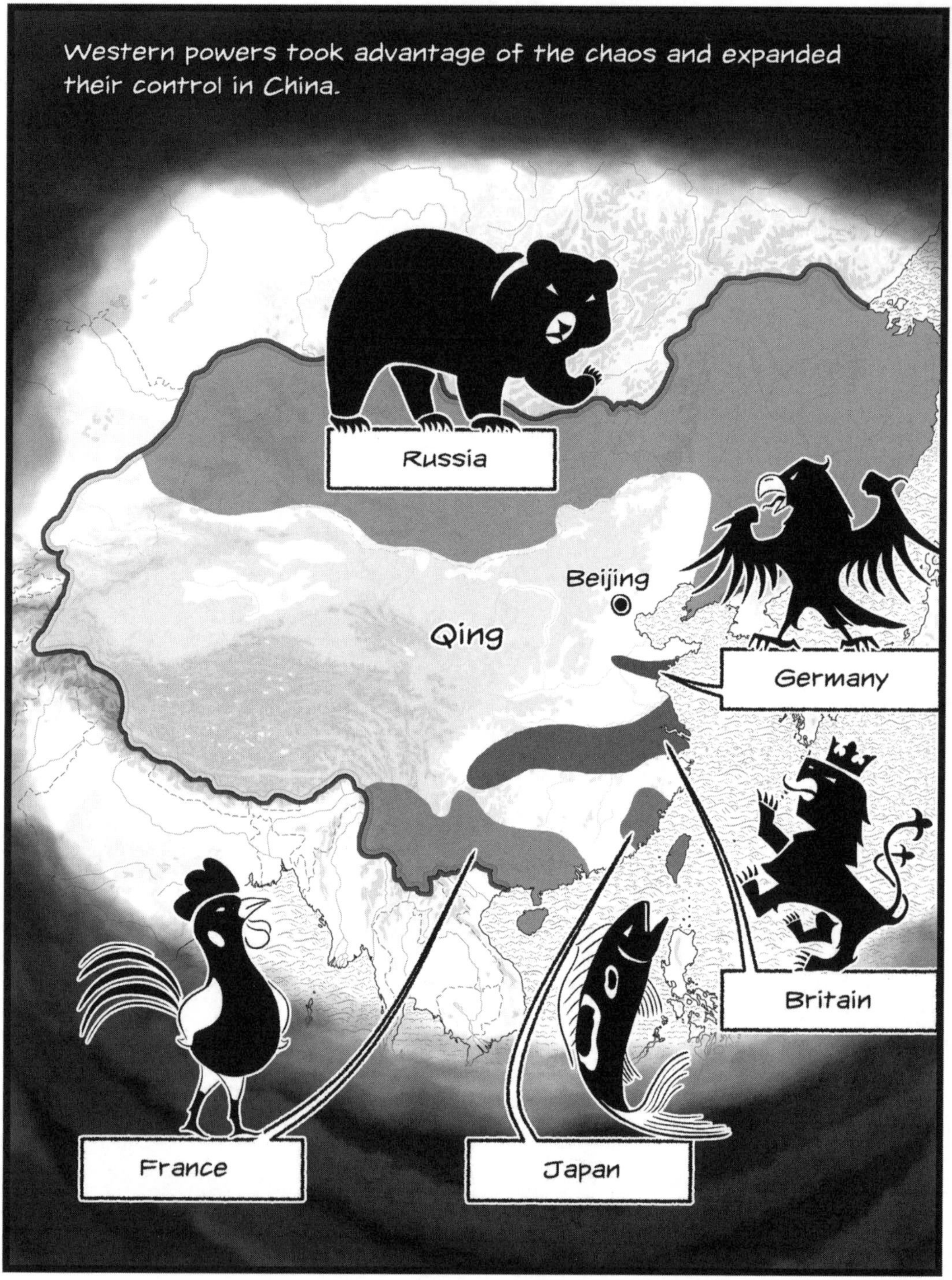
Western powers took advantage of the chaos and expanded their control in China.
Russia
Beijing
Qing
Germany
Britain
France
Japan

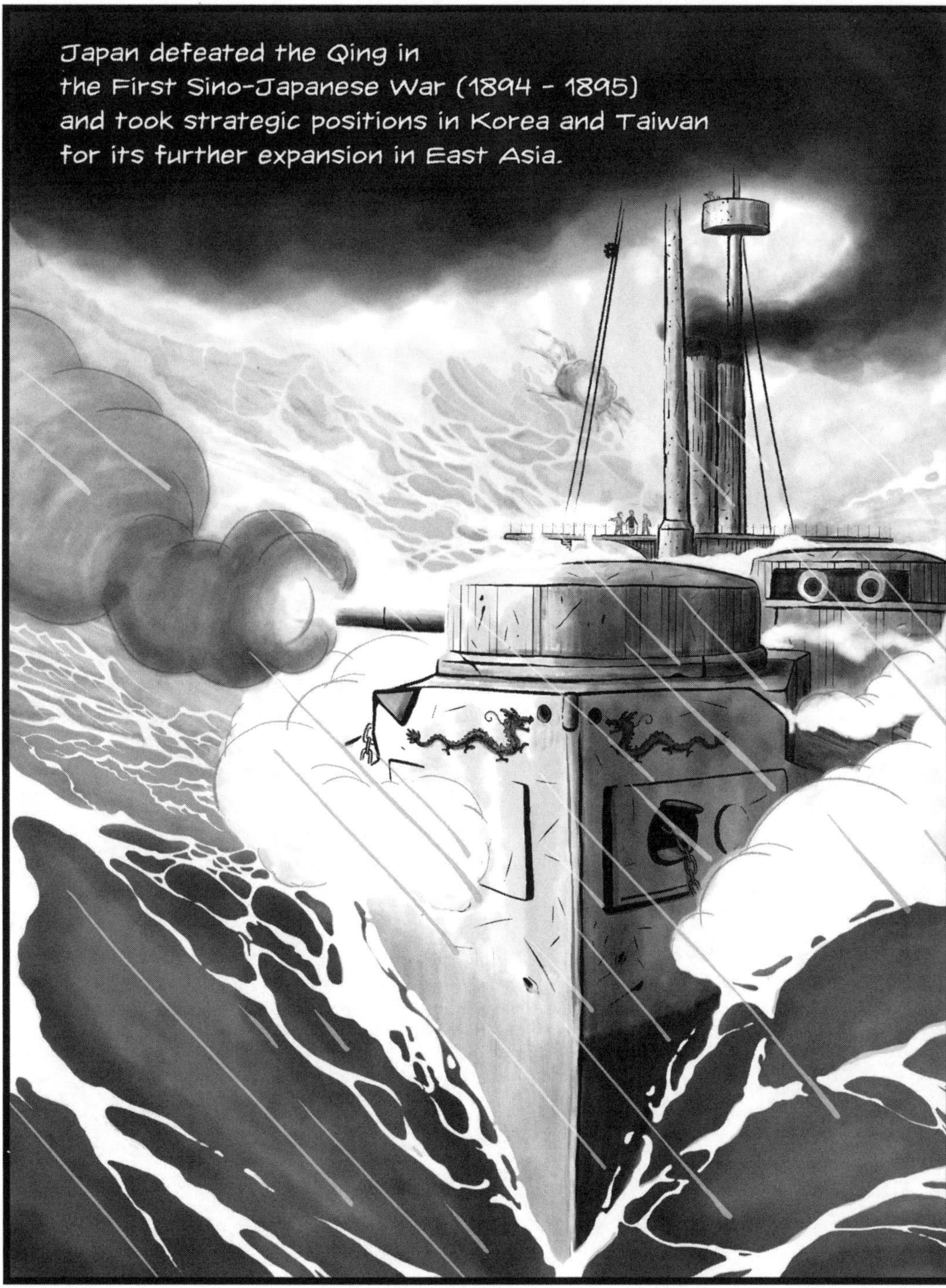
Japan defeated the Qing in
the First Sino-Japanese War (1894 - 1895)
and took strategic positions in Korea and Taiwan
for its further expansion in East Asia.

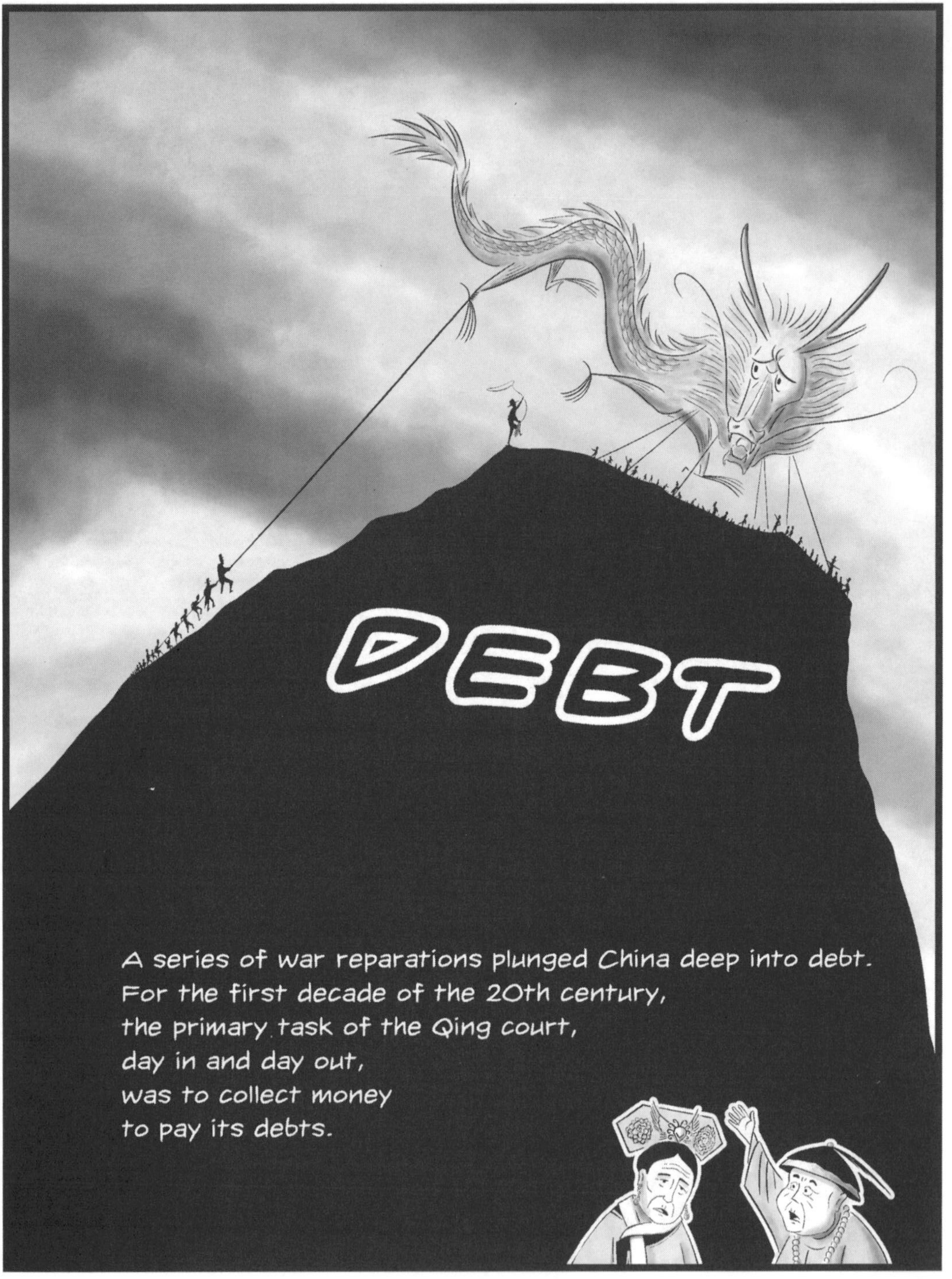
DEBT
A series of war reparations plunged China deep into debt.
For the first decade of the 20th century,
the primary task of the Qing court,
day in and day out,
was to collect money
to pay its debts.

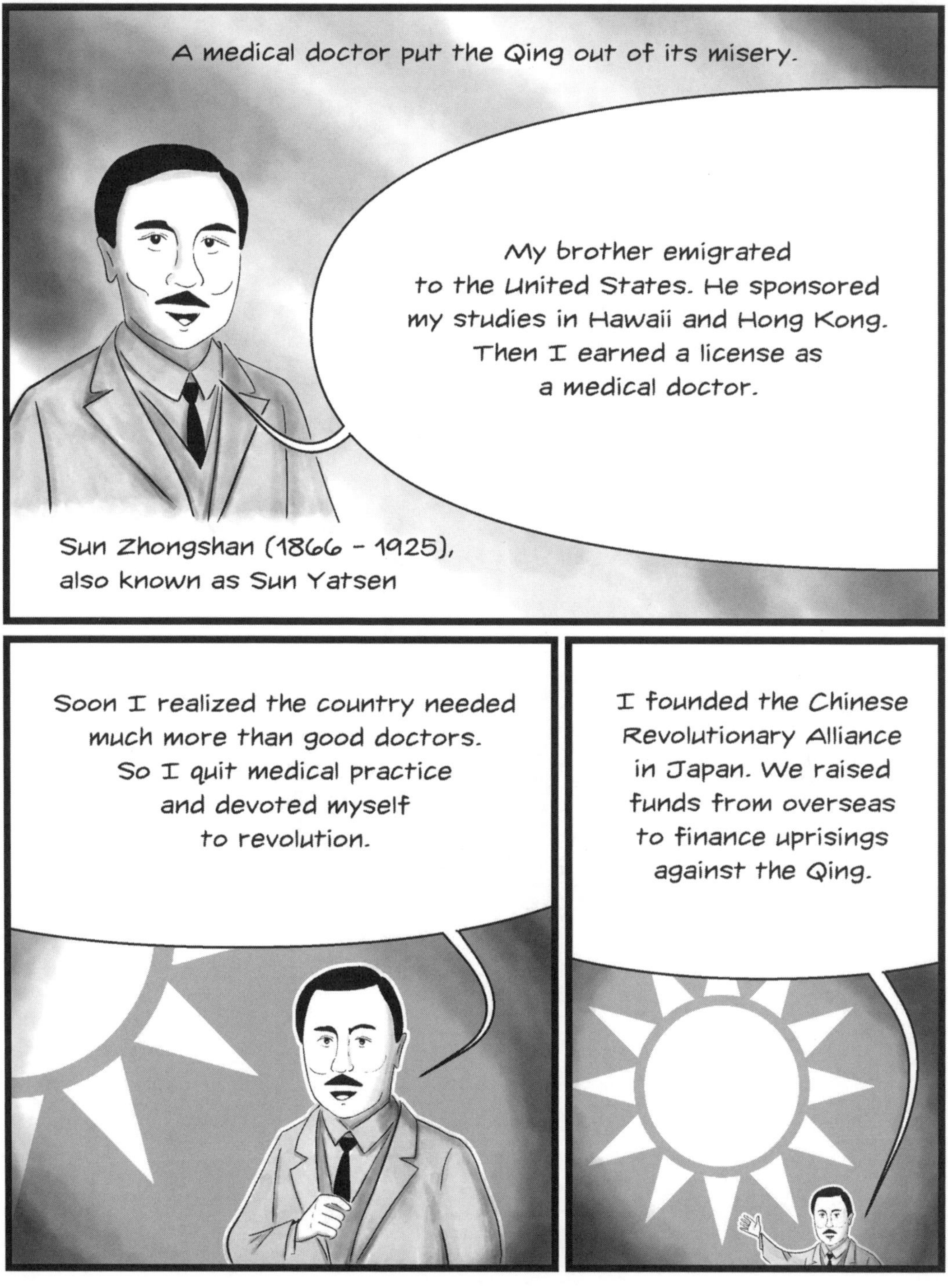
A medical doctor put the Qing out of its misery.
My brother emigrated to the United States. He sponsored my studies in Hawaii and Hong Kong. Then I earned a license as a medical doctor.
Sun Zhongshan (1866 - 1925), also known as Sun Yatsen
Soon I realized the country needed much more than good doctors. So I quit medical practice and devoted myself to revolution.
I founded the Chinese Revolutionary Alliance in Japan. We raised funds from overseas to finance uprisings against the Qing.

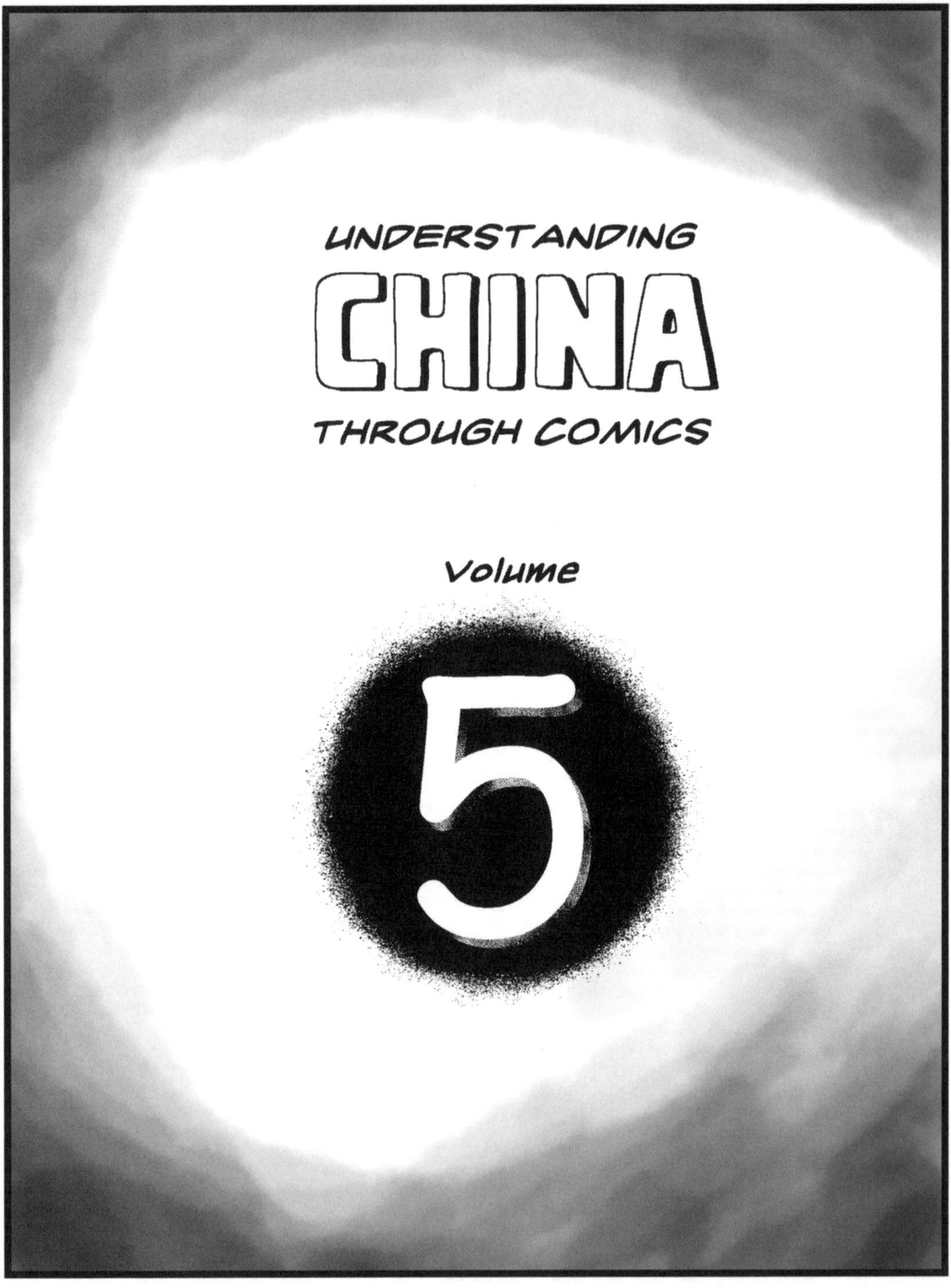
UNDERSTANDING
CHINA
THROUGH COMICS
Volume
5

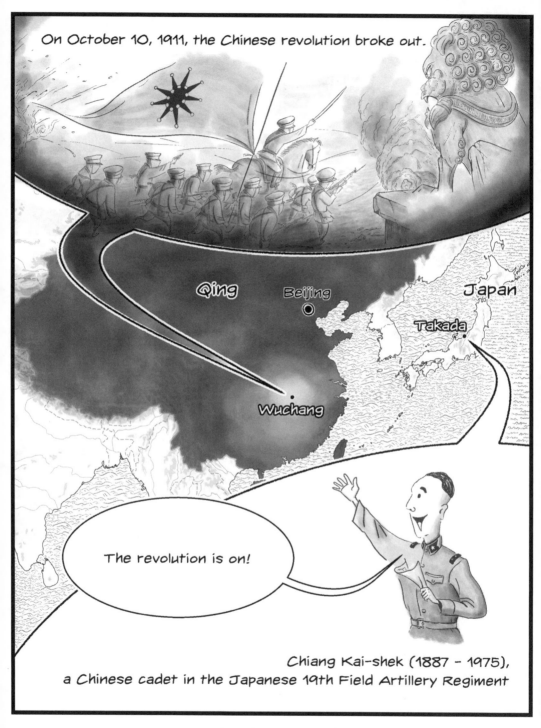

On October 10, 1911, the Chinese revolution broke out.

Qing

Beijing

Japan

Takada

Wuchang

The revolution is on!

Chiang Kai-shek (1887 – 1975),
a Chinese cadet in the Japanese 19th Field Artillery Regiment

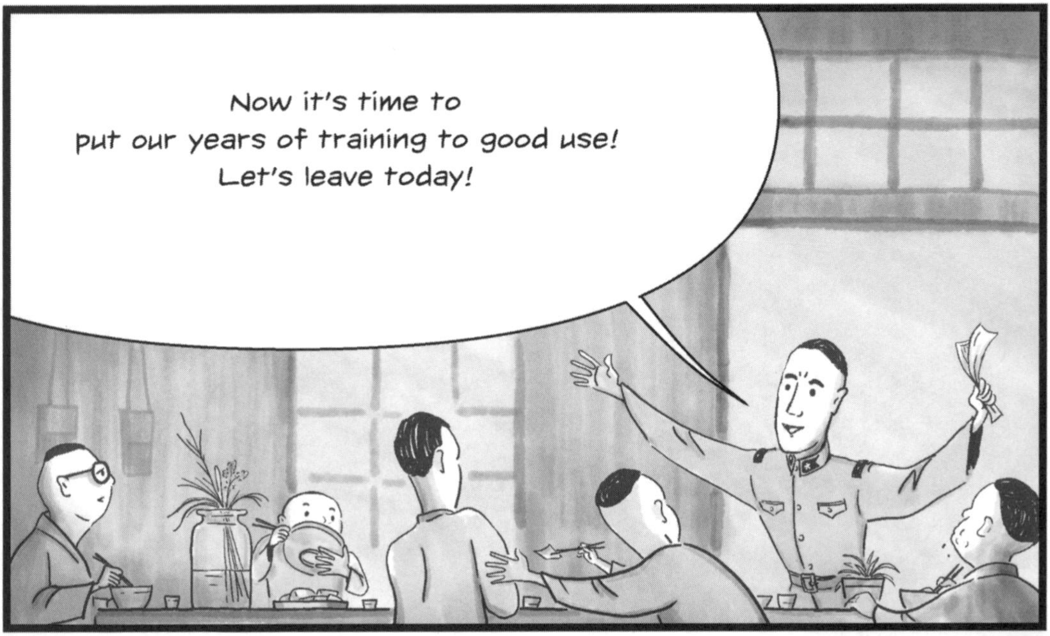
Now it's time to put our years of training to good use! Let's leave today!

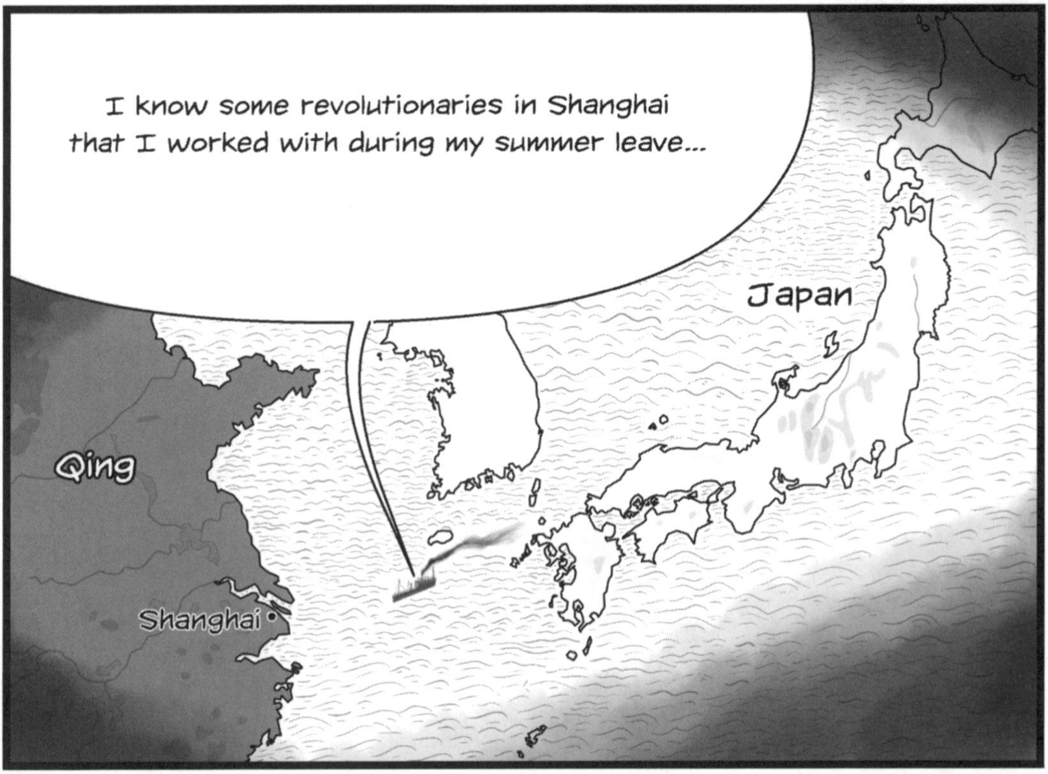
I know some revolutionaries in Shanghai that I worked with during my summer leave...
Japan
Qing
Shanghai

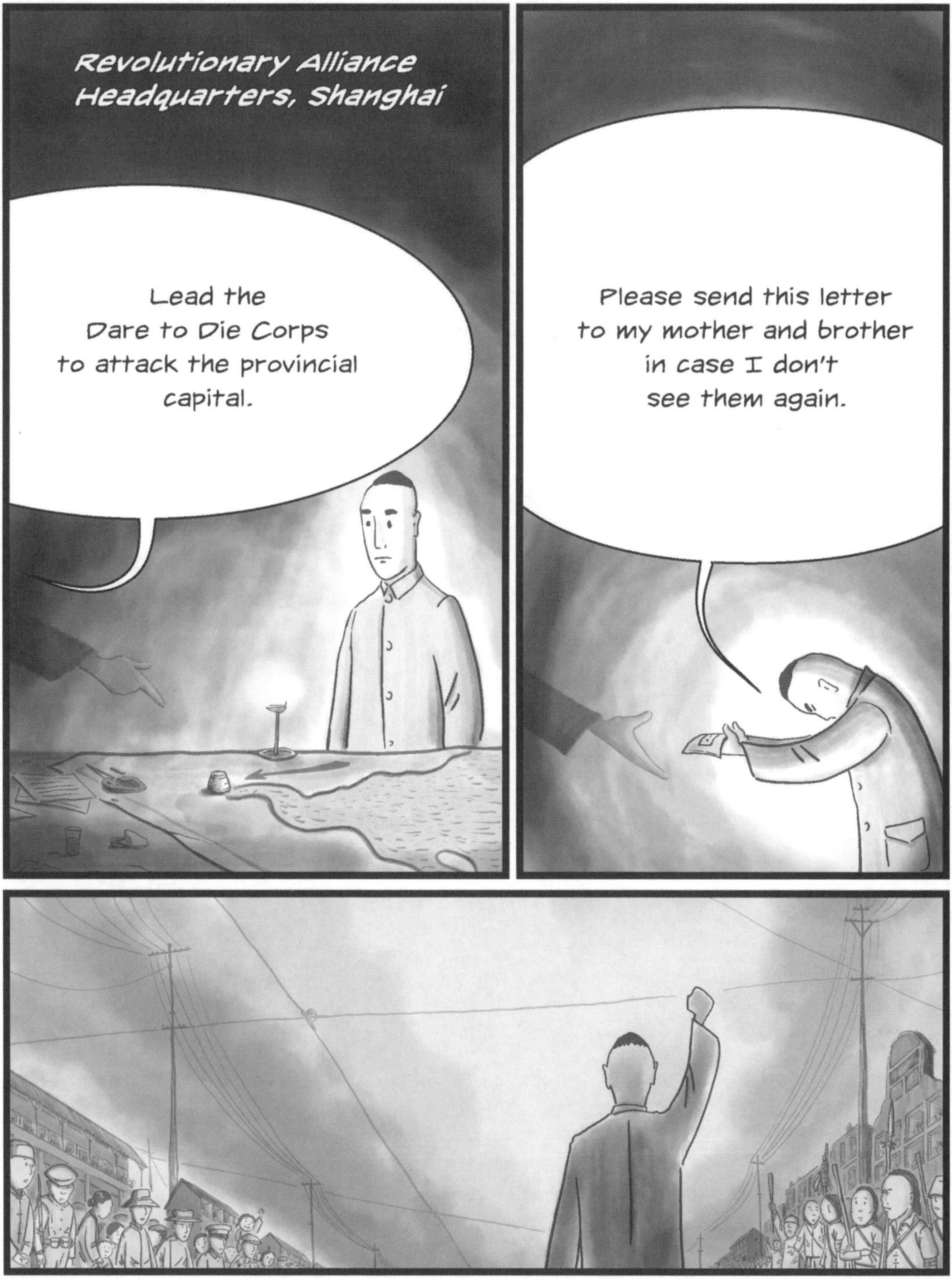
Revolutionary Alliance Headquarters, Shanghai
Lead the Dare to Die Corps to attack the provincial capital.
Please send this letter to my mother and brother in case I don't see them again.

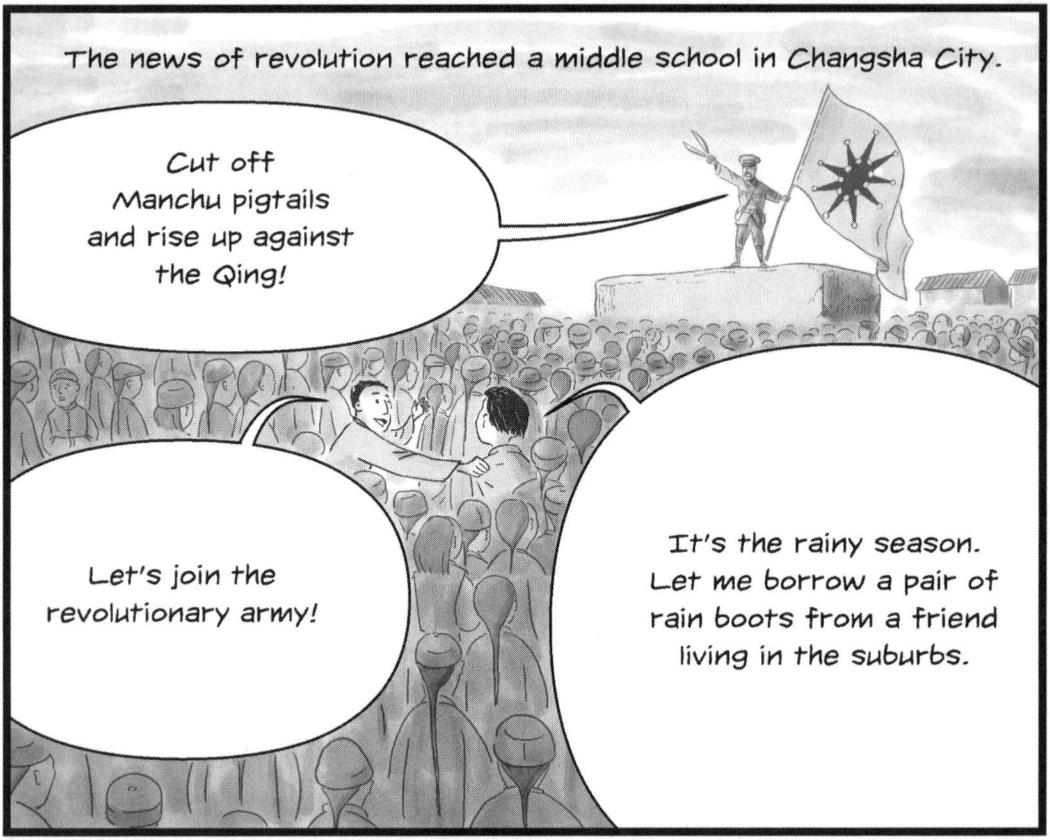
The news of revolution reached a middle school in Changsha City.
Cut off Manchu pigtails and rise up against the Qing!
Let's join the revolutionary army!
It's the rainy season. Let me borrow a pair of rain boots from a friend living in the suburbs.

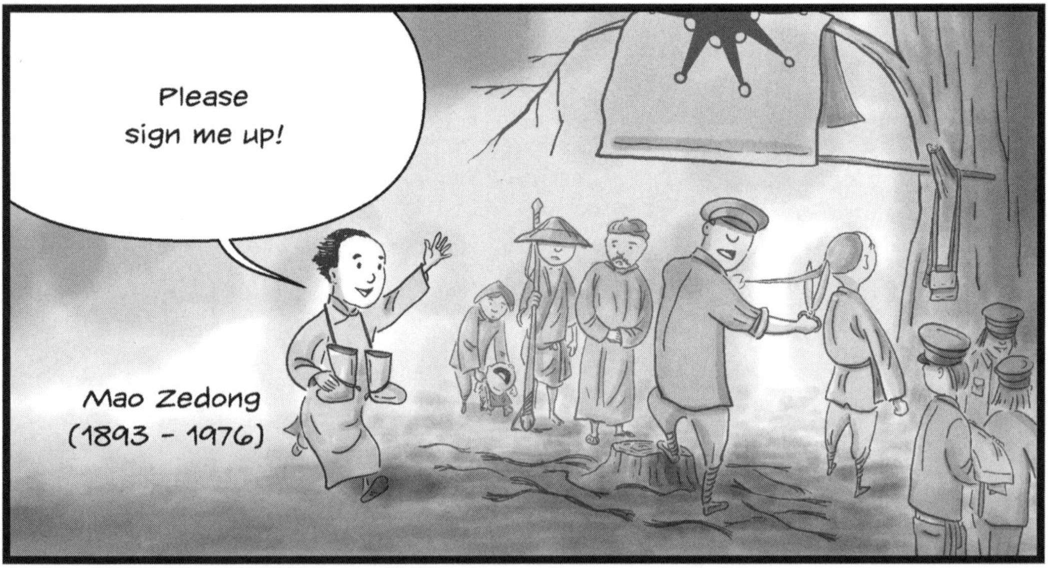
Please sign me up!
Mao Zedong (1893 - 1976)

EARLY REPUBLIC

1912 - 1916

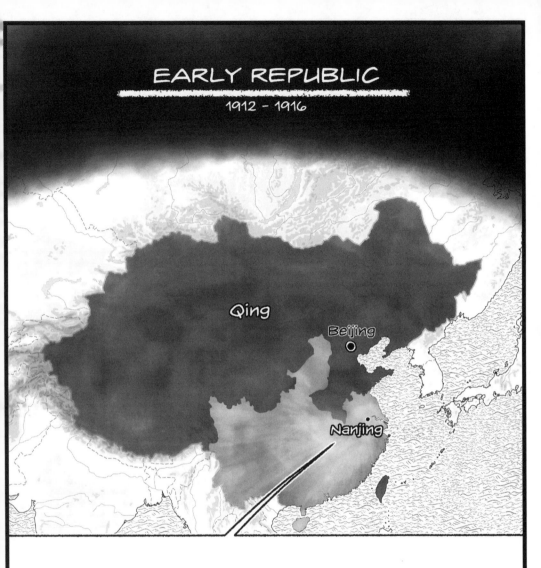

Qing

Beijing

Nanjing

Within two months of the Wuchang uprising,
15 provinces declared independence from the Qing dynasty.
Provincial representatives met in Nanjing and
elected Sun Zhongshan provisional president of
the Republic of China on December 29, 1911.

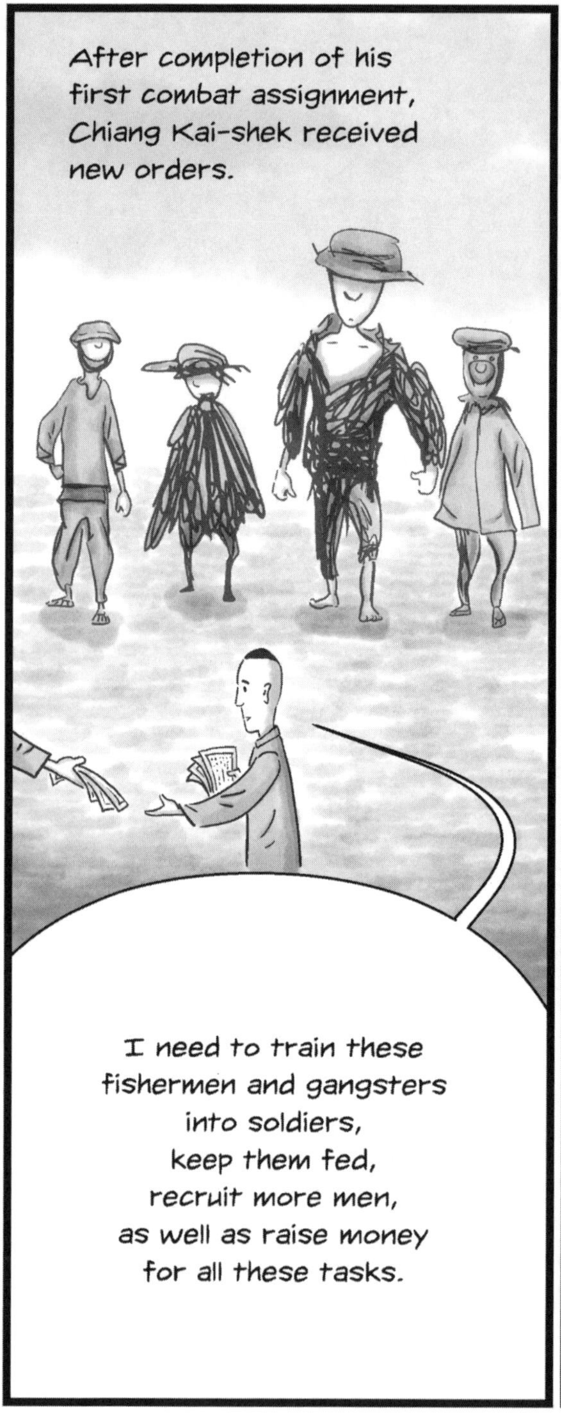
After completion of his first combat assignment, Chiang Kai-shek received new orders.
I need to train these fishermen and gangsters into soldiers, keep them fed, recruit more men, as well as raise money for all these tasks.

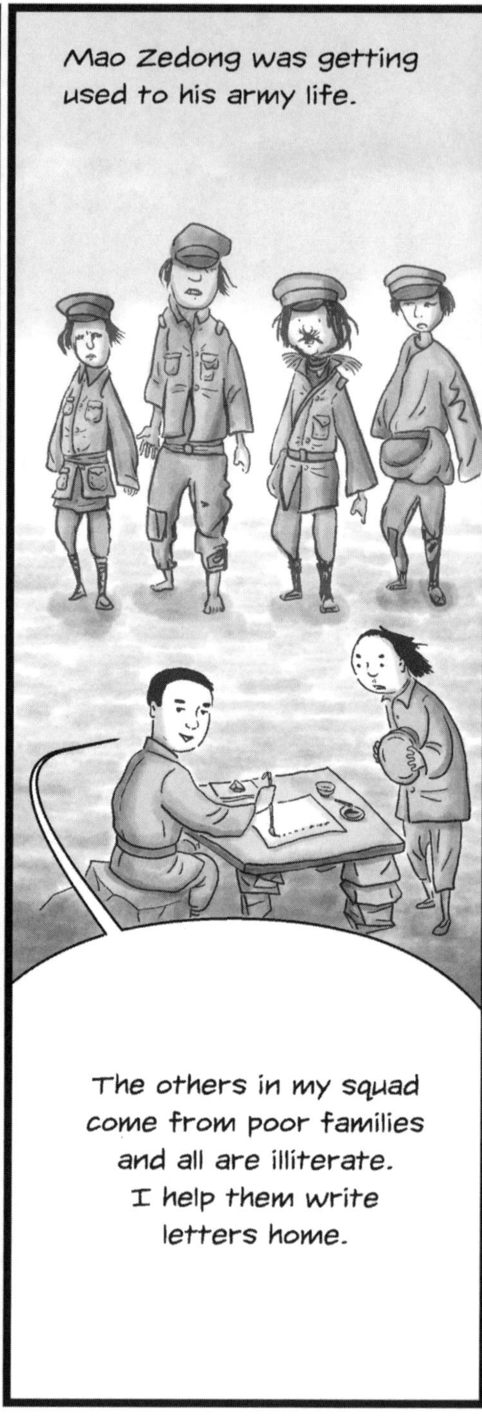
Mao Zedong was getting used to his army life.
The others in my squad come from poor families and all are illiterate. I help them write letters home.

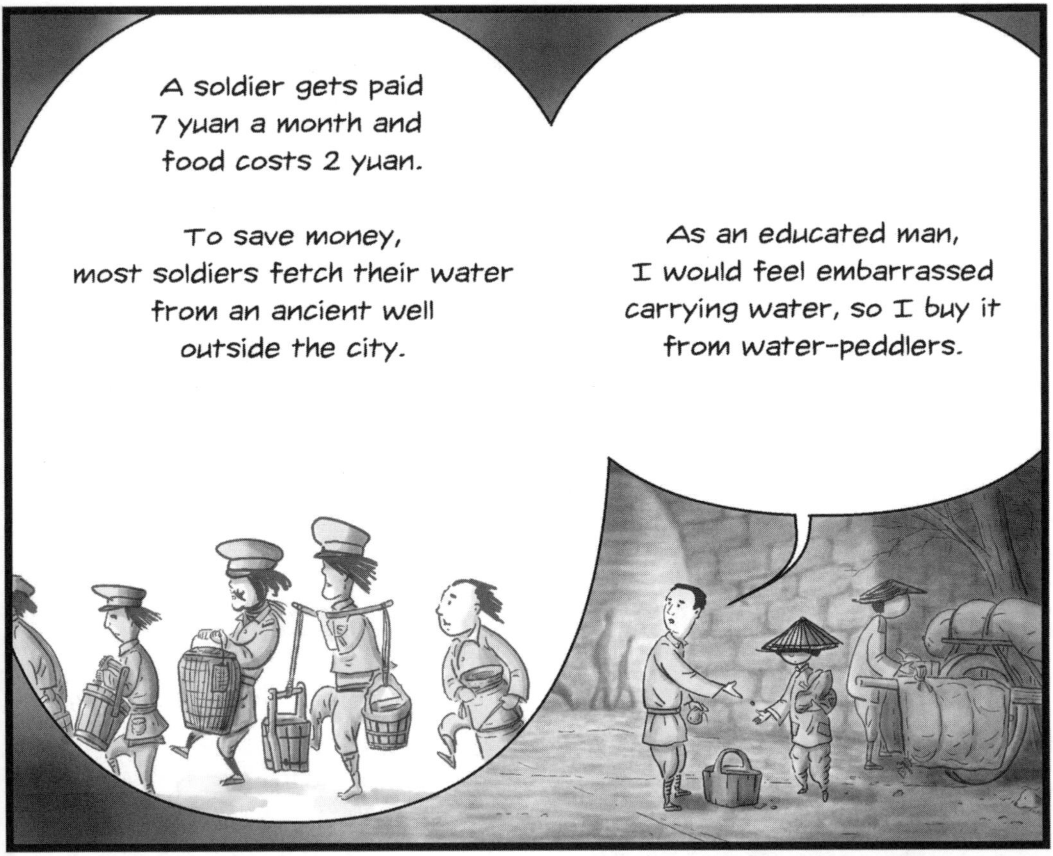
A soldier gets paid 7 yuan a month and food costs 2 yuan.
To save money, most soldiers fetch their water from an ancient well outside the city.
As an educated man, I would feel embarrassed carrying water, so I buy it from water-peddlers.

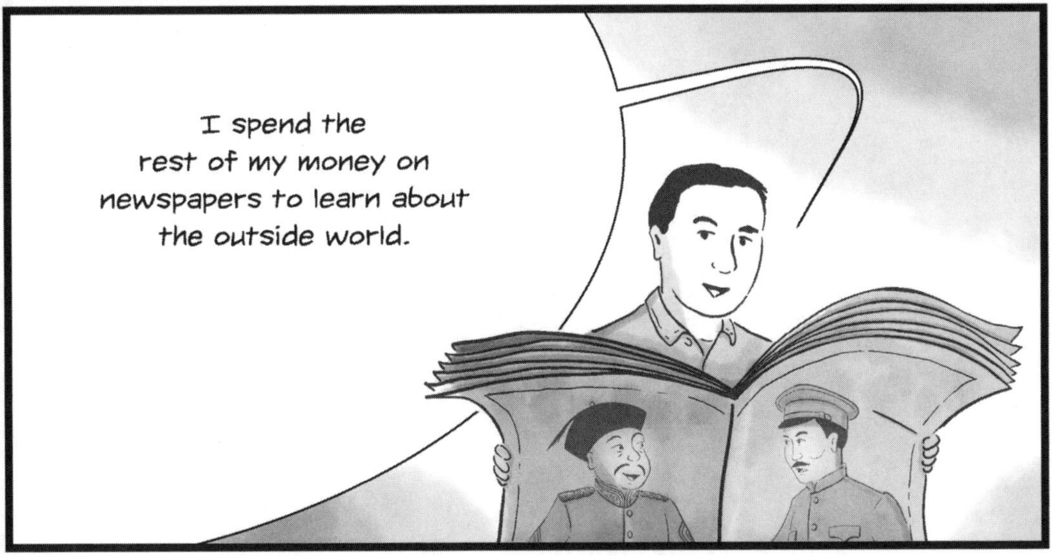
I spend the rest of my money on newspapers to learn about the outside world.

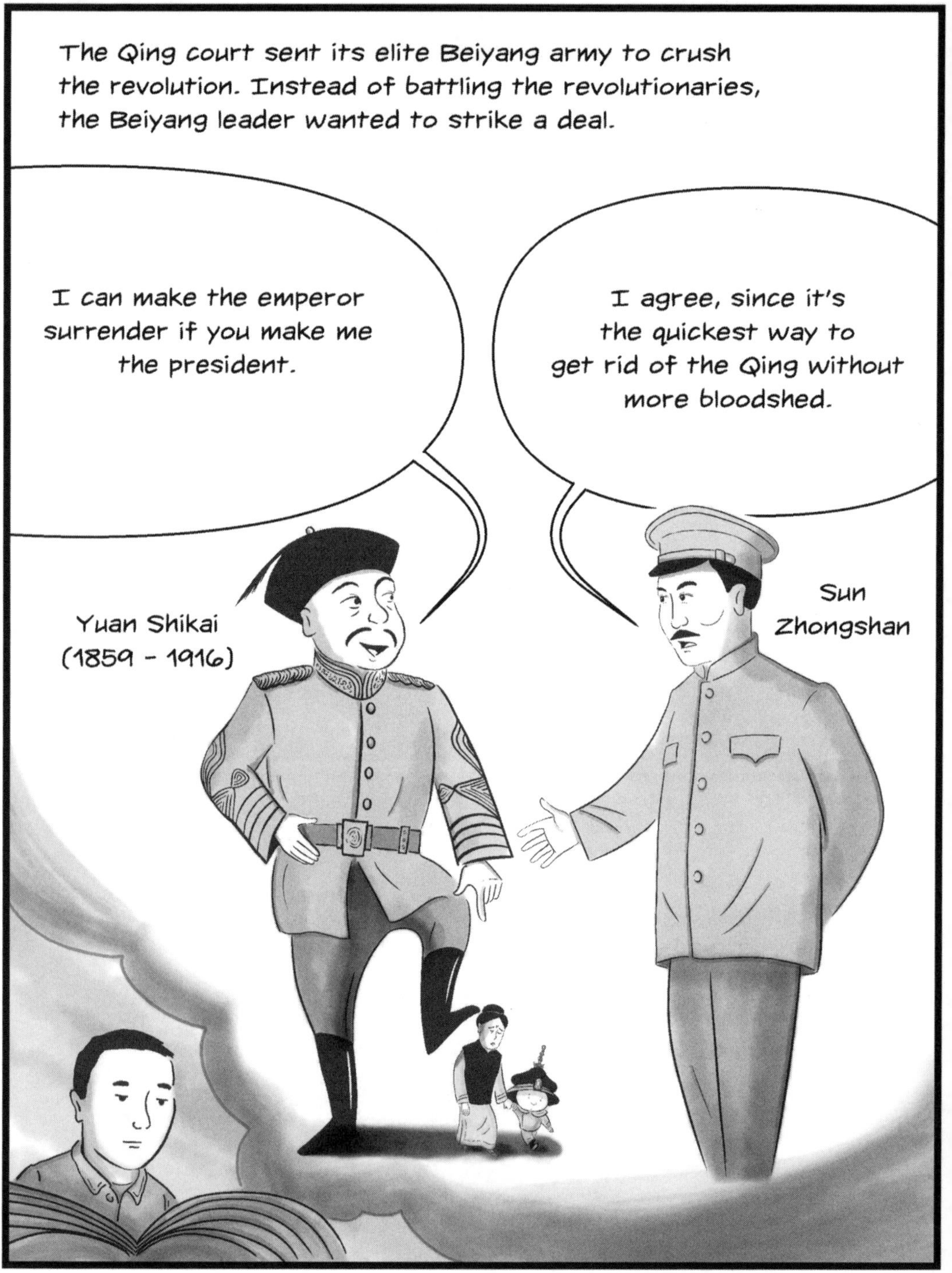
The Qing court sent its elite Beiyang army to crush the revolution. Instead of battling the revolutionaries, the Beiyang leader wanted to strike a deal.
I can make the emperor surrender if you make me the president.
I agree, since it's the quickest way to get rid of the Qing without more bloodshed.
Yuan Shikai (1859 - 1916)
Sun Zhongshan

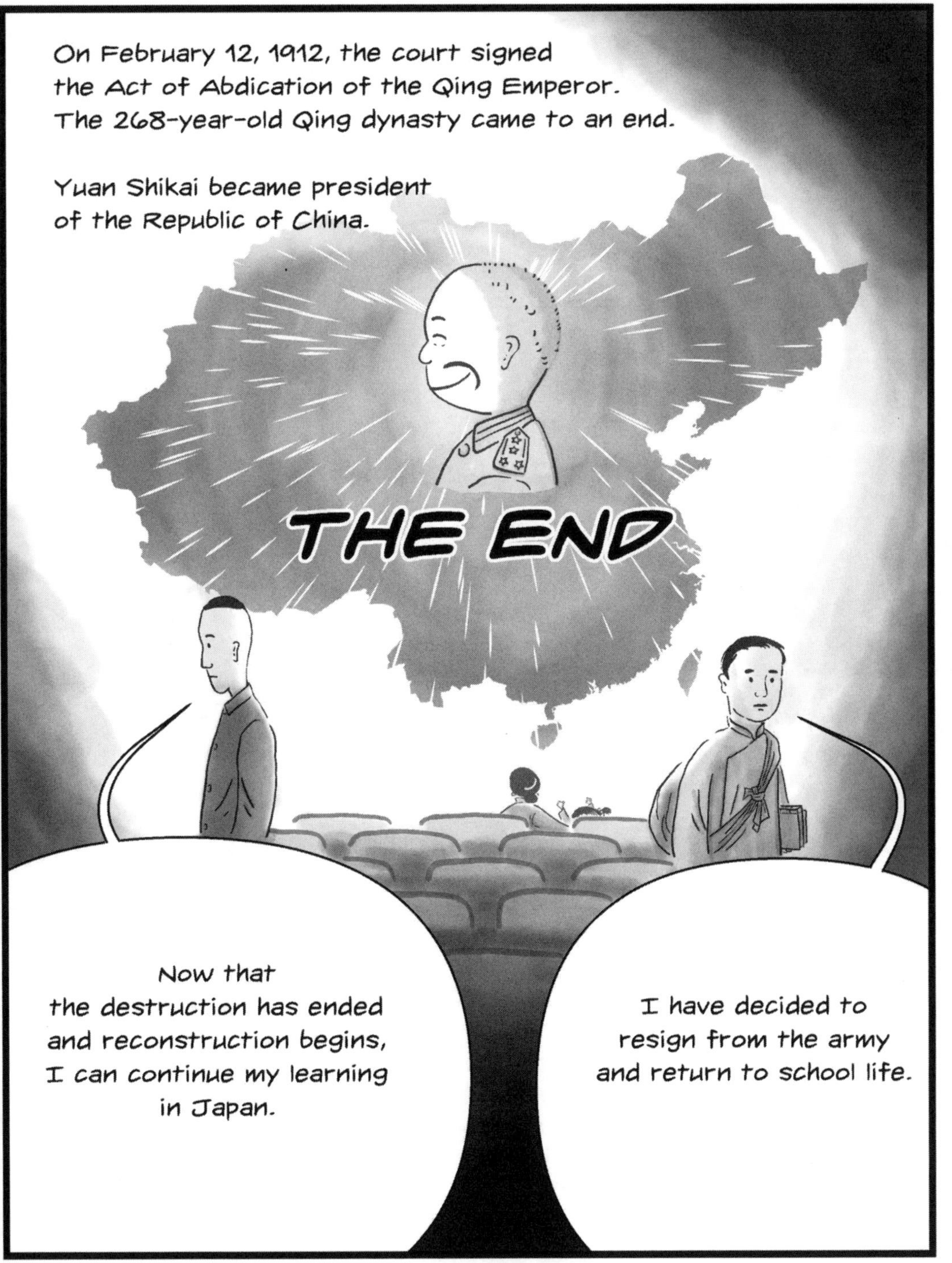
On February 12, 1912, the court signed the Act of Abdication of the Qing Emperor. The 268-year-old Qing dynasty came to an end.
Yuan Shikai became president of the Republic of China.
THE END
Now that the destruction has ended and reconstruction begins, I can continue my learning in Japan.
I have decided to resign from the army and return to school life.

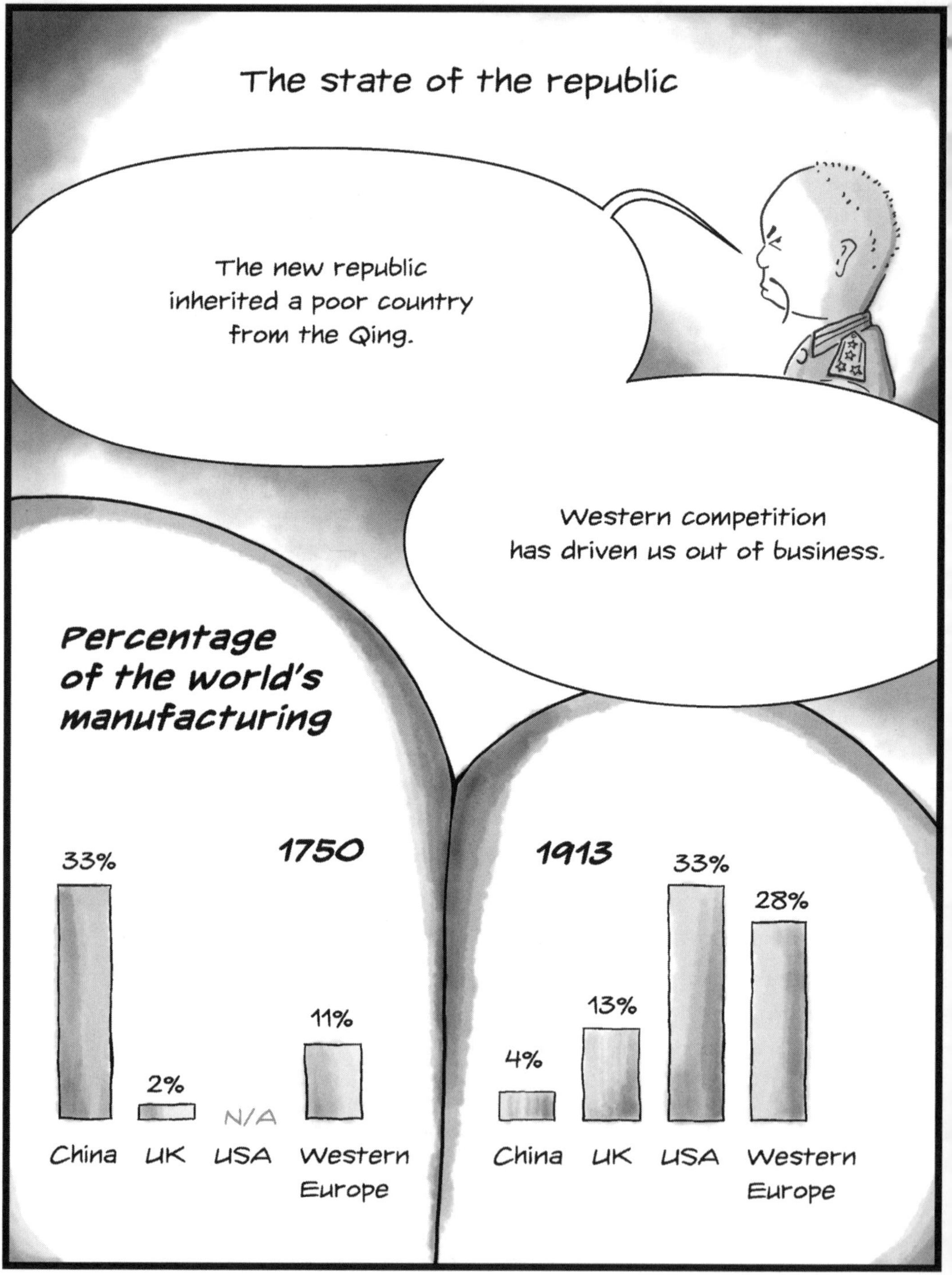

The state of the republic

The new republic inherited a poor country from the Qing.

Western competition has driven us out of business.

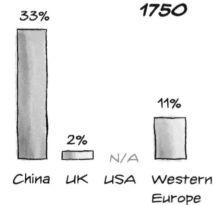

Percentage of the world's manufacturing

1750

- China 33%
- UK 2%
- USA N/A
- Western Europe 11%

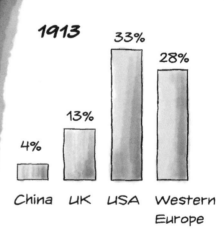

1913

- China 4%
- UK 13%
- USA 33%
- Western Europe 28%

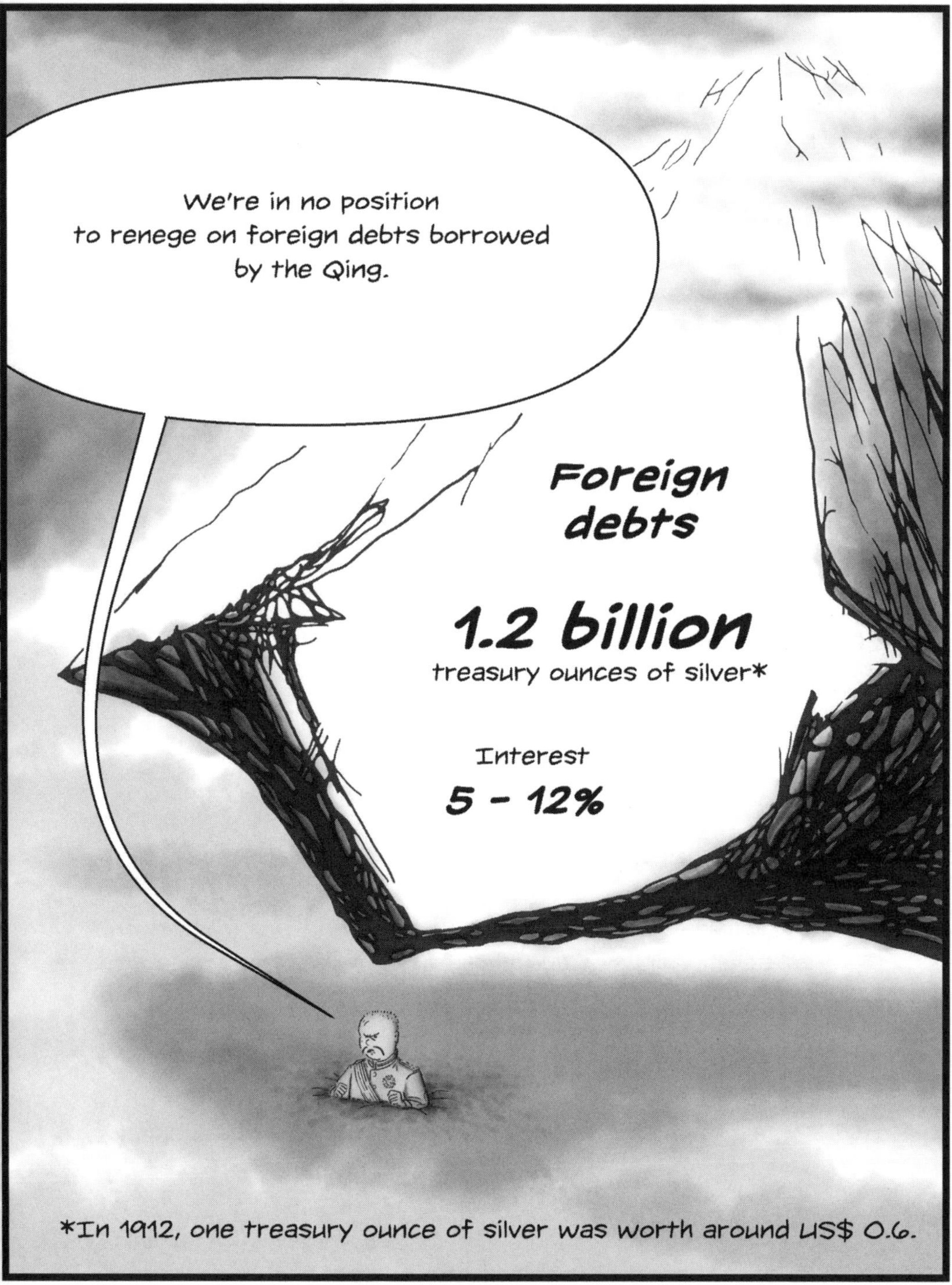
We're in no position to renege on foreign debts borrowed by the Qing.
Foreign debts
1.2 billion
treasury ounces of silver*
Interest
5 - 12%
*In 1912, one treasury ounce of silver was worth around US$ 0.6.

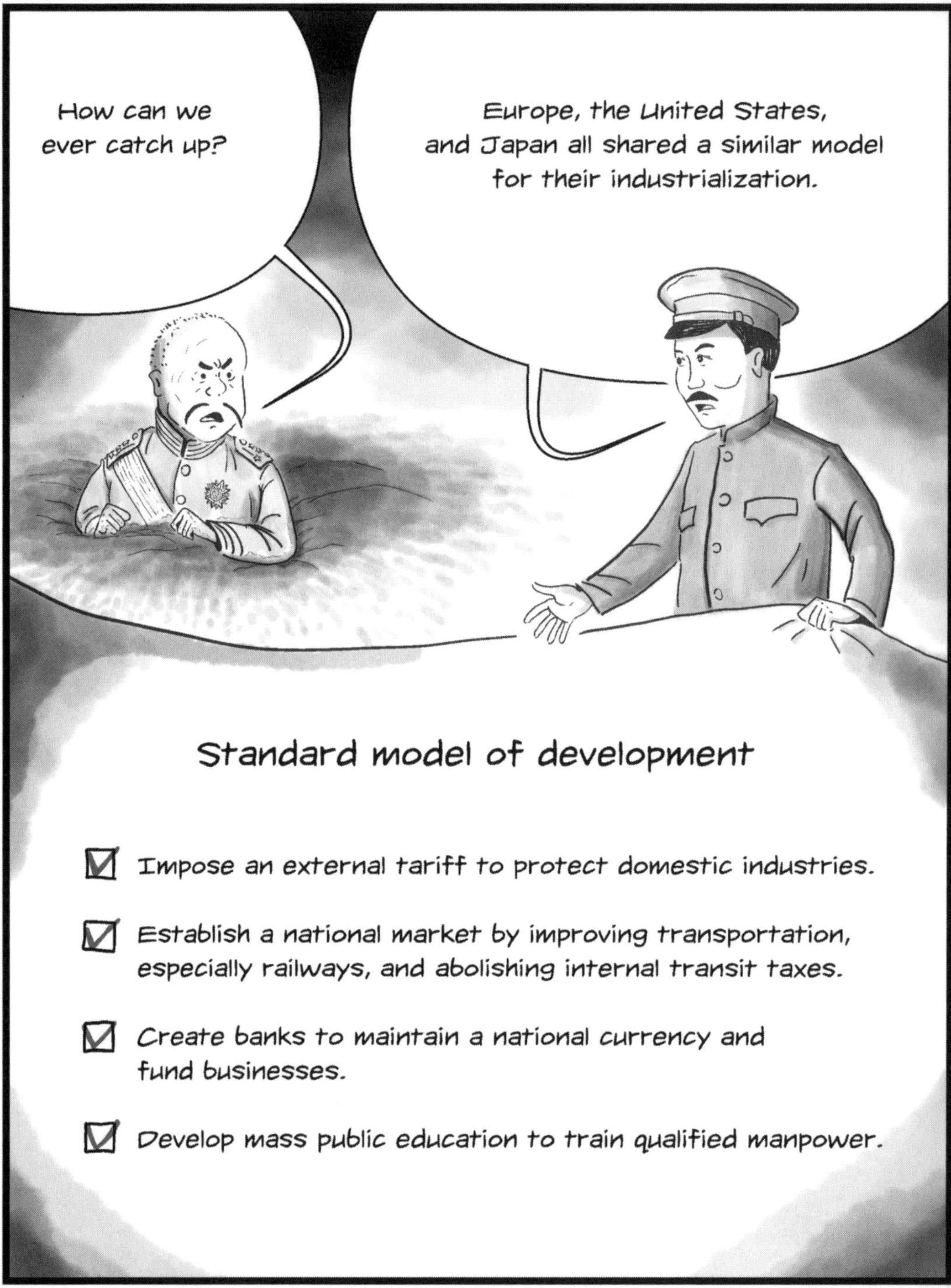
How can we ever catch up?
Europe, the United States, and Japan all shared a similar model for their industrialization.
Standard model of development
Impose an external tariff to protect domestic industries.
Establish a national market by improving transportation, especially railways, and abolishing internal transit taxes.
Create banks to maintain a national currency and fund businesses.
Develop mass public education to train qualified manpower.

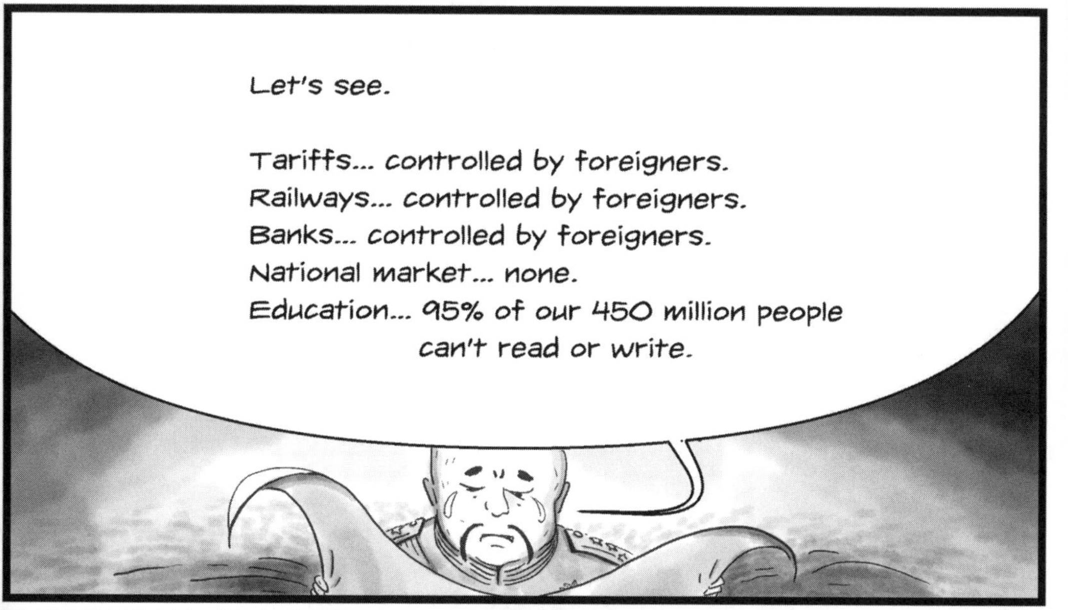
Let's see.
Tariffs... controlled by foreigners.
Railways... controlled by foreigners.
Banks... controlled by foreigners.
National market... none.
Education... 95% of our 450 million people can't read or write.

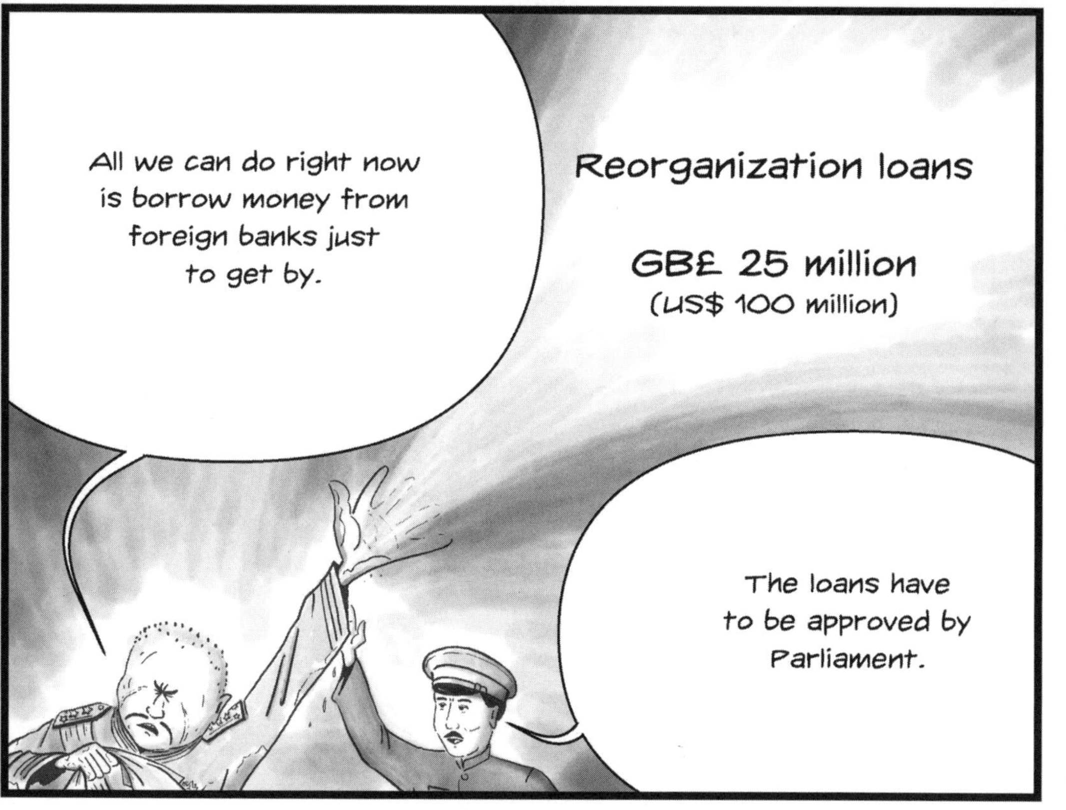
All we can do right now is borrow money from foreign banks just to get by.
Reorganization loans
GB£ 25 million
(US$ 100 million)
The loans have to be approved by Parliament.

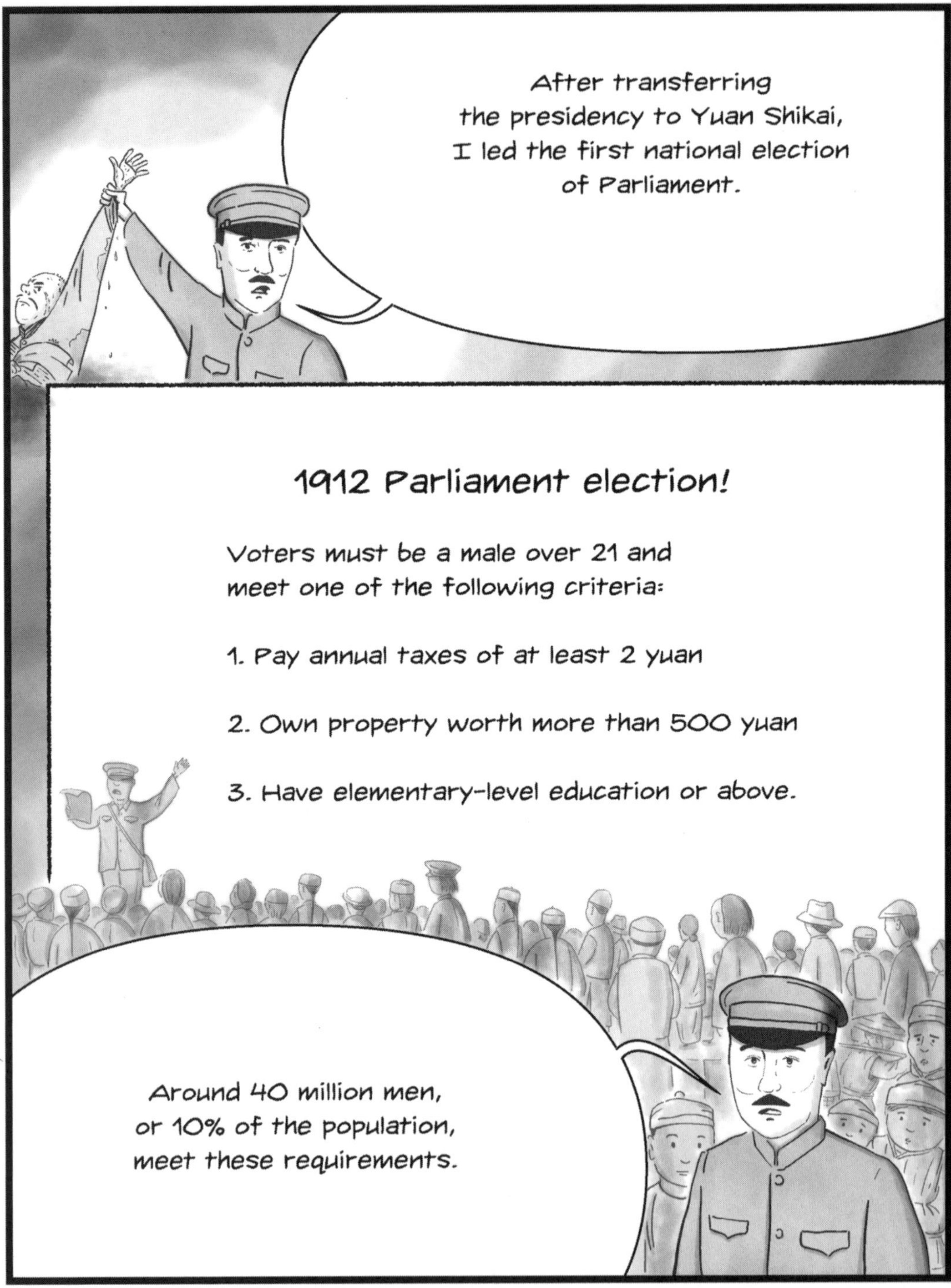
After transferring the presidency to Yuan Shikai, I led the first national election of Parliament.
1912 Parliament election!
Voters must be a male over 21 and meet one of the following criteria:
1. Pay annual taxes of at least 2 yuan
2. Own property worth more than 500 yuan
3. Have elementary-level education or above.
Around 40 million men, or 10% of the population, meet these requirements.

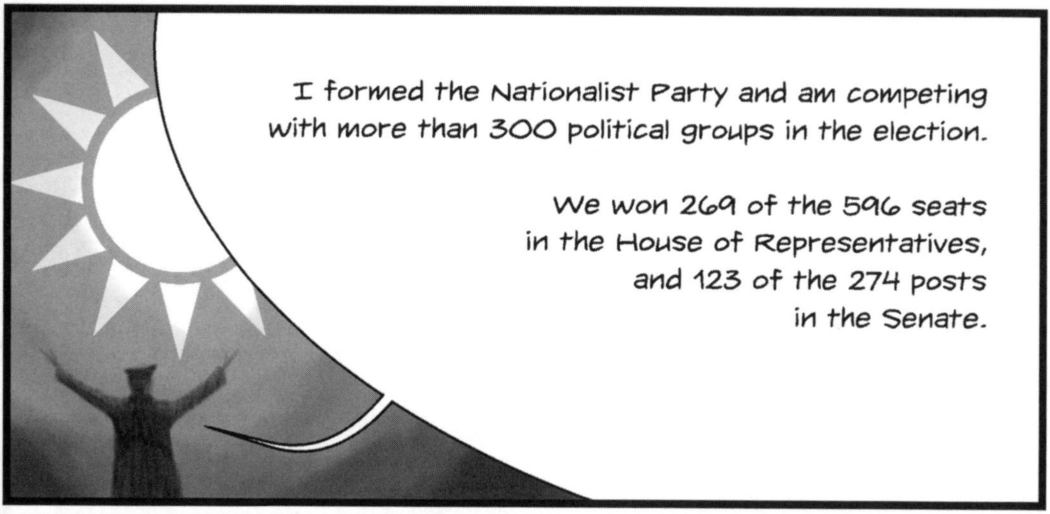
I formed the Nationalist Party and am competing with more than 300 political groups in the election.
We won 269 of the 596 seats in the House of Representatives, and 123 of the 274 posts in the Senate.

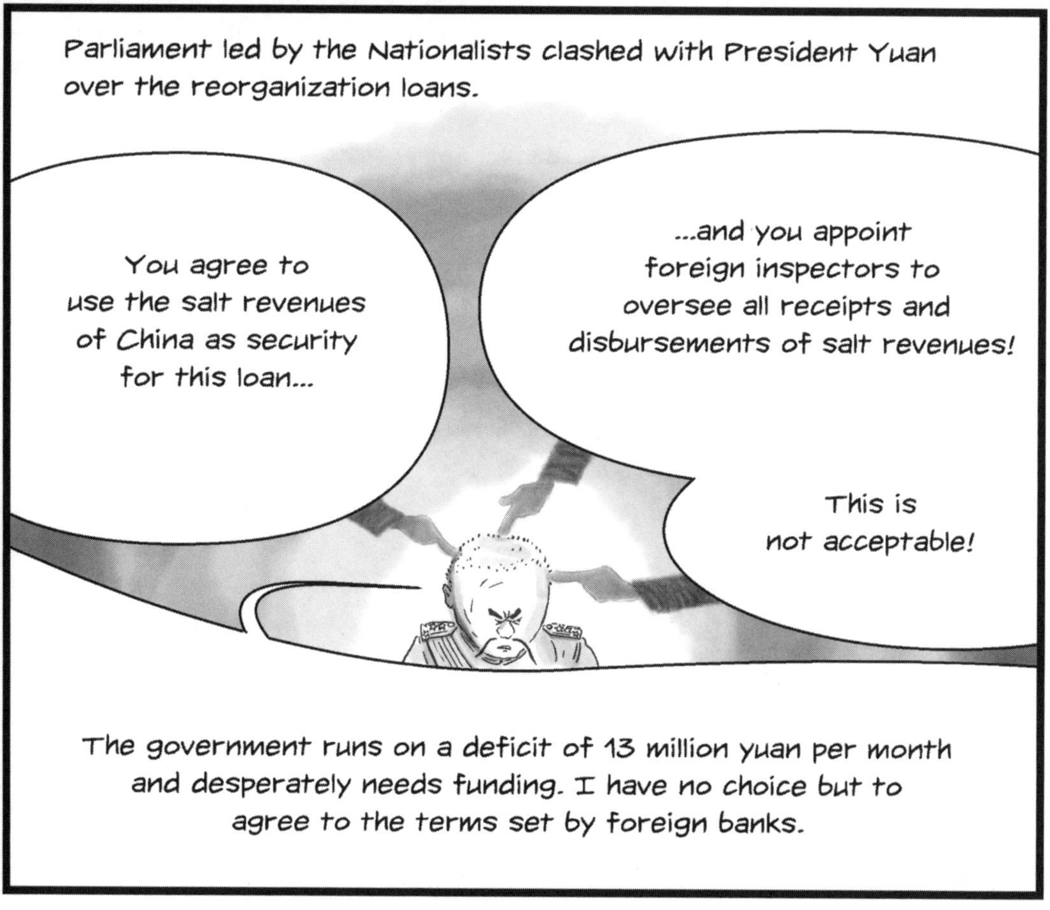
Parliament led by the Nationalists clashed with President Yuan over the reorganization loans.
You agree to use the salt revenues of China as security for this loan...
...and you appoint foreign inspectors to oversee all receipts and disbursements of salt revenues!
This is not acceptable!
The government runs on a deficit of 13 million yuan per month and desperately needs funding. I have no choice but to agree to the terms set by foreign banks.

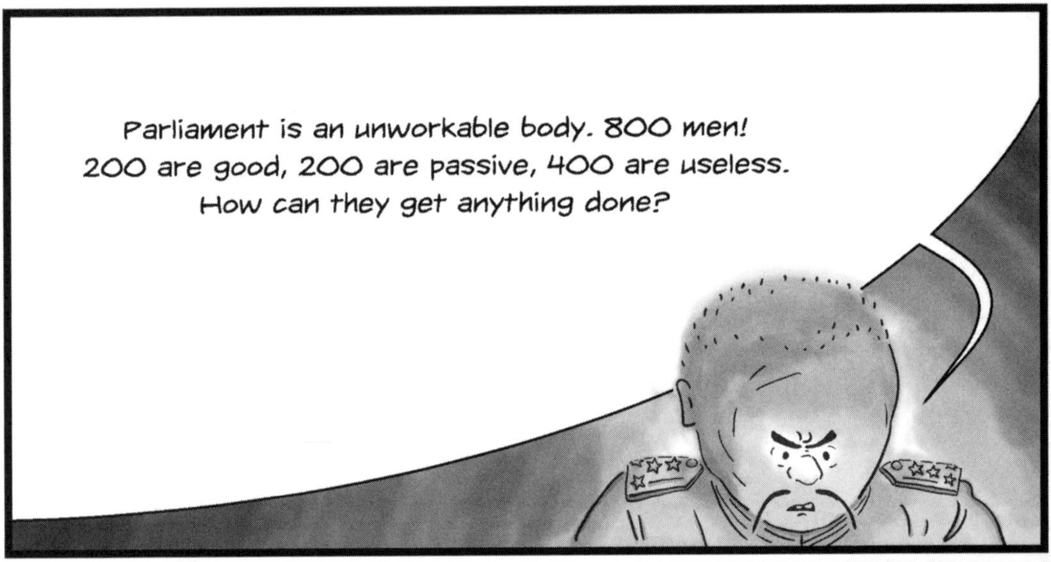
Parliament is an unworkable body. 800 men! 200 are good, 200 are passive, 400 are useless. How can they get anything done?

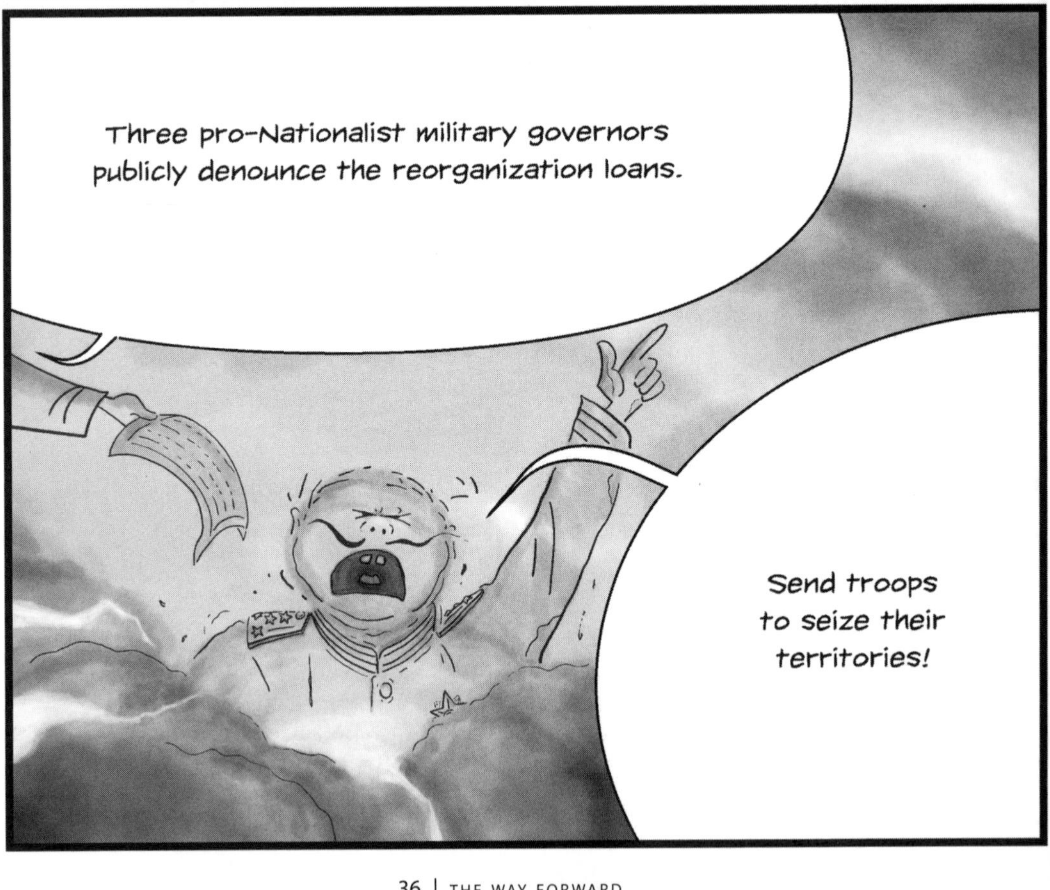
Three pro-Nationalist military governors publicly denounce the reorganization loans.
Send troops to seize their territories!

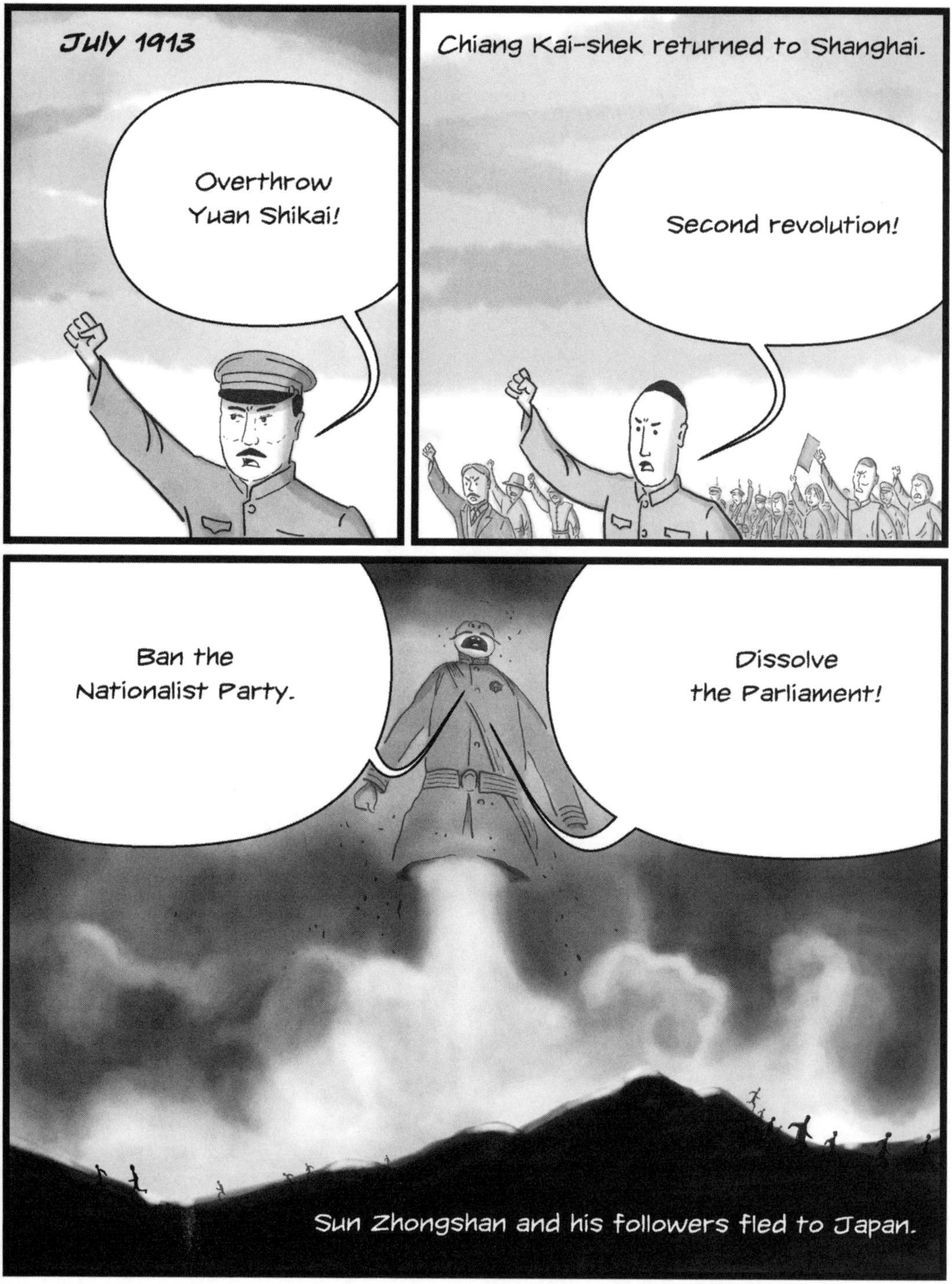
July 1913
Overthrow Yuan Shikai!
Chiang Kai-shek returned to Shanghai.
Second revolution!
Ban the Nationalist Party.
Dissolve the Parliament!
Sun Zhongshan and his followers fled to Japan.

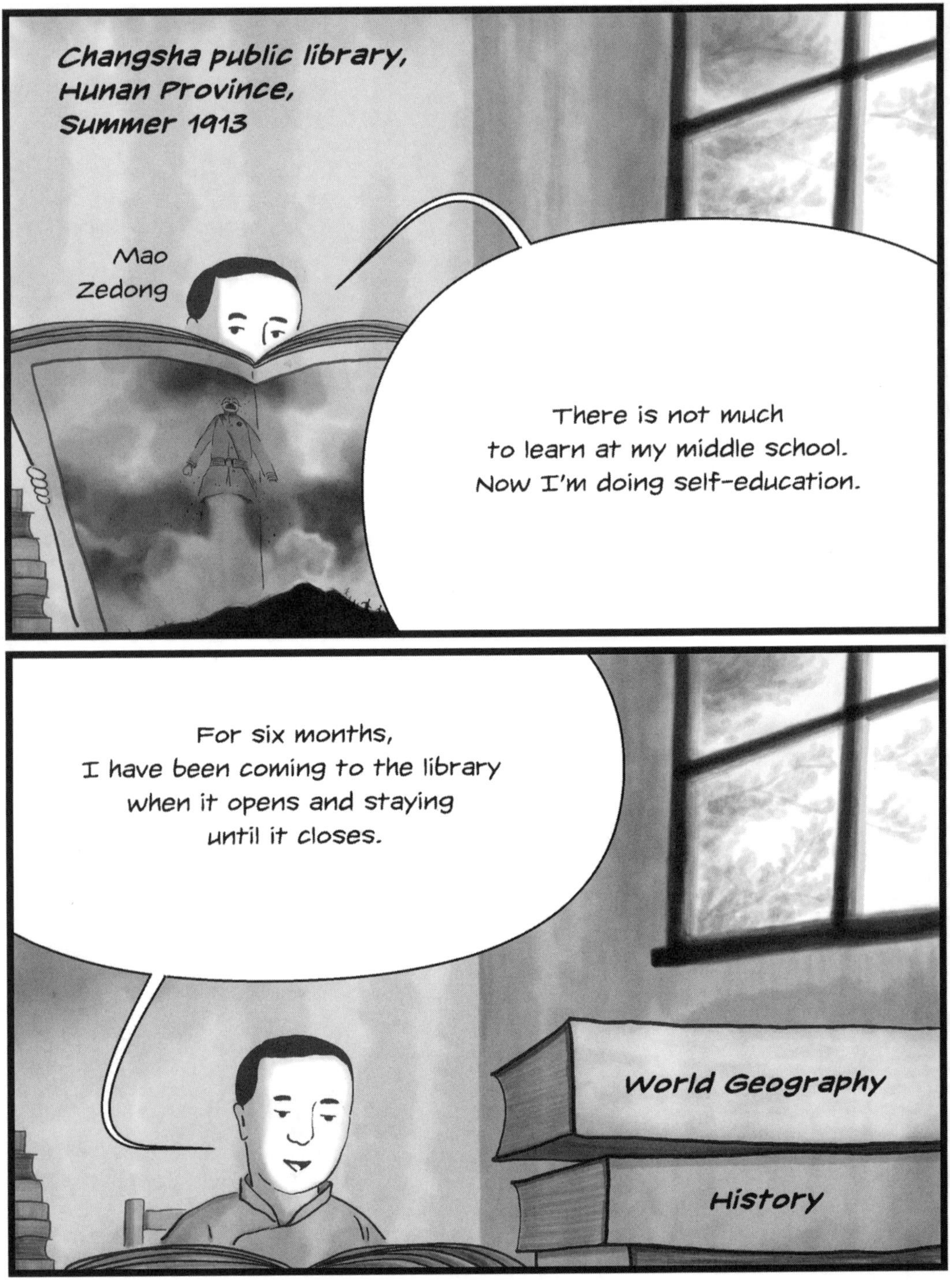
Changsha public library, Hunan Province, Summer 1913
Mao Zedong
There is not much to learn at my middle school. Now I'm doing self-education.
For six months, I have been coming to the library when it opens and staying until it closes.
World Geography
History

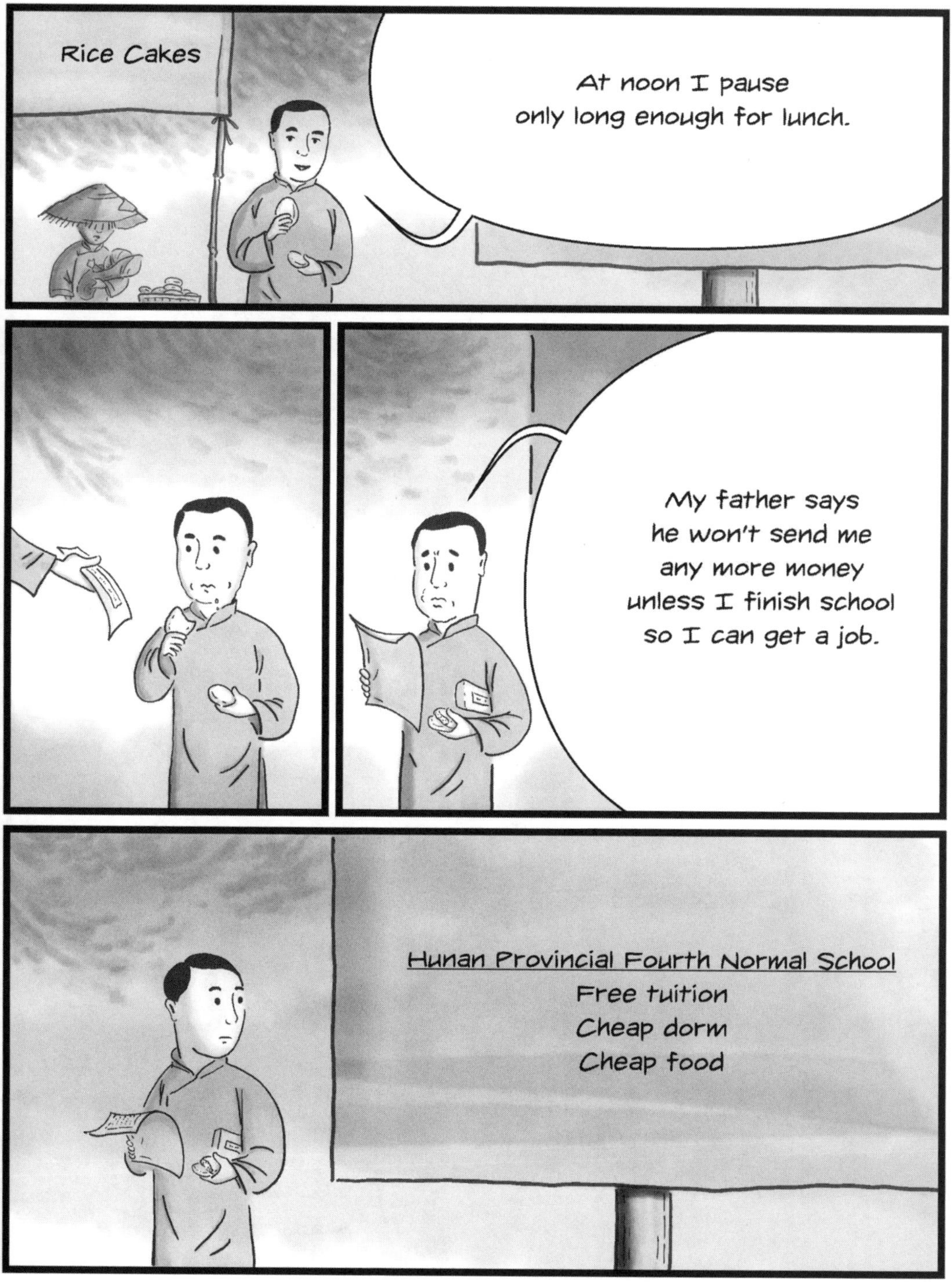
Rice Cakes
At noon I pause only long enough for lunch.
My father says he won't send me any more money unless I finish school so I can get a job.
Hunan Provincial Fourth Normal School
Free tuition
Cheap dorm
Cheap food

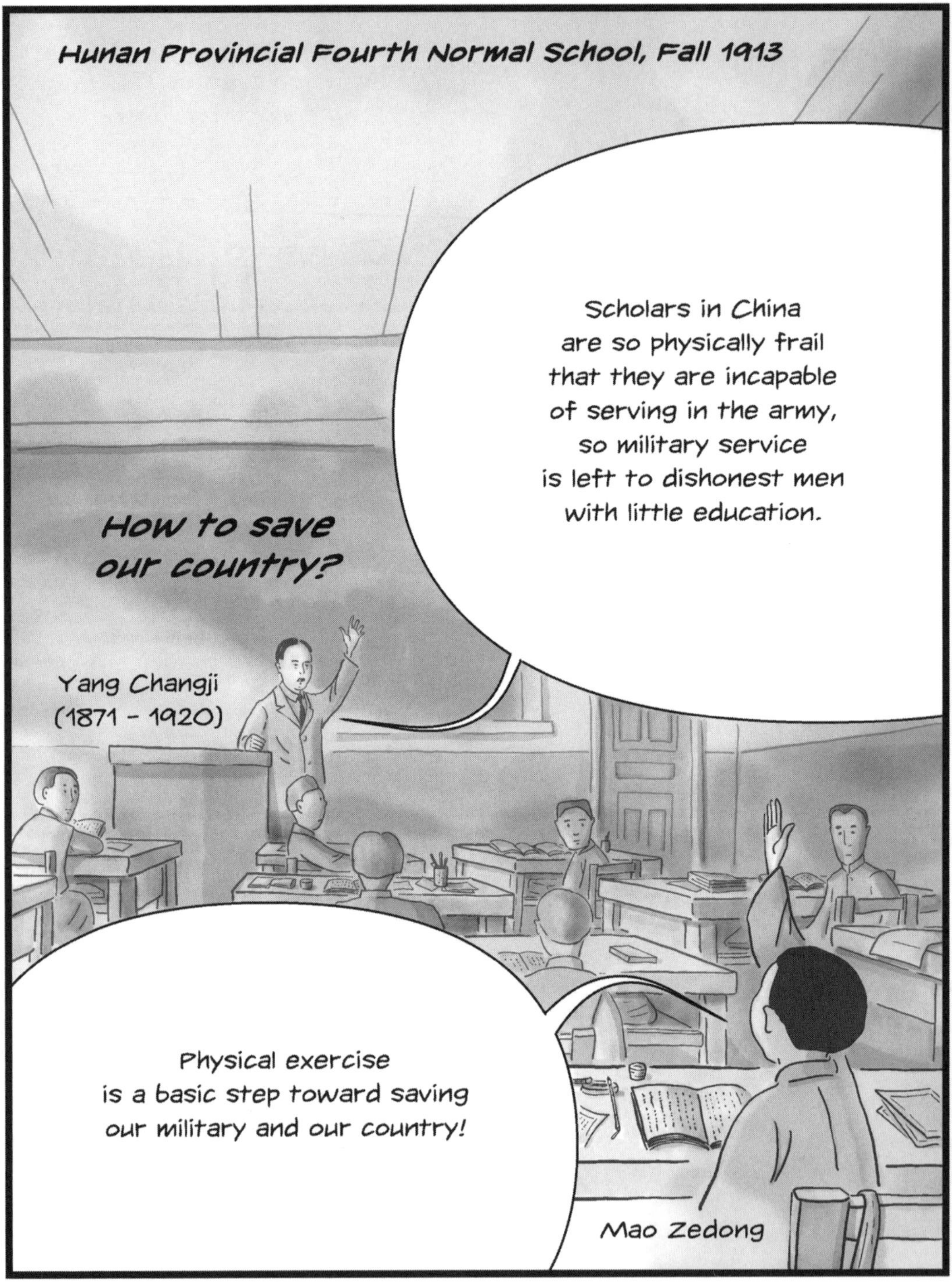
Hunan Provincial Fourth Normal School, Fall 1913
How to save our country?
Yang Changji (1871 - 1920)
Scholars in China are so physically frail that they are incapable of serving in the army, so military service is left to dishonest men with little education.
Physical exercise is a basic step toward saving our military and our country!
Mao Zedong

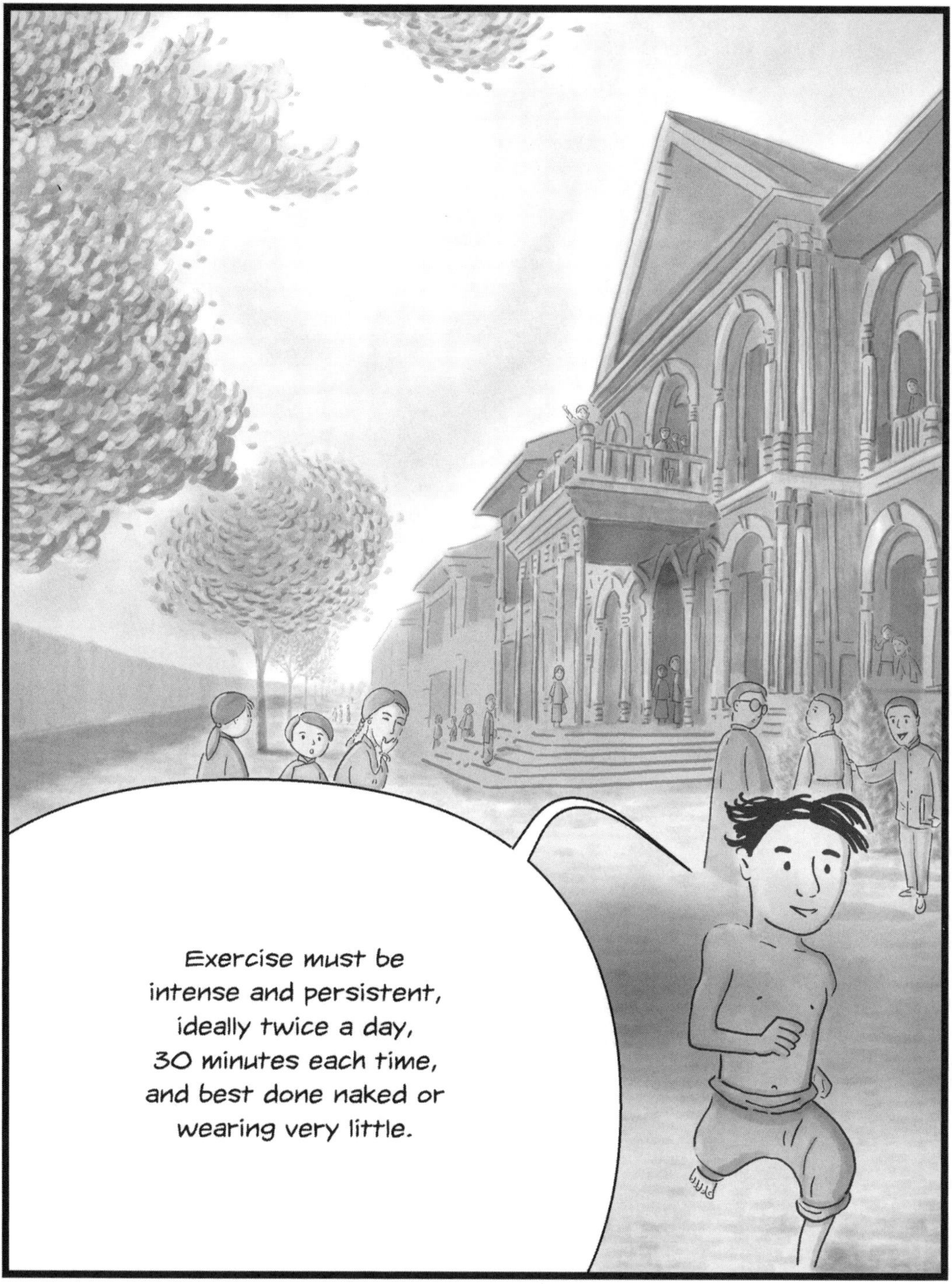
Exercise must be intense and persistent, ideally twice a day, 30 minutes each time, and best done naked or wearing very little.

World War I

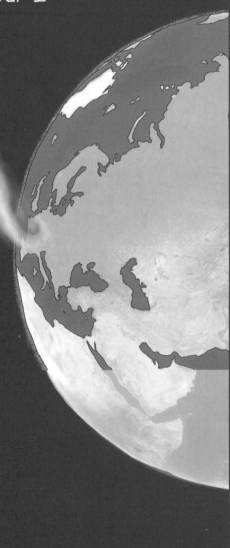

In the late 19th and
early 20th centuries,
among the Western imperialists
there was a renewed race
to establish colonies
in Africa and Asia.
The imperial competition for
new markets and resources
contributed to the outbreak
of World War I (1914 – 1918).

WWI was the first major war
between industrialized countries.
The main warring blocs were
the Allied powers of France,
Britain, and Russia
and the Central powers
of Germany, Austro-Hungary,
and Italy. The United States
entered the war in 1917.

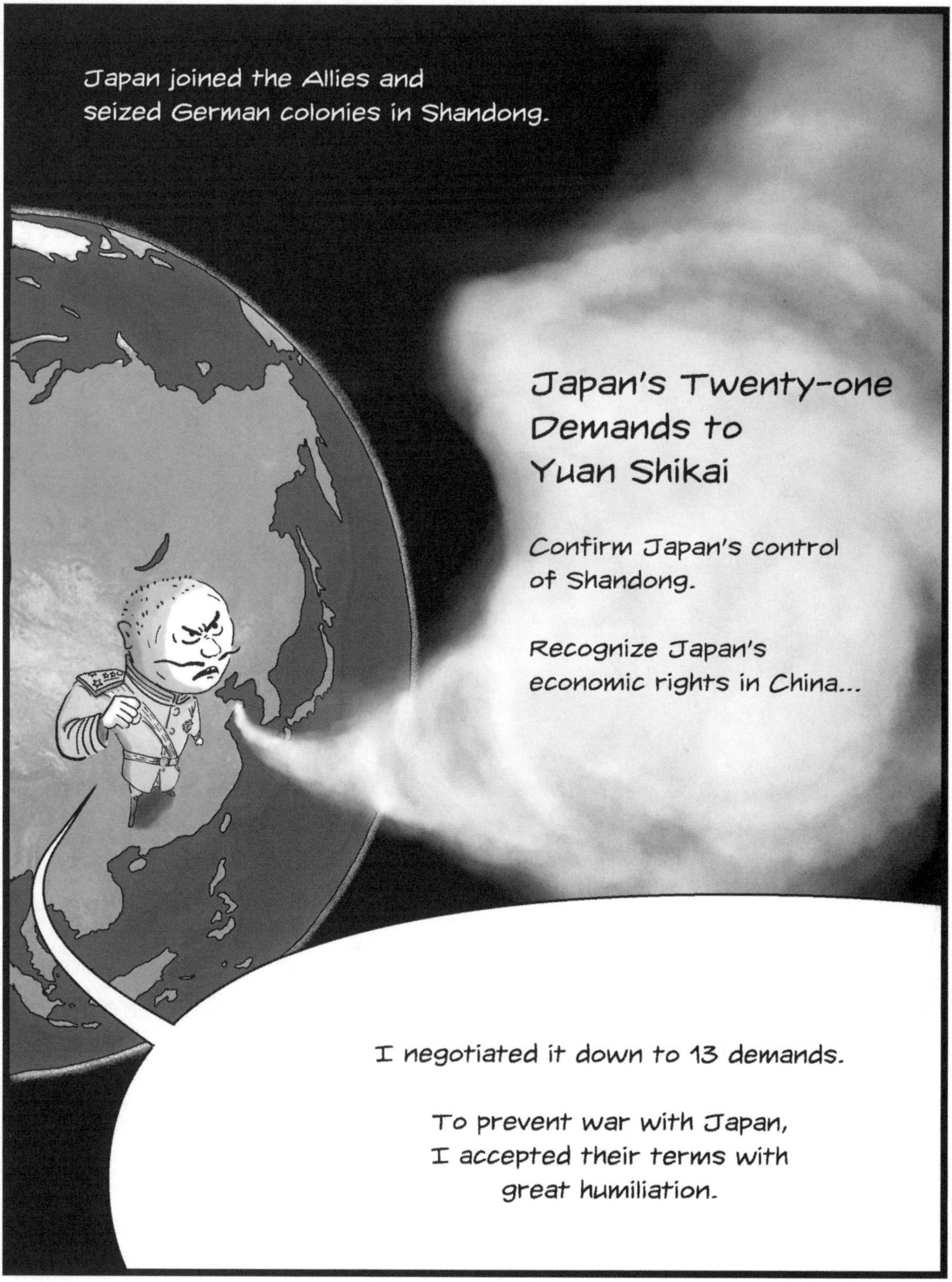
Japan joined the Allies and
seized German colonies in Shandong.
Japan's Twenty-one
Demands to
Yuan Shikai
Confirm Japan's control
of Shandong.
Recognize Japan's
economic rights in China...
I negotiated it down to 13 demands.
To prevent war with Japan,
I accepted their terms with
great humiliation.

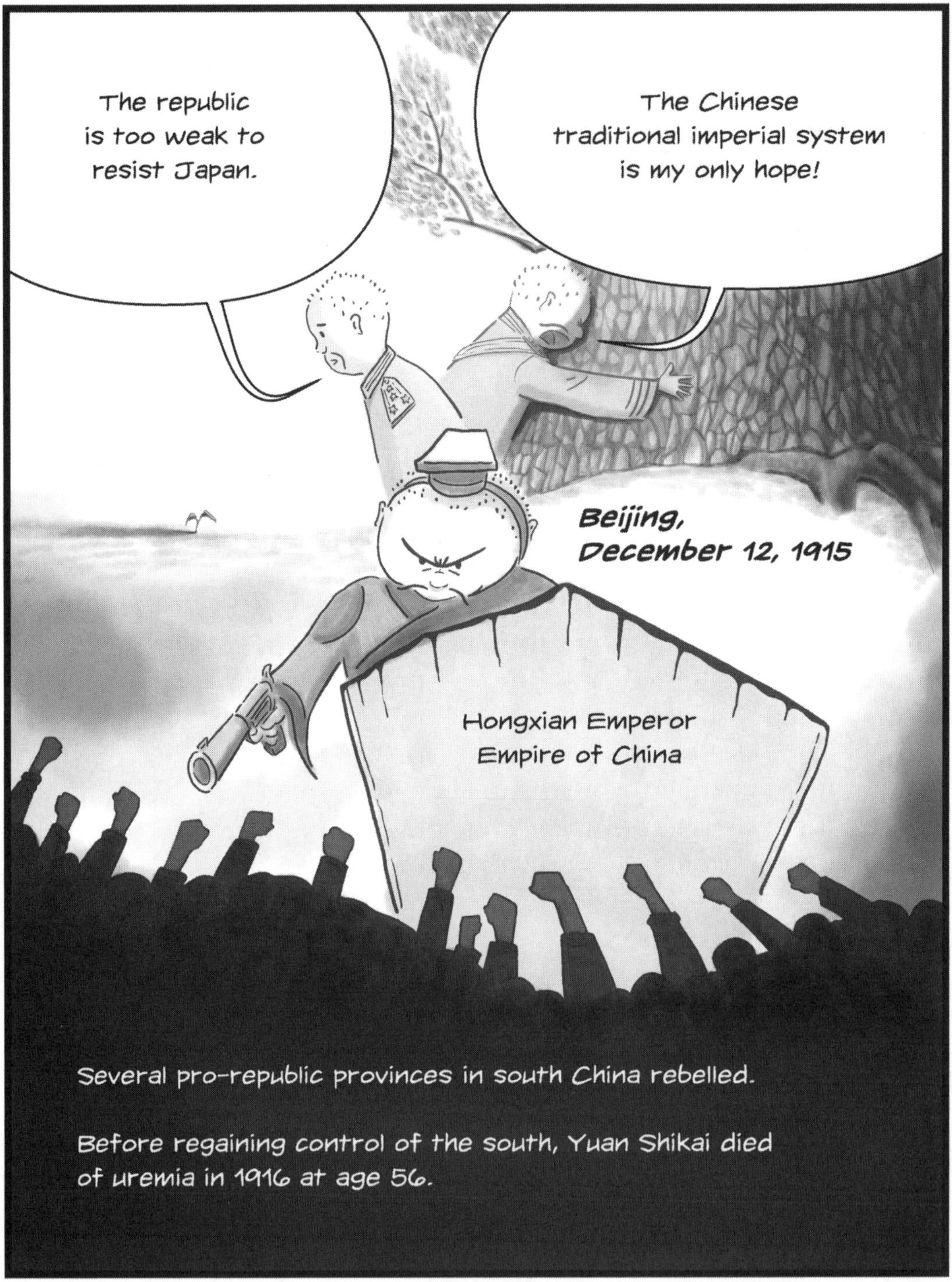
The republic is too weak to resist Japan.
The Chinese traditional imperial system is my only hope!
Beijing, December 12, 1915
Hongxian Emperor Empire of China
Several pro-republic provinces in south China rebelled.
Before regaining control of the south, Yuan Shikai died of uremia in 1916 at age 56.

WARLORD ERA
1916 – 1928

After Yuan died, Parliament was restored, but it only existed in name. Former Beiyang generals fought over the control of Beijing while small private armies were scattered all over the country. Their bases ranged from a few provinces to a handful of towns. The Warlord Era had begun.

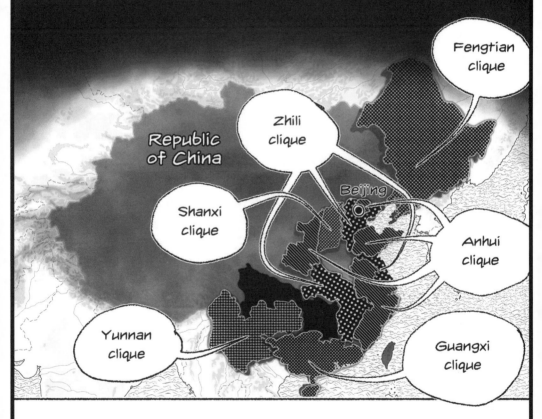

Fengtian clique

Zhili clique

Republic of China

Shanxi clique

Beijing

Anhui clique

Yunnan clique

Guangxi clique

 Major battlegrounds between the northern and southern warlords

 Areas nominally submissive to Beijing

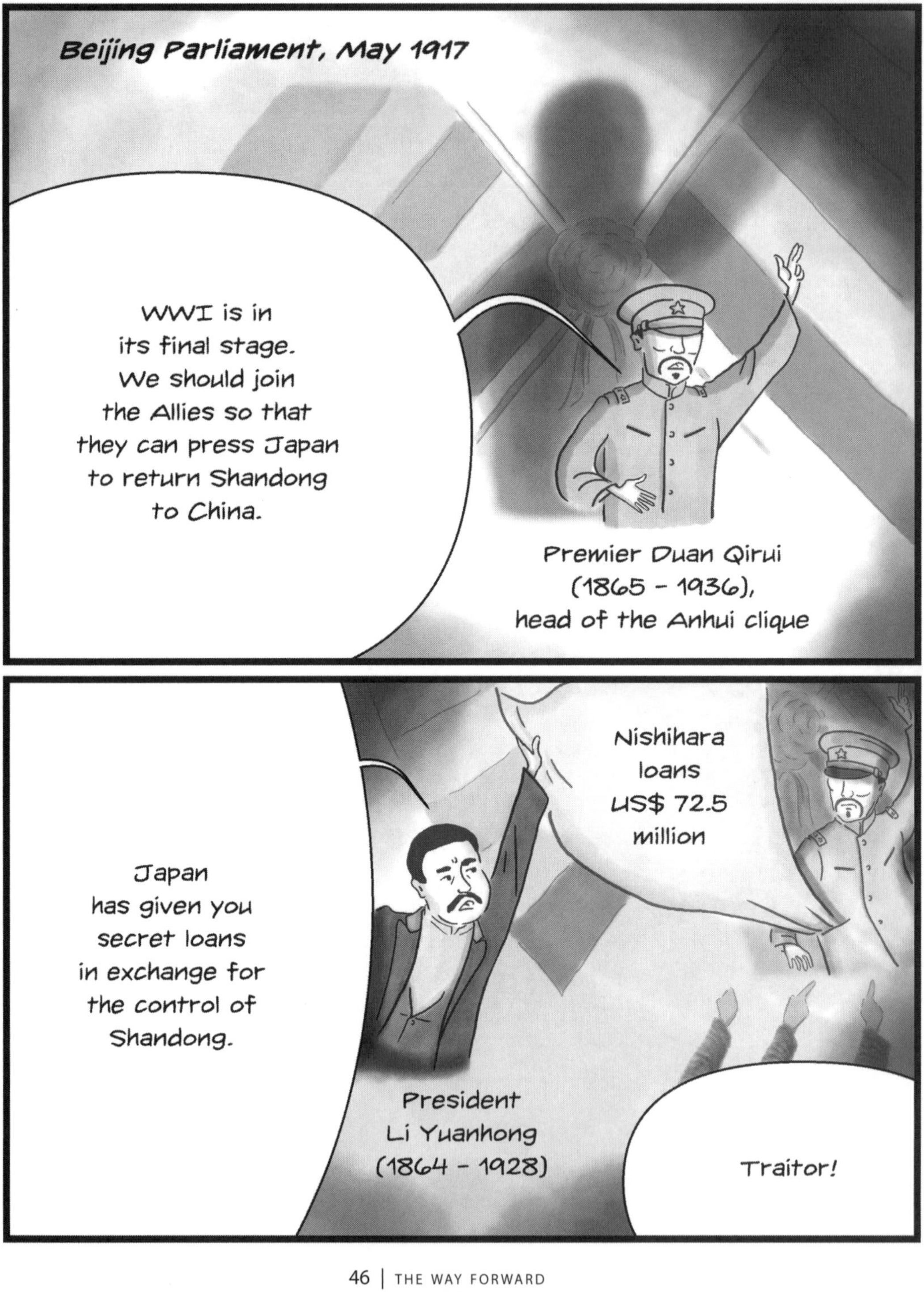

Beijing Parliament, May 1917
WWI is in its final stage. We should join the Allies so that they can press Japan to return Shandong to China.
Premier Duan Qirui (1865 - 1936), head of the Anhui clique
Japan has given you secret loans in exchange for the control of Shandong.
Nishihara loans US$ 72.5 million
President Li Yuanhong (1864 - 1928)
Traitor!

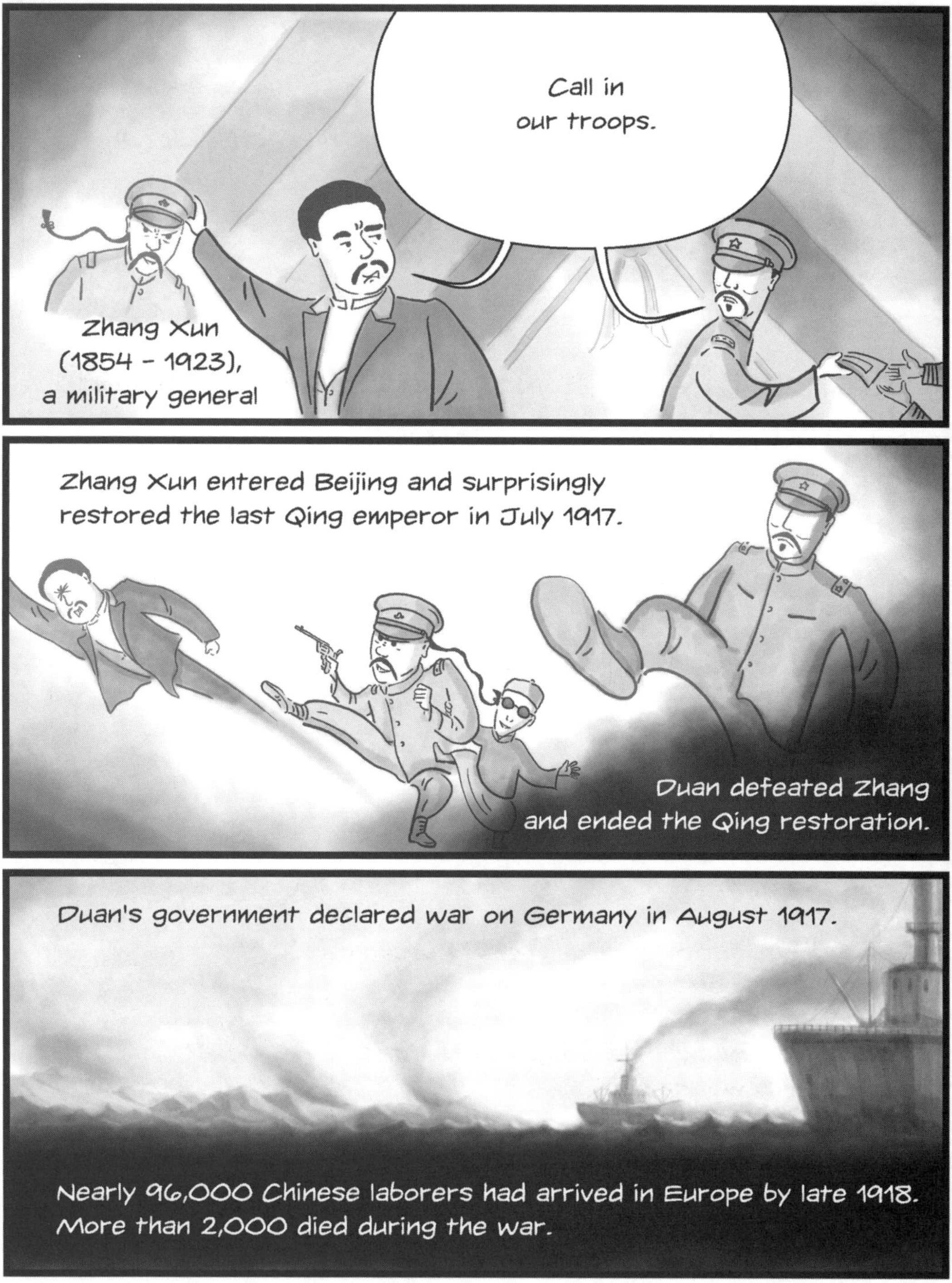
Call in our troops.
Zhang Xun (1854 - 1923), a military general
Zhang Xun entered Beijing and surprisingly restored the last Qing emperor in July 1917.
Duan defeated Zhang and ended the Qing restoration.
Duan's government declared war on Germany in August 1917.
Nearly 96,000 Chinese laborers had arrived in Europe by late 1918. More than 2,000 died during the war.

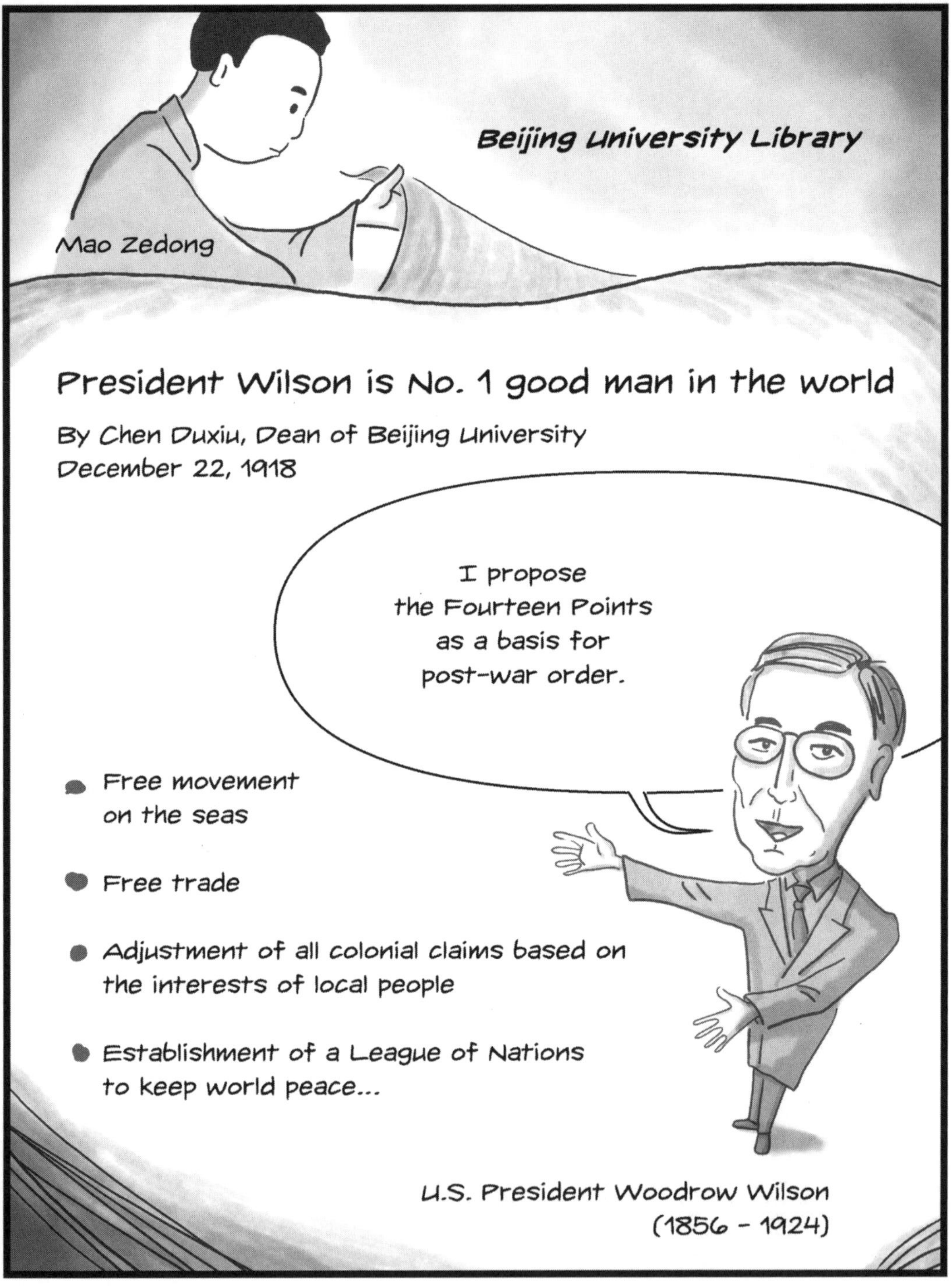
Beijing University Library
Mao Zedong
President Wilson is No. 1 good man in the world
By Chen Duxiu, Dean of Beijing University
December 22, 1918
I propose the Fourteen Points as a basis for post-war order.
Free movement on the seas
Free trade
Adjustment of all colonial claims based on the interests of local people
Establishment of a League of Nations to keep world peace...
U.S. President Woodrow Wilson (1856 - 1924)

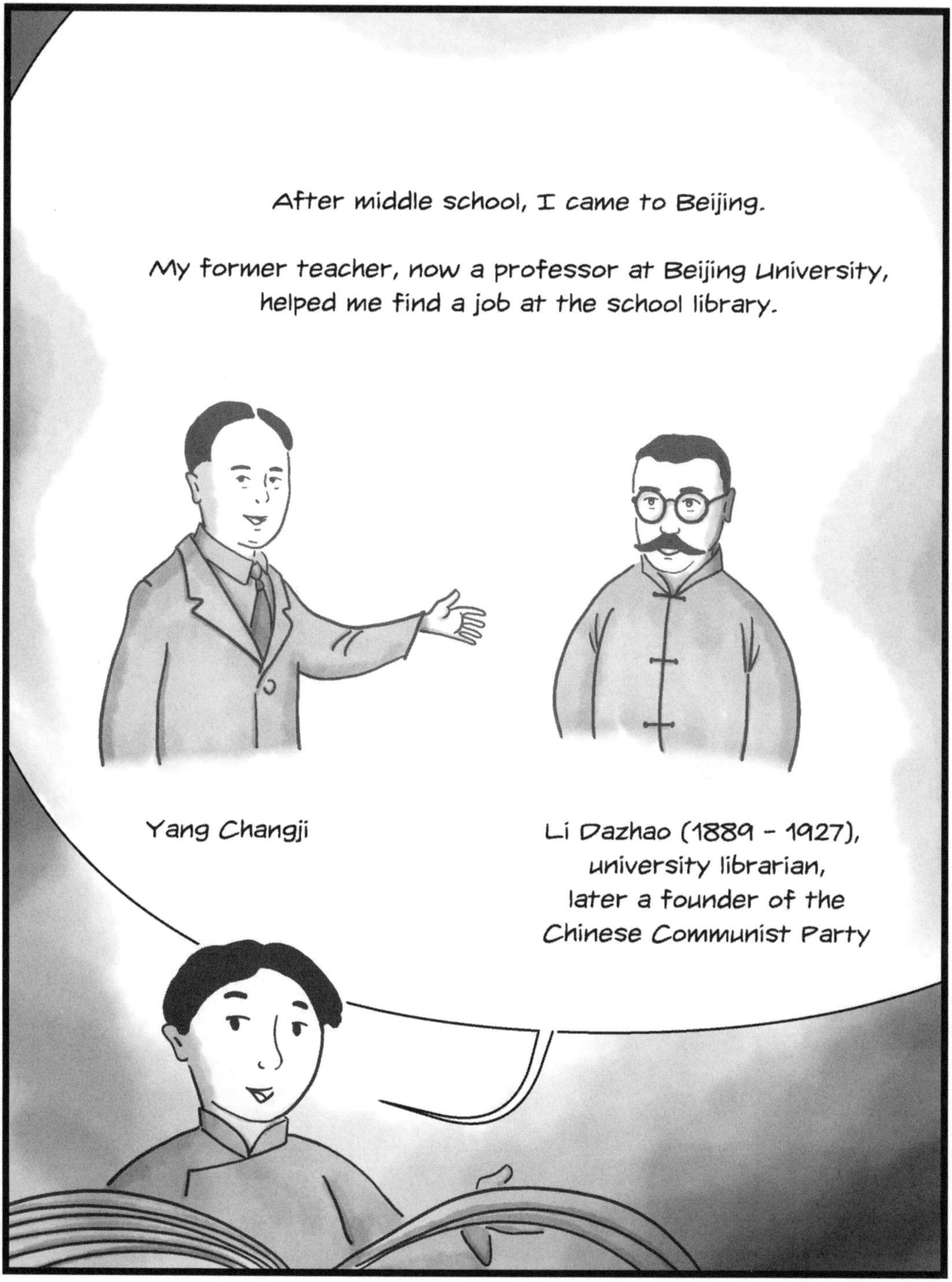
After middle school, I came to Beijing.
My former teacher, now a professor at Beijing University, helped me find a job at the school library.
Yang Changji
Li Dazhao (1889 – 1927), university librarian, later a founder of the Chinese Communist Party

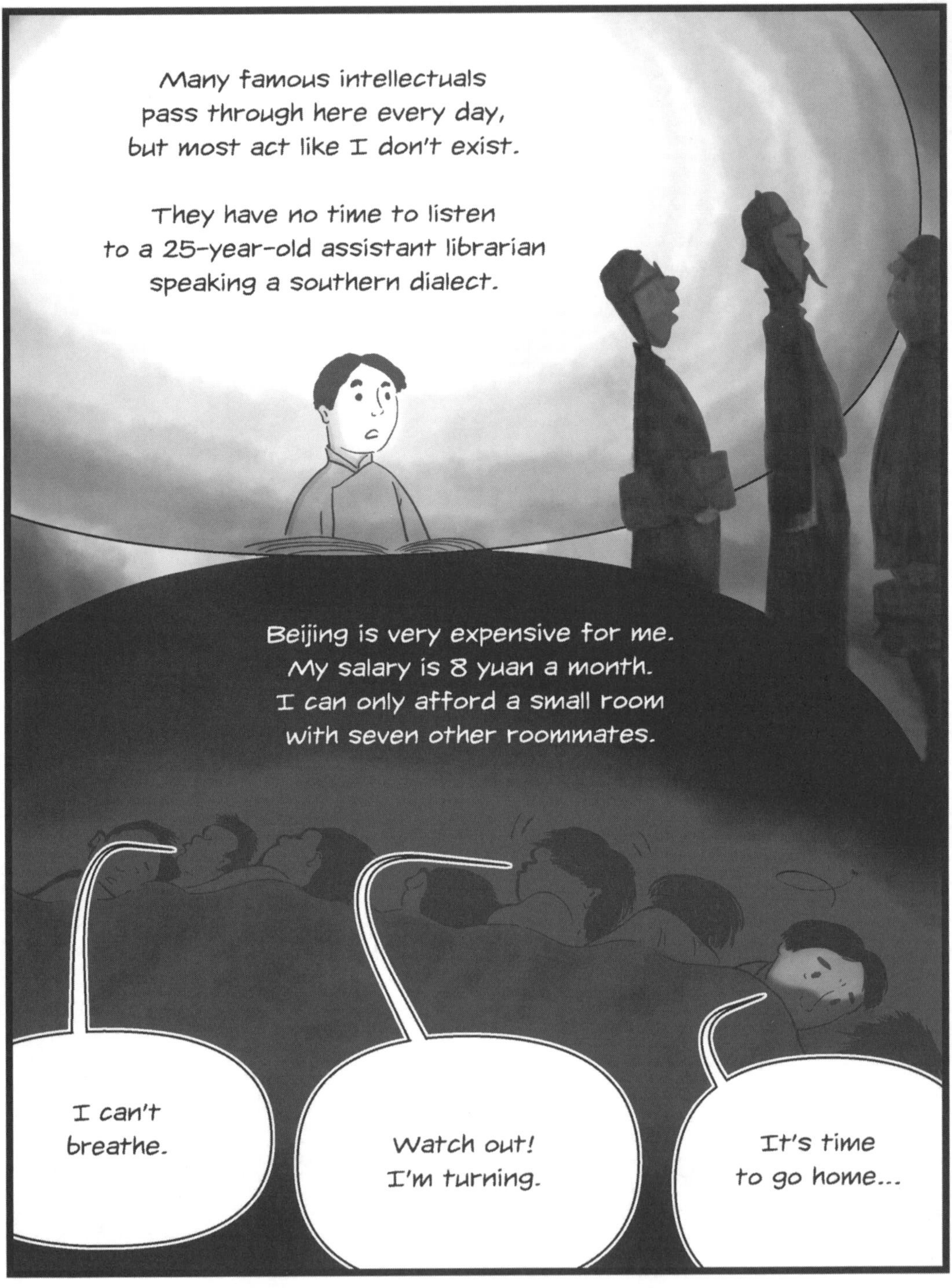
Many famous intellectuals pass through here every day, but most act like I don't exist.
They have no time to listen to a 25-year-old assistant librarian speaking a southern dialect.
Beijing is very expensive for me. My salary is 8 yuan a month. I can only afford a small room with seven other roommates.
I can't breathe.
Watch out! I'm turning.
It's time to go home...

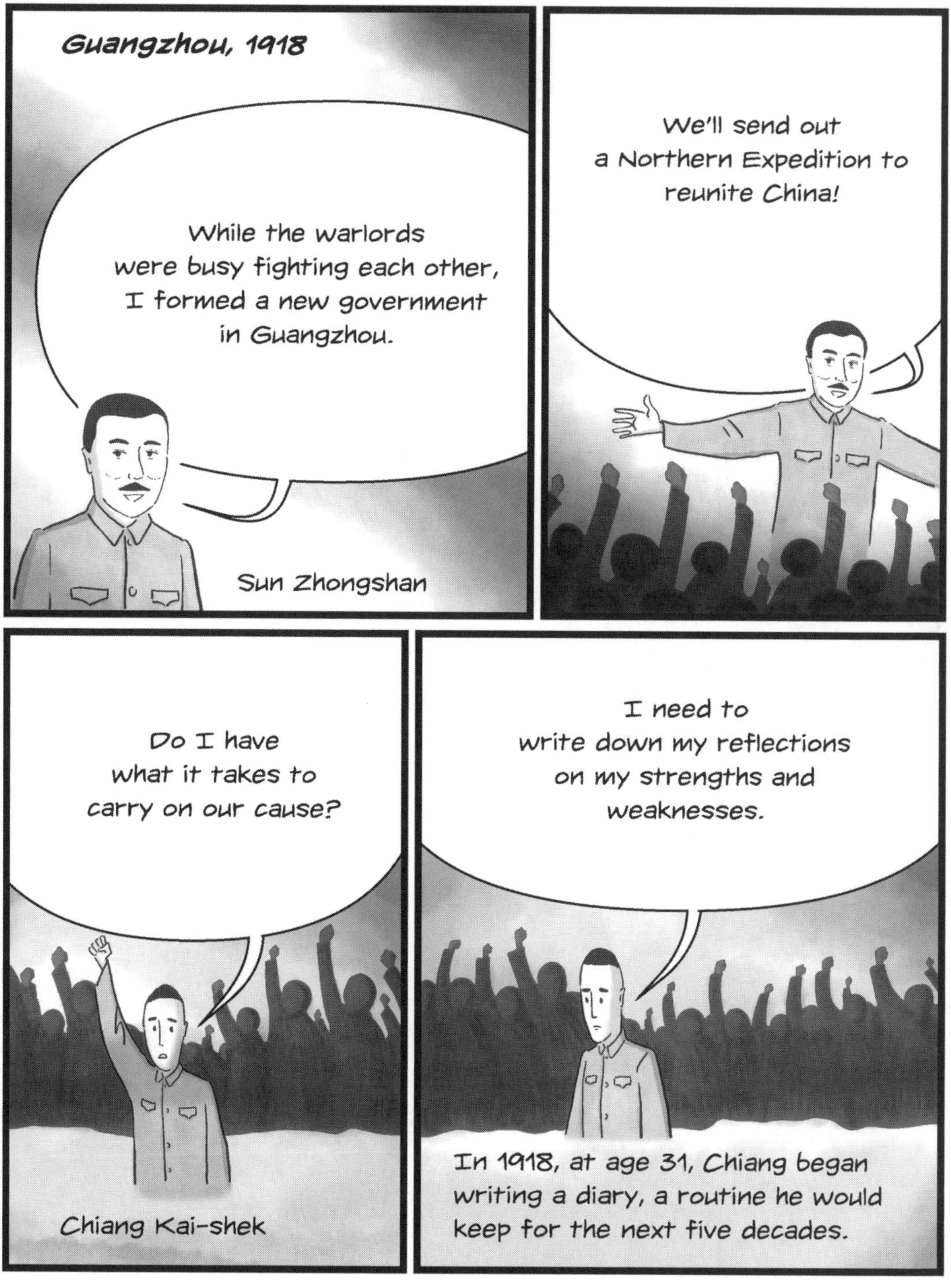
Guangzhou, 1918
While the warlords were busy fighting each other, I formed a new government in Guangzhou.
Sun Zhongshan
We'll send out a Northern Expedition to reunite China!
Do I have what it takes to carry on our cause?
Chiang Kai-shek
I need to write down my reflections on my strengths and weaknesses.
In 1918, at age 31, Chiang began writing a diary, a routine he would keep for the next five decades.

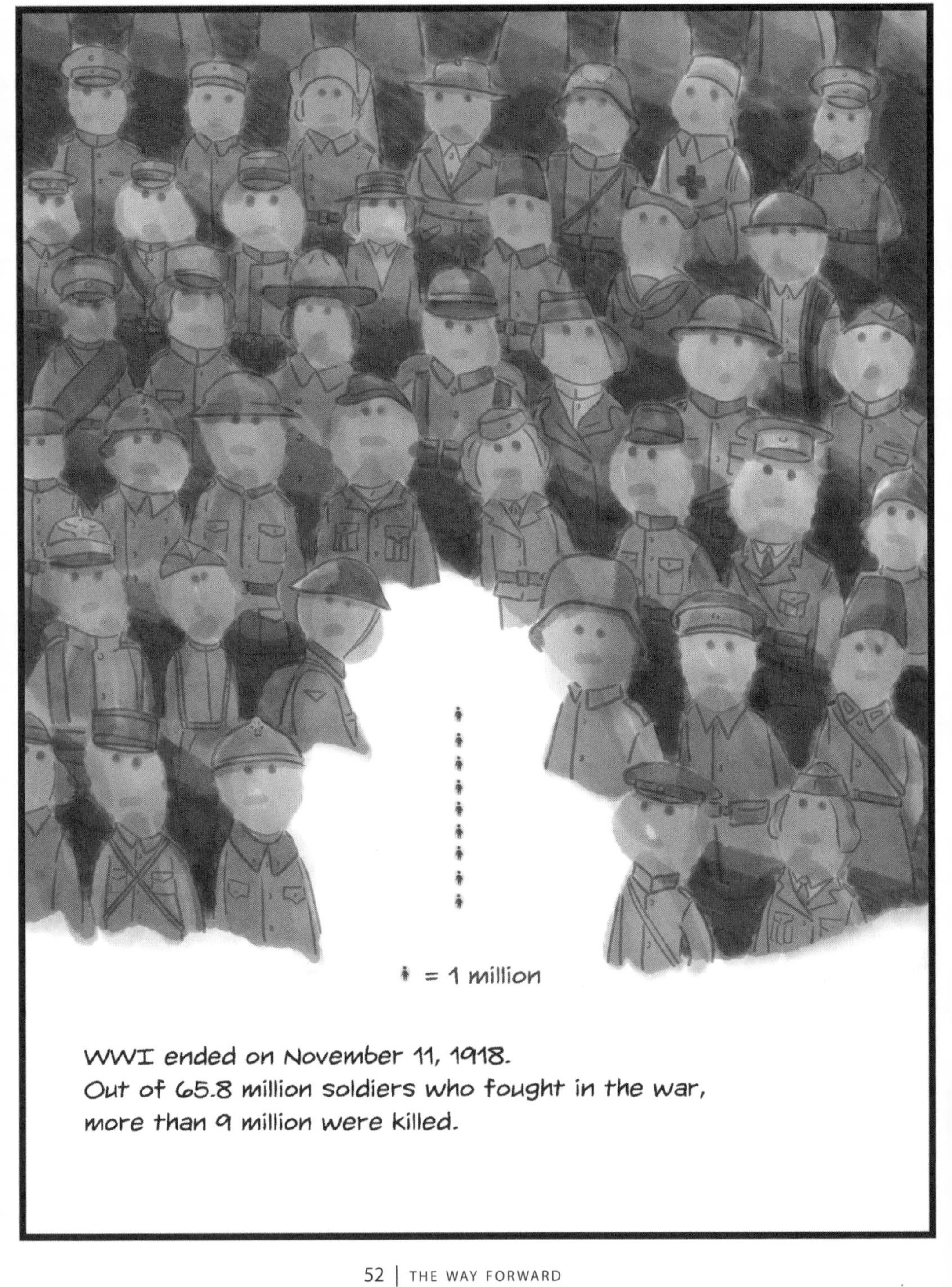
= 1 million

WWI ended on November 11, 1918.
Out of 65.8 million soldiers who fought in the war,
more than 9 million were killed.

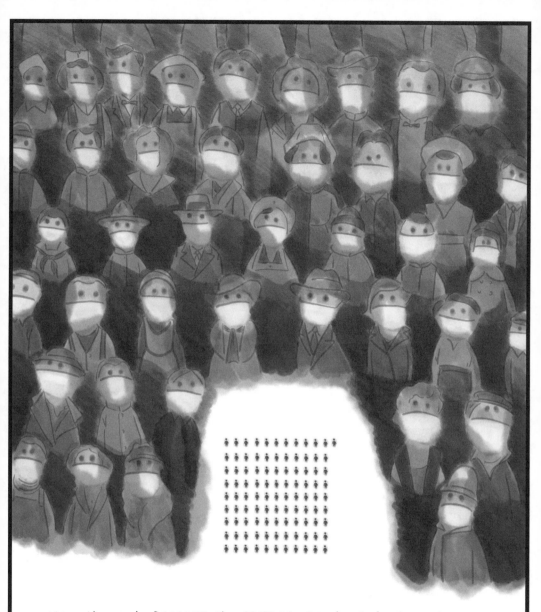

Near the end of WWI, the 1918 Flu Pandemic broke out. Overcrowded barracks, war hospitals, and modern transportation helped the virus spread. Between 1918 and 1919, 500 million people were infected and around 100 million, or 5% of the global population at the time, died.

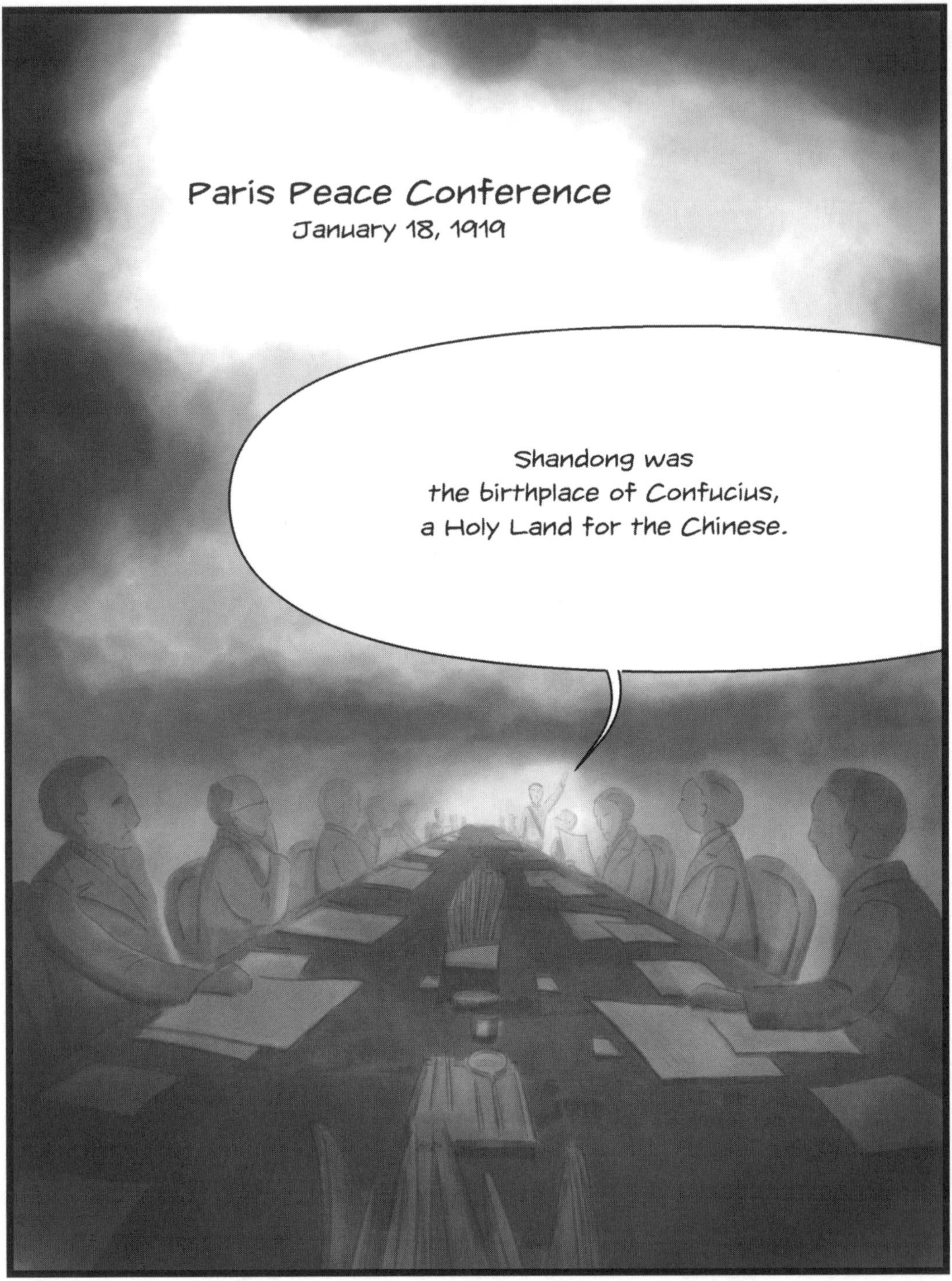
Paris Peace Conference
January 18, 1919
Shandong was the birthplace of Confucius, a Holy Land for the Chinese.

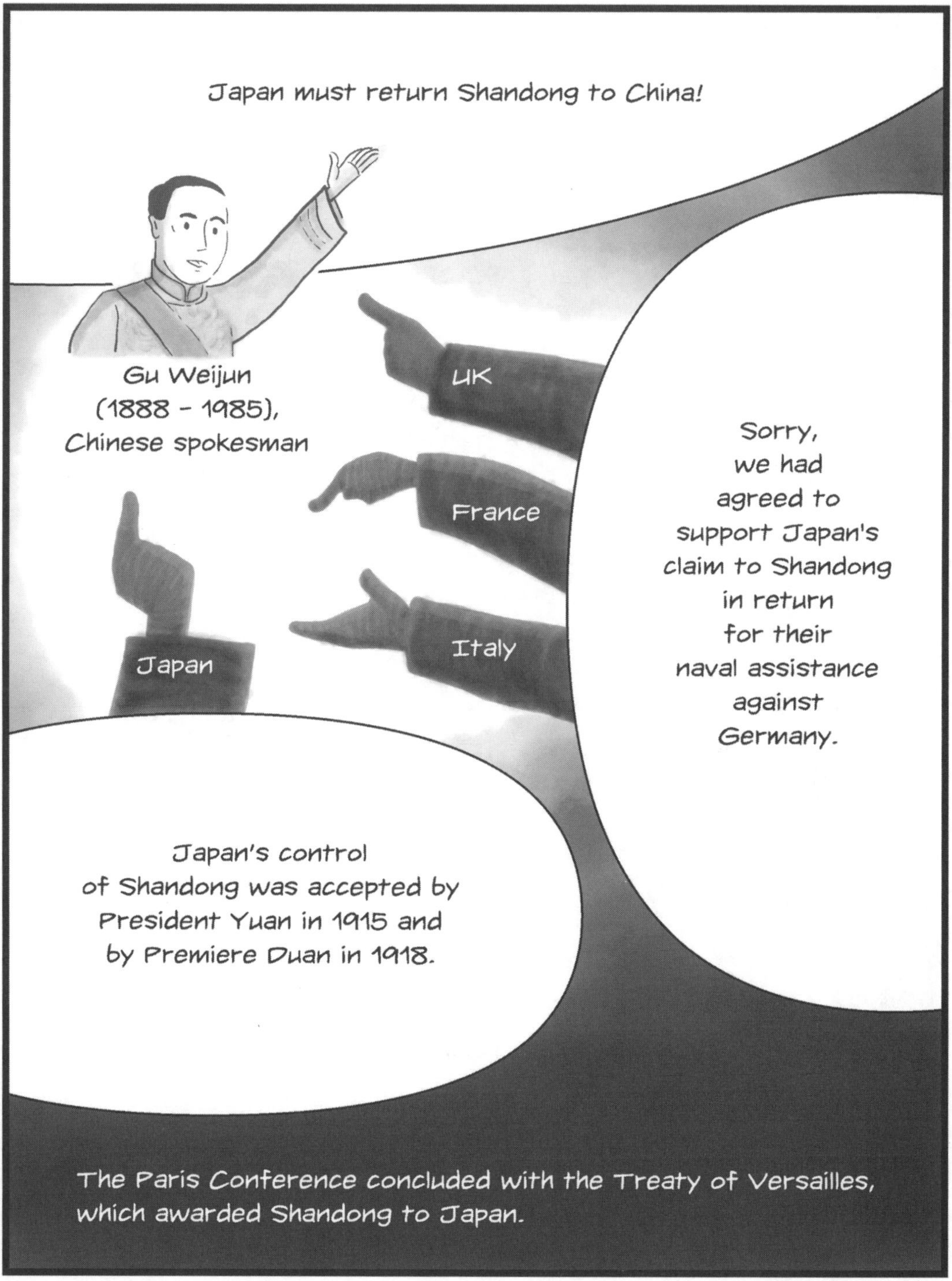
Japan must return Shandong to China!
Gu Weijun
(1888 - 1985),
Chinese spokesman
UK
France
Italy
Japan
Sorry, we had agreed to support Japan's claim to Shandong in return for their naval assistance against Germany.
Japan's control of Shandong was accepted by President Yuan in 1915 and by Premiere Duan in 1918.
The Paris Conference concluded with the Treaty of Versailles, which awarded Shandong to Japan.

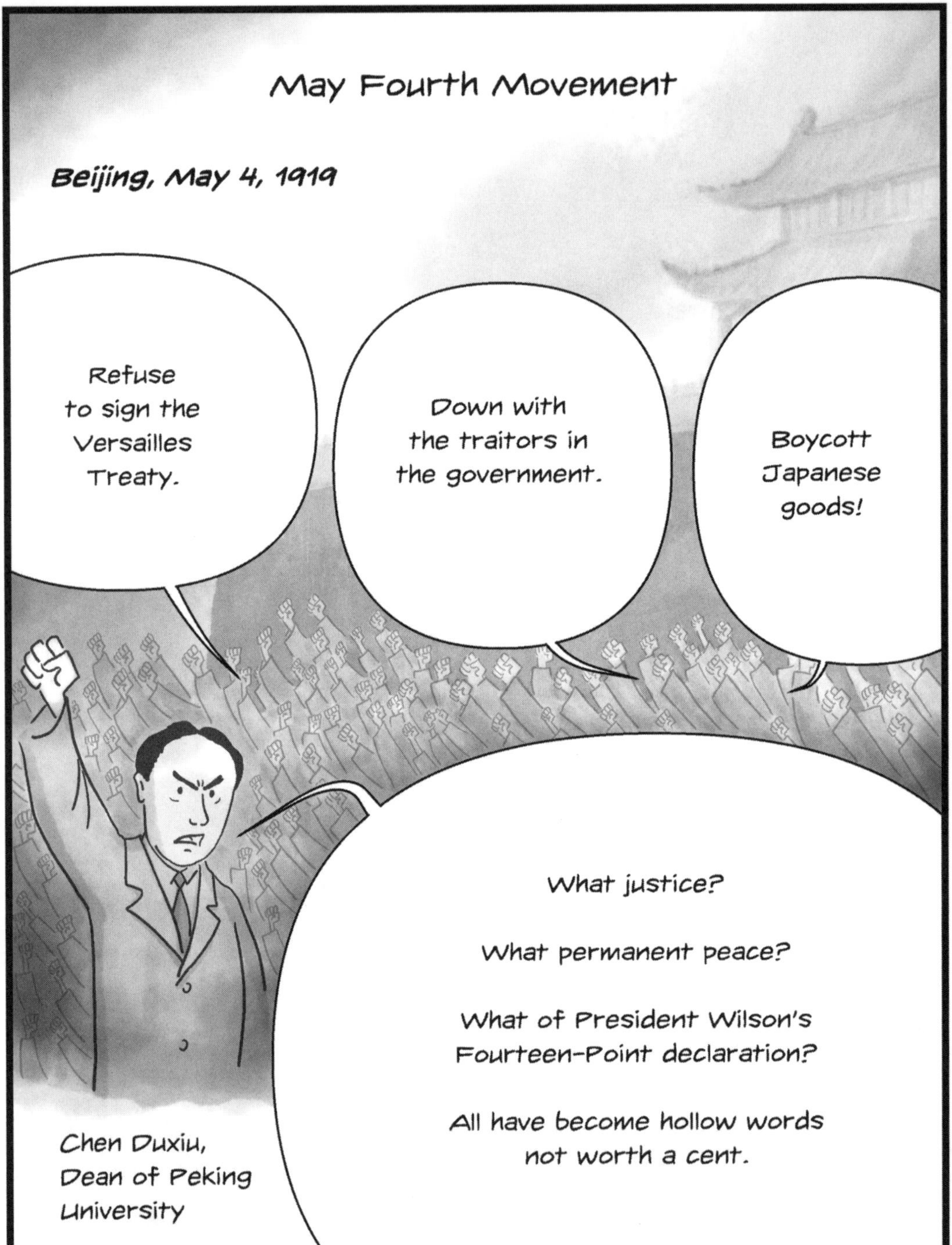
May Fourth Movement
Beijing, May 4, 1919
Refuse to sign the Versailles Treaty.
Down with the traitors in the government.
Boycott Japanese goods!
What justice?
What permanent peace?
What of President Wilson's Fourteen-Point declaration?
All have become hollow words not worth a cent.
Chen Duxiu, Dean of Peking University

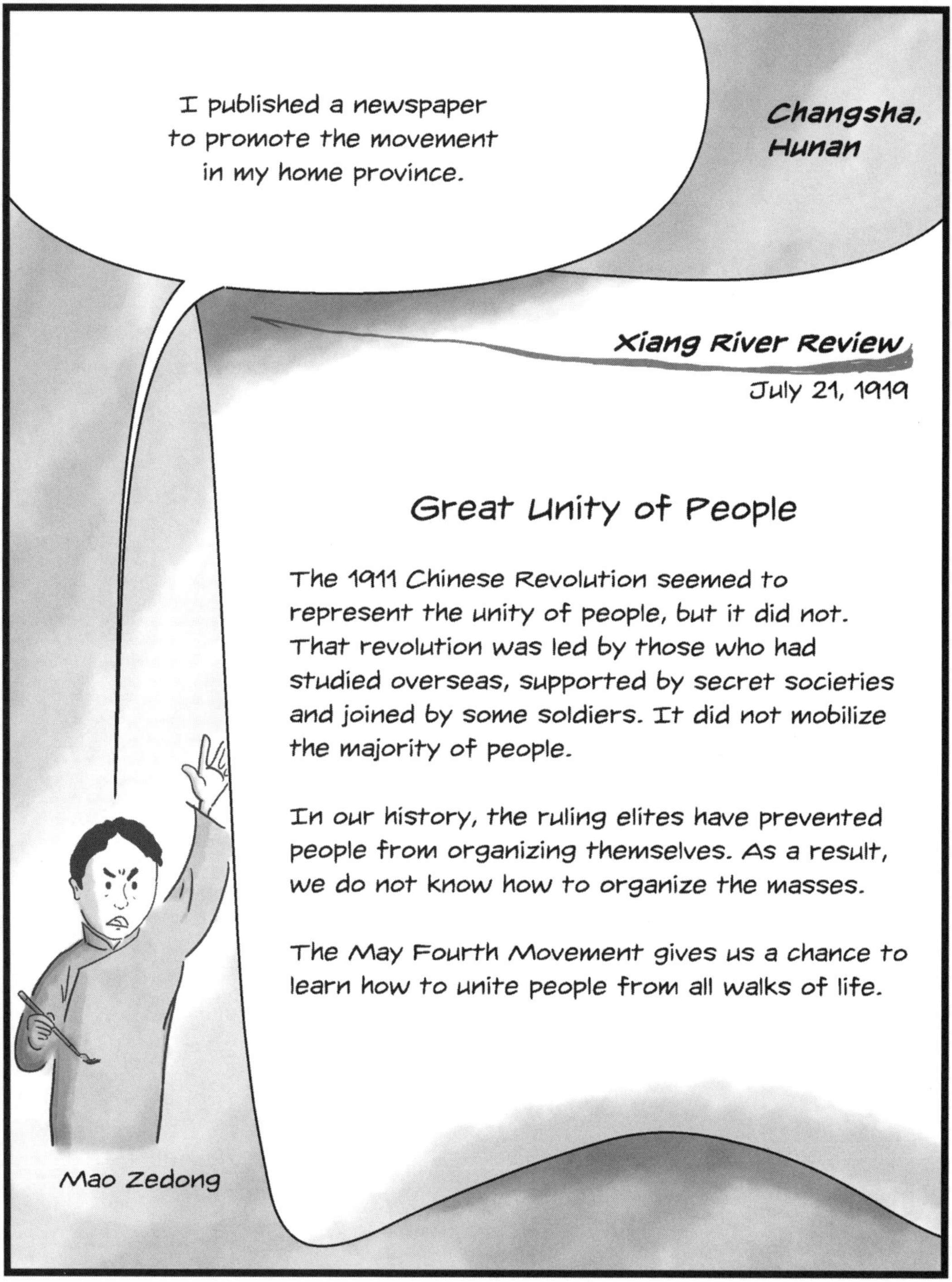
I published a newspaper to promote the movement in my home province.
Changsha, Hunan
Xiang River Review
July 21, 1919
Great Unity of People
The 1911 Chinese Revolution seemed to represent the unity of people, but it did not. That revolution was led by those who had studied overseas, supported by secret societies and joined by some soldiers. It did not mobilize the majority of people.
In our history, the ruling elites have prevented people from organizing themselves. As a result, we do not know how to organize the masses.
The May Fourth Movement gives us a chance to learn how to unite people from all walks of life.
Mao Zedong

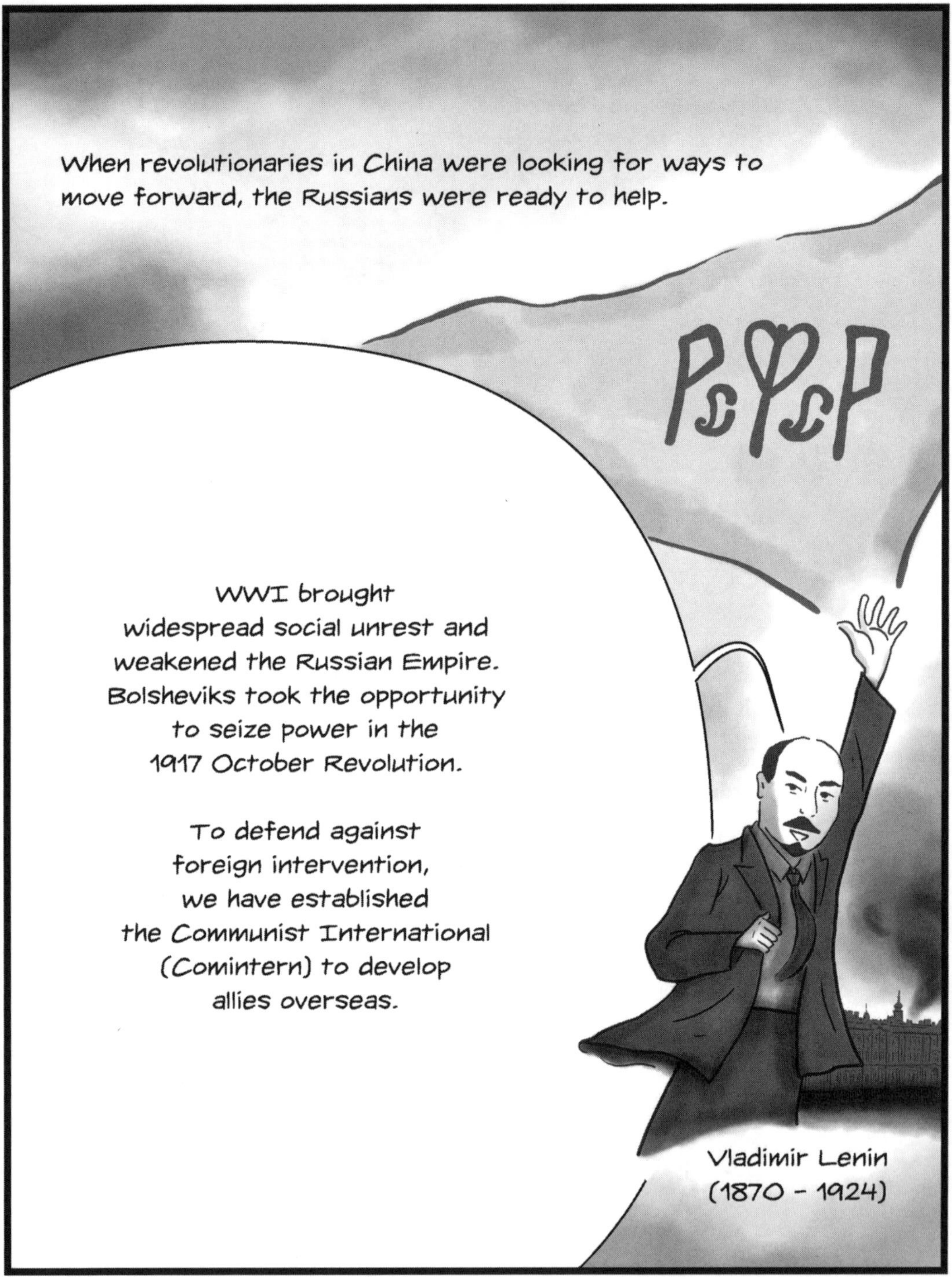
When revolutionaries in China were looking for ways to move forward, the Russians were ready to help.
PCΦCP
WWI brought widespread social unrest and weakened the Russian Empire. Bolsheviks took the opportunity to seize power in the 1917 October Revolution.
To defend against foreign intervention, we have established the Communist International (Comintern) to develop allies overseas.
Vladimir Lenin (1870 - 1924)

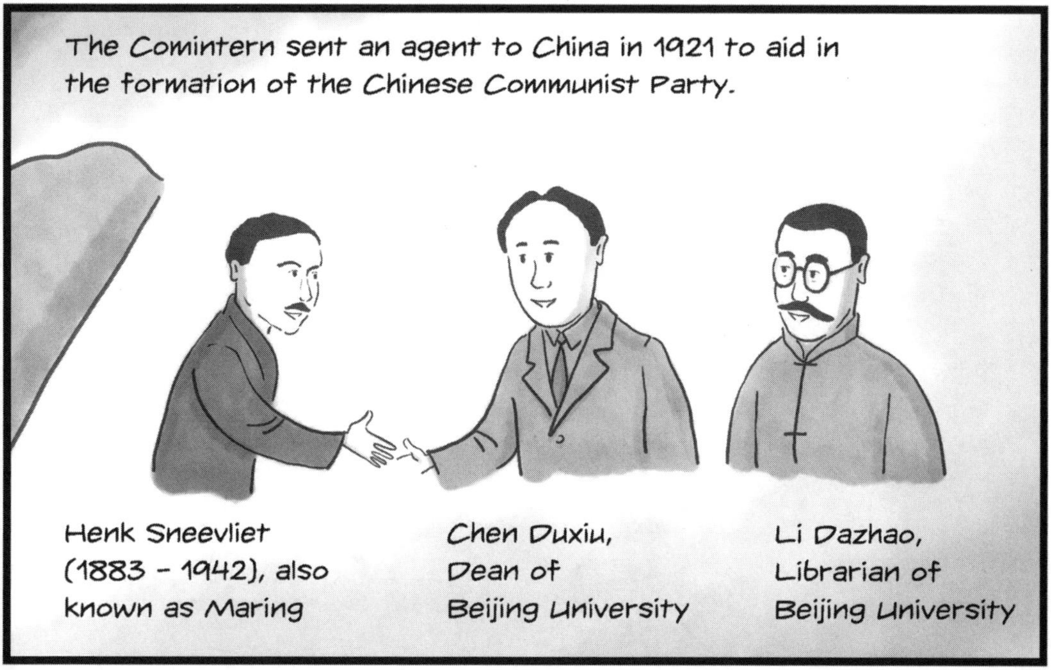
The Comintern sent an agent to China in 1921 to aid in the formation of the Chinese Communist Party.
Henk Sneevliet (1883 – 1942), also known as Maring
Chen Duxiu, Dean of Beijing University
Li Dazhao, Librarian of Beijing University

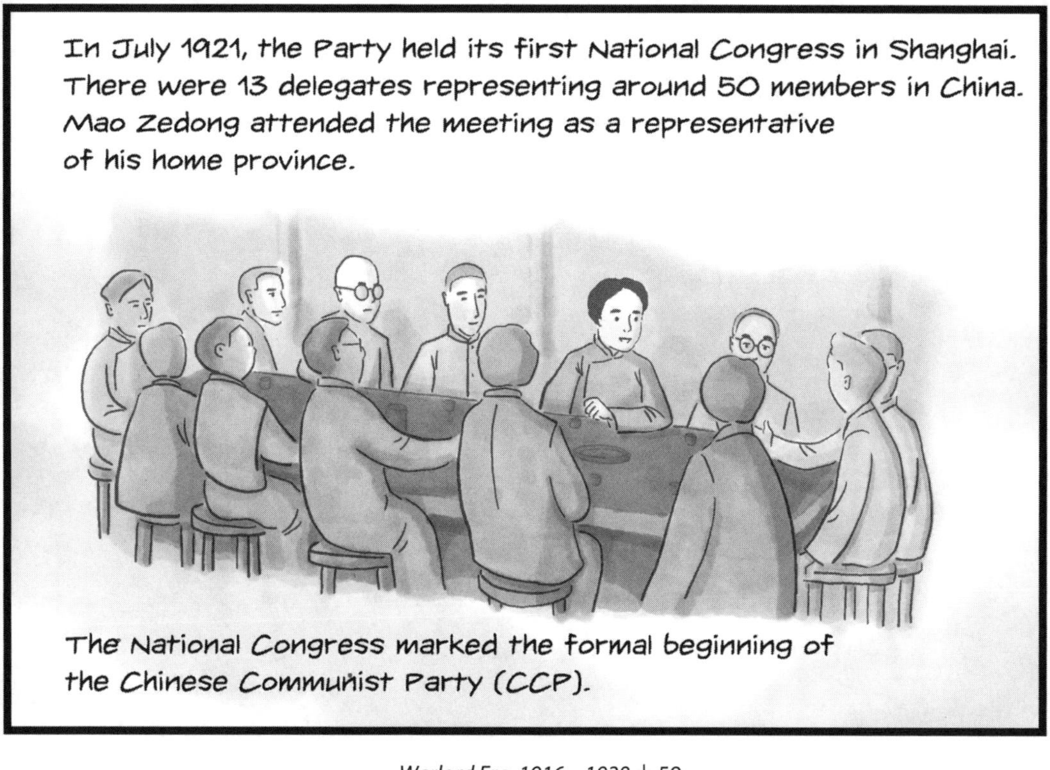
In July 1921, the Party held its first National Congress in Shanghai. There were 13 delegates representing around 50 members in China. Mao Zedong attended the meeting as a representative of his home province.
The National Congress marked the formal beginning of the Chinese Communist Party (CCP).

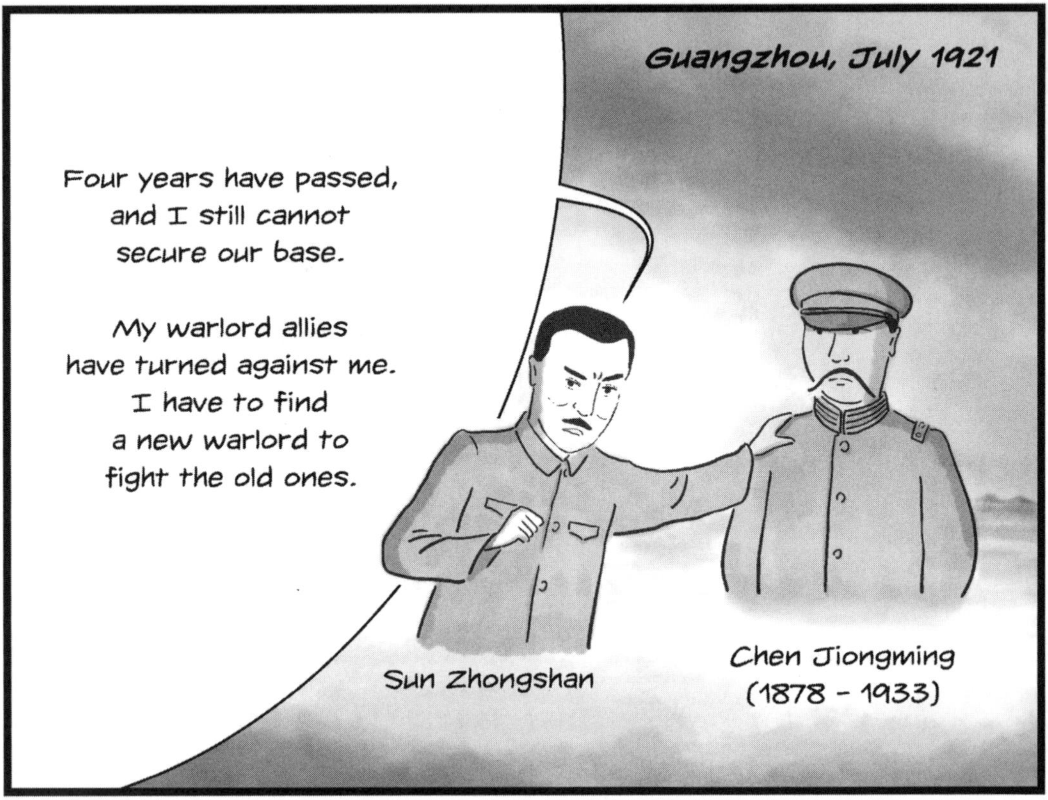
Guangzhou, July 1921
Four years have passed, and I still cannot secure our base.
My warlord allies have turned against me. I have to find a new warlord to fight the old ones.
Sun Zhongshan
Chen Jiongming (1878 - 1933)

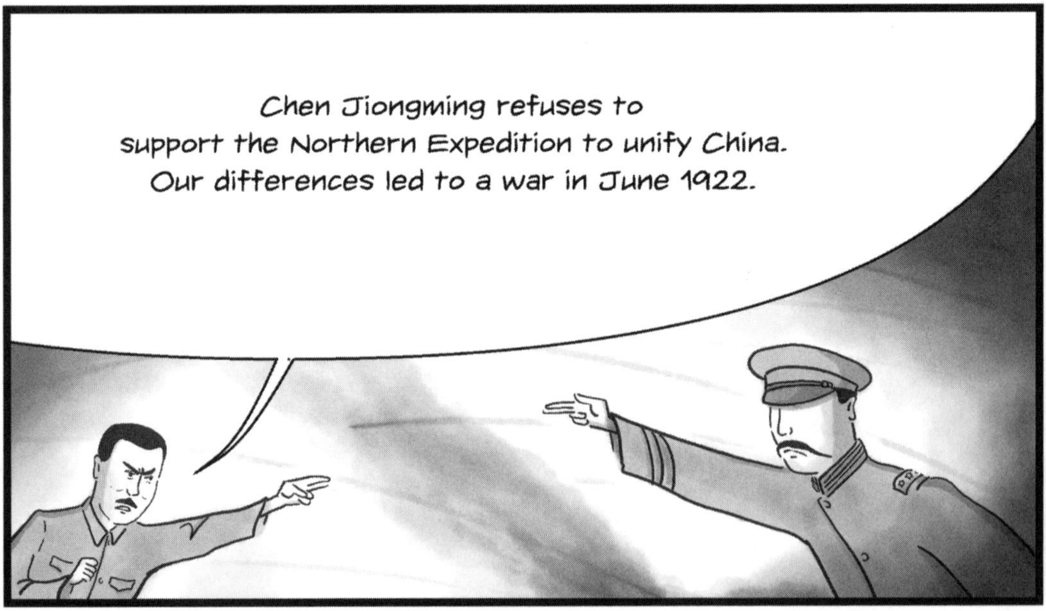
Chen Jiongming refuses to support the Northern Expedition to unify China. Our differences led to a war in June 1922.

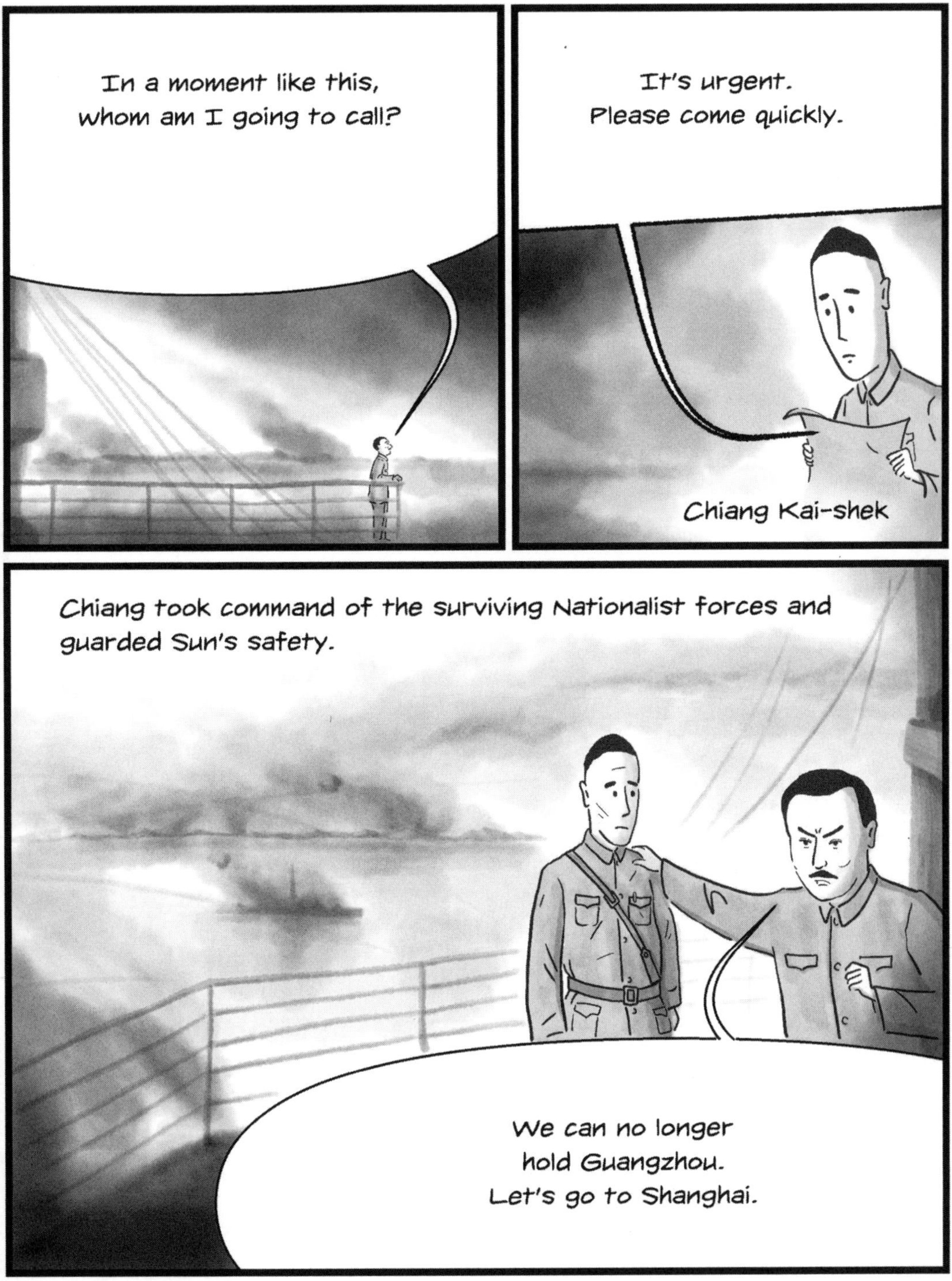

In a moment like this, whom am I going to call?
It's urgent. Please come quickly.
Chiang Kai-shek
Chiang took command of the surviving Nationalist forces and guarded Sun's safety.
We can no longer hold Guangzhou. Let's go to Shanghai.

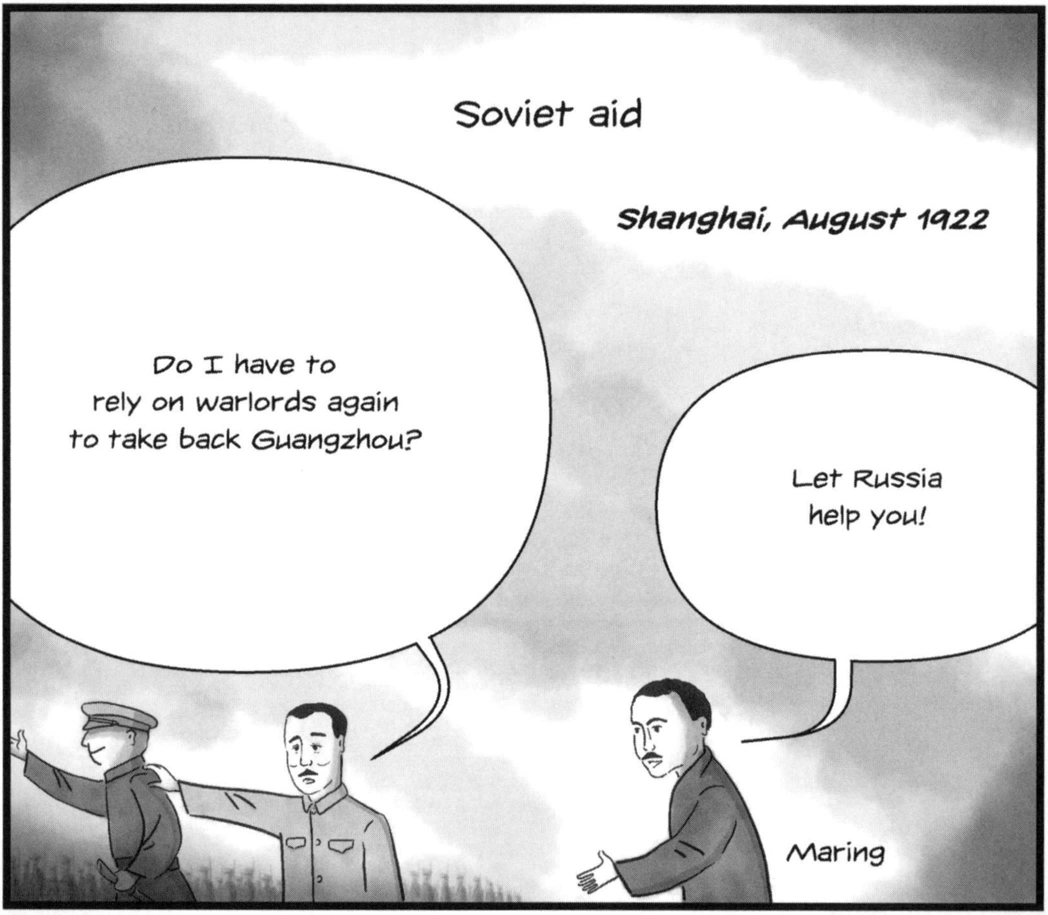
Soviet aid
Shanghai, August 1922
Do I have to rely on warlords again to take back Guangzhou?
Let Russia help you!
Maring

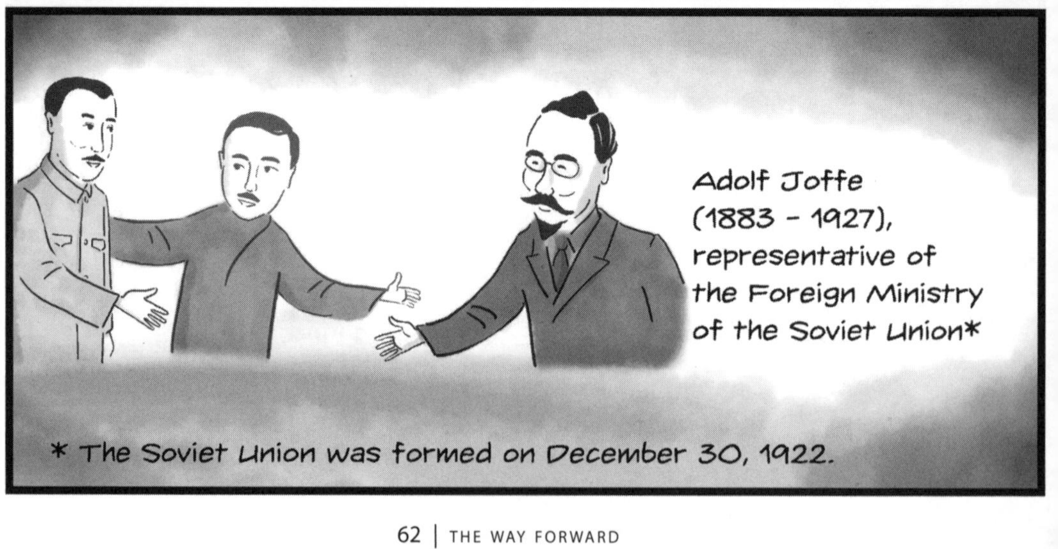
Adolf Joffe (1883 - 1927), representative of the Foreign Ministry of the Soviet Union*
* The Soviet Union was formed on December 30, 1922.

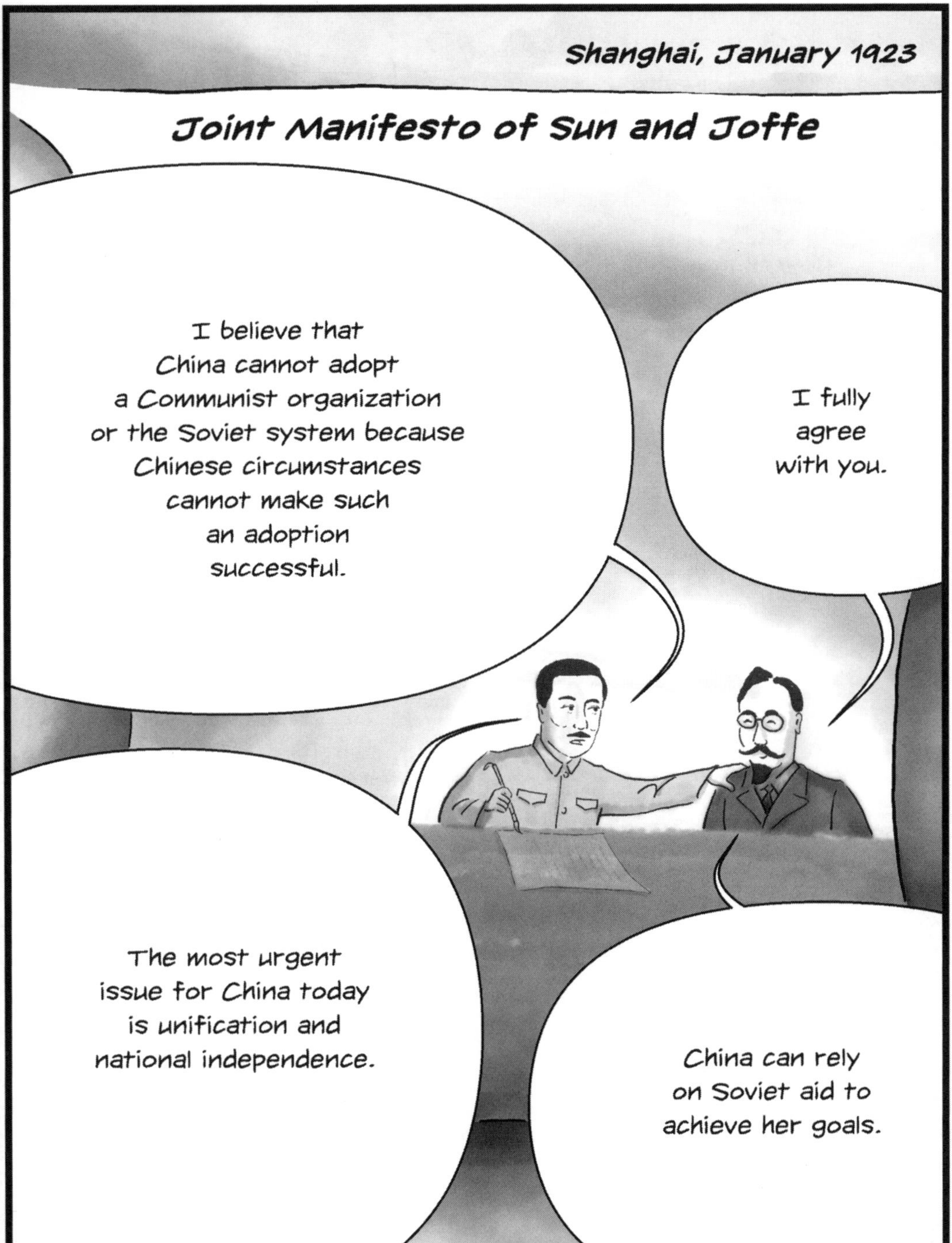
Shanghai, January 1923
Joint Manifesto of Sun and Joffe
I believe that China cannot adopt a Communist organization or the Soviet system because Chinese circumstances cannot make such an adoption successful.
I fully agree with you.
The most urgent issue for China today is unification and national independence.
China can rely on Soviet aid to achieve her goals.

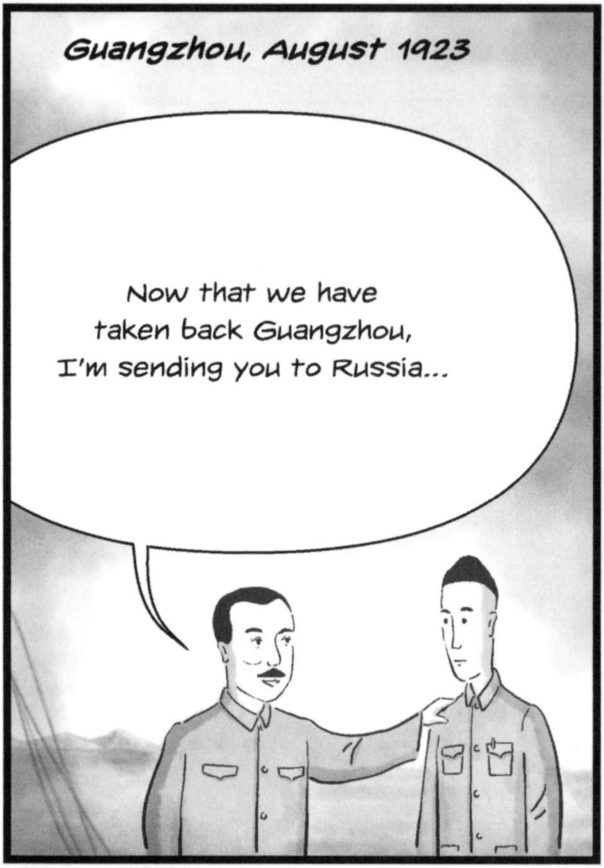
Guangzhou, August 1923
Now that we have taken back Guangzhou, I'm sending you to Russia...

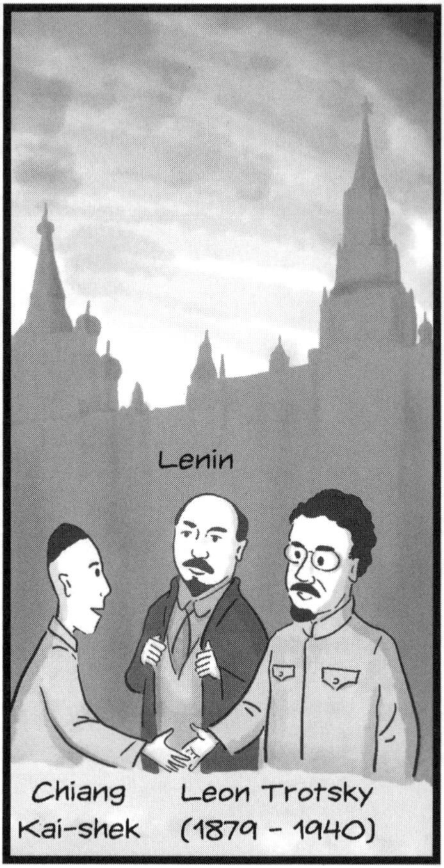
Lenin
Chiang Kai-shek
Leon Trotsky (1879 - 1940)

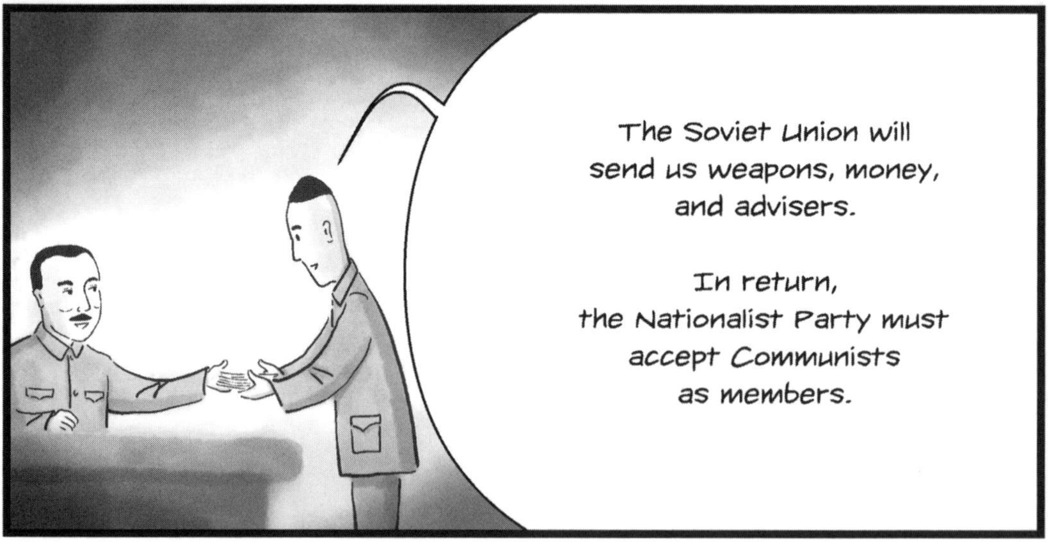
The Soviet Union will send us weapons, money, and advisers.
In return, the Nationalist Party must accept Communists as members.

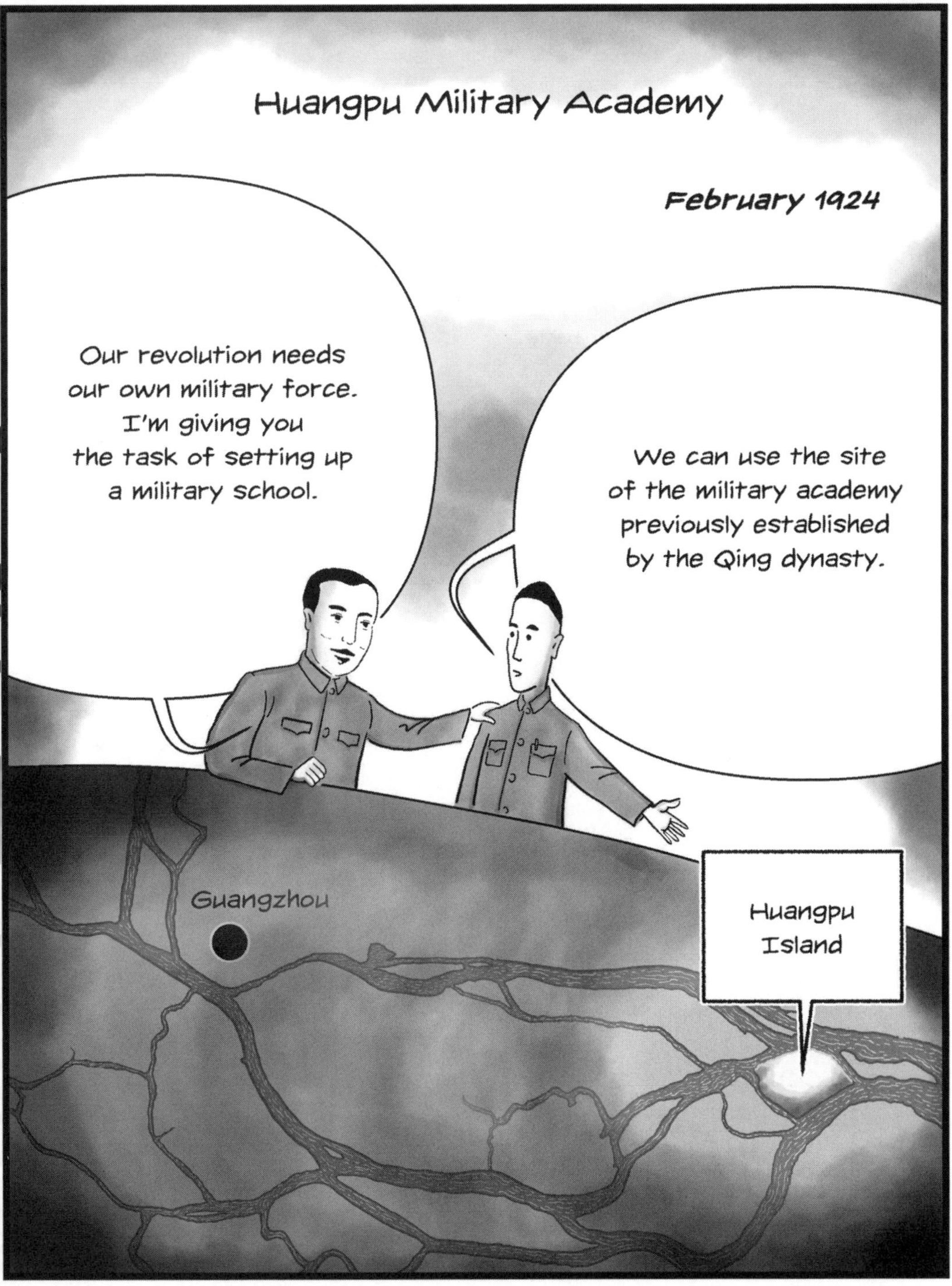

Huangpu Military Academy
February 1924
Our revolution needs our own military force. I'm giving you the task of setting up a military school.
We can use the site of the military academy previously established by the Qing dynasty.
Guangzhou
Huangpu Island

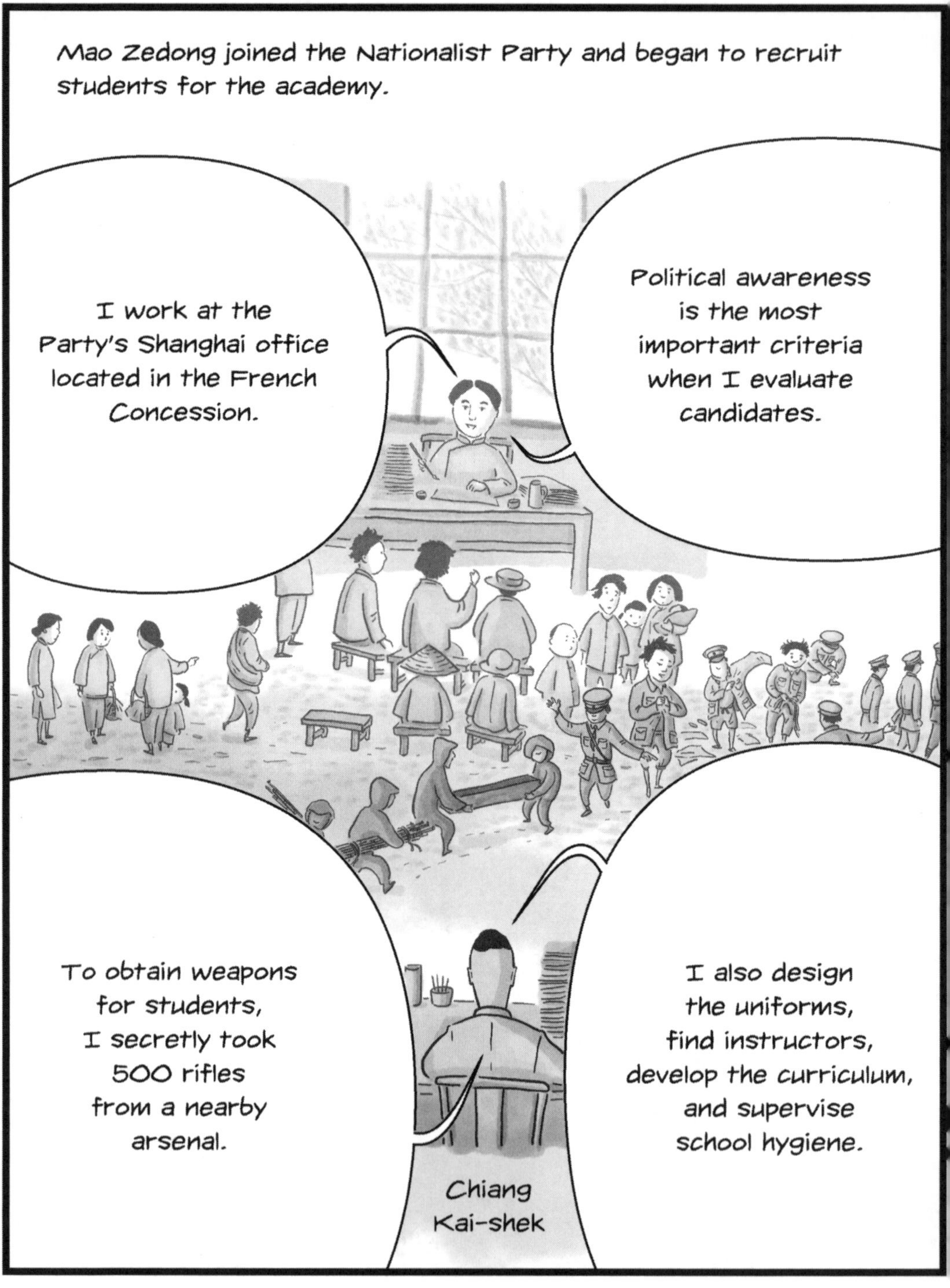
Mao Zedong joined the Nationalist Party and began to recruit students for the academy.
I work at the Party's Shanghai office located in the French Concession.
Political awareness is the most important criteria when I evaluate candidates.
To obtain weapons for students, I secretly took 500 rifles from a nearby arsenal.
I also design the uniforms, find instructors, develop the curriculum, and supervise school hygiene.
Chiang Kai-shek

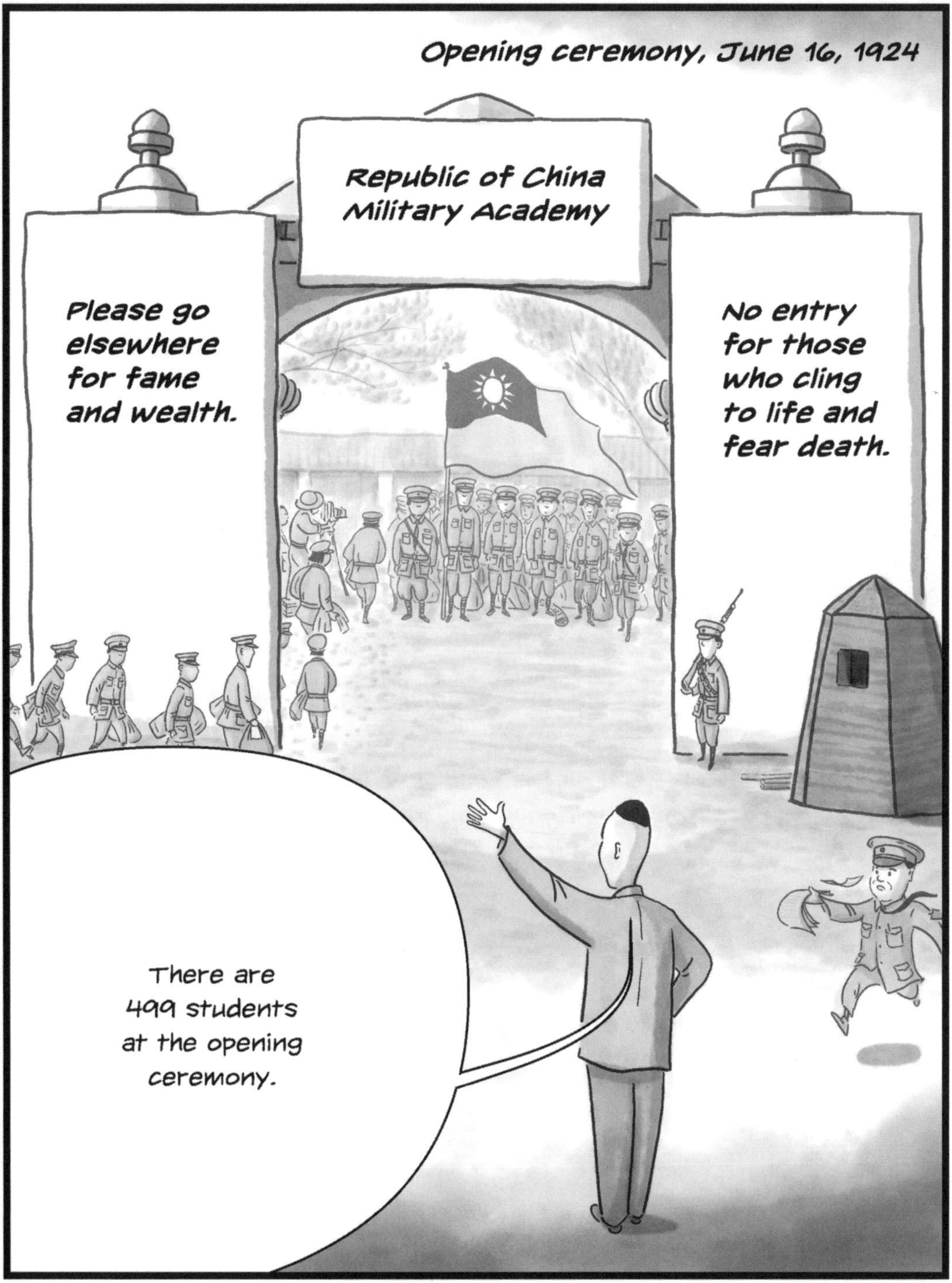
Opening ceremony, June 16, 1924
Republic of China Military Academy
Please go elsewhere for fame and wealth.
No entry for those who cling to life and fear death.
There are 499 students at the opening ceremony.

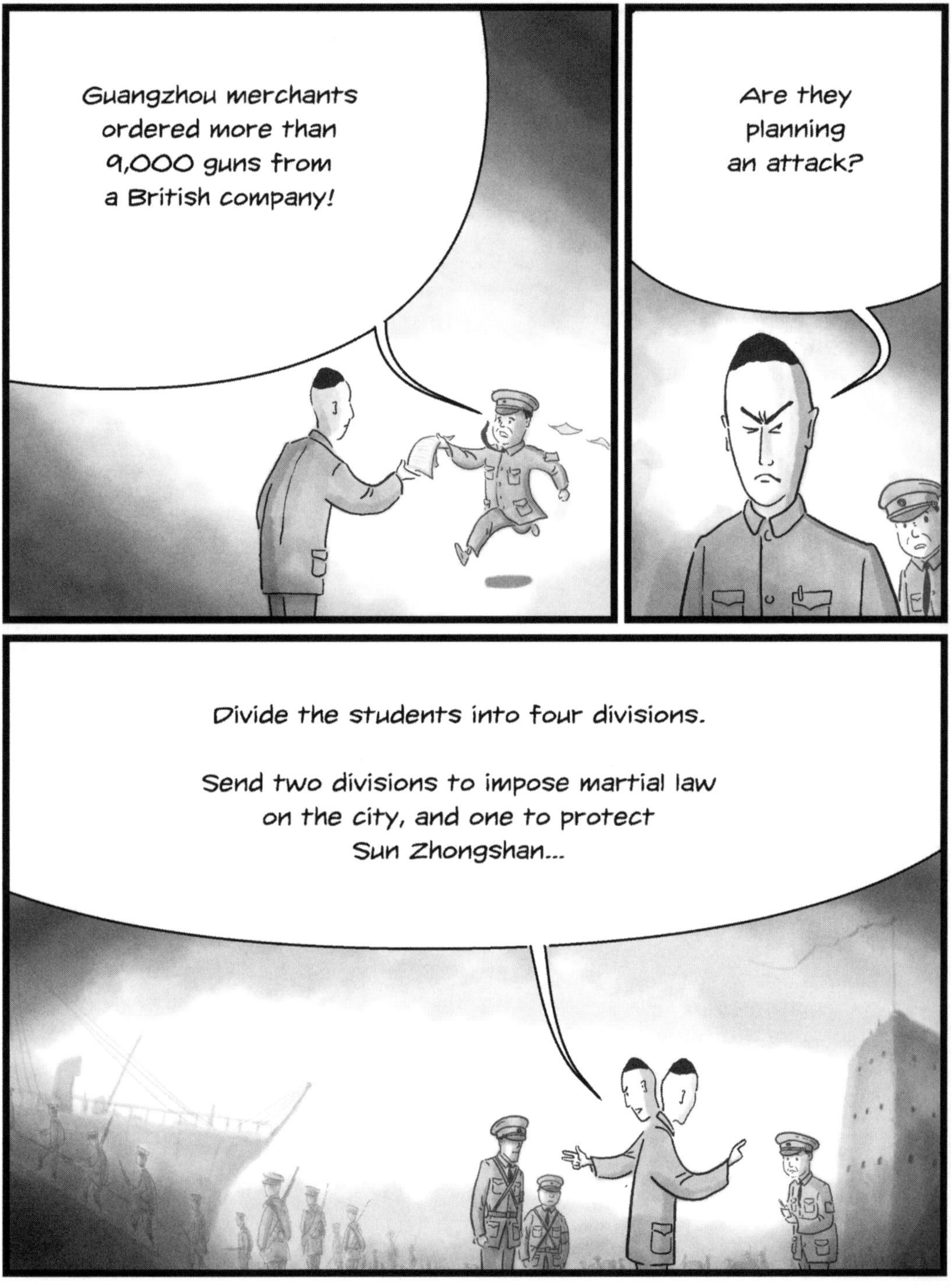
Guangzhou merchants ordered more than 9,000 guns from a British company!
Are they planning an attack?
Divide the students into four divisions.
Send two divisions to impose martial law on the city, and one to protect Sun Zhongshan...

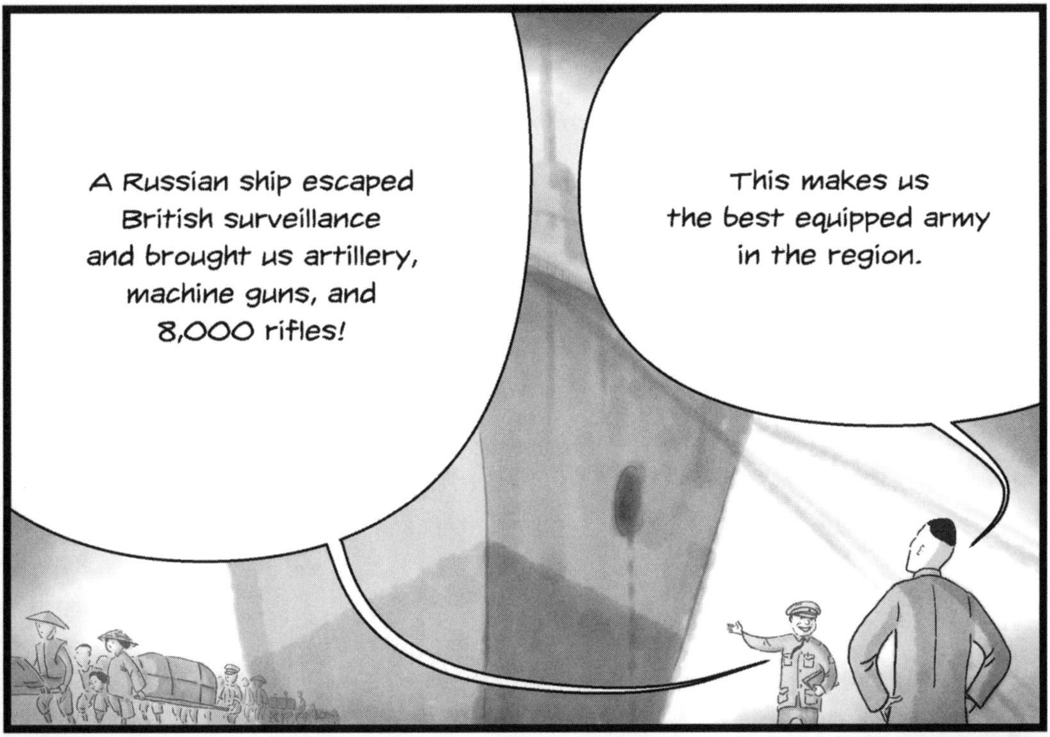
A Russian ship escaped British surveillance and brought us artillery, machine guns, and 8,000 rifles!
This makes us the best equipped army in the region.

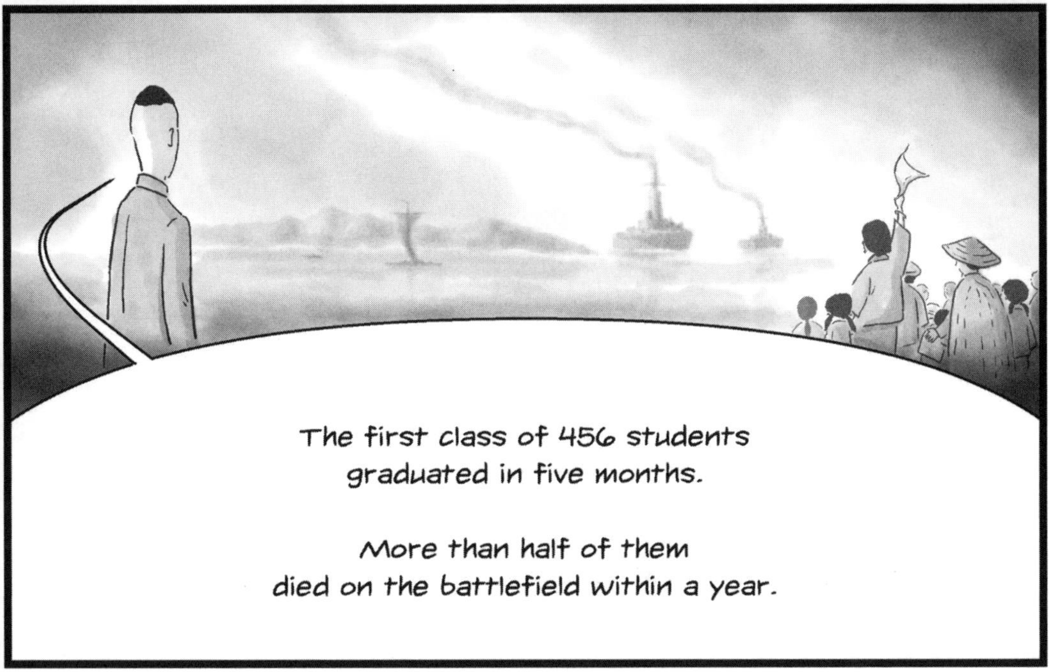
The first class of 456 students graduated in five months.
More than half of them died on the battlefield within a year.

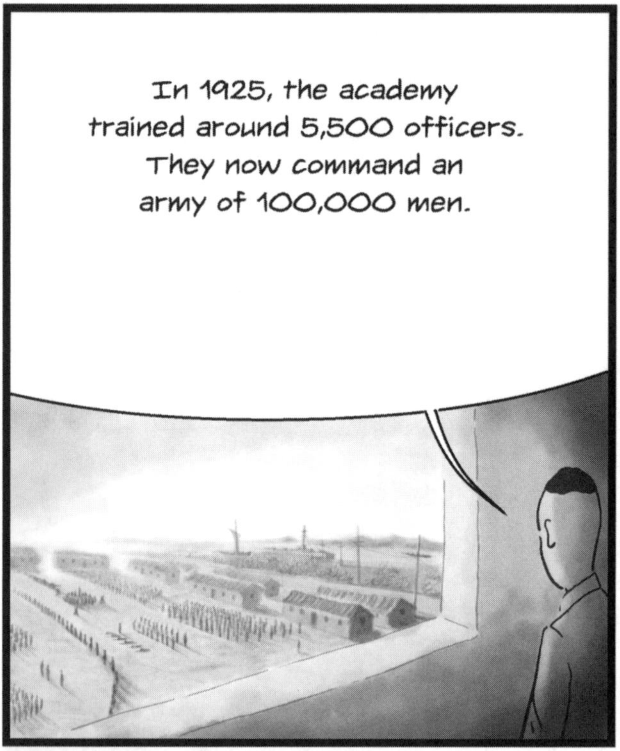
In 1925, the academy trained around 5,500 officers. They now command an army of 100,000 men.

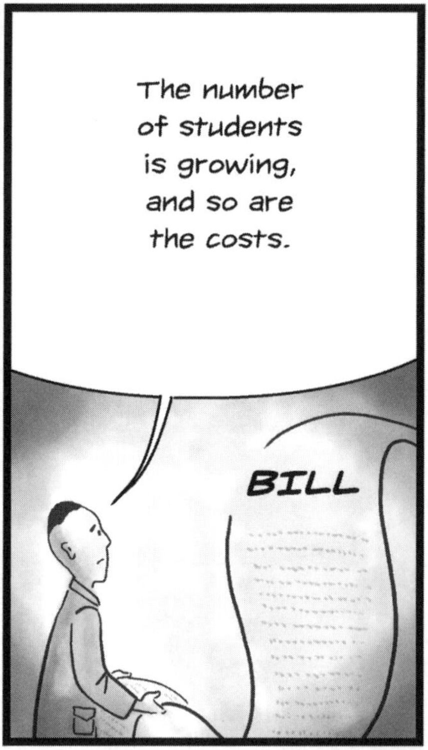
The number of students is growing, and so are the costs.
BILL

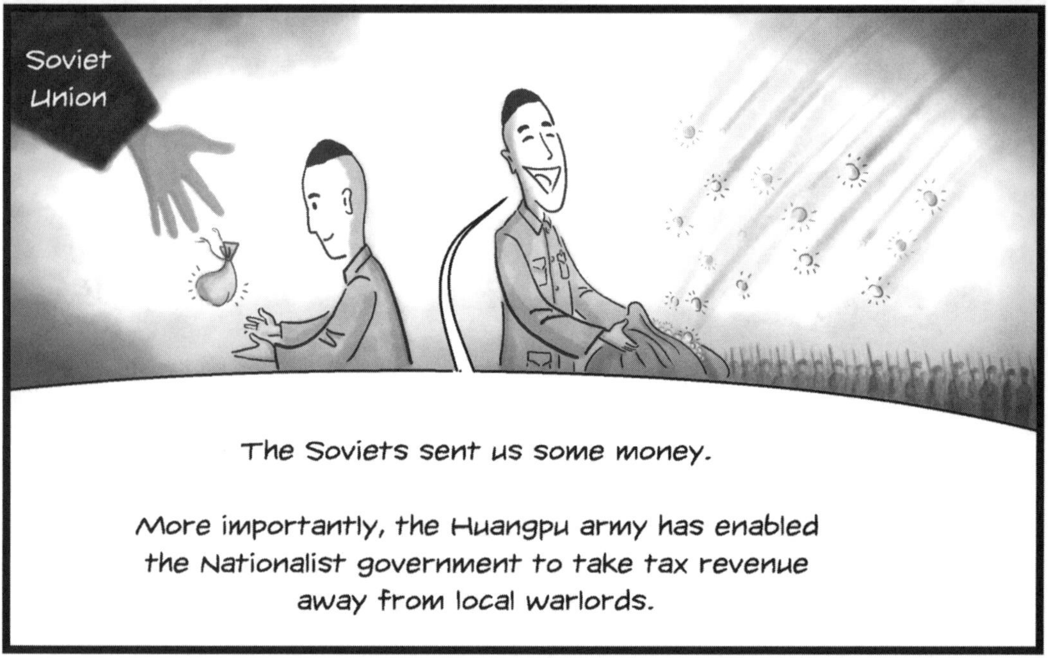
Soviet Union
The Soviets sent us some money.
More importantly, the Huangpu army has enabled the Nationalist government to take tax revenue away from local warlords.

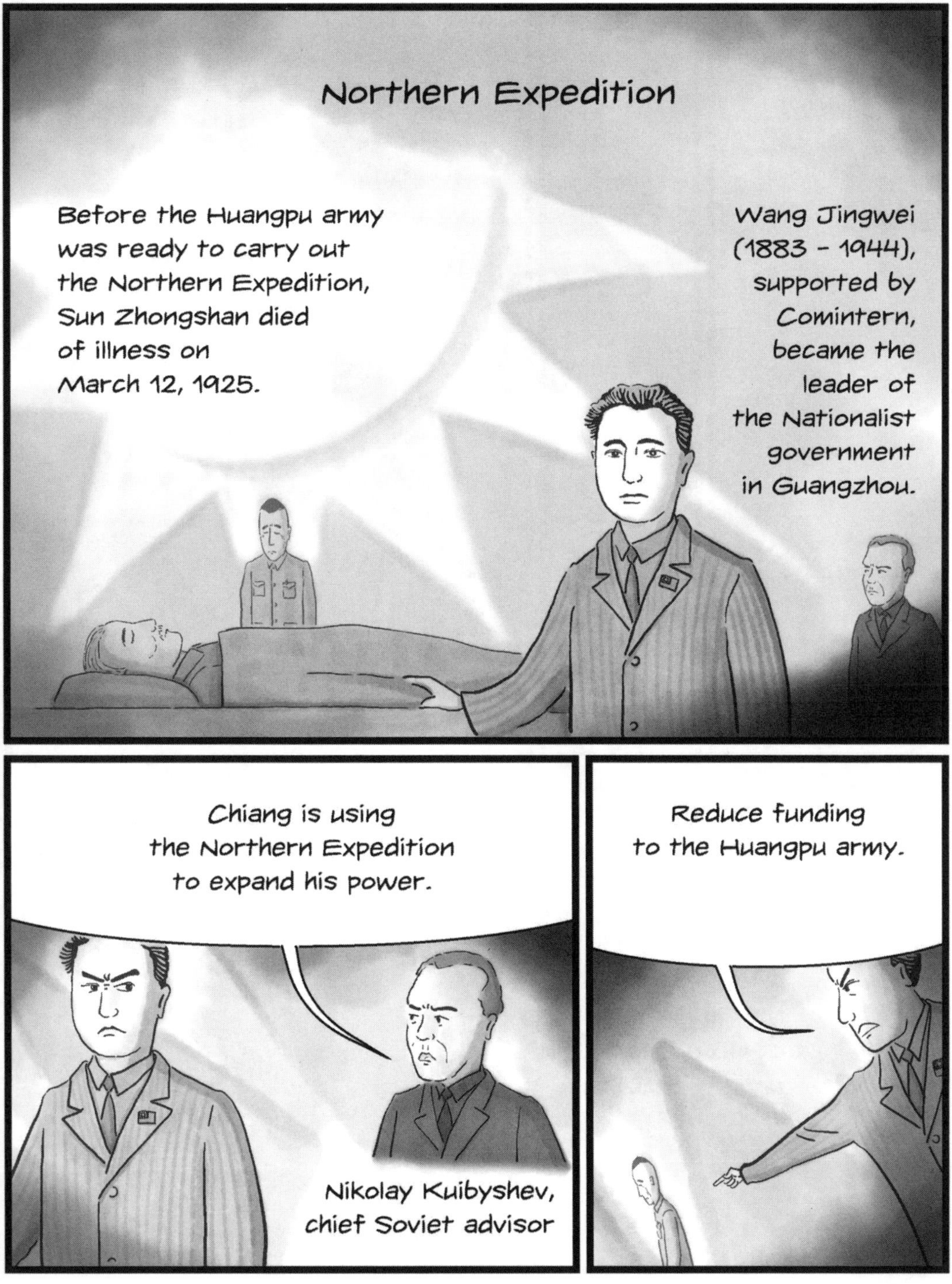
Northern Expedition
Before the Huangpu army was ready to carry out the Northern Expedition, Sun Zhongshan died of illness on March 12, 1925.
Wang Jingwei (1883 - 1944), supported by Comintern, became the leader of the Nationalist government in Guangzhou.
Chiang is using the Northern Expedition to expand his power.
Nikolay Kuibyshev, chief Soviet advisor
Reduce funding to the Huangpu army.

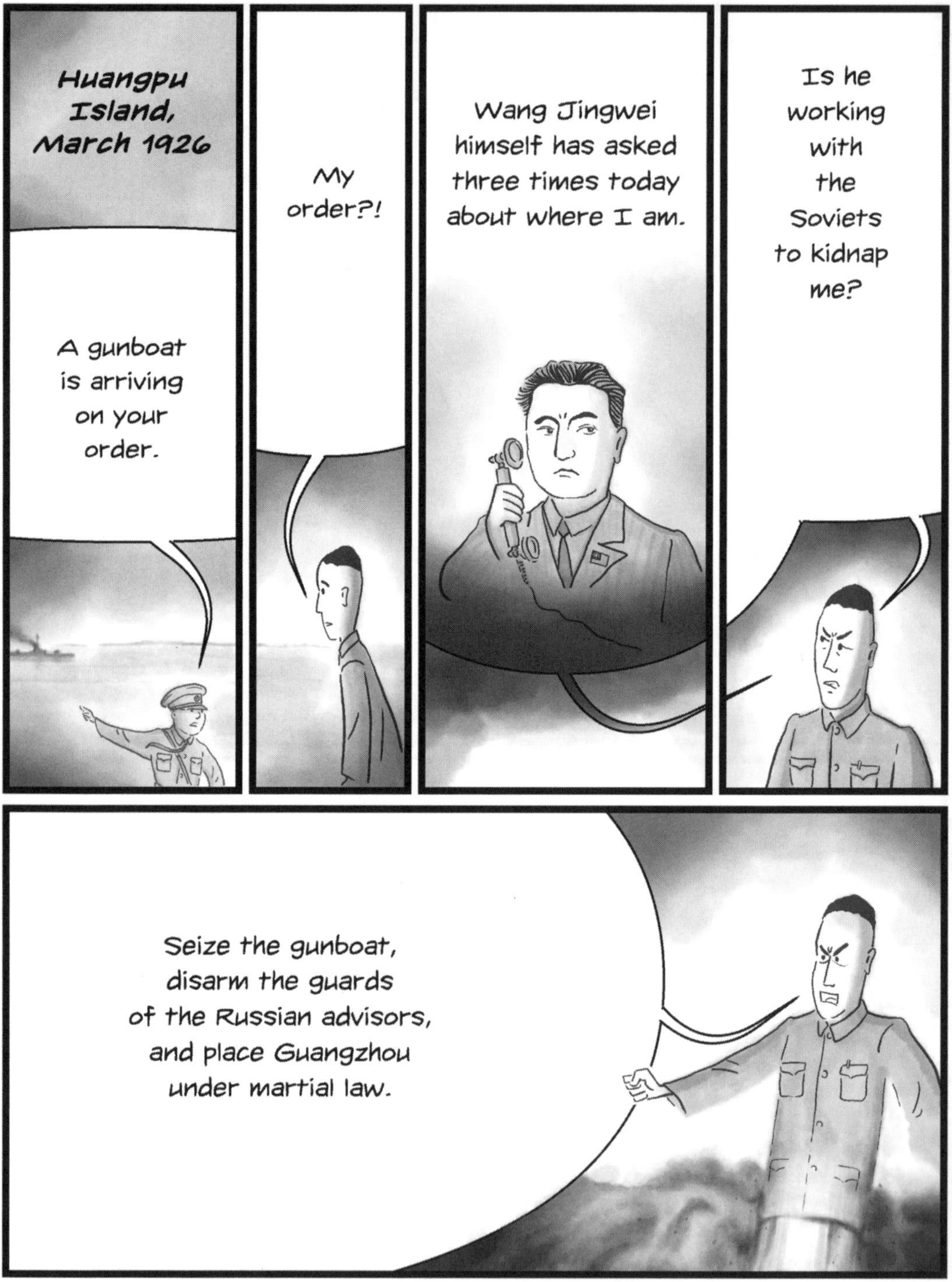
Huangpu Island, March 1926
A gunboat is arriving on your order.
My order?!
Wang Jingwei himself has asked three times today about where I am.
Is he working with the Soviets to kidnap me?
Seize the gunboat, disarm the guards of the Russian advisors, and place Guangzhou under martial law.

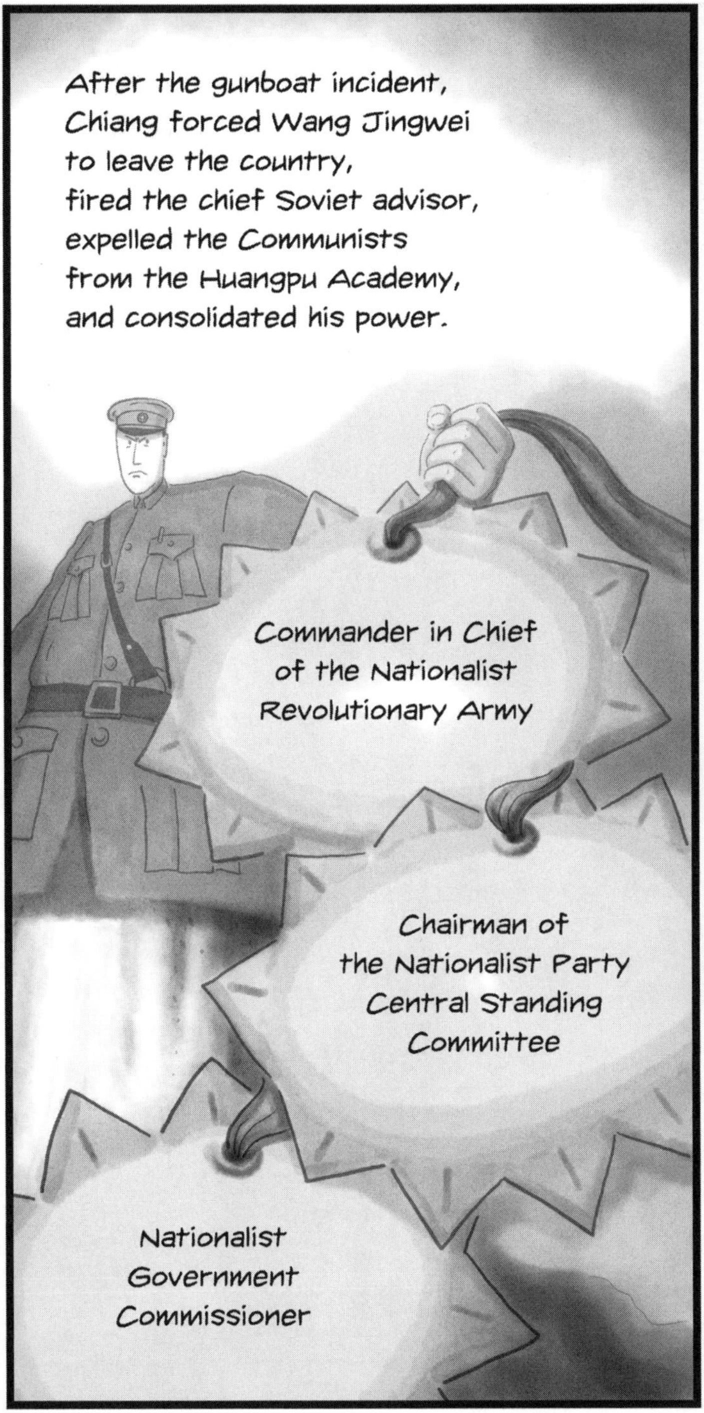
After the gunboat incident, Chiang forced Wang Jingwei to leave the country, fired the chief Soviet advisor, expelled the Communists from the Huangpu Academy, and consolidated his power.
Commander in Chief of the Nationalist Revolutionary Army
Chairman of the Nationalist Party Central Standing Committee
Nationalist Government Commissioner

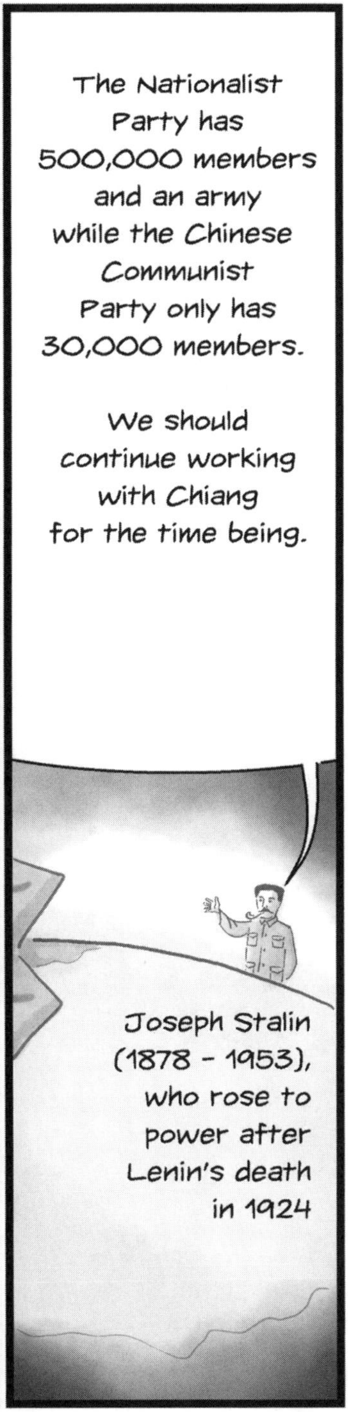
The Nationalist Party has 500,000 members and an army while the Chinese Communist Party only has 30,000 members.
We should continue working with Chiang for the time being.
Joseph Stalin (1878 - 1953), who rose to power after Lenin's death in 1924

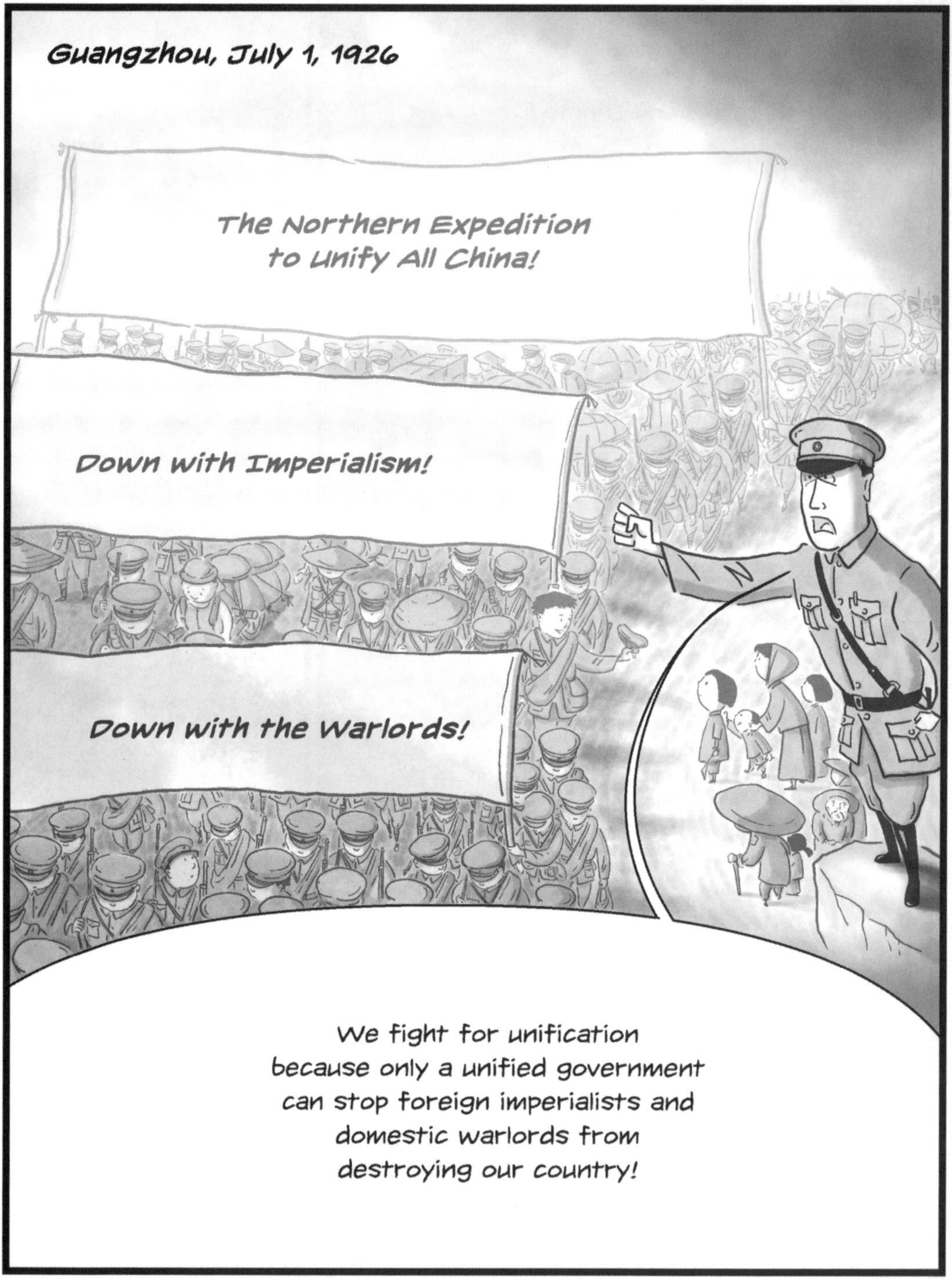
Guangzhou, July 1, 1926
The Northern Expedition to Unify All China!
Down with Imperialism!
Down with the Warlords!
We fight for unification because only a unified government can stop foreign imperialists and domestic warlords from destroying our country!

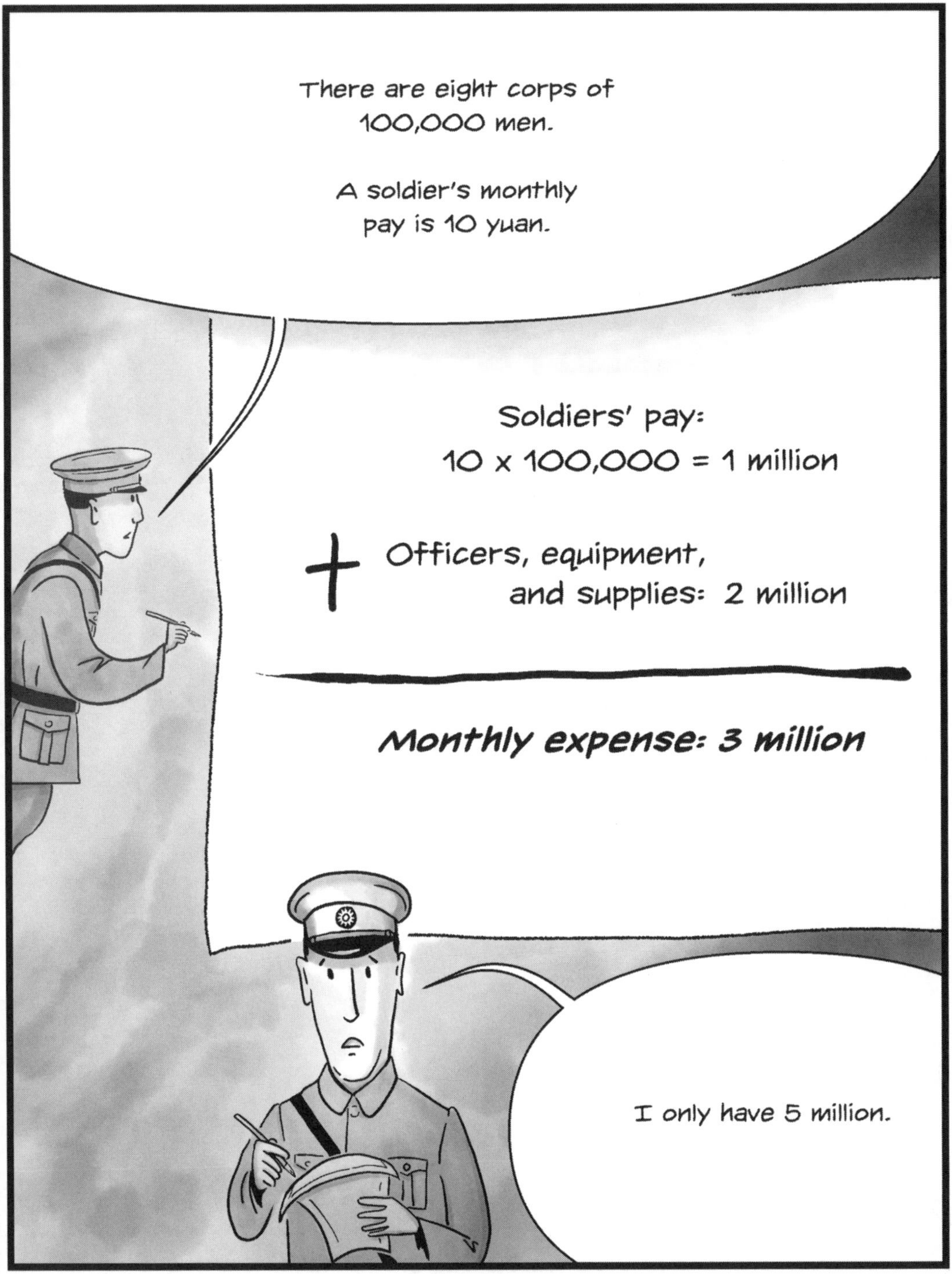
There are eight corps of 100,000 men.
A soldier's monthly pay is 10 yuan.
Soldiers' pay:
10 x 100,000 = 1 million
+ Officers, equipment, and supplies: 2 million
Monthly expense: 3 million
I only have 5 million.

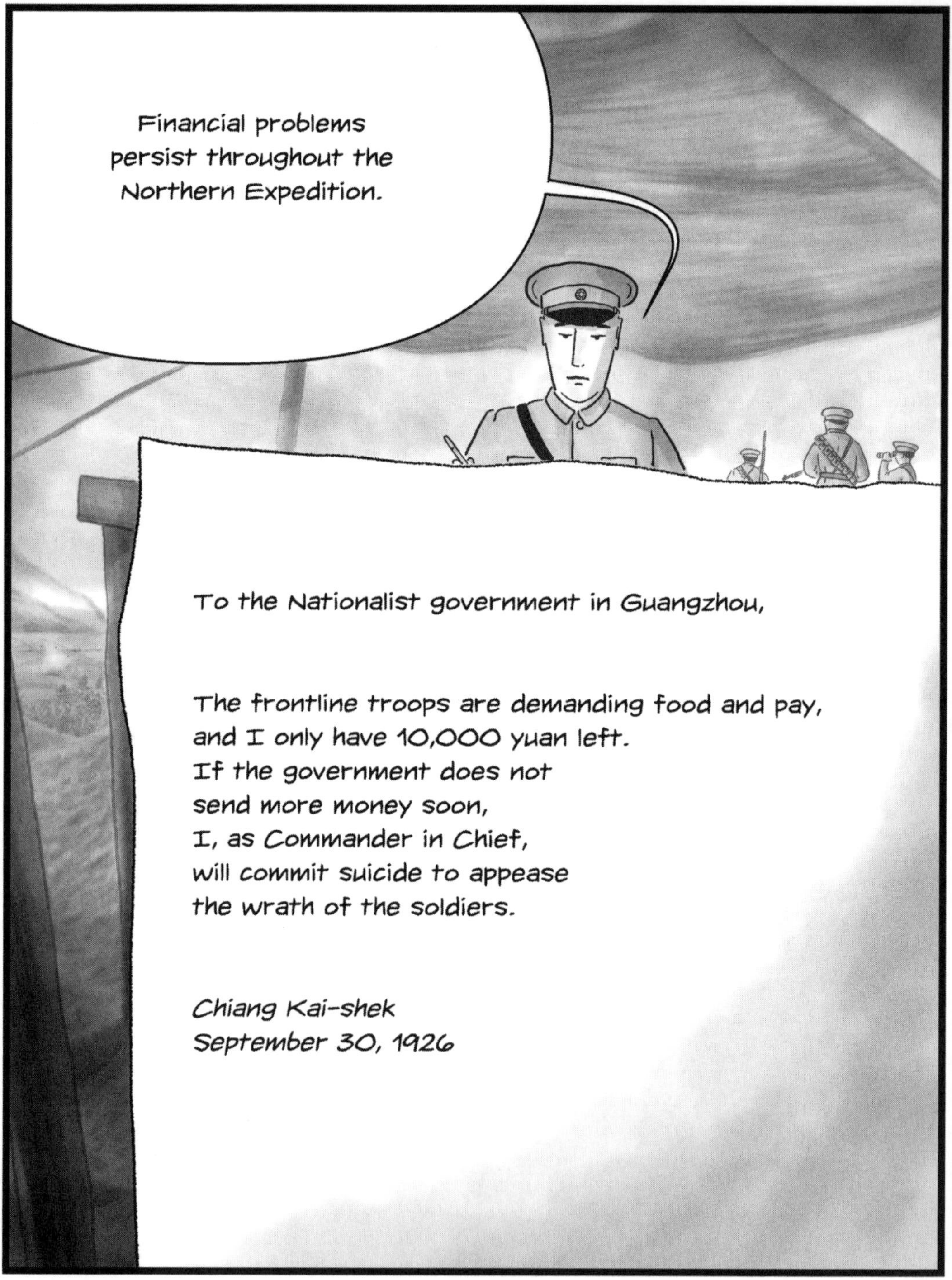
Financial problems persist throughout the Northern Expedition.
To the Nationalist government in Guangzhou,
The frontline troops are demanding food and pay, and I only have 10,000 yuan left. If the government does not send more money soon, I, as Commander in Chief, will commit suicide to appease the wrath of the soldiers.
Chiang Kai-shek
September 30, 1926

To defeat the enemies quickly,
I offer their generals higher ranks to tempt them to defect.
As a result, the Nationalist army has nearly doubled
to 15 corps in less than three months.

In just four months, the Nationalist army
has defeated two major warlords and
captured three provincial capitals!

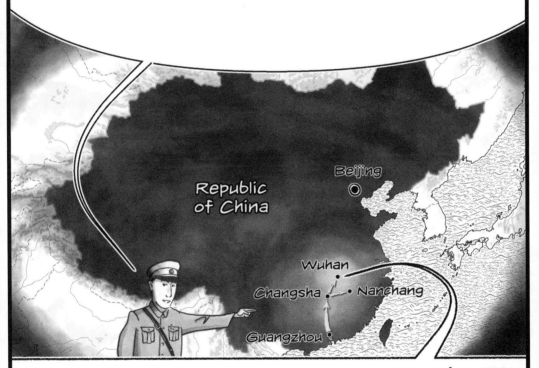

Beijing

Republic
of China

Wuhan

Changsha • Nanchang

Guangzhou

December 1926

The Nationalist Government and
the Nationalist Party Central Committee
moved from Guangzhou to Wuhan.

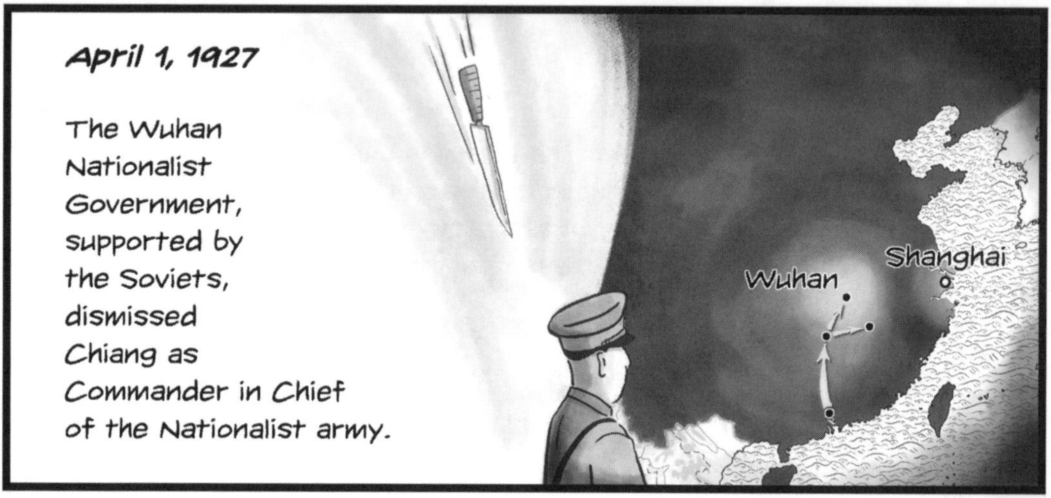
April 1, 1927
The Wuhan Nationalist Government, supported by the Soviets, dismissed Chiang as Commander in Chief of the Nationalist army.
Shanghai
Wuhan

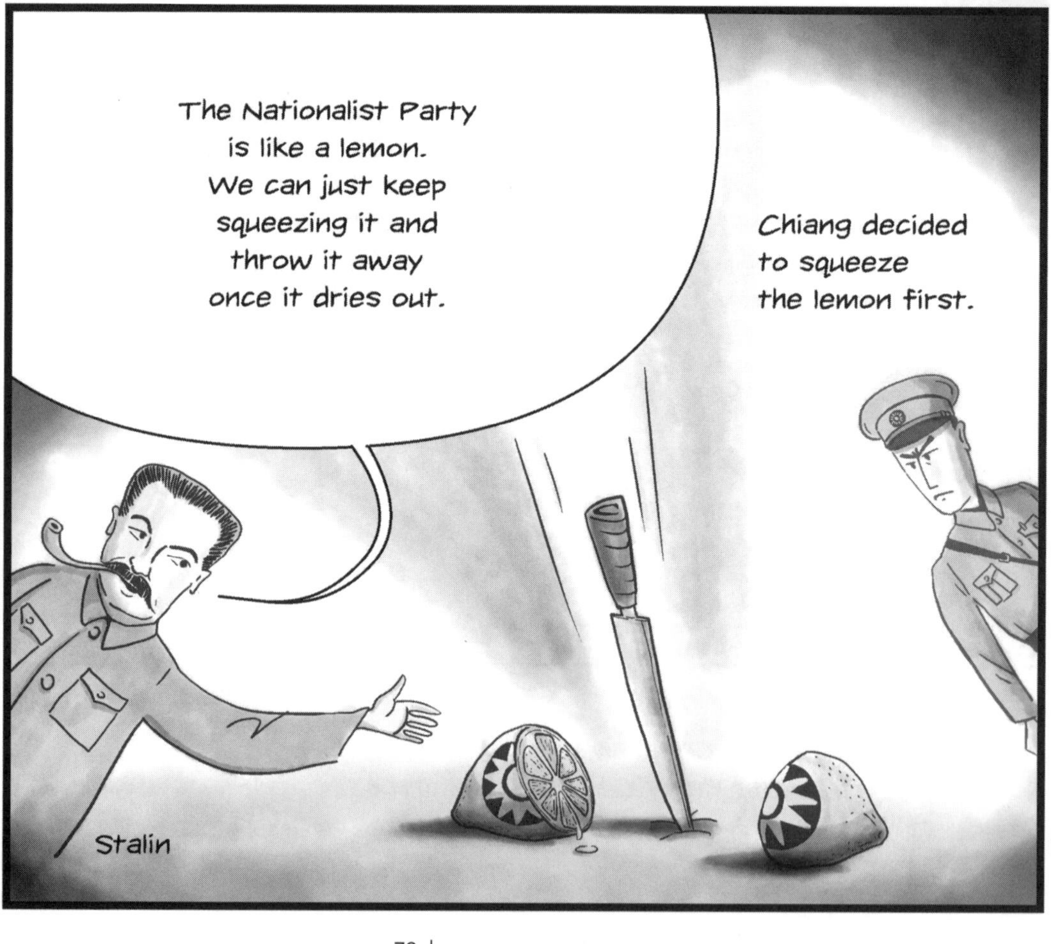
The Nationalist Party is like a lemon. We can just keep squeezing it and throw it away once it dries out.
Chiang decided to squeeze the lemon first.
Stalin

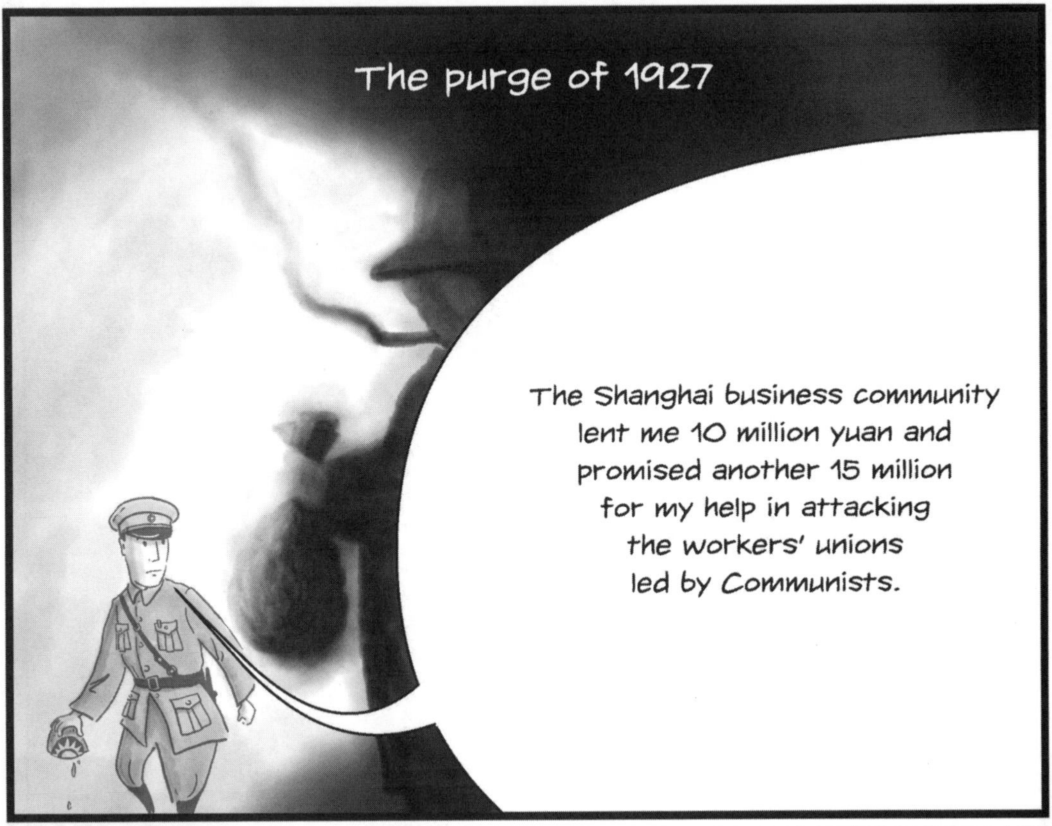
The purge of 1927
The Shanghai business community lent me 10 million yuan and promised another 15 million for my help in attacking the workers' unions led by Communists.

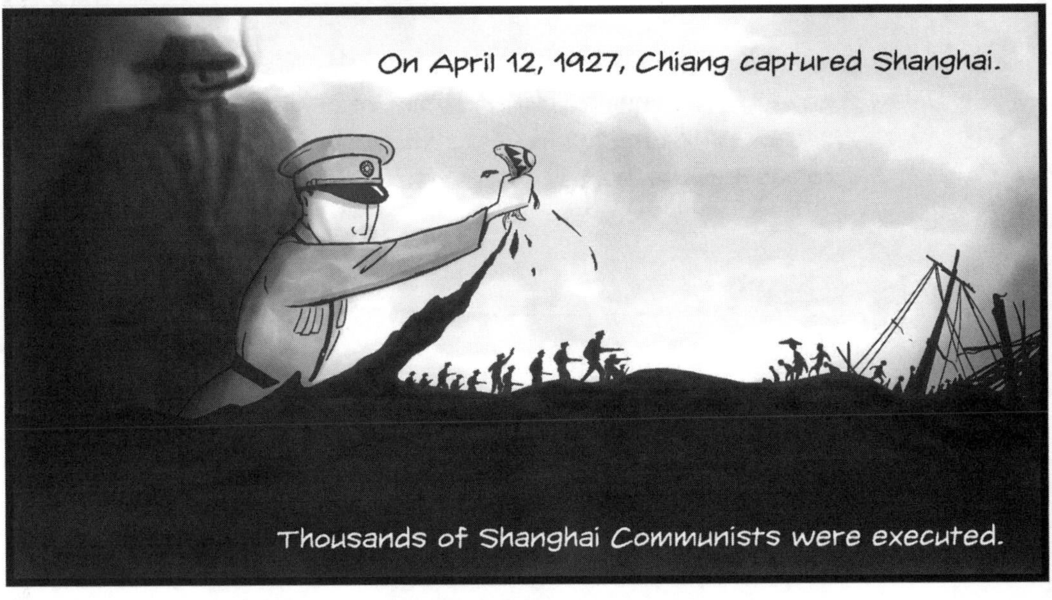
On April 12, 1927, Chiang captured Shanghai.
Thousands of Shanghai Communists were executed.

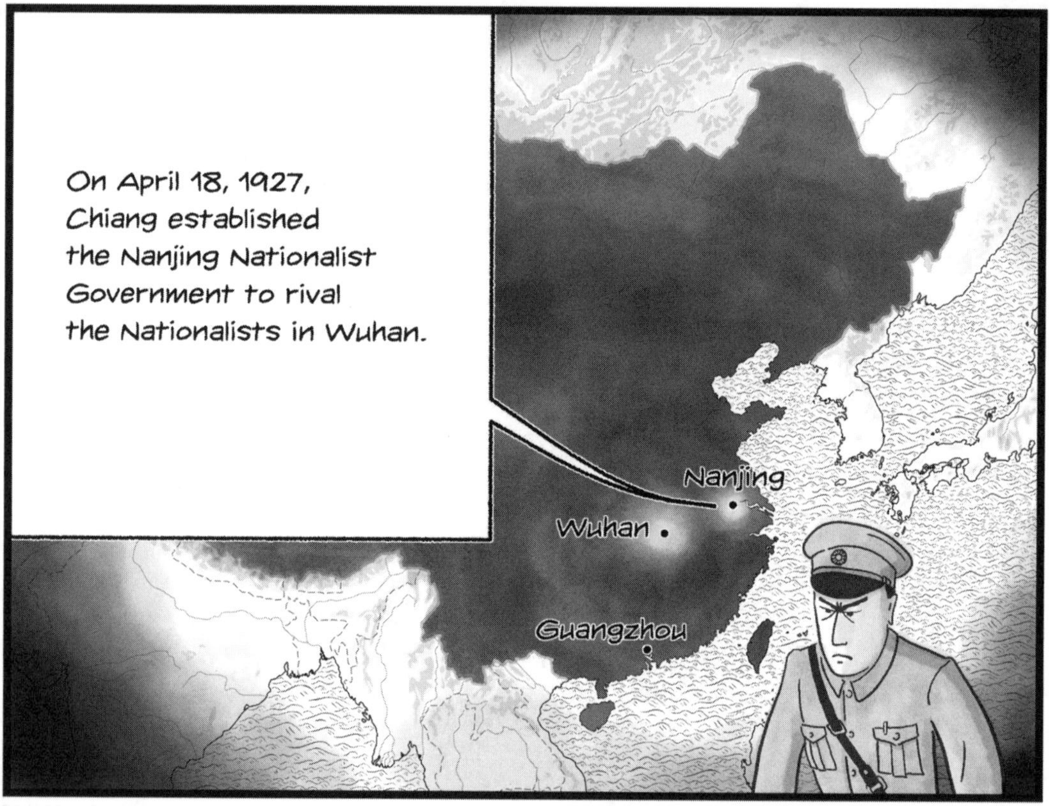
On April 18, 1927, Chiang established the Nanjing Nationalist Government to rival the Nationalists in Wuhan.
Nanjing
Wuhan
Guangzhou

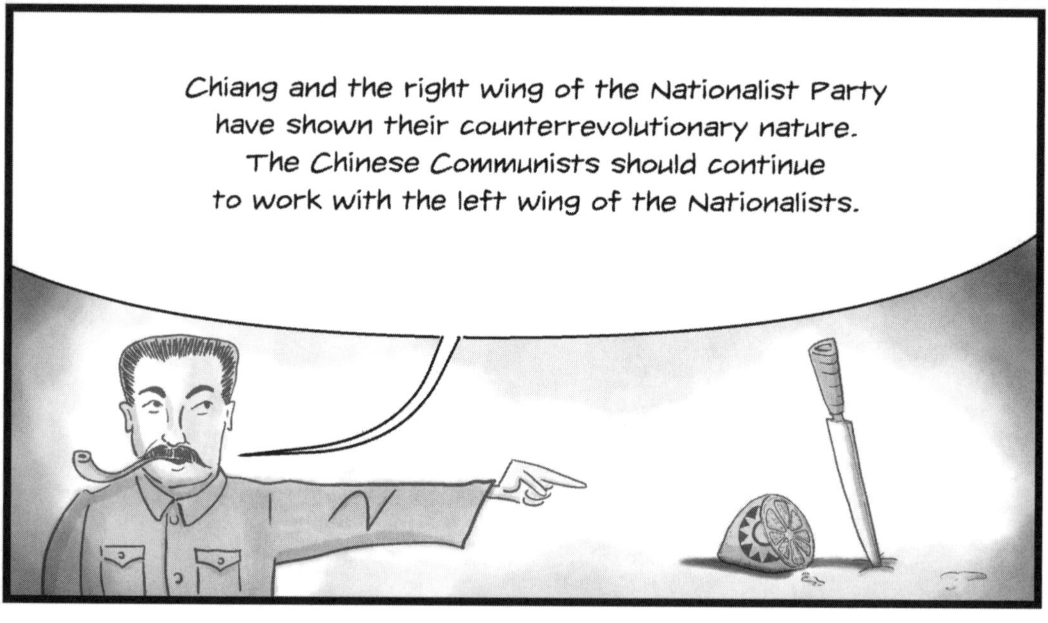
Chiang and the right wing of the Nationalist Party have shown their counterrevolutionary nature. The Chinese Communists should continue to work with the left wing of the Nationalists.

  I came to Wuhan as an alternate member of the Nationalist Central Committee.

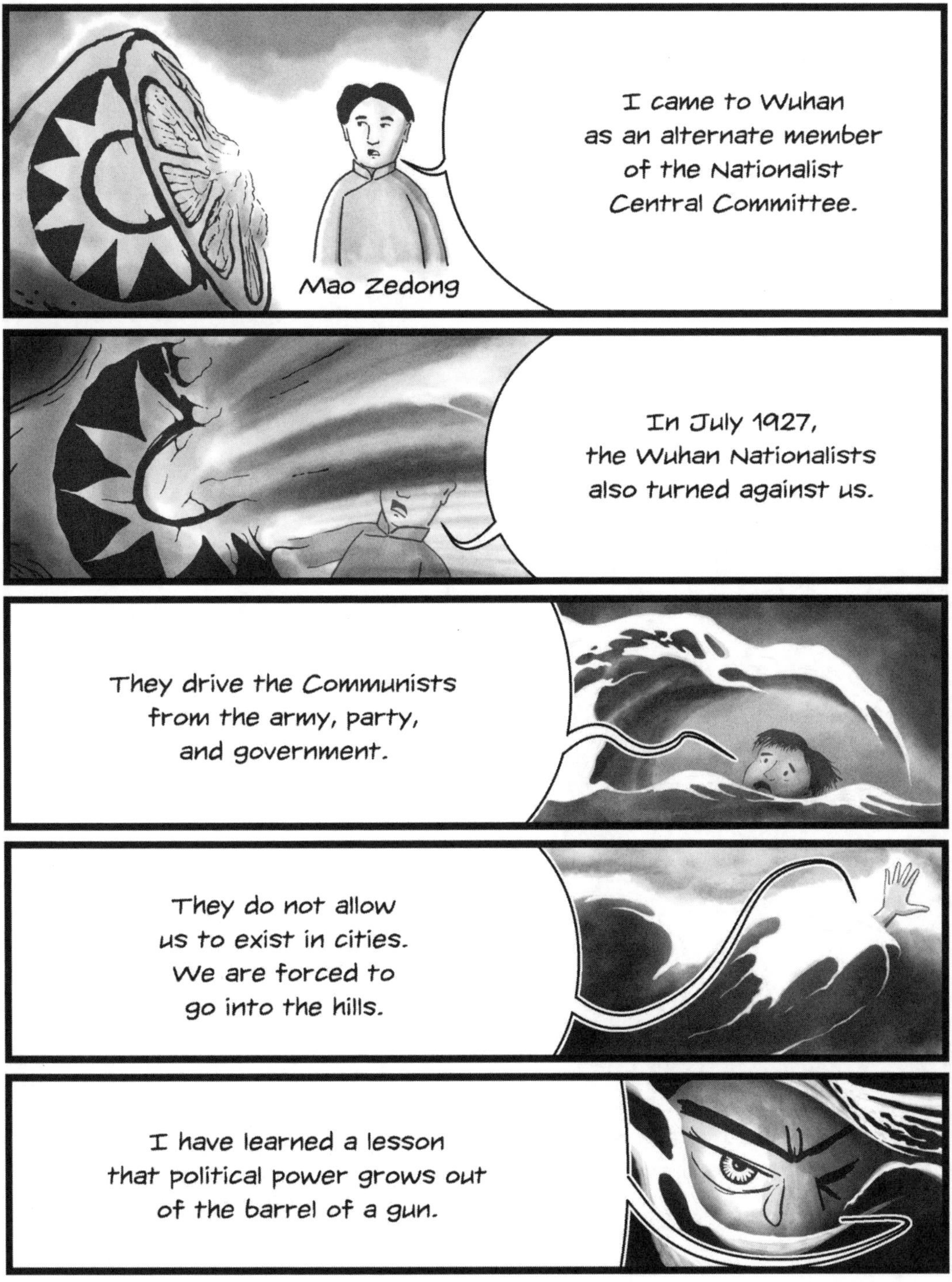

Mao Zedong

 In July 1927, the Wuhan Nationalists also turned against us.

They drive the Communists from the army, party, and government.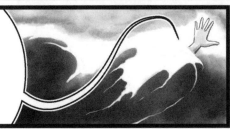

They do not allow us to exist in cities. We are forced to go into the hills.

I have learned a lesson that political power grows out of the barrel of a gun.

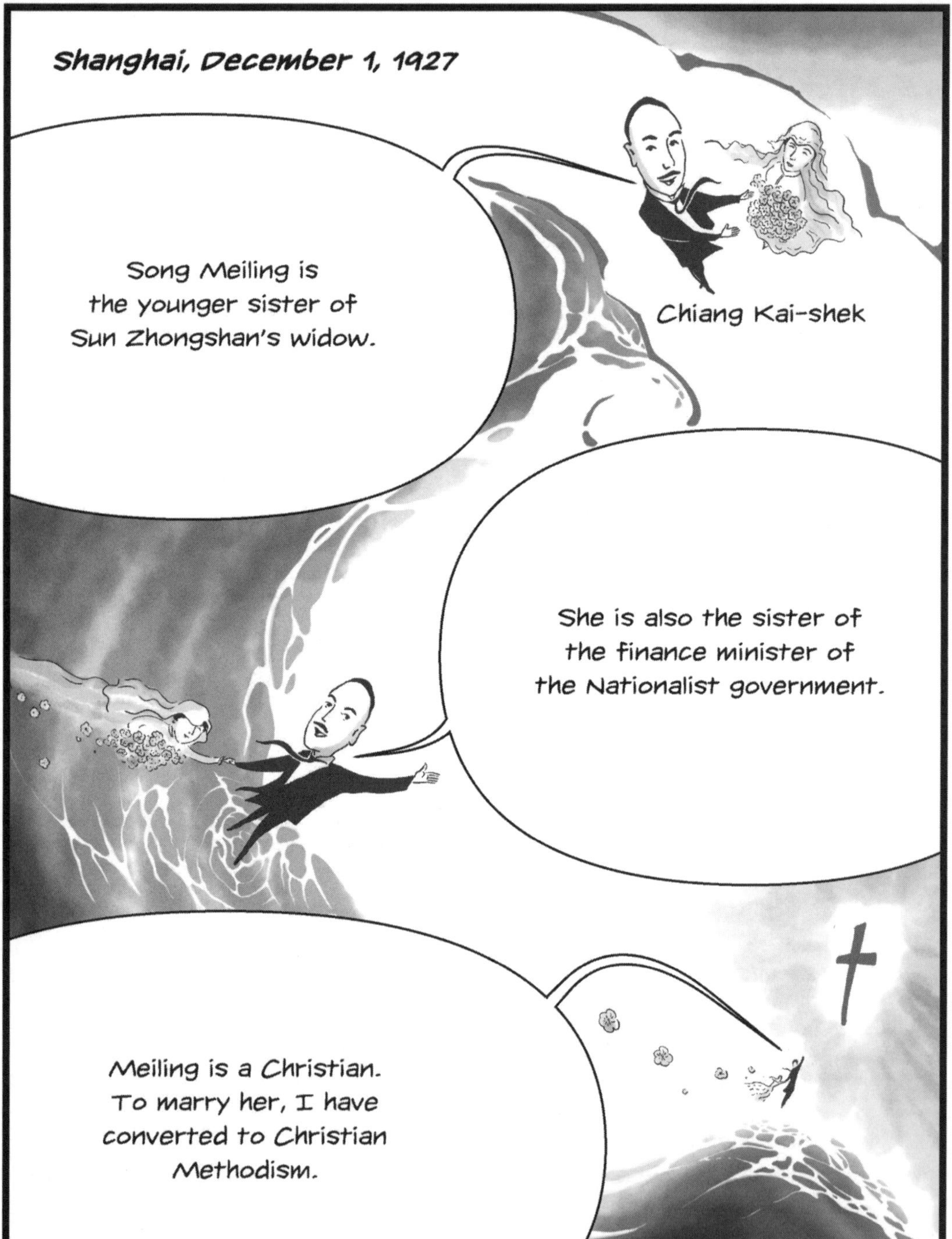
Shanghai, December 1, 1927
Song Meiling is the younger sister of Sun Zhongshan's widow.
Chiang Kai-shek
She is also the sister of the finance minister of the Nationalist government.
Meiling is a Christian. To marry her, I have converted to Christian Methodism.

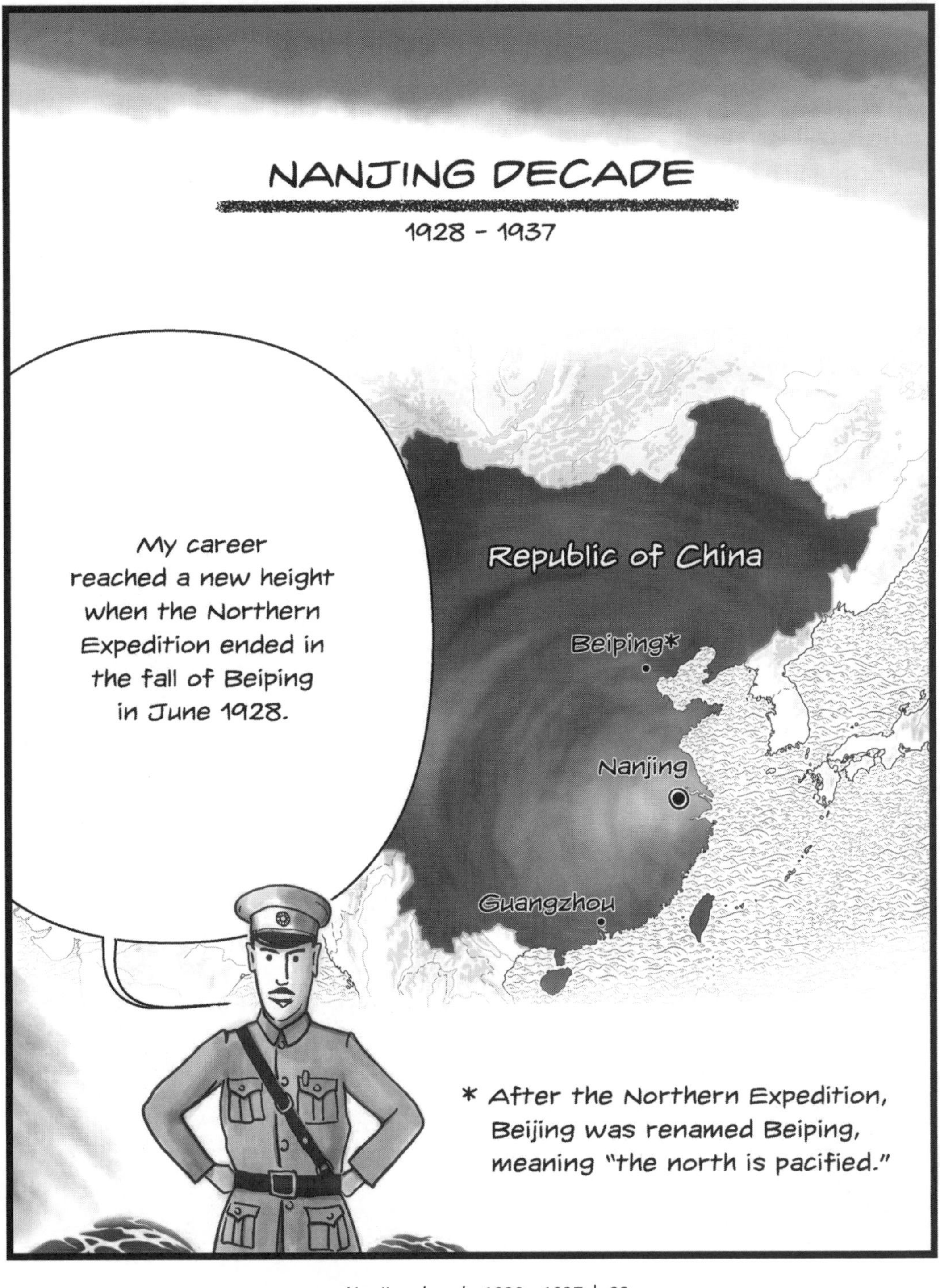
NANJING DECADE
1928 - 1937
My career reached a new height when the Northern Expedition ended in the fall of Beiping in June 1928.
Republic of China
Beiping*
Nanjing
Guangzhou
* After the Northern Expedition, Beijing was renamed Beiping, meaning "the north is pacified."

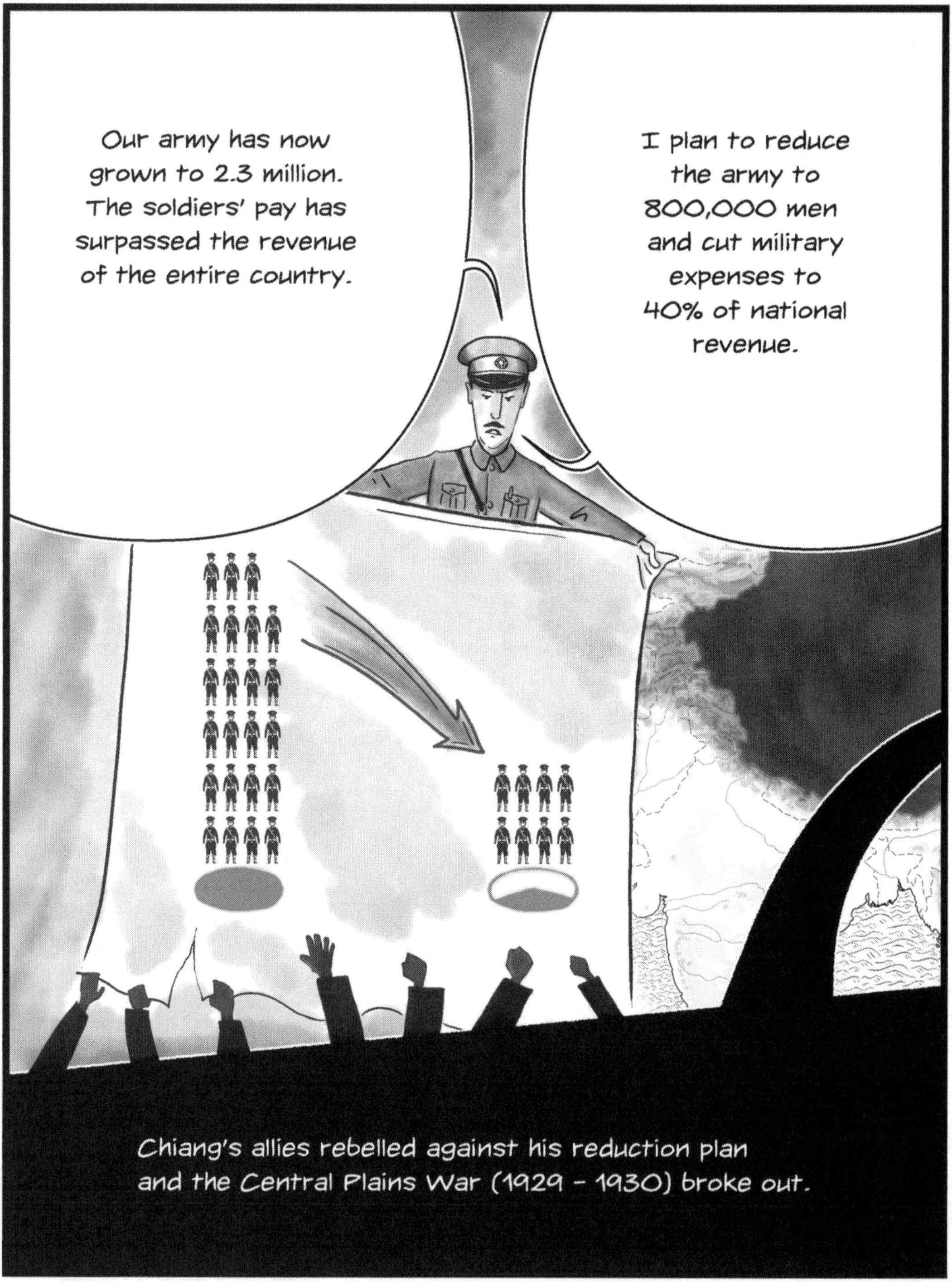
Our army has now grown to 2.3 million. The soldiers' pay has surpassed the revenue of the entire country.
I plan to reduce the army to 800,000 men and cut military expenses to 40% of national revenue.
Chiang's allies rebelled against his reduction plan and the Central Plains War (1929 - 1930) broke out.

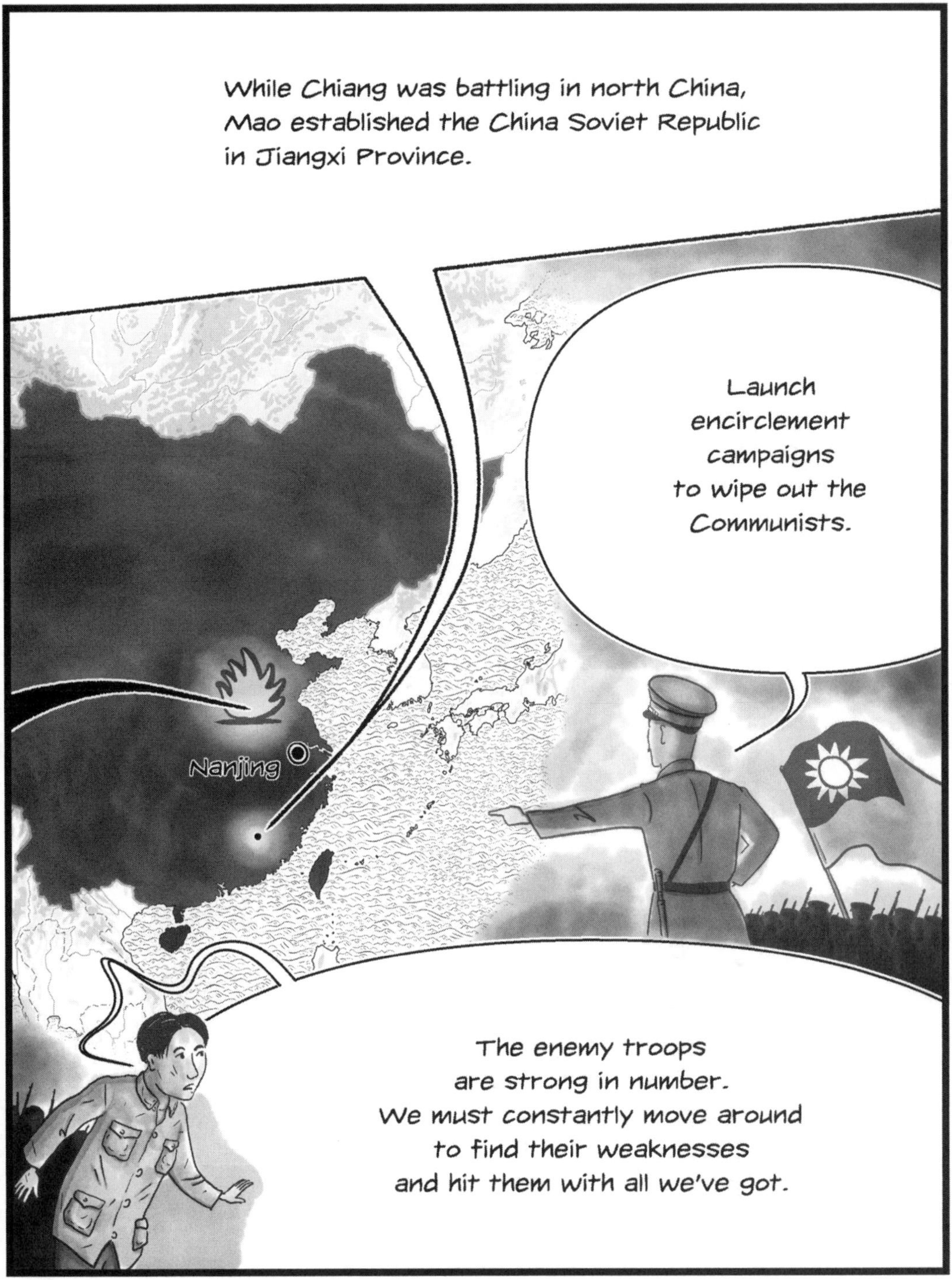

While Chiang was battling in north China, Mao established the China Soviet Republic in Jiangxi Province.
Nanjing
Launch encirclement campaigns to wipe out the Communists.
The enemy troops are strong in number. We must constantly move around to find their weaknesses and hit them with all we've got.

	1st encirclement campaign	2nd encirclement campaign	3rd encirclement campaign
Start date:	November 27, 1930	May 16, 1931	July 1, 1931
Duration:	7 days	15 days	80 days
Nationalist army:	100,000 local troops	200,000 local troops	300,000 including 100,000 elite Central Government Army
Communist army:	40,000	30,000	30,000
Result:	Communist victory	Communist victory	

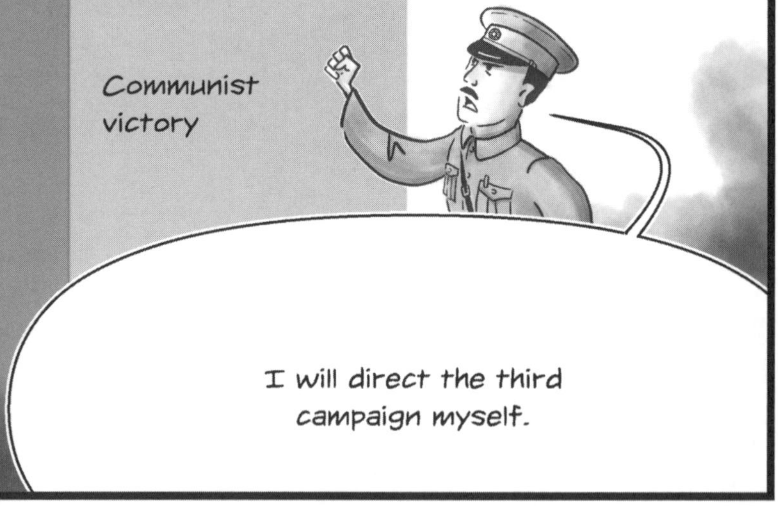
I will direct the third campaign myself.

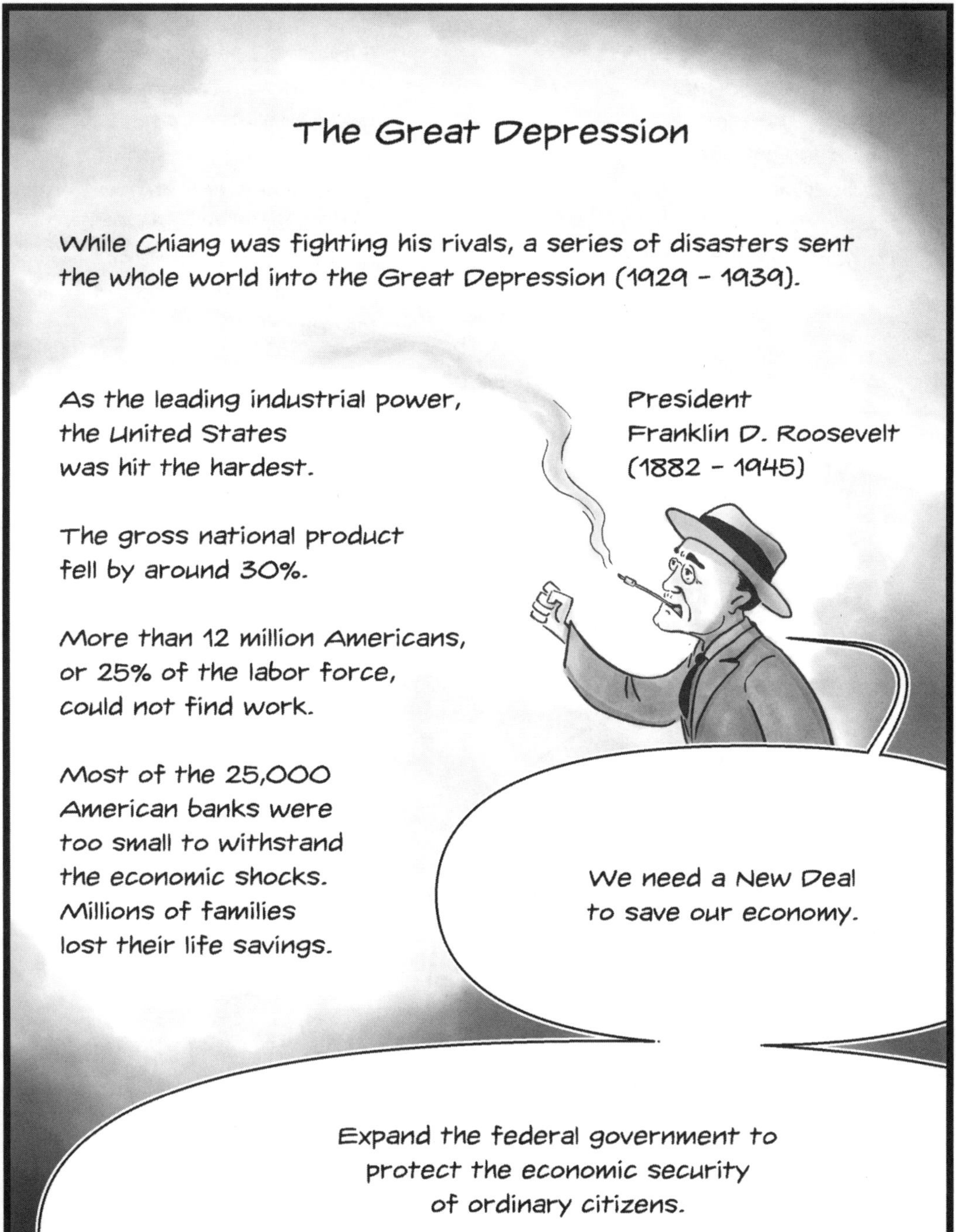
The Great Depression
While Chiang was fighting his rivals, a series of disasters sent the whole world into the Great Depression (1929 - 1939).
As the leading industrial power, the United States was hit the hardest.
The gross national product fell by around 30%.
More than 12 million Americans, or 25% of the labor force, could not find work.
Most of the 25,000 American banks were too small to withstand the economic shocks. Millions of families lost their life savings.
President Franklin D. Roosevelt (1882 - 1945)
We need a New Deal to save our economy.
Expand the federal government to protect the economic security of ordinary citizens.

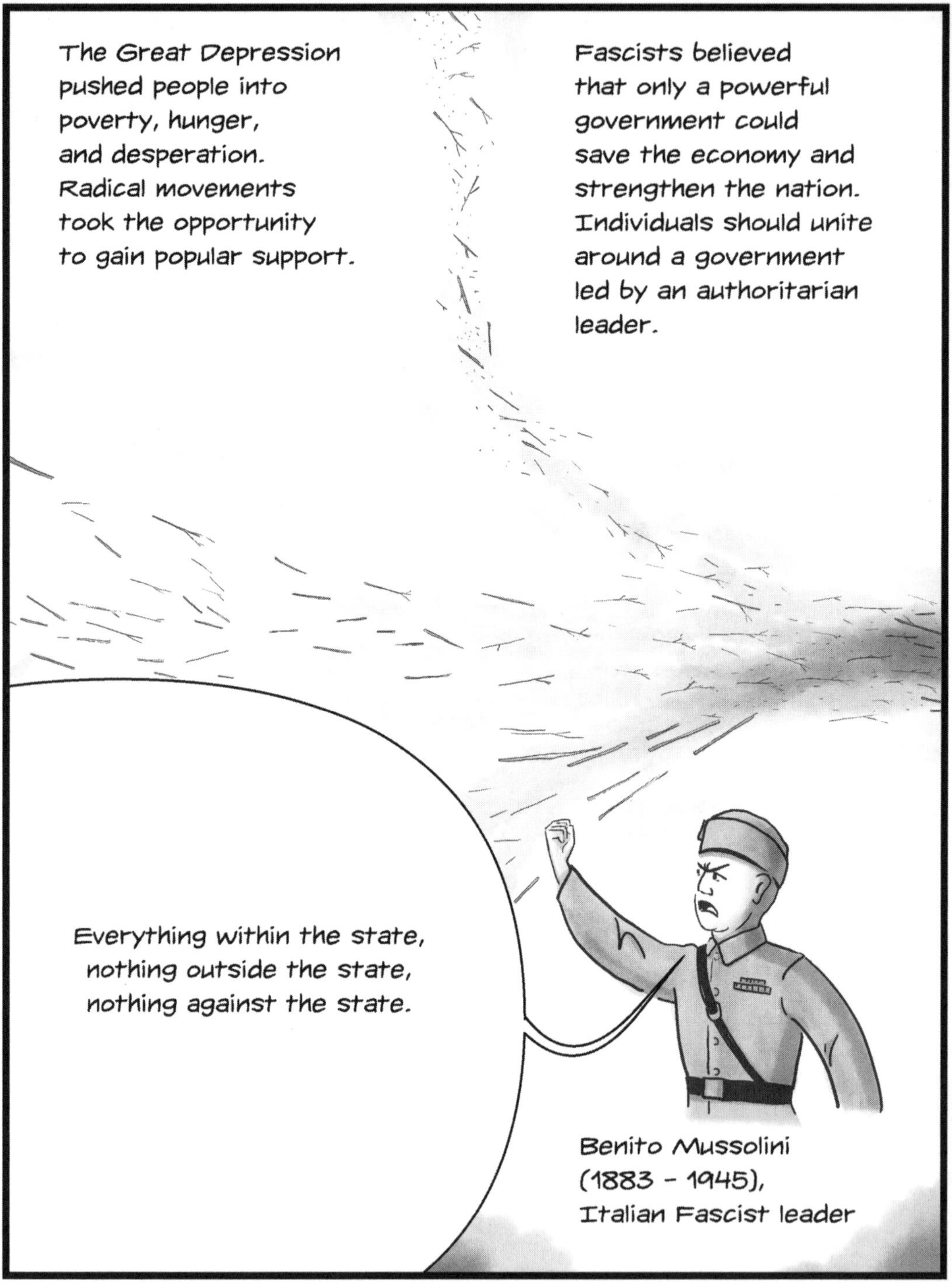
The Great Depression pushed people into poverty, hunger, and desperation. Radical movements took the opportunity to gain popular support.
Fascists believed that only a powerful government could save the economy and strengthen the nation. Individuals should unite around a government led by an authoritarian leader.
Everything within the state, nothing outside the state, nothing against the state.
Benito Mussolini (1883 - 1945), Italian Fascist leader

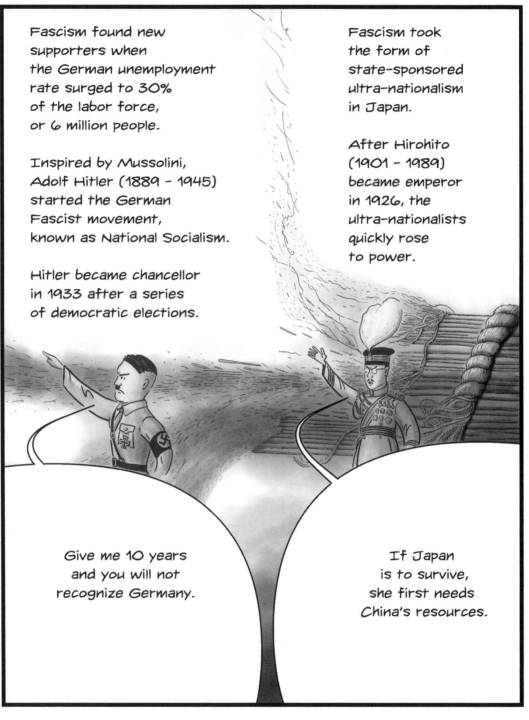

Fascism found new supporters when the German unemployment rate surged to 30% of the labor force, or 6 million people.

Inspired by Mussolini, Adolf Hitler (1889 – 1945) started the German Fascist movement, known as National Socialism.

Hitler became chancellor in 1933 after a series of democratic elections.

Fascism took the form of state-sponsored ultra-nationalism in Japan.

After Hirohito (1901 – 1989) became emperor in 1926, the ultra-nationalists quickly rose to power.

Give me 10 years and you will not recognize Germany.

If Japan is to survive, she first needs China's resources.

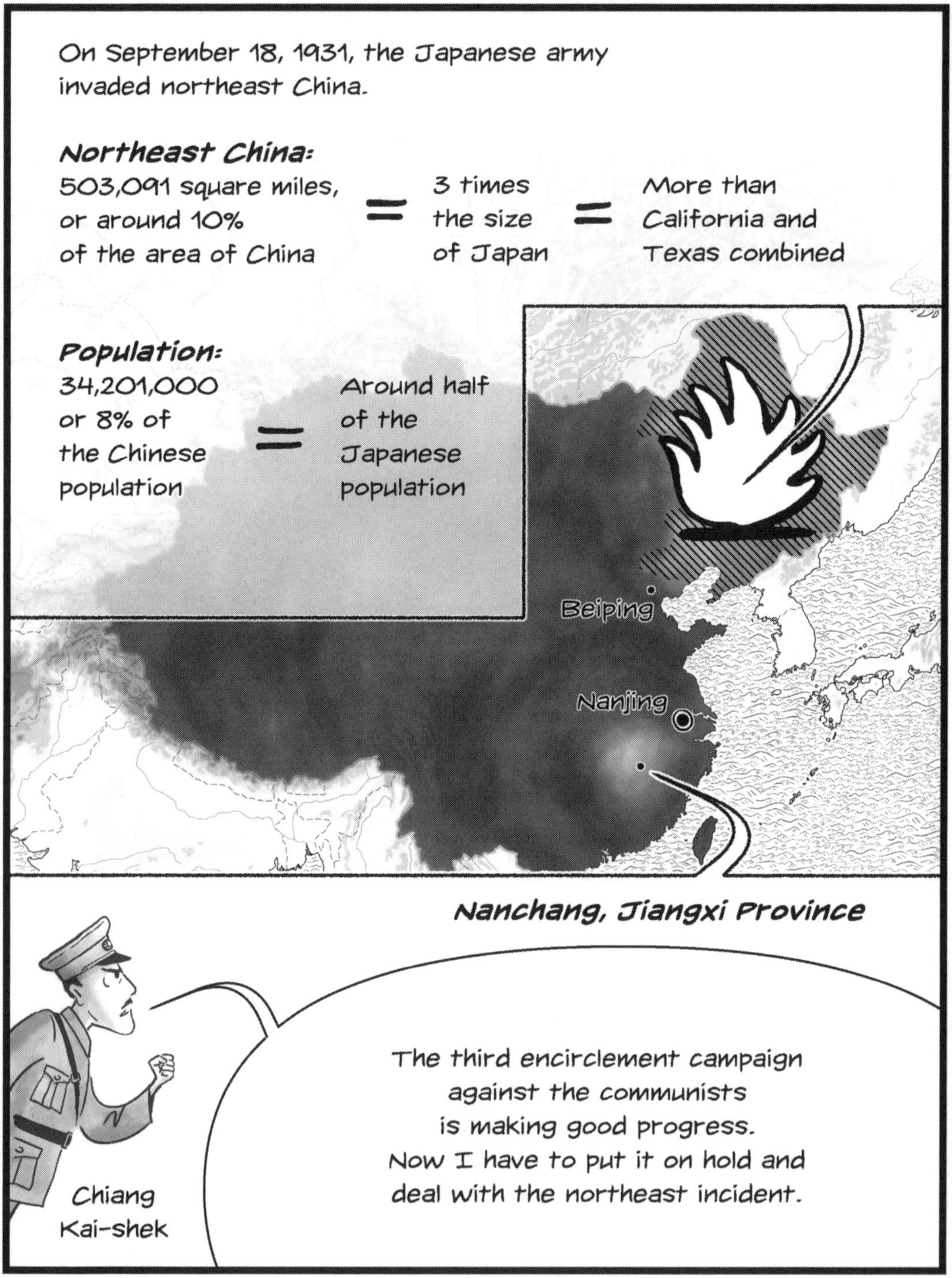

On September 18, 1931, the Japanese army invaded northeast China.
Northeast China:
503,091 square miles, or around 10% of the area of China
=
3 times the size of Japan
=
More than California and Texas combined
Population:
34,201,000 or 8% of the Chinese population
=
Around half of the Japanese population
Beiping
Nanjing
Nanchang, Jiangxi Province
The third encirclement campaign against the communists is making good progress. Now I have to put it on hold and deal with the northeast incident.
Chiang Kai-shek

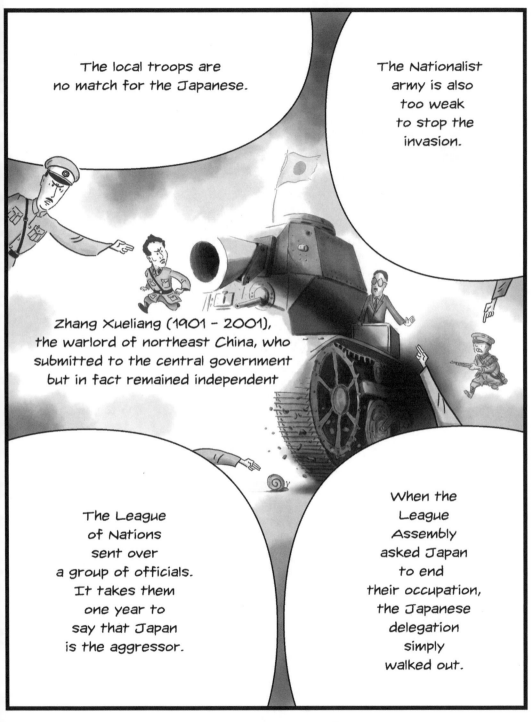

The local troops are no match for the Japanese.

The Nationalist army is also too weak to stop the invasion.

Zhang Xueliang (1901 – 2001), the warlord of northeast China, who submitted to the central government but in fact remained independent

The League of Nations sent over a group of officials. It takes them one year to say that Japan is the aggressor.

When the League Assembly asked Japan to end their occupation, the Japanese delegation simply walked out.

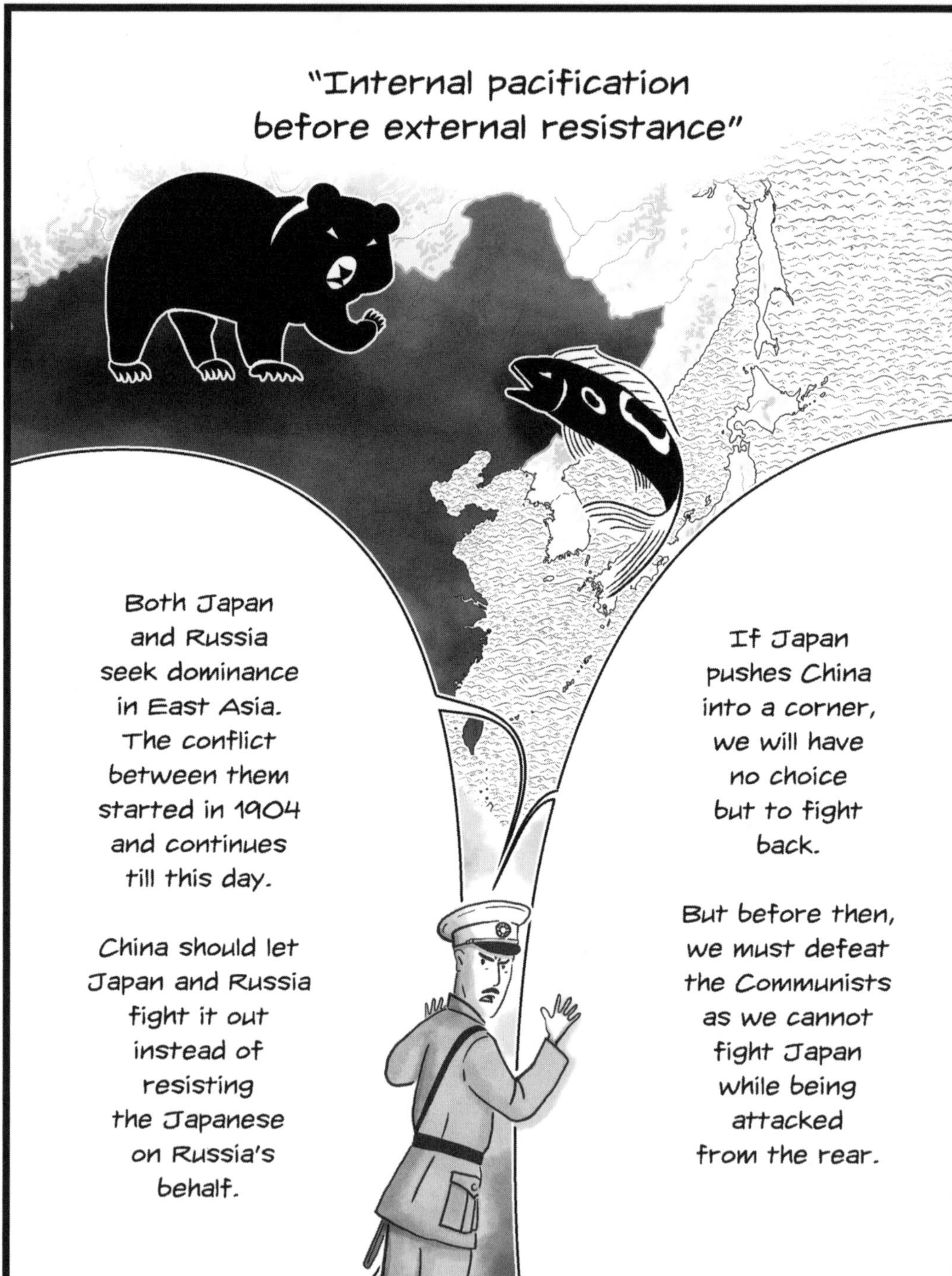
"Internal pacification before external resistance"
Both Japan and Russia seek dominance in East Asia. The conflict between them started in 1904 and continues till this day.
China should let Japan and Russia fight it out instead of resisting the Japanese on Russia's behalf.
If Japan pushes China into a corner, we will have no choice but to fight back.
But before then, we must defeat the Communists as we cannot fight Japan while being attacked from the rear.

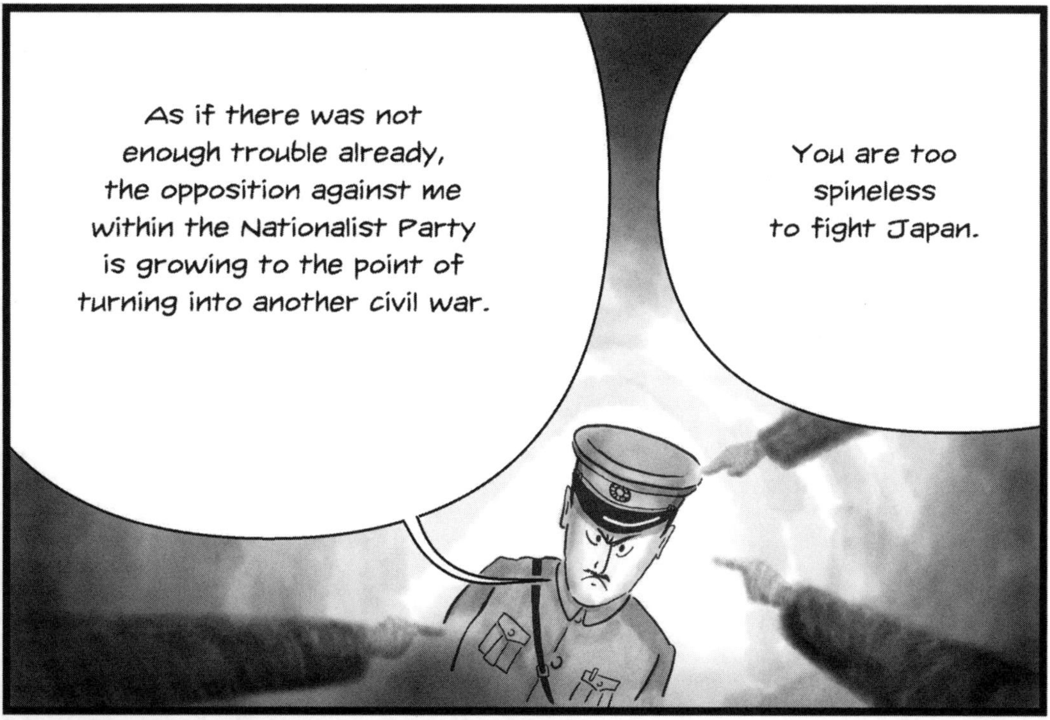
As if there was not enough trouble already, the opposition against me within the Nationalist Party is growing to the point of turning into another civil war.
You are too spineless to fight Japan.

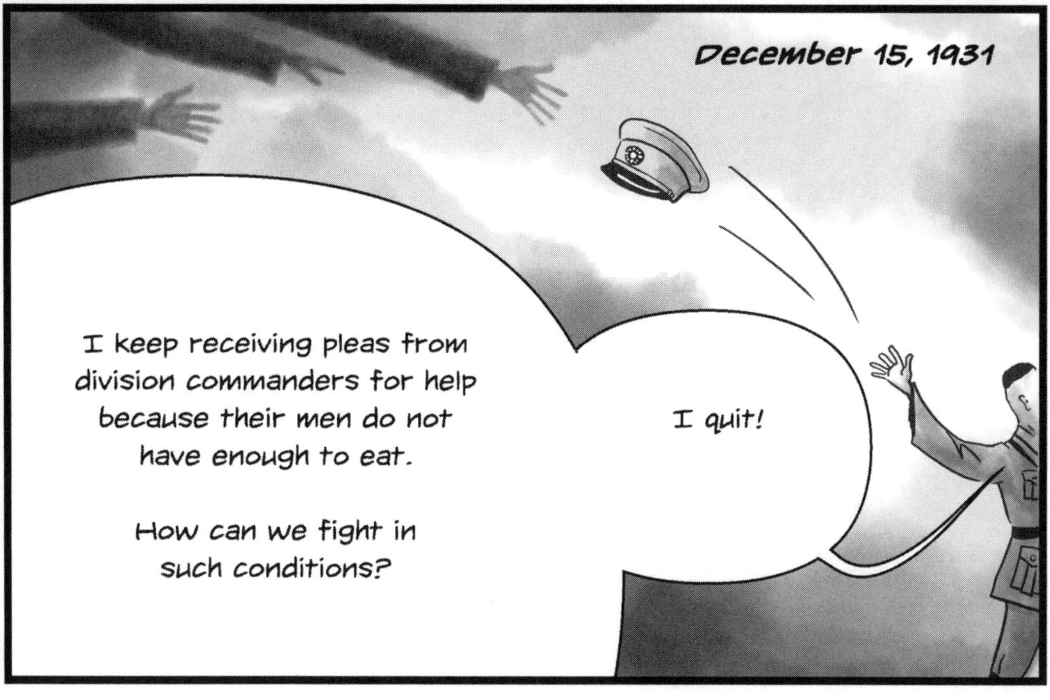
December 15, 1931
I keep receiving pleas from division commanders for help because their men do not have enough to eat.
How can we fight in such conditions?
I quit!

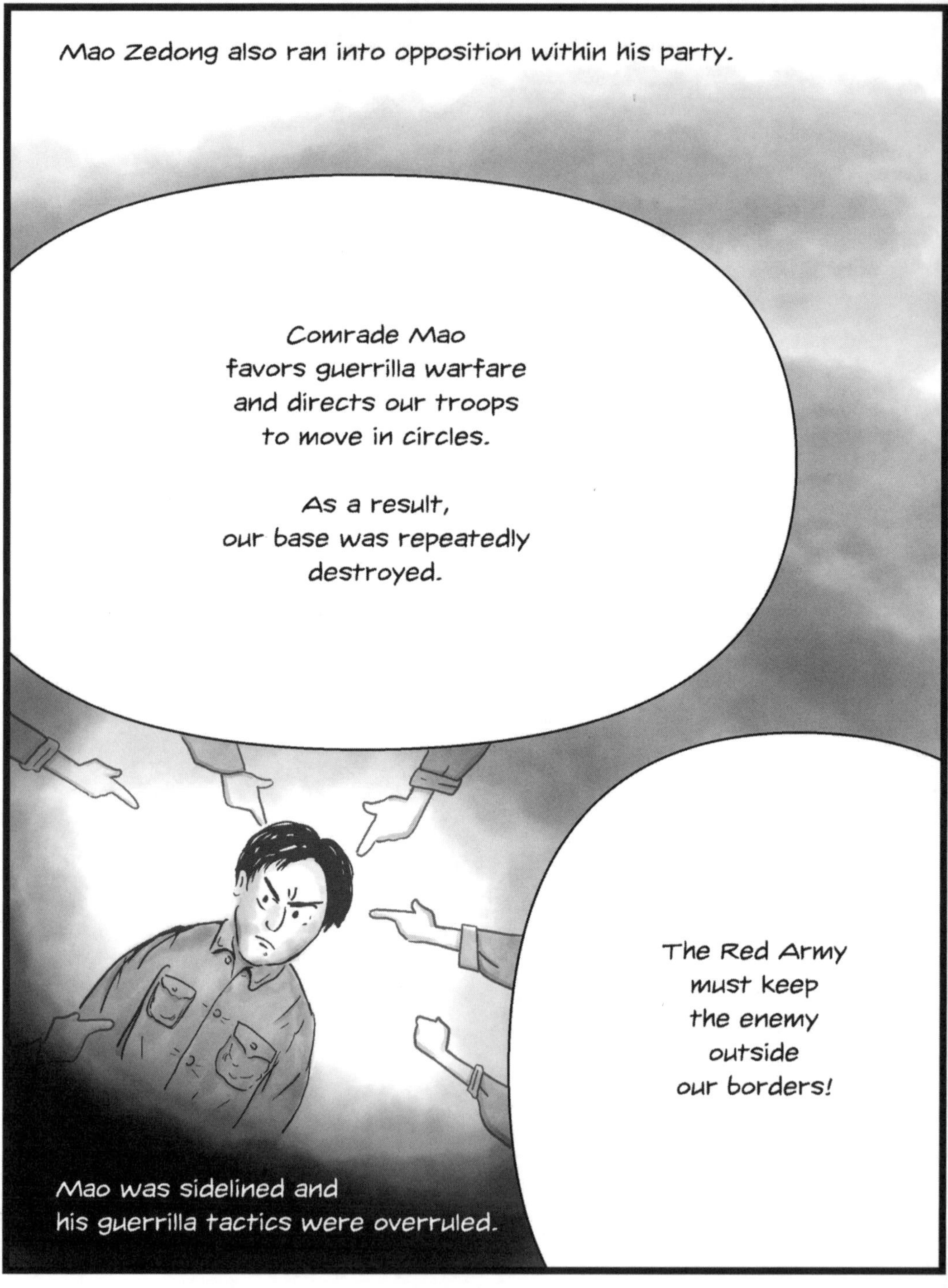
Mao Zedong also ran into opposition within his party.
Comrade Mao favors guerrilla warfare and directs our troops to move in circles.
As a result, our base was repeatedly destroyed.
The Red Army must keep the enemy outside our borders!
Mao was sidelined and his guerrilla tactics were overruled.

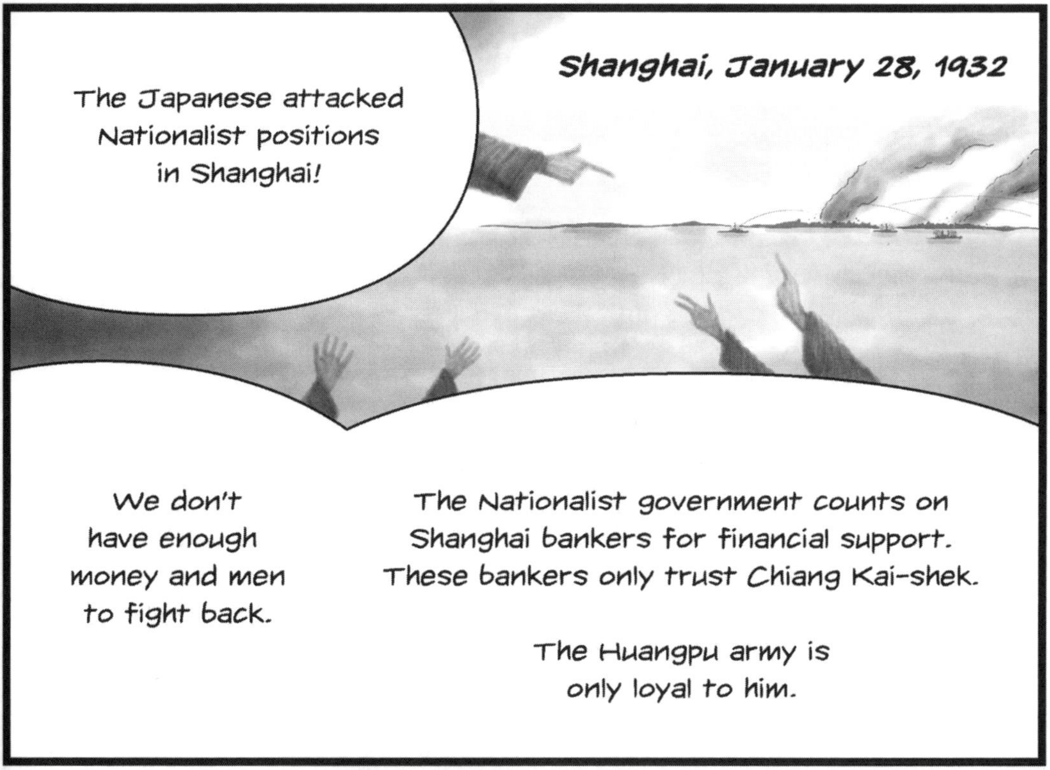
Shanghai, January 28, 1932
The Japanese attacked Nationalist positions in Shanghai!
We don't have enough money and men to fight back.
The Nationalist government counts on Shanghai bankers for financial support. These bankers only trust Chiang Kai-shek.
The Huangpu army is only loyal to him.

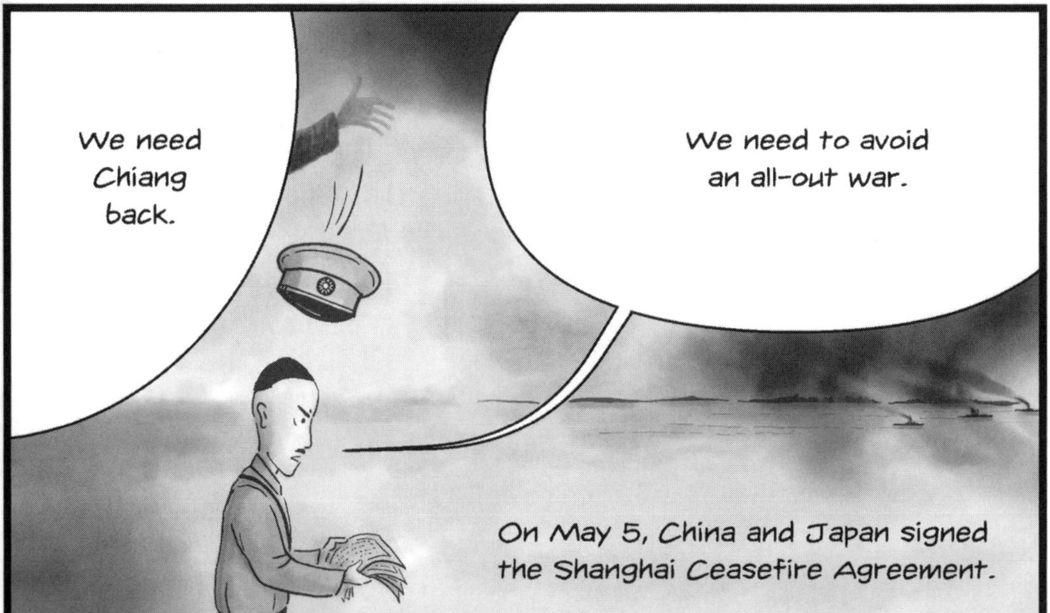
We need Chiang back.
We need to avoid an all-out war.
On May 5, China and Japan signed the Shanghai Ceasefire Agreement.

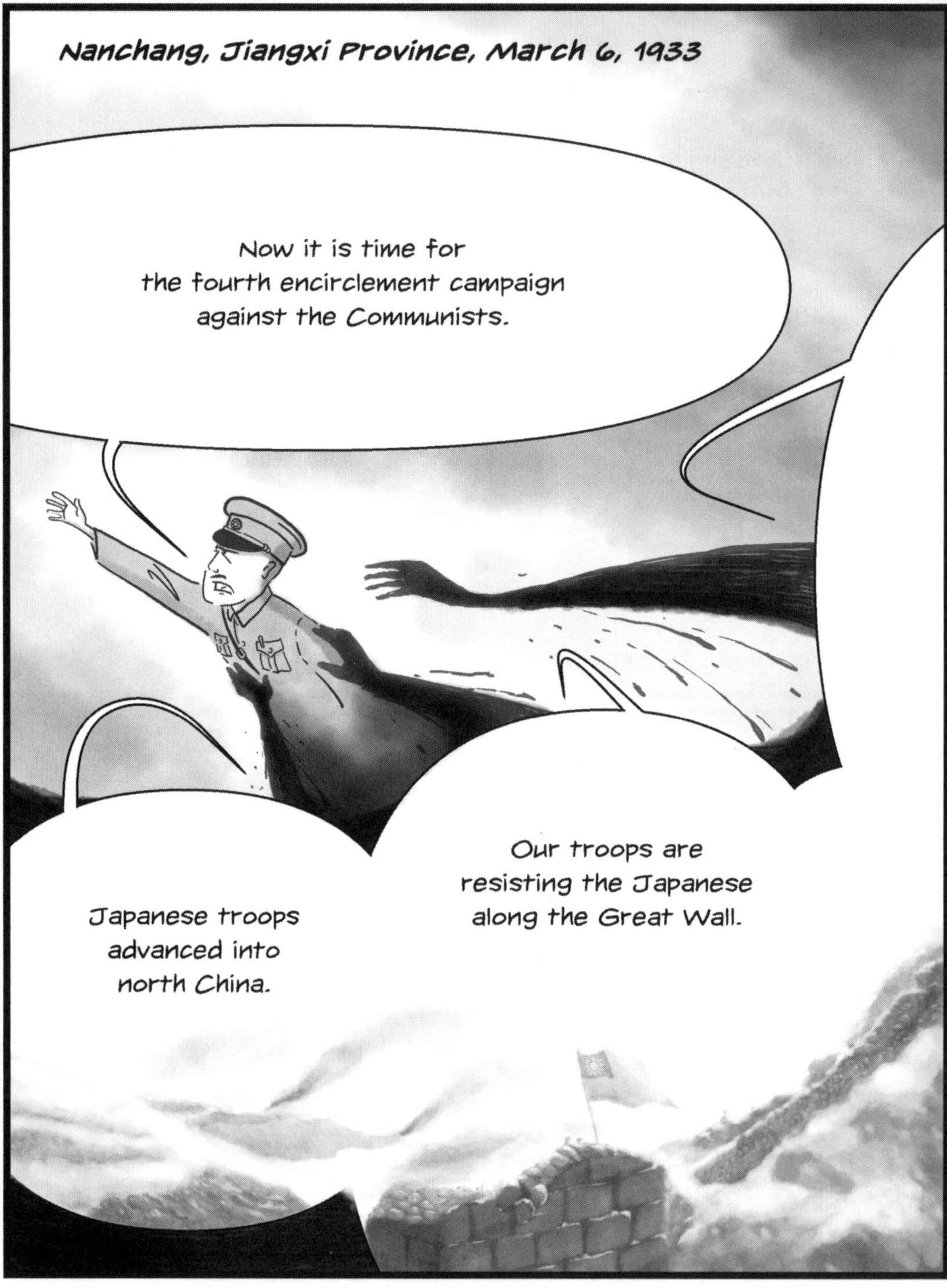
Nanchang, Jiangxi Province, March 6, 1933
Now it is time for the fourth encirclement campaign against the Communists.
Japanese troops advanced into north China.
Our troops are resisting the Japanese along the Great Wall.

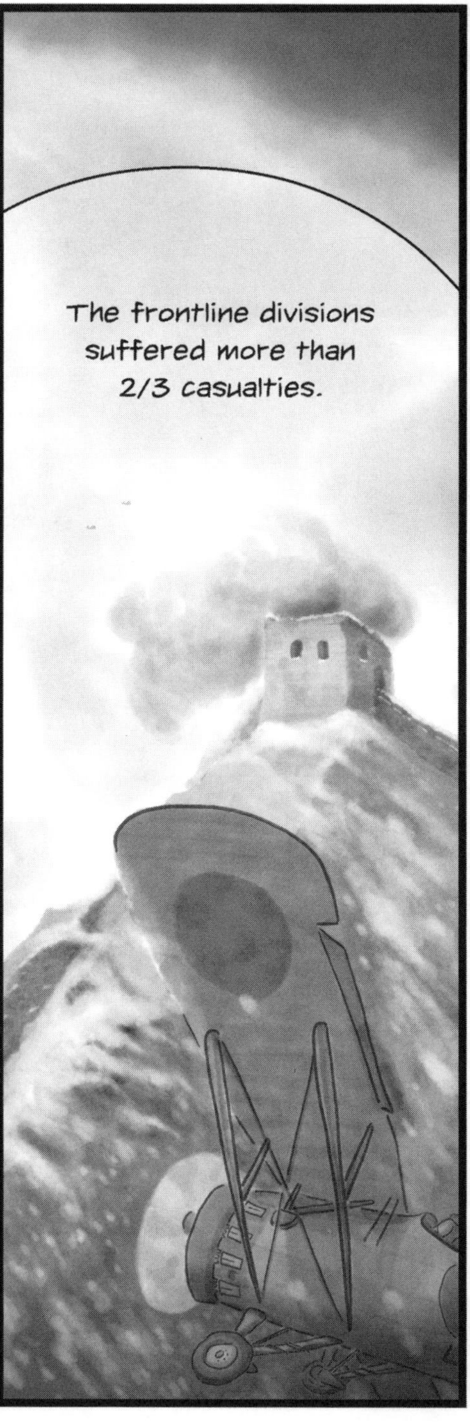
The frontline divisions suffered more than 2/3 casualties.

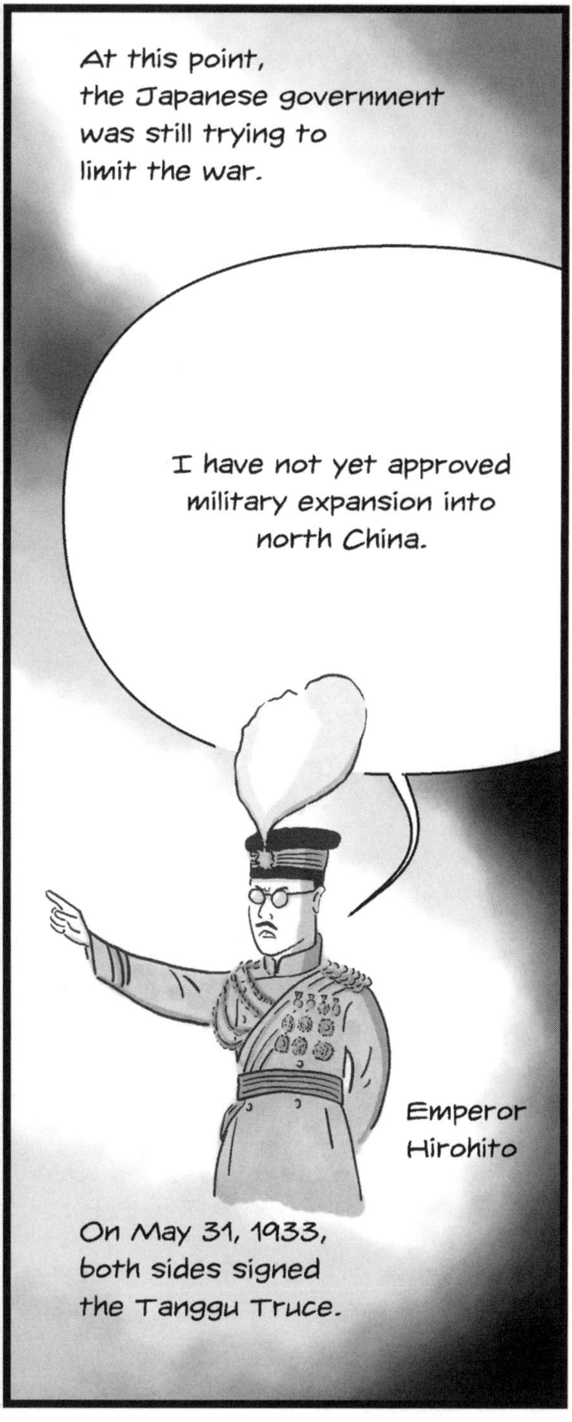
At this point, the Japanese government was still trying to limit the war.
I have not yet approved military expansion into north China.
Emperor Hirohito
On May 31, 1933, both sides signed the Tanggu Truce.

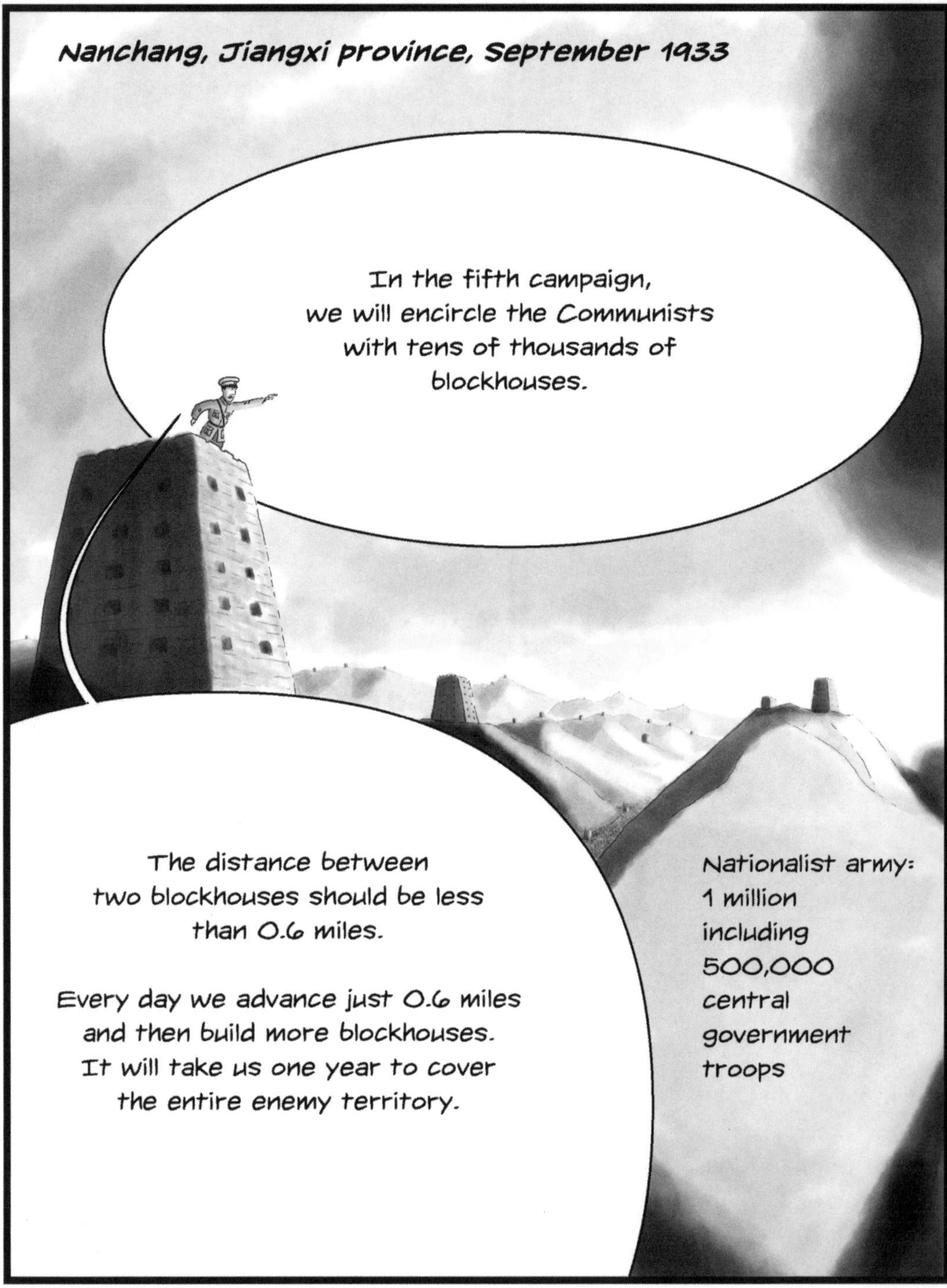
Nanchang, Jiangxi province, September 1933
In the fifth campaign, we will encircle the Communists with tens of thousands of blockhouses.
The distance between two blockhouses should be less than 0.6 miles.
Every day we advance just 0.6 miles and then build more blockhouses. It will take us one year to cover the entire enemy territory.
Nationalist army: 1 million including 500,000 central government troops

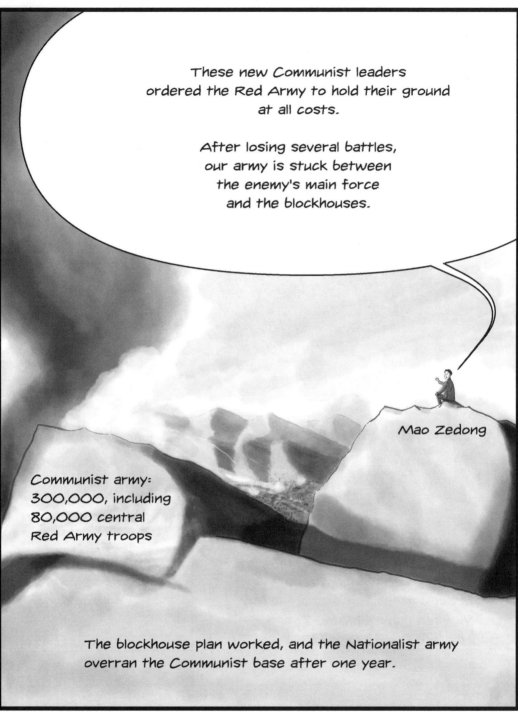

These new Communist leaders ordered the Red Army to hold their ground at all costs.

After losing several battles, our army is stuck between the enemy's main force and the blockhouses.

Mao Zedong

Communist army: 300,000, including 80,000 central Red Army troops

The blockhouse plan worked, and the Nationalist army overran the Communist base after one year.

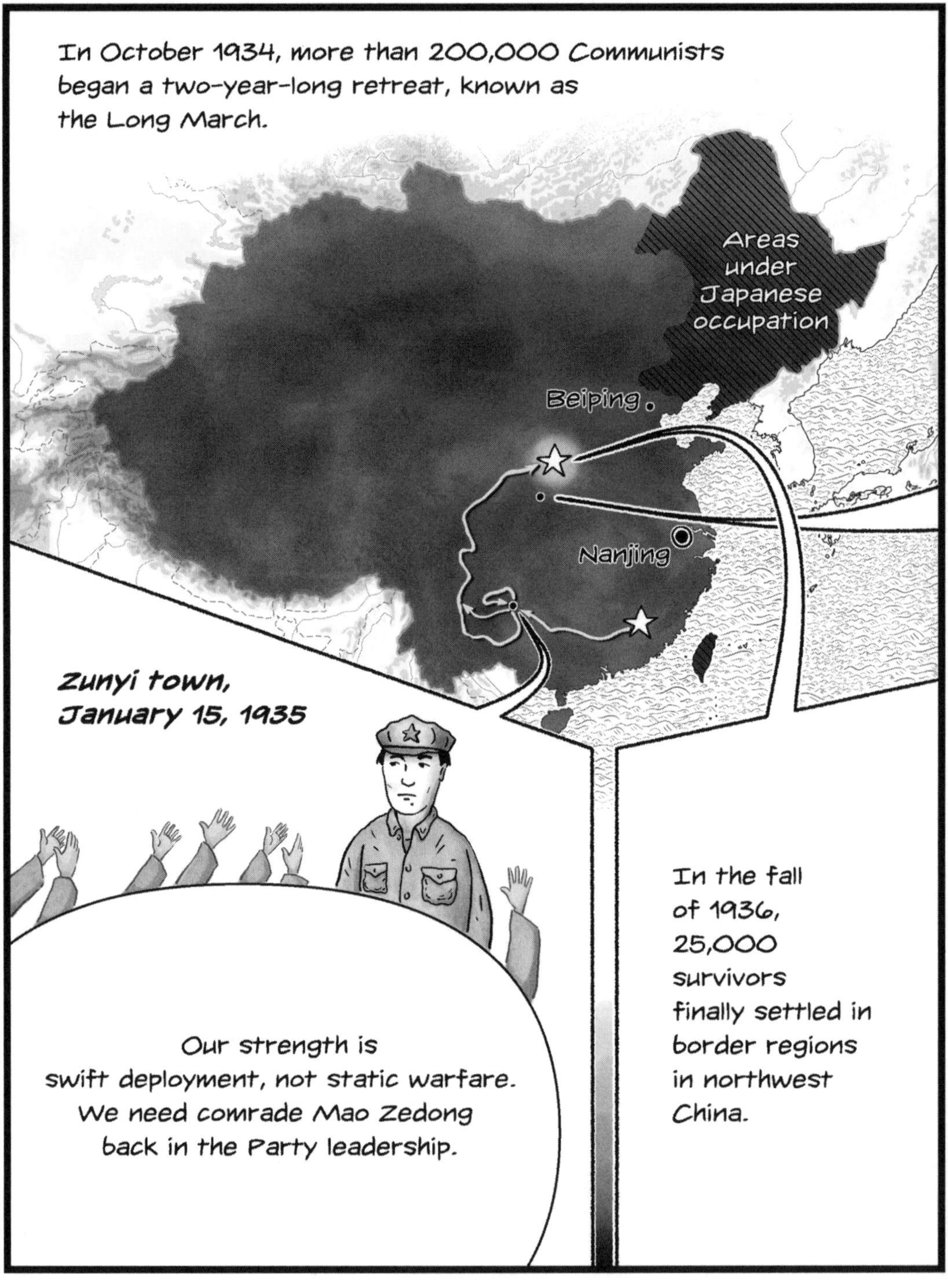
In October 1934, more than 200,000 Communists began a two-year-long retreat, known as the Long March.
Areas under Japanese occupation
Beiping
Nanjing
Zunyi town, January 15, 1935
Our strength is swift deployment, not static warfare. We need comrade Mao Zedong back in the Party leadership.
In the fall of 1936, 25,000 survivors finally settled in border regions in northwest China.

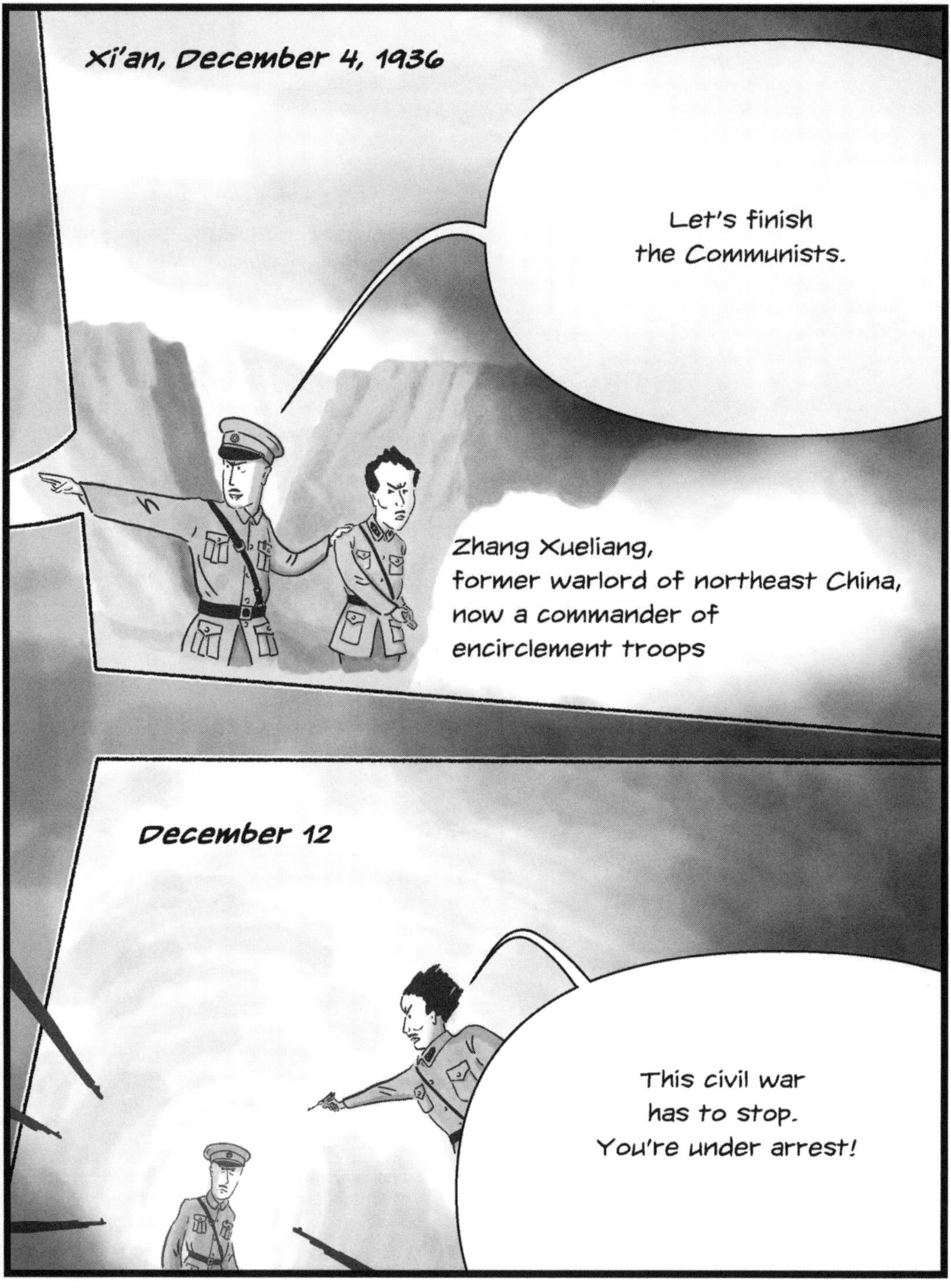
Xi'an, December 4, 1936
Let's finish the Communists.
Zhang Xueliang, former warlord of northeast China, now a commander of encirclement troops
December 12
This civil war has to stop. You're under arrest!

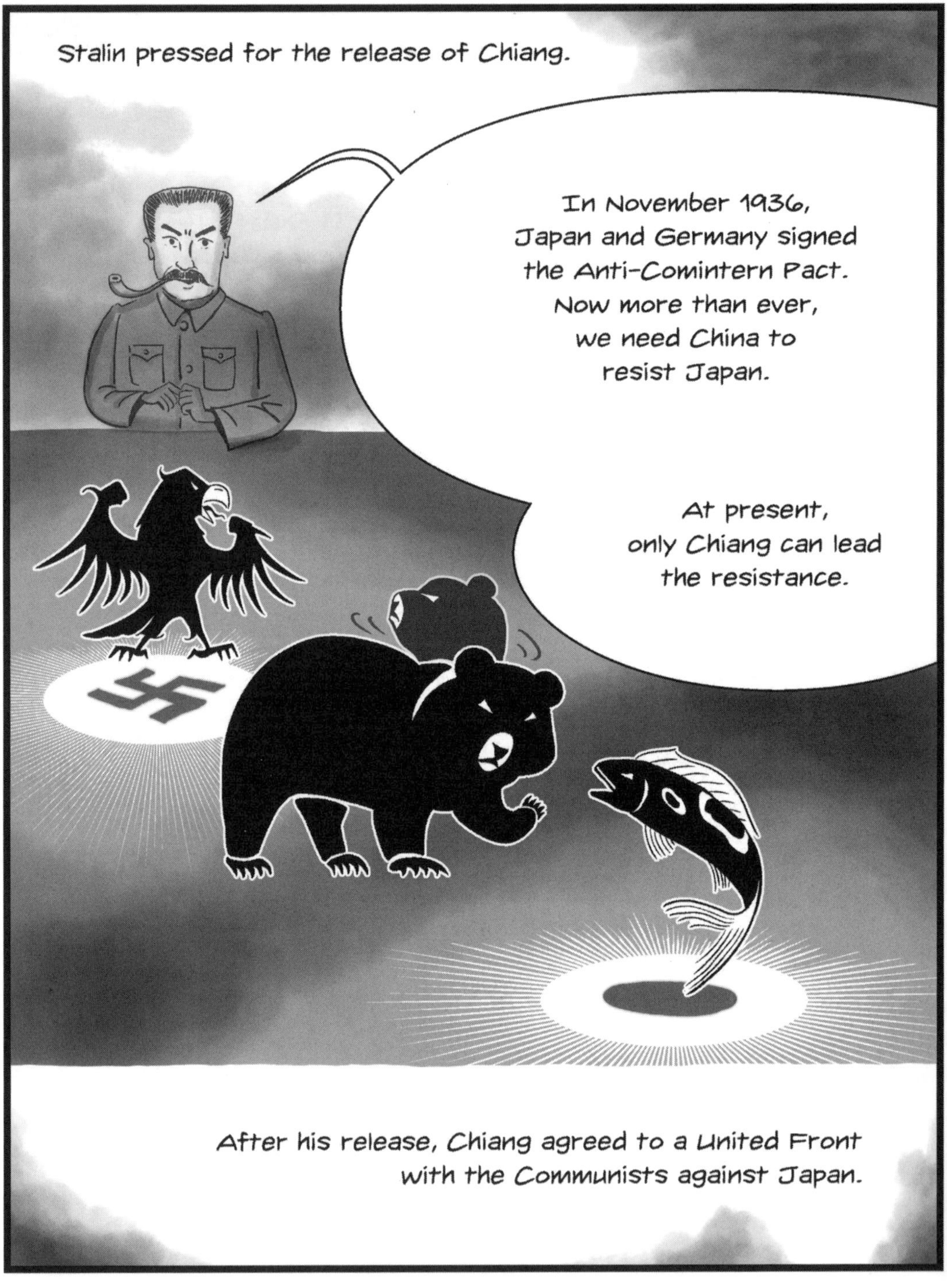
Stalin pressed for the release of Chiang.
In November 1936, Japan and Germany signed the Anti-Comintern Pact. Now more than ever, we need China to resist Japan.
At present, only Chiang can lead the resistance.
After his release, Chiang agreed to a United Front with the Communists against Japan.

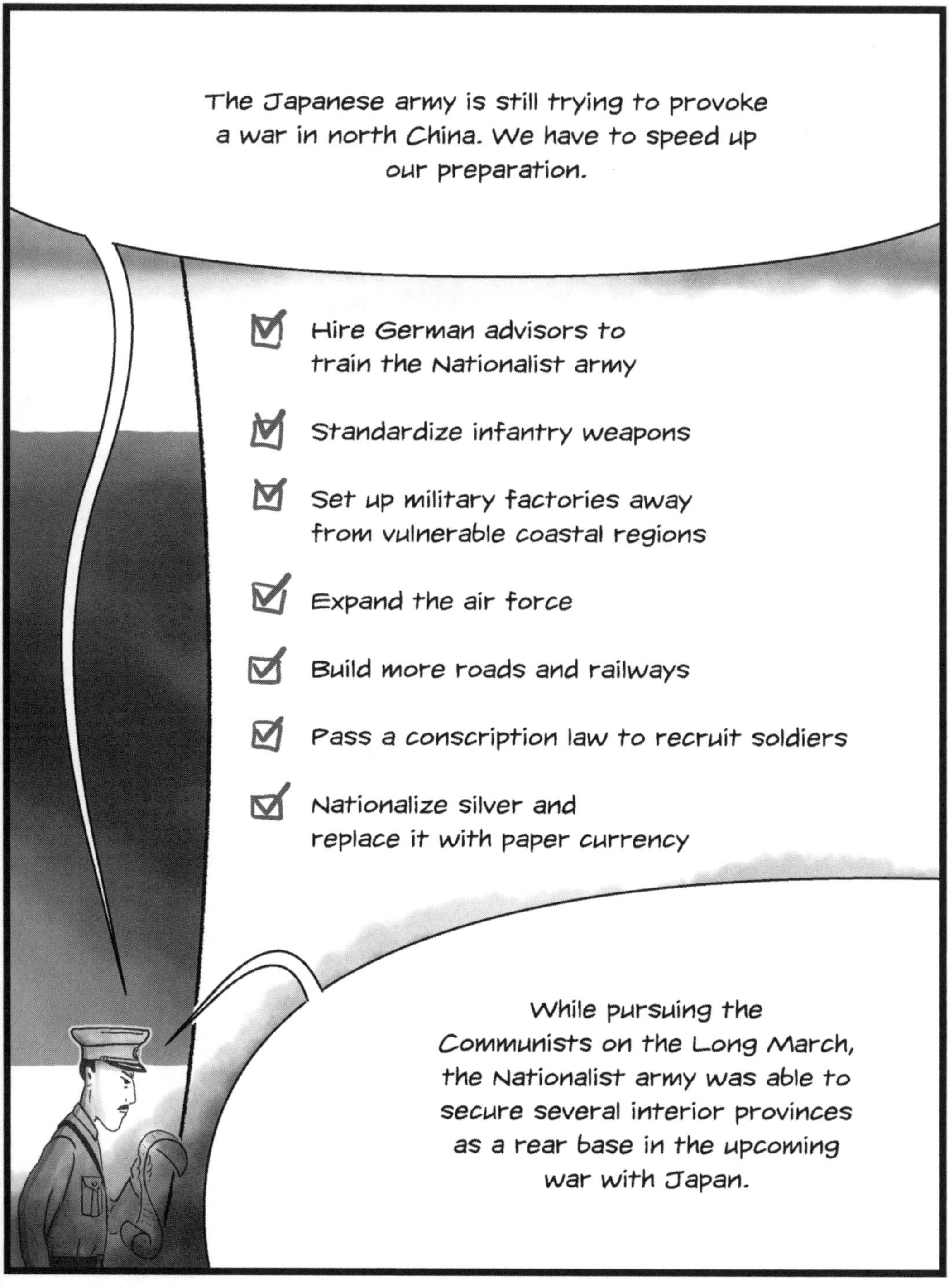
The Japanese army is still trying to provoke a war in north China. We have to speed up our preparation.
Hire German advisors to train the Nationalist army
Standardize infantry weapons
Set up military factories away from vulnerable coastal regions
Expand the air force
Build more roads and railways
Pass a conscription law to recruit soldiers
Nationalize silver and replace it with paper currency
While pursuing the Communists on the Long March, the Nationalist army was able to secure several interior provinces as a rear base in the upcoming war with Japan.

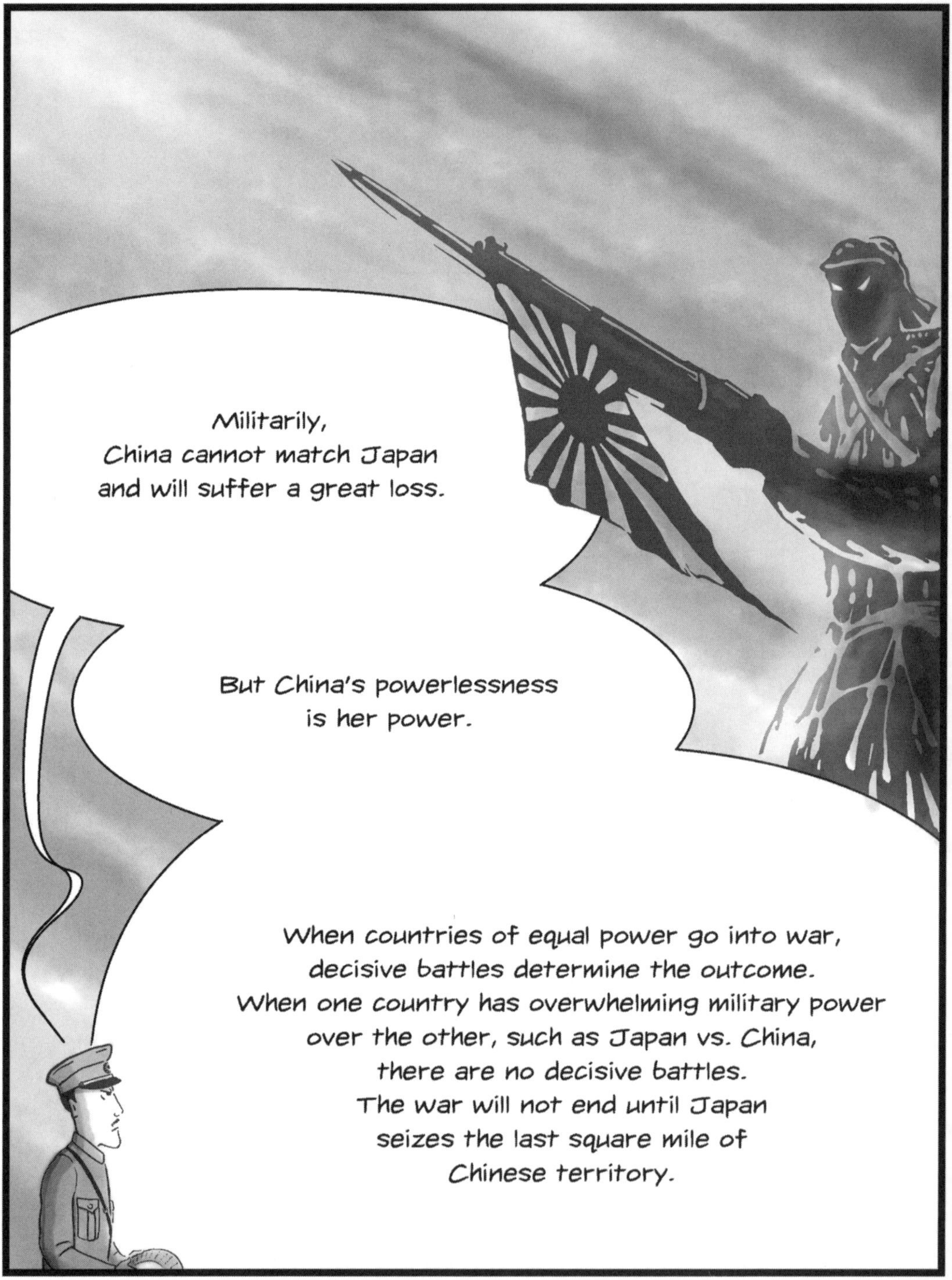
Militarily, China cannot match Japan and will suffer a great loss.
But China's powerlessness is her power.
When countries of equal power go into war, decisive battles determine the outcome. When one country has overwhelming military power over the other, such as Japan vs. China, there are no decisive battles. The war will not end until Japan seizes the last square mile of Chinese territory.

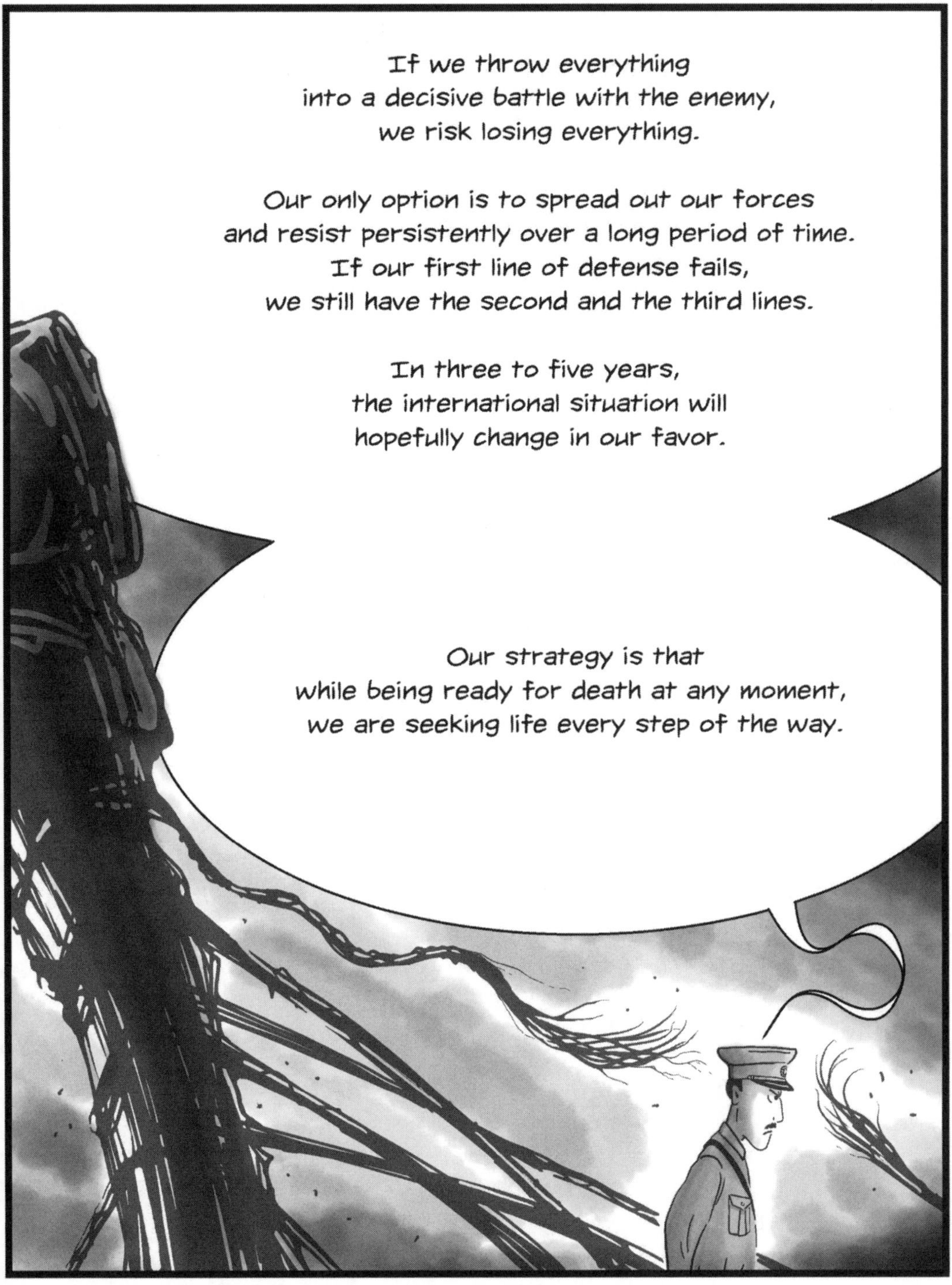
If we throw everything into a decisive battle with the enemy, we risk losing everything.
Our only option is to spread out our forces and resist persistently over a long period of time. If our first line of defense fails, we still have the second and the third lines.
In three to five years, the international situation will hopefully change in our favor.
Our strategy is that while being ready for death at any moment, we are seeking life every step of the way.

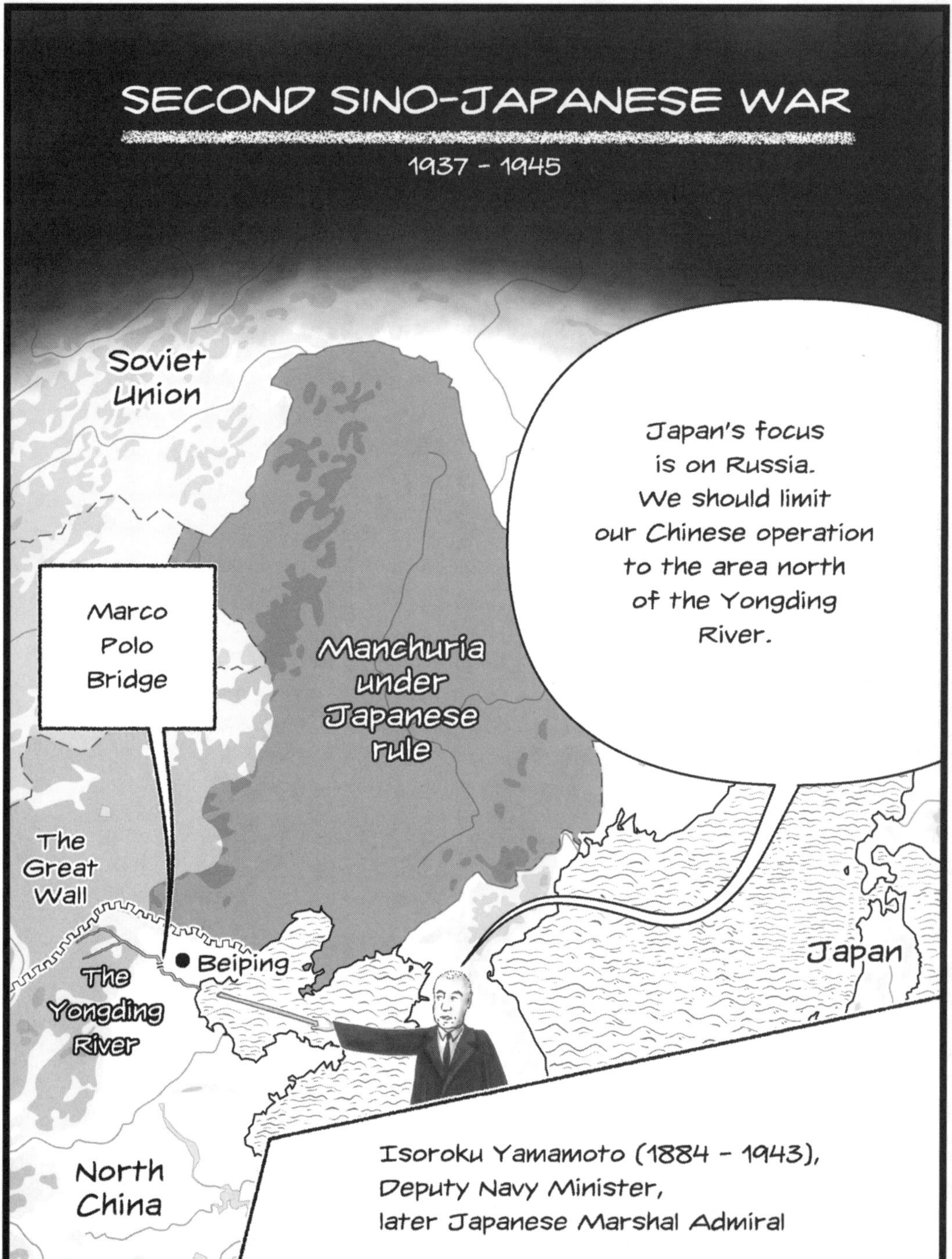
SECOND SINO-JAPANESE WAR
1937 - 1945
Soviet Union
Japan's focus is on Russia. We should limit our Chinese operation to the area north of the Yongding River.
Marco Polo Bridge
Manchuria under Japanese rule
The Great Wall
Beiping
The Yongding River
Japan
North China
Isoroku Yamamoto (1884 - 1943), Deputy Navy Minister, later Japanese Marshal Admiral

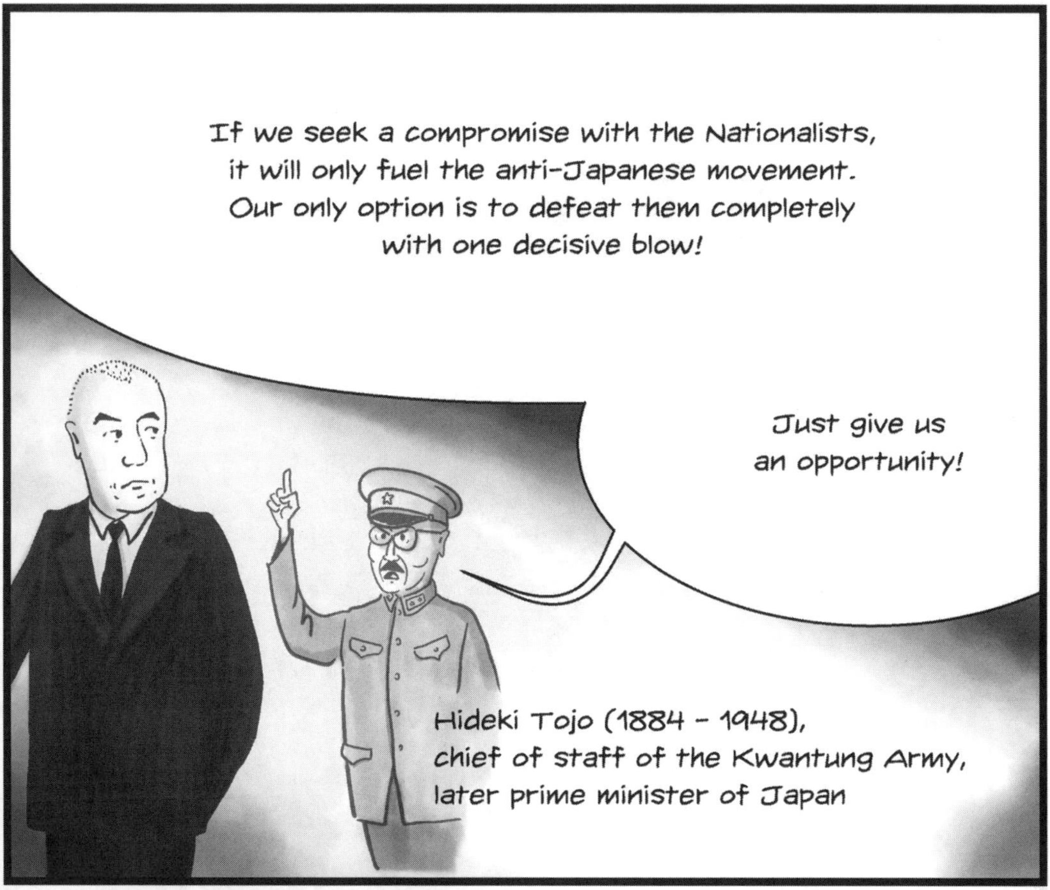
If we seek a compromise with the Nationalists,
it will only fuel the anti-Japanese movement.
Our only option is to defeat them completely
with one decisive blow!
Just give us
an opportunity!
Hideki Tojo (1884 – 1948),
chief of staff of the Kwantung Army,
later prime minister of Japan

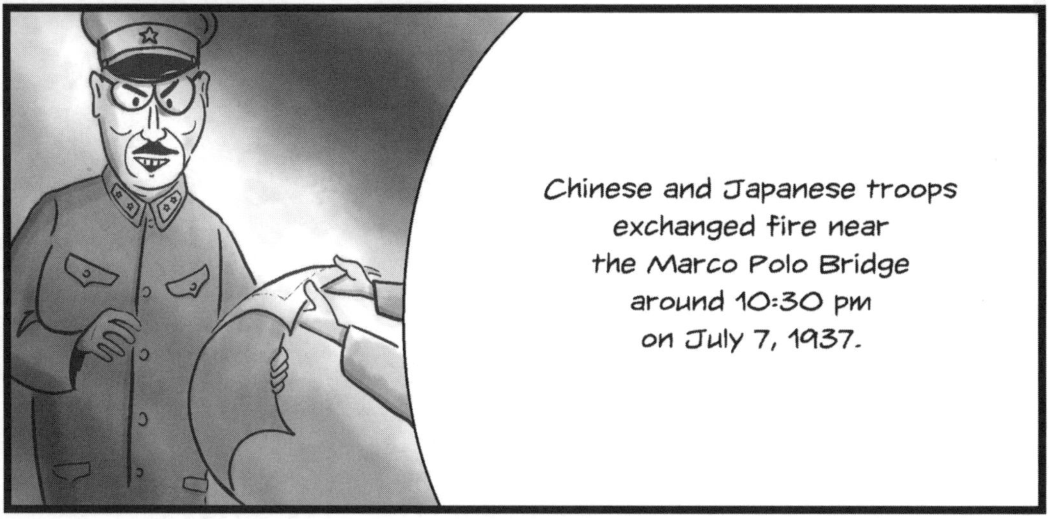
Chinese and Japanese troops
exchanged fire near
the Marco Polo Bridge
around 10:30 pm
on July 7, 1937.

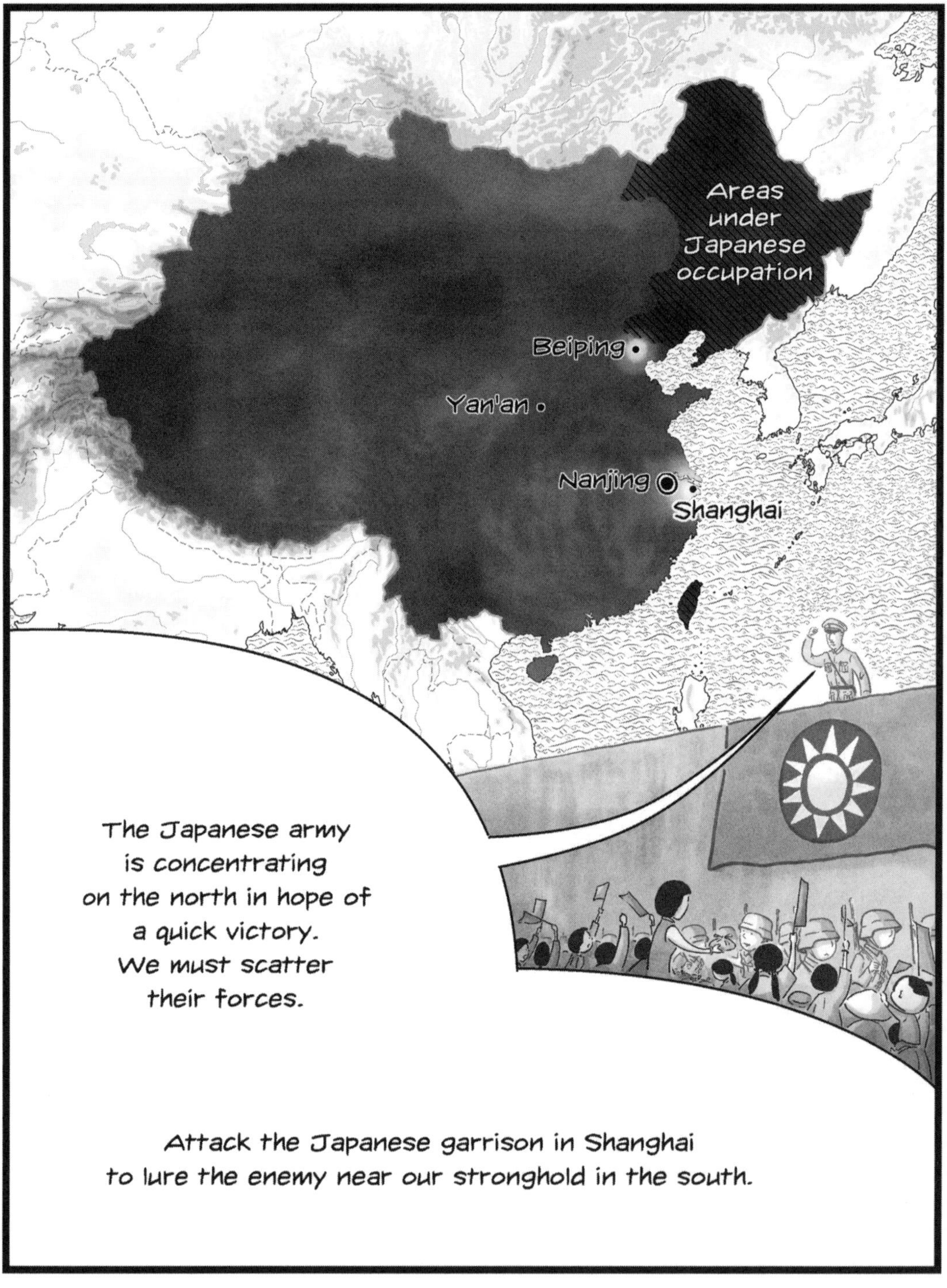

Areas under Japanese occupation
Beiping
Yan'an
Nanjing
Shanghai
The Japanese army is concentrating on the north in hope of a quick victory. We must scatter their forces.
Attack the Japanese garrison in Shanghai to lure the enemy near our stronghold in the south.

The Battle of Shanghai began on August 13, 1937 and lasted three months.

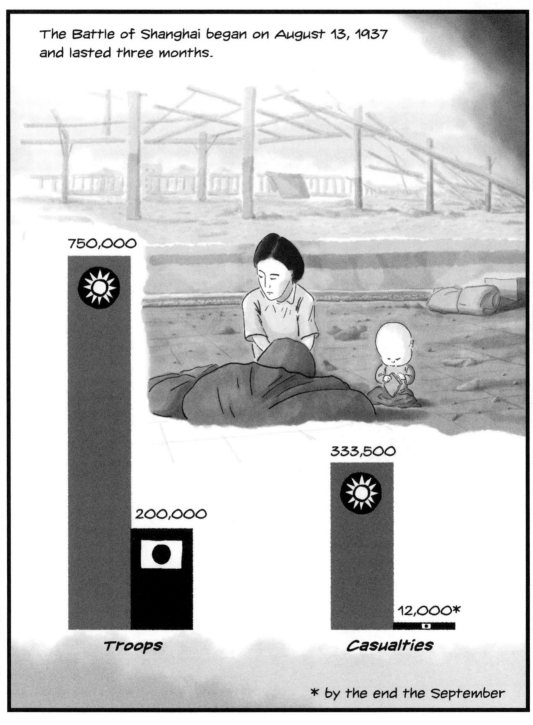

750,000

200,000

333,500

12,000*

Troops

Casualties

* by the end the September

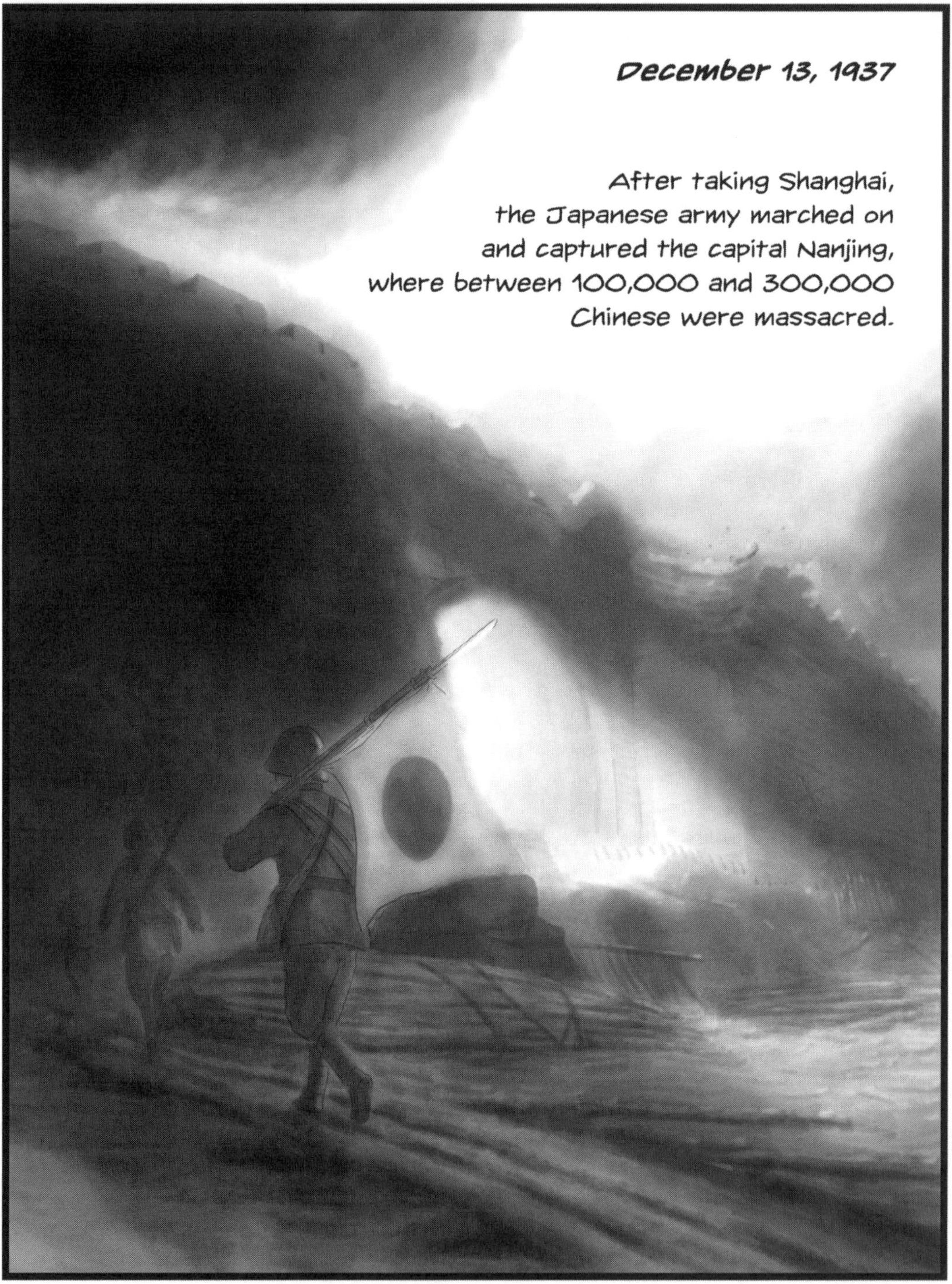
December 13, 1937
After taking Shanghai, the Japanese army marched on and captured the capital Nanjing, where between 100,000 and 300,000 Chinese were massacred.

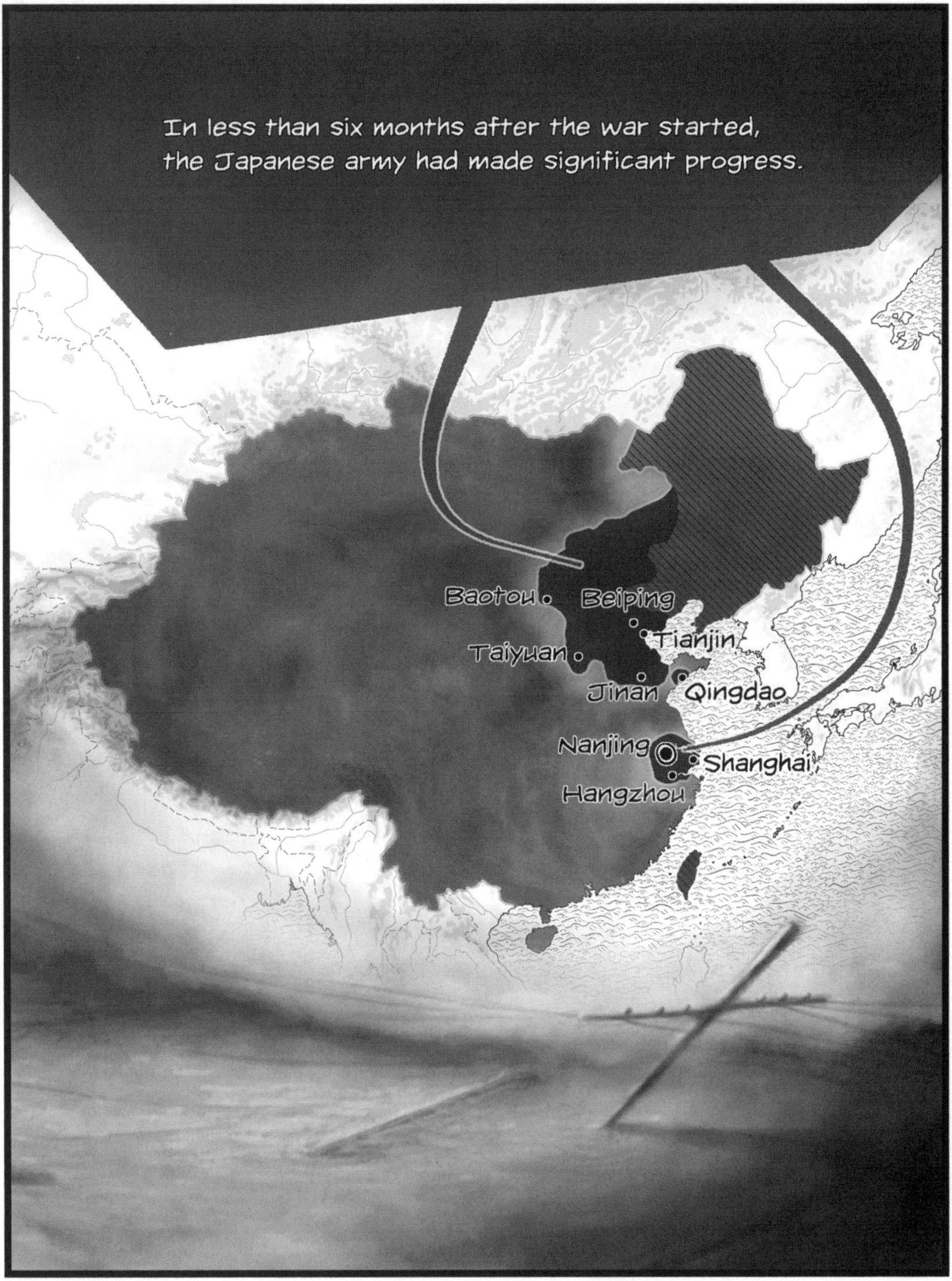
In less than six months after the war started, the Japanese army had made significant progress.
Baotou
Beiping
Tianjin
Taiyuan
Jinan
Qingdao
Nanjing
Shanghai
Hangzhou

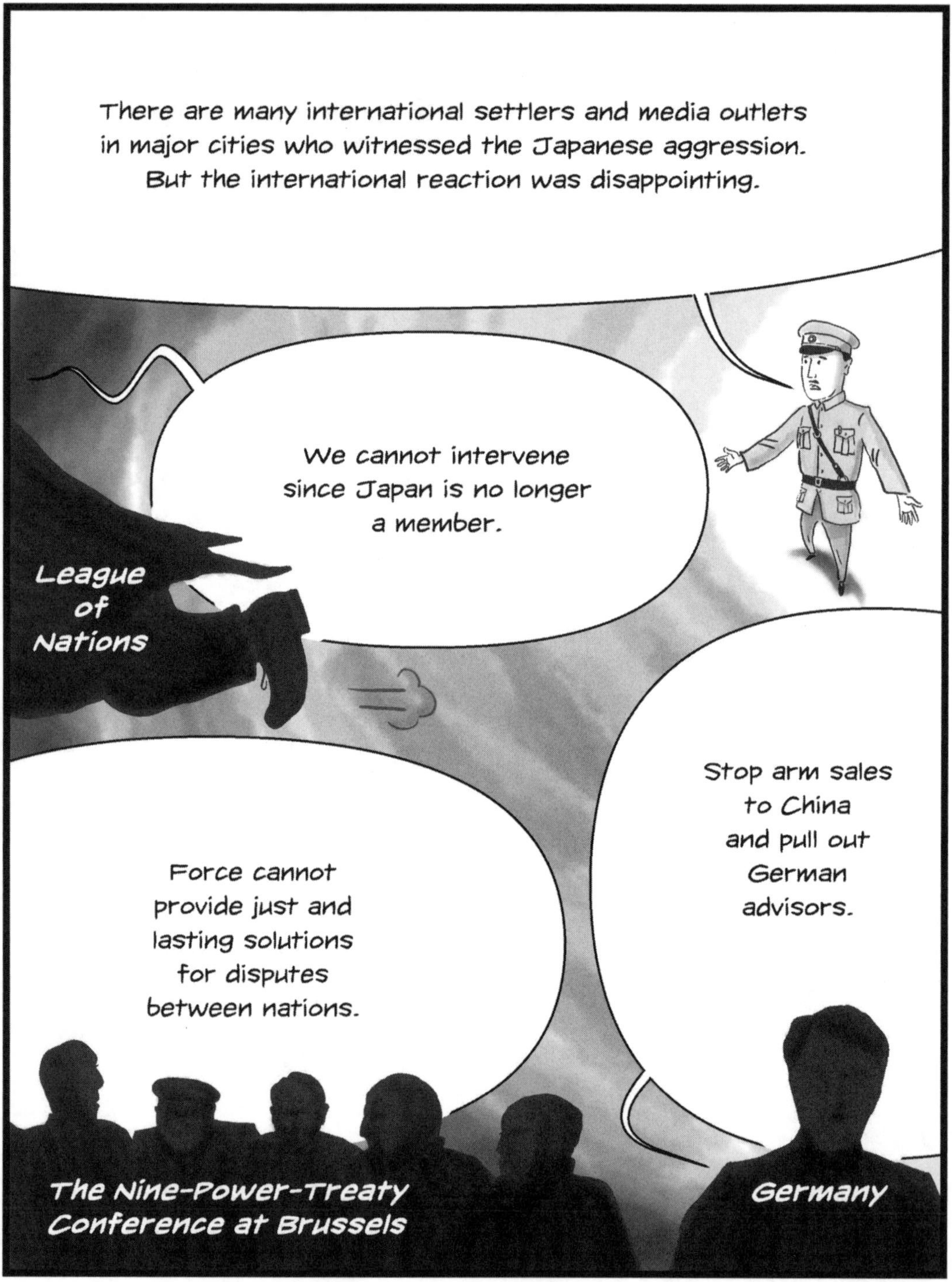
There are many international settlers and media outlets in major cities who witnessed the Japanese aggression. But the international reaction was disappointing.
We cannot intervene since Japan is no longer a member.
League of Nations
Force cannot provide just and lasting solutions for disputes between nations.
Stop arm sales to China and pull out German advisors.
The Nine-Power-Treaty Conference at Brussels
Germany

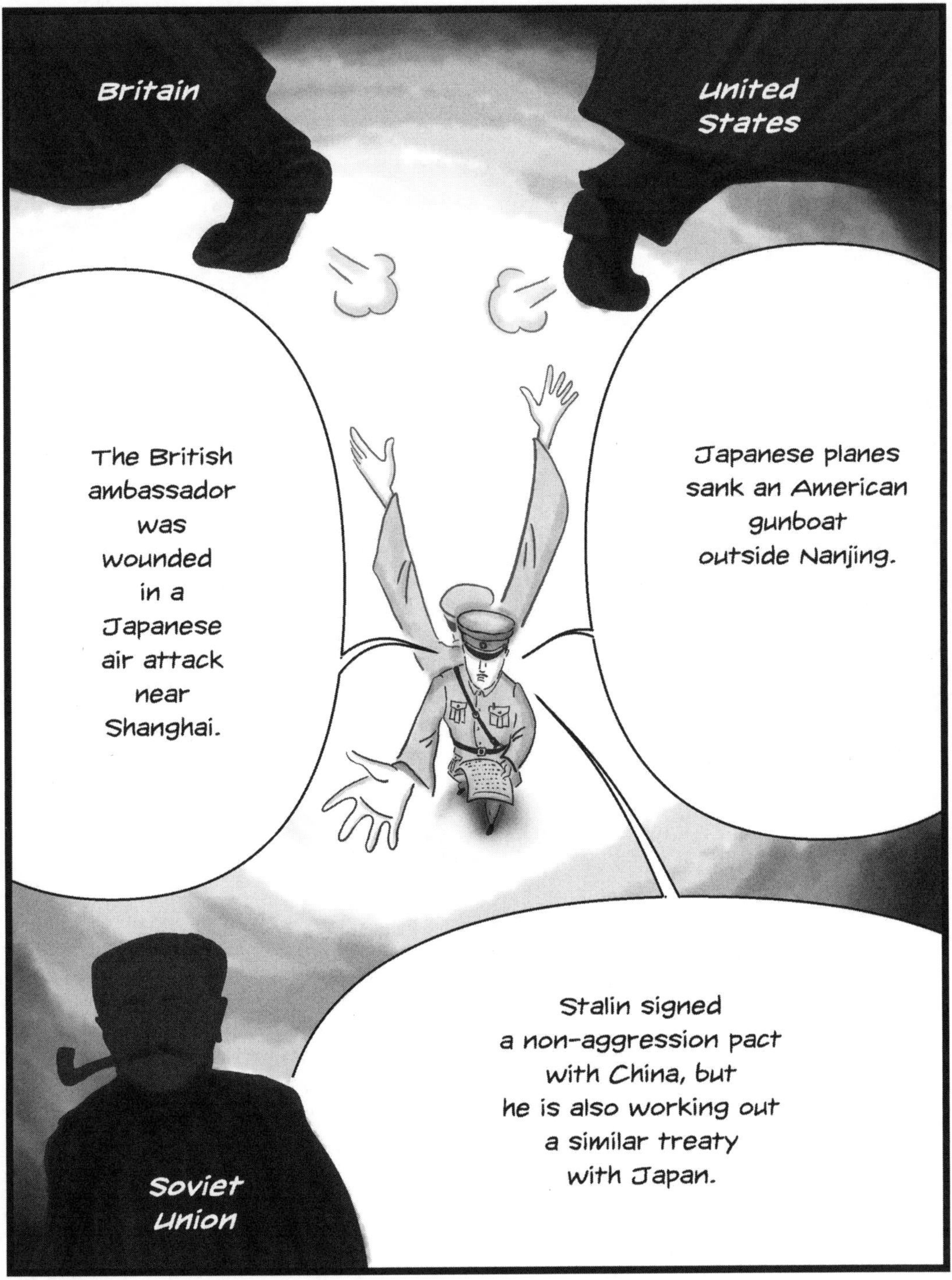
Britain
United States
The British ambassador was wounded in a Japanese air attack near Shanghai.
Japanese planes sank an American gunboat outside Nanjing.
Soviet Union
Stalin signed a non-aggression pact with China, but he is also working out a similar treaty with Japan.

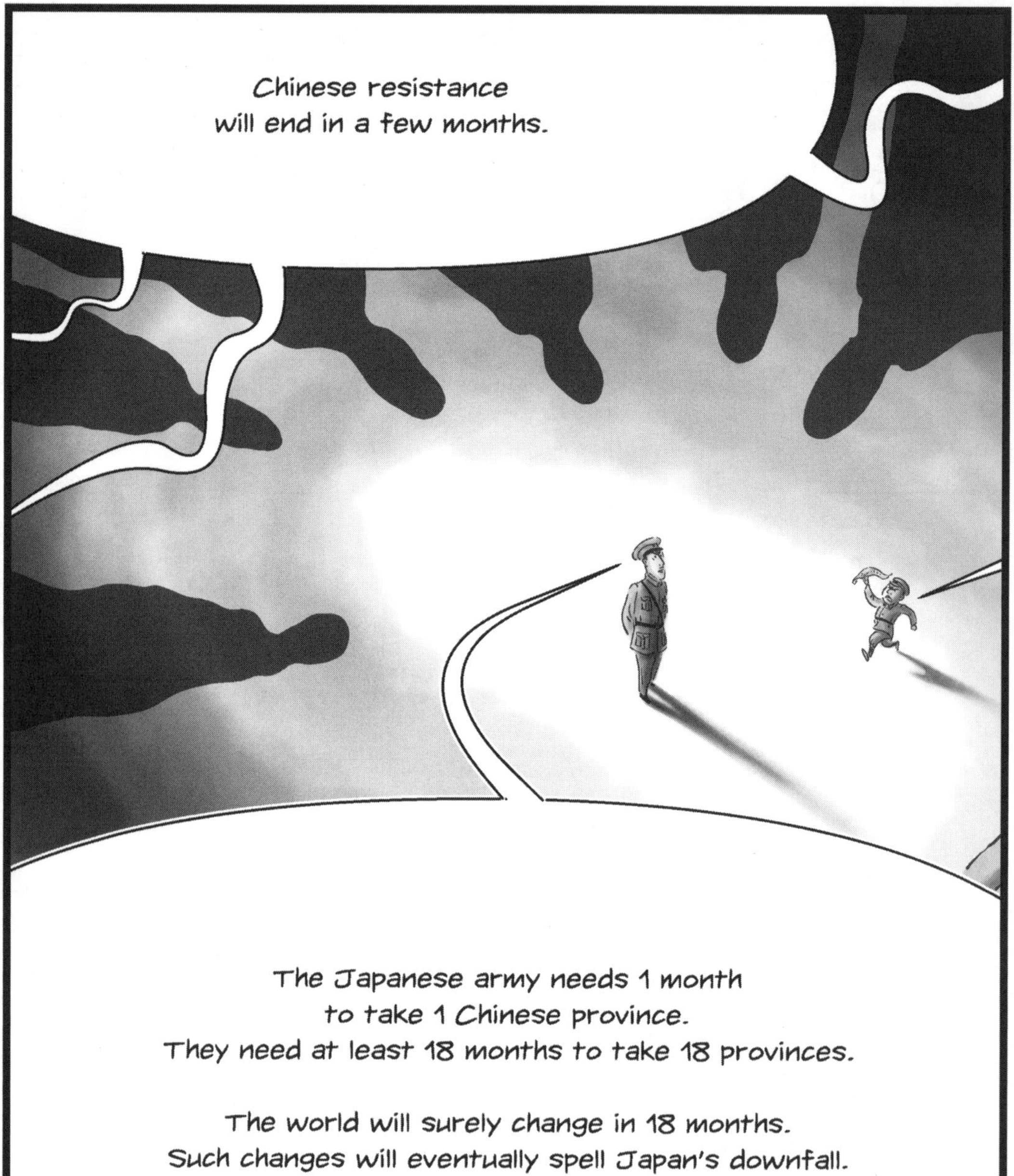

Chinese resistance will end in a few months.
The Japanese army needs 1 month to take 1 Chinese province. They need at least 18 months to take 18 provinces.
The world will surely change in 18 months. Such changes will eventually spell Japan's downfall. Why don't the Japanese just wake up and withdraw already?

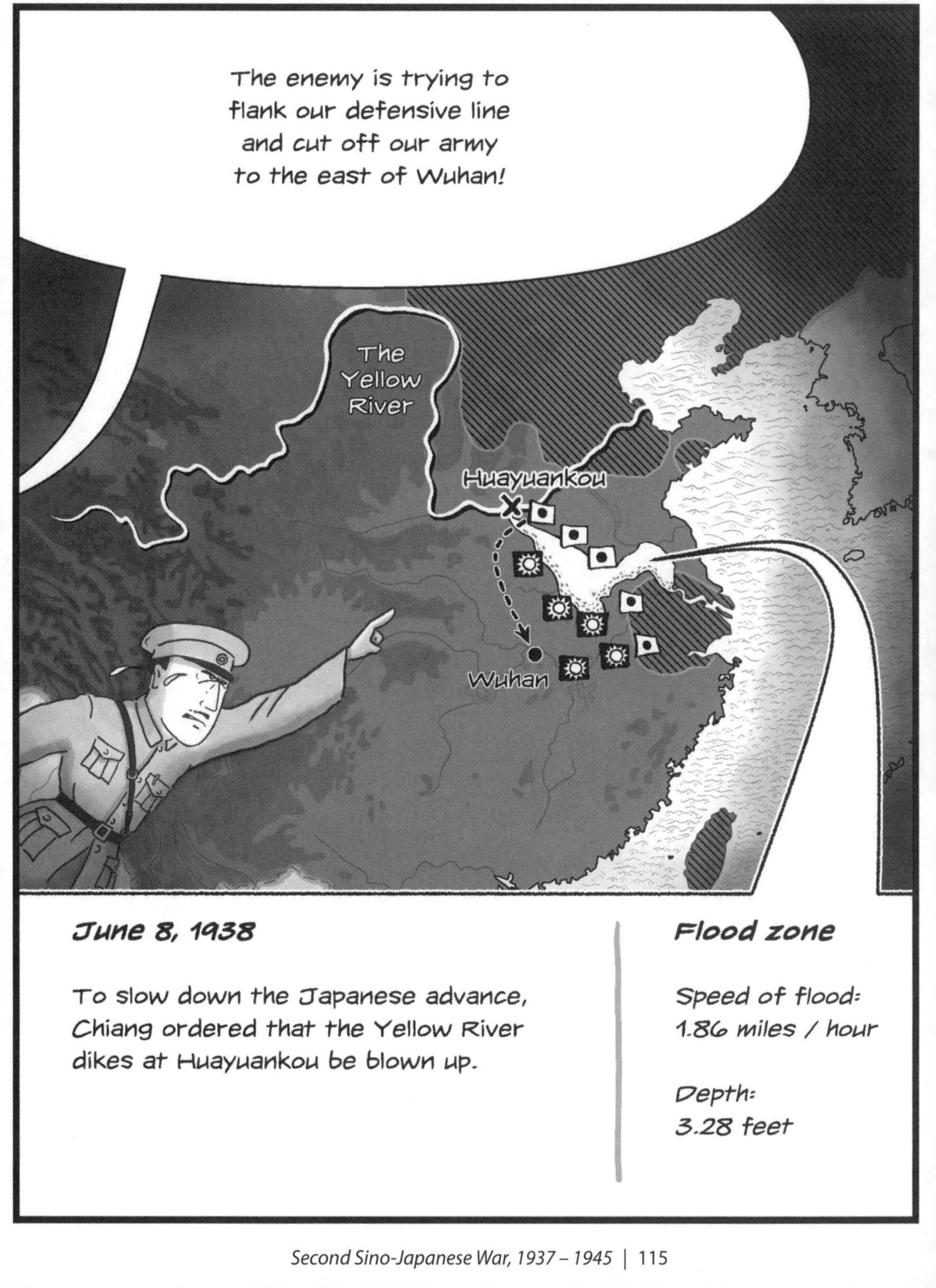
The enemy is trying to flank our defensive line and cut off our army to the east of Wuhan!
The Yellow River
Huayuankou
Wuhan

June 8, 1938

To slow down the Japanese advance, Chiang ordered that the Yellow River dikes at Huayuankou be blown up.

Flood zone

Speed of flood:
1.86 miles / hour

Depth:
3.28 feet

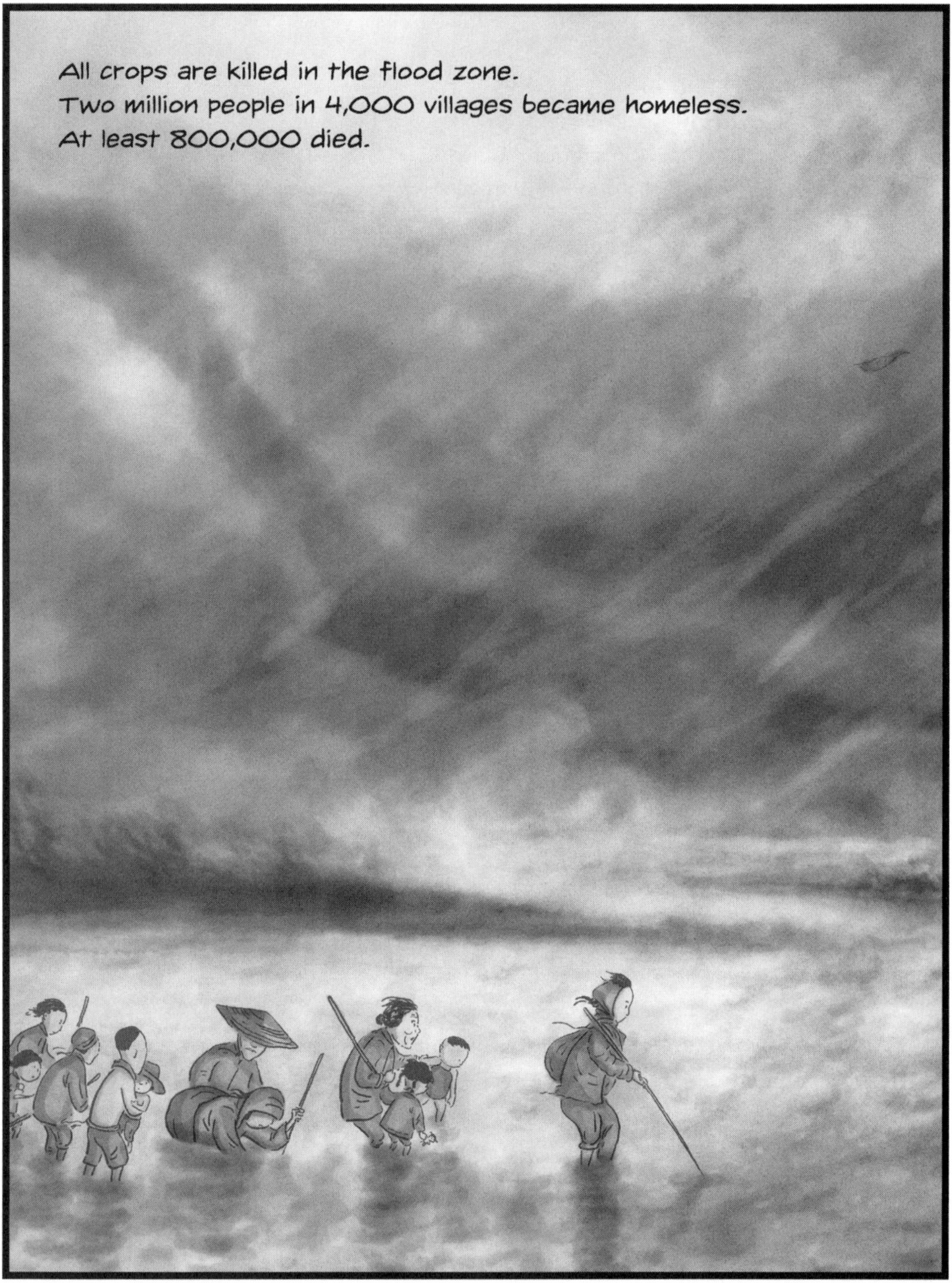
All crops are killed in the flood zone.
Two million people in 4,000 villages became homeless.
At least 800,000 died.

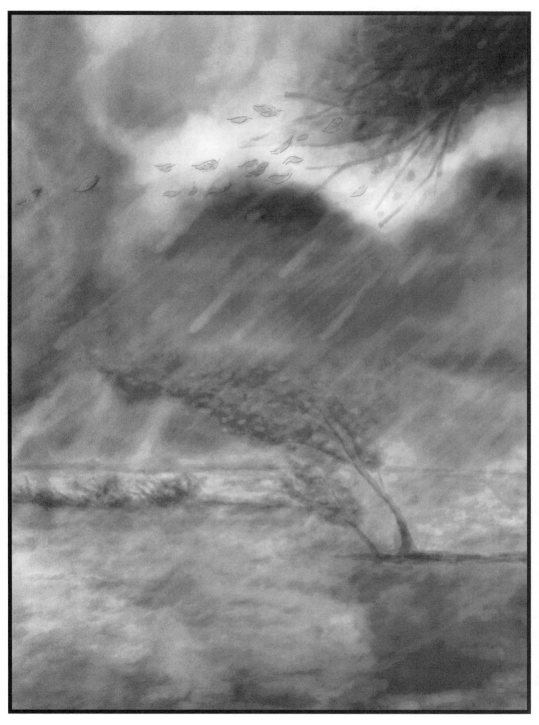

Second Sino-Japanese War, 1937 – 1945 | 117

State of Free China

In October 1938, the war entered a stalemate.

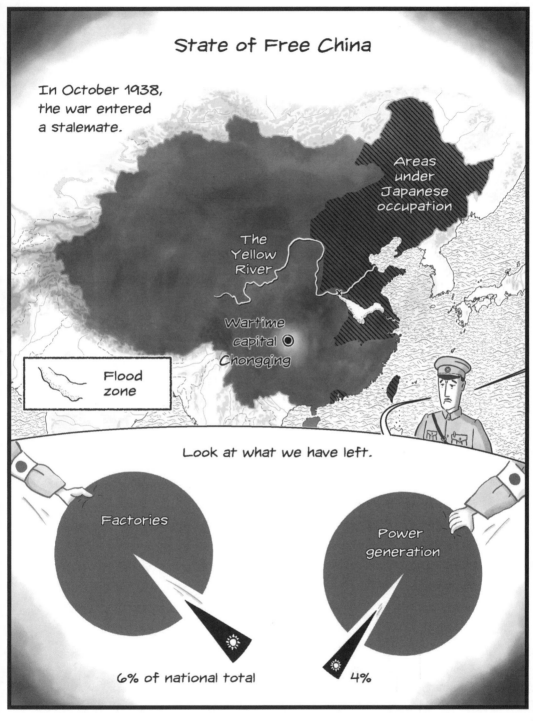

Areas under Japanese occupation

The Yellow River

Wartime capital ◉ Chongqing

Flood zone

Look at what we have left.

Factories

6% of national total

Power generation

4%

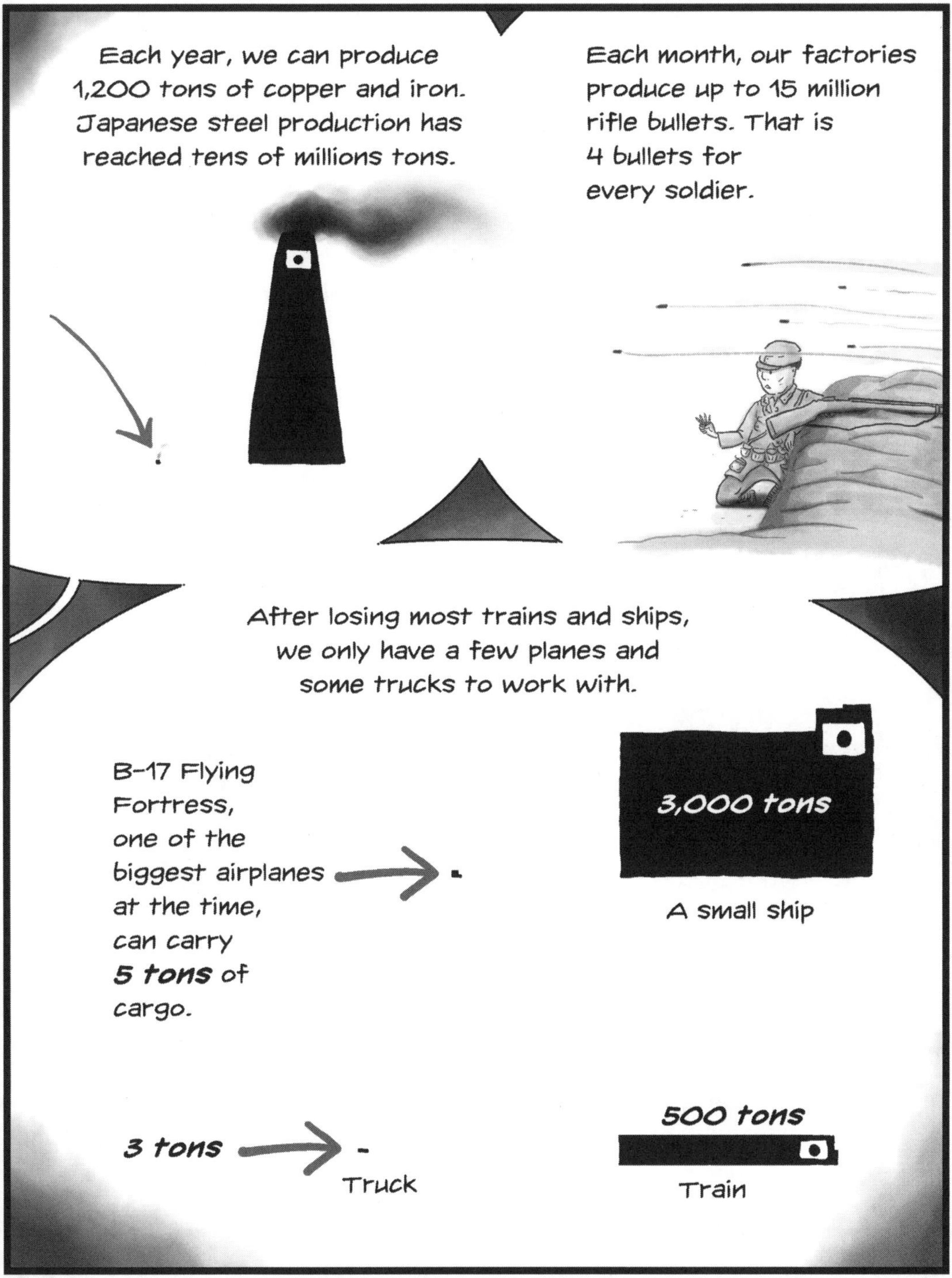

Each year, we can produce 1,200 tons of copper and iron. Japanese steel production has reached tens of millions tons.
Each month, our factories produce up to 15 million rifle bullets. That is 4 bullets for every soldier.
After losing most trains and ships, we only have a few planes and some trucks to work with.
B-17 Flying Fortress, one of the biggest airplanes at the time, can carry 5 tons of cargo.
3,000 tons
A small ship
3 tons
Truck
500 tons
Train

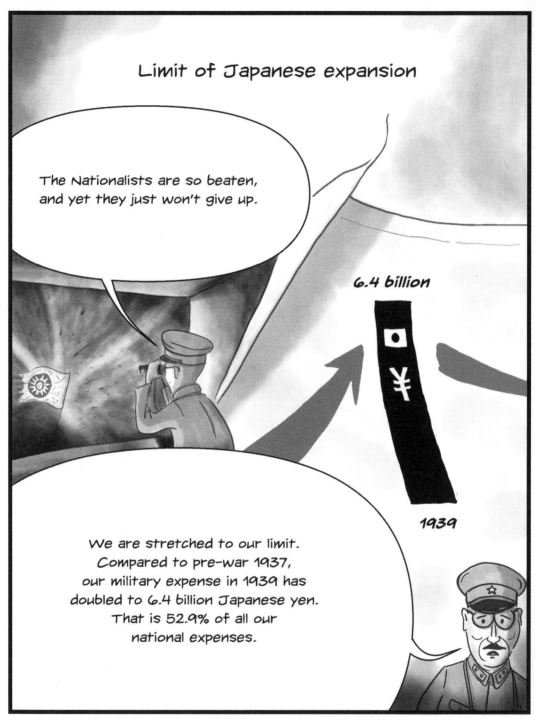

Limit of Japanese expansion

The Nationalists are so beaten, and yet they just won't give up.

6.4 billion

1939

We are stretched to our limit. Compared to pre-war 1937, our military expense in 1939 has doubled to 6.4 billion Japanese yen. That is 52.9% of all our national expenses.

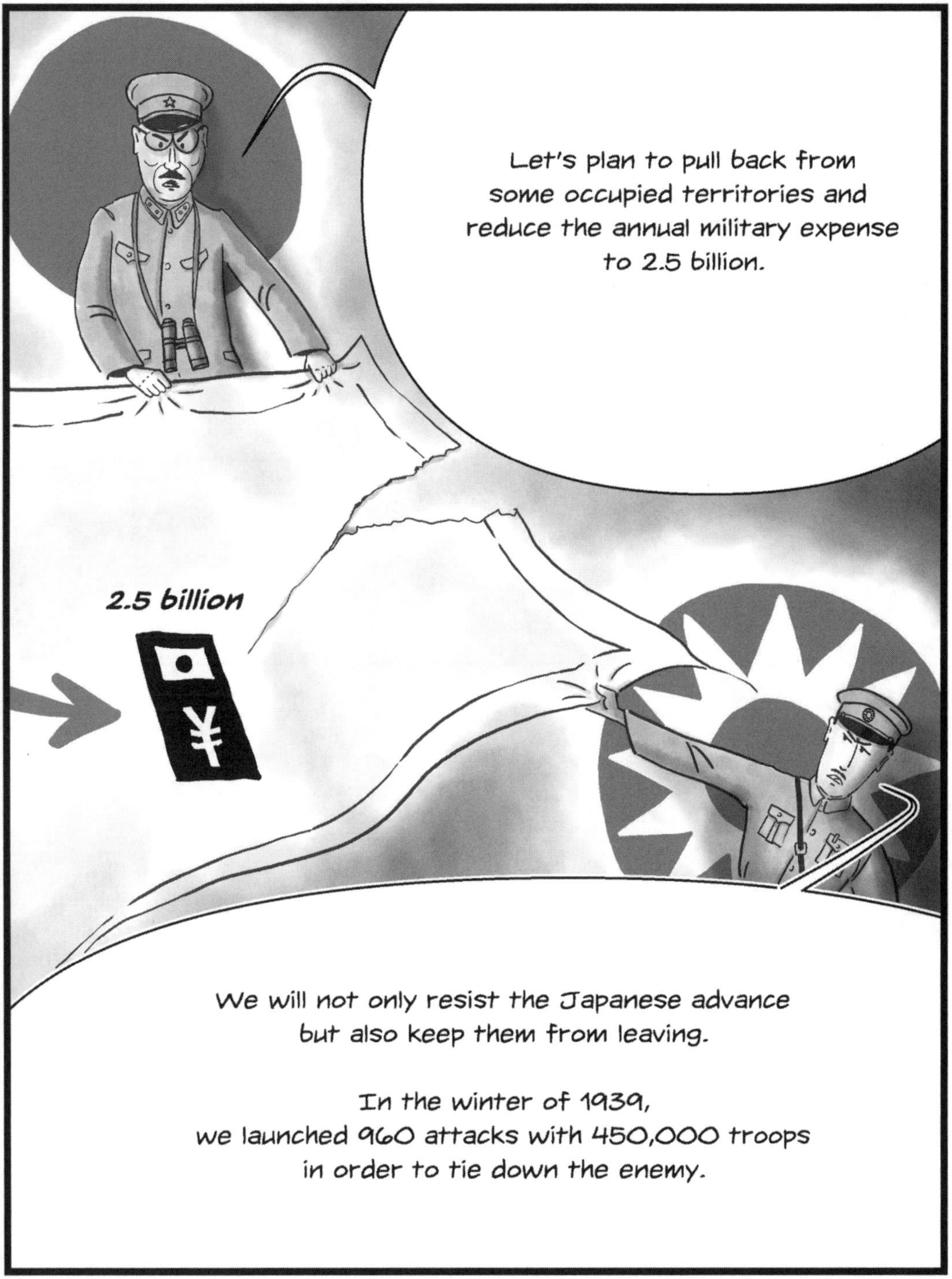
Let's plan to pull back from some occupied territories and reduce the annual military expense to 2.5 billion.
2.5 billion
We will not only resist the Japanese advance but also keep them from leaving.
In the winter of 1939, we launched 960 attacks with 450,000 troops in order to tie down the enemy.

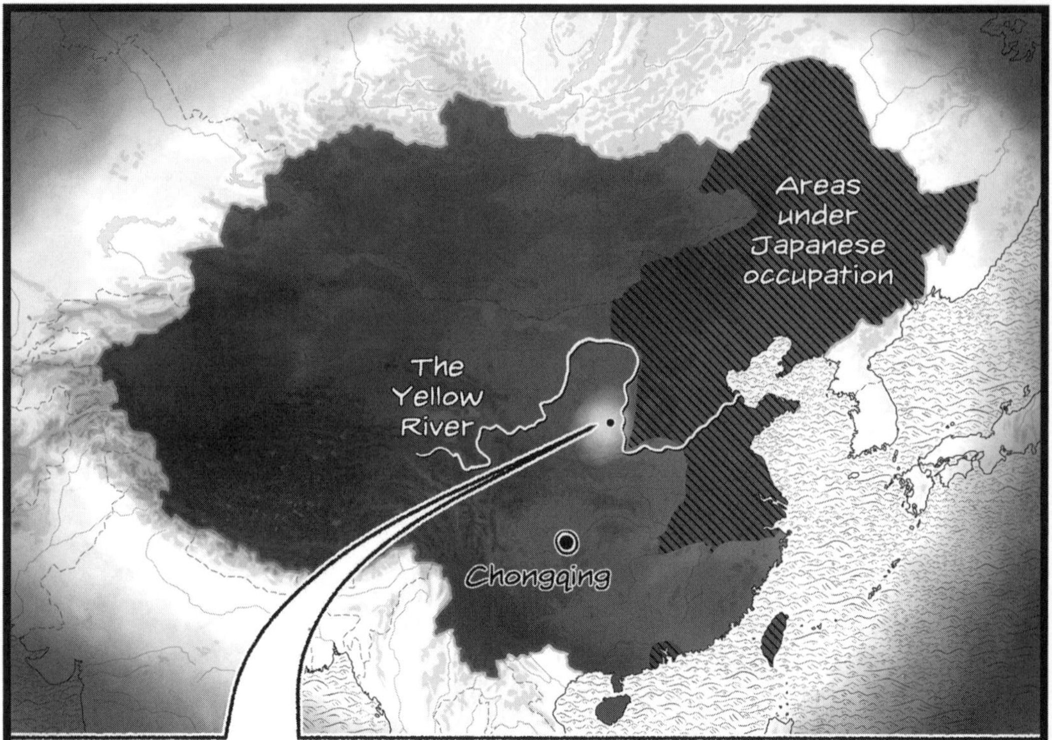
Areas under Japanese occupation
The Yellow River
Chongqing

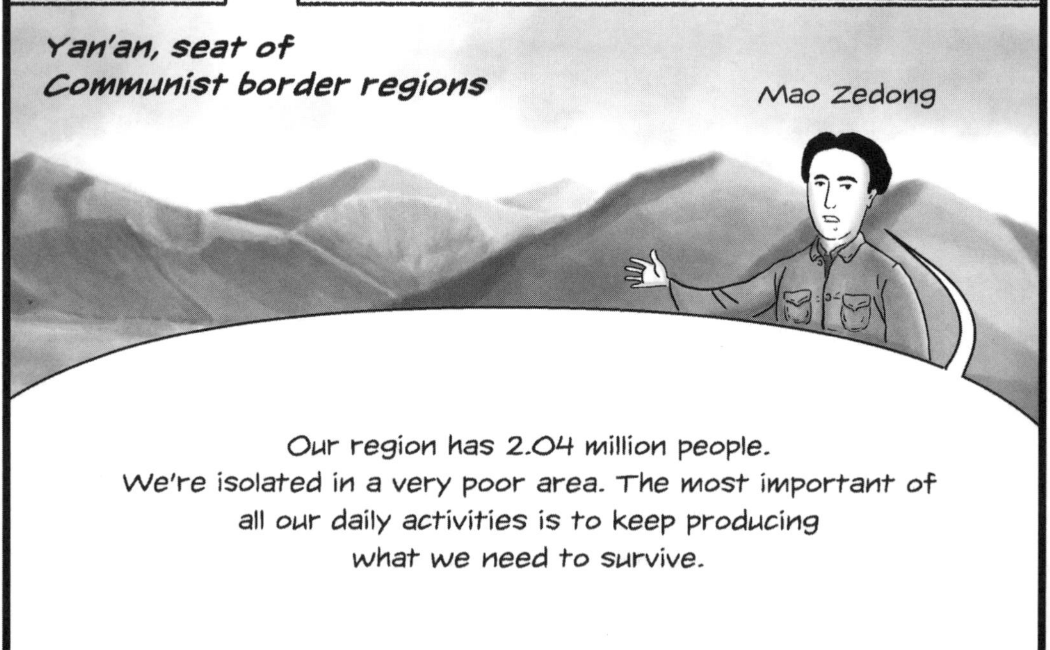
Yan'an, seat of Communist border regions
Mao Zedong
Our region has 2.04 million people.
We're isolated in a very poor area. The most important of all our daily activities is to keep producing what we need to survive.

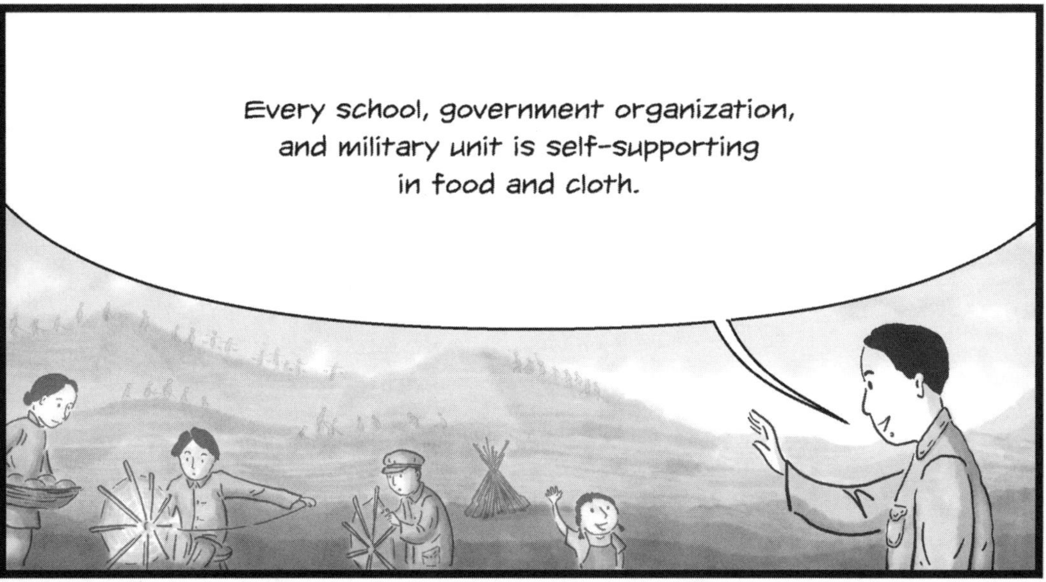
Every school, government organization, and military unit is self-supporting in food and cloth.

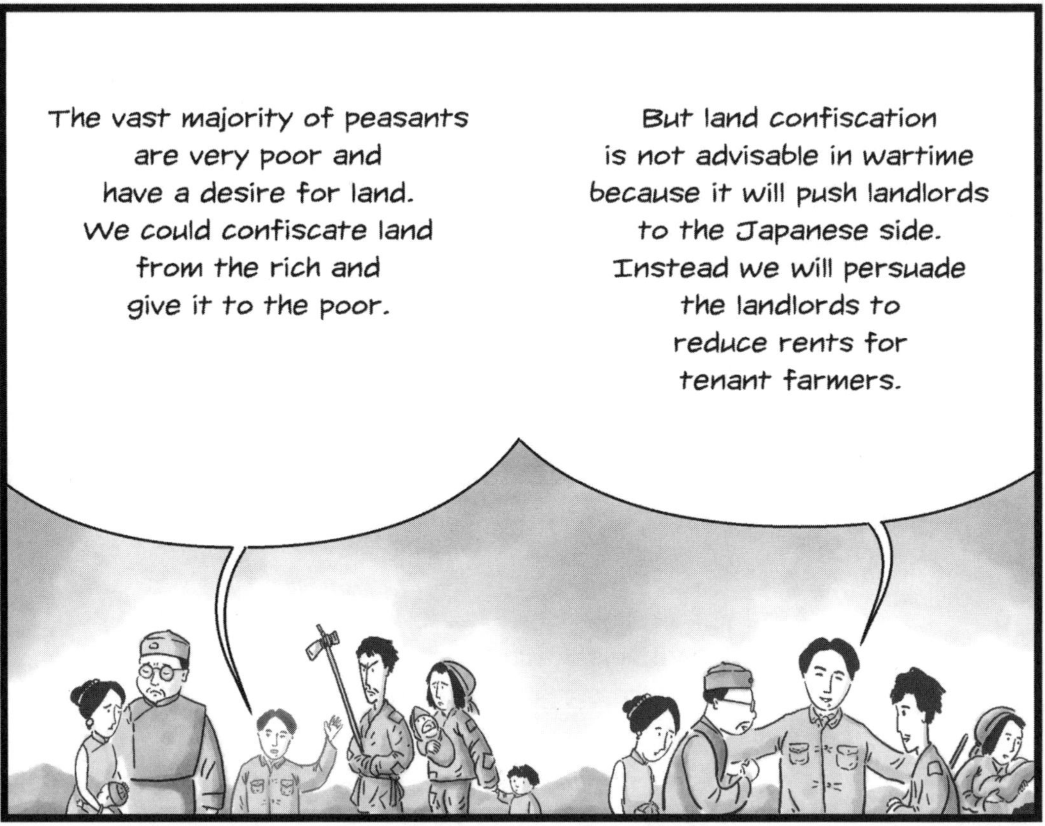
The vast majority of peasants are very poor and have a desire for land. We could confiscate land from the rich and give it to the poor.
But land confiscation is not advisable in wartime because it will push landlords to the Japanese side. Instead we will persuade the landlords to reduce rents for tenant farmers.

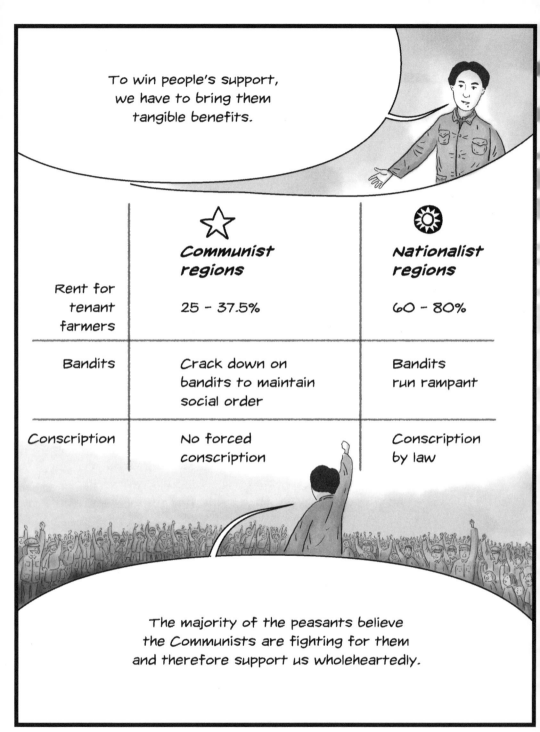

To win people's support, we have to bring them tangible benefits.

	☆ Communist regions	☀ Nationalist regions
Rent for tenant farmers	25 – 37.5%	60 – 80%
Bandits	Crack down on bandits to maintain social order	Bandits run rampant
Conscription	No forced conscription	Conscription by law

The majority of the peasants believe the Communists are fighting for them and therefore support us wholeheartedly.

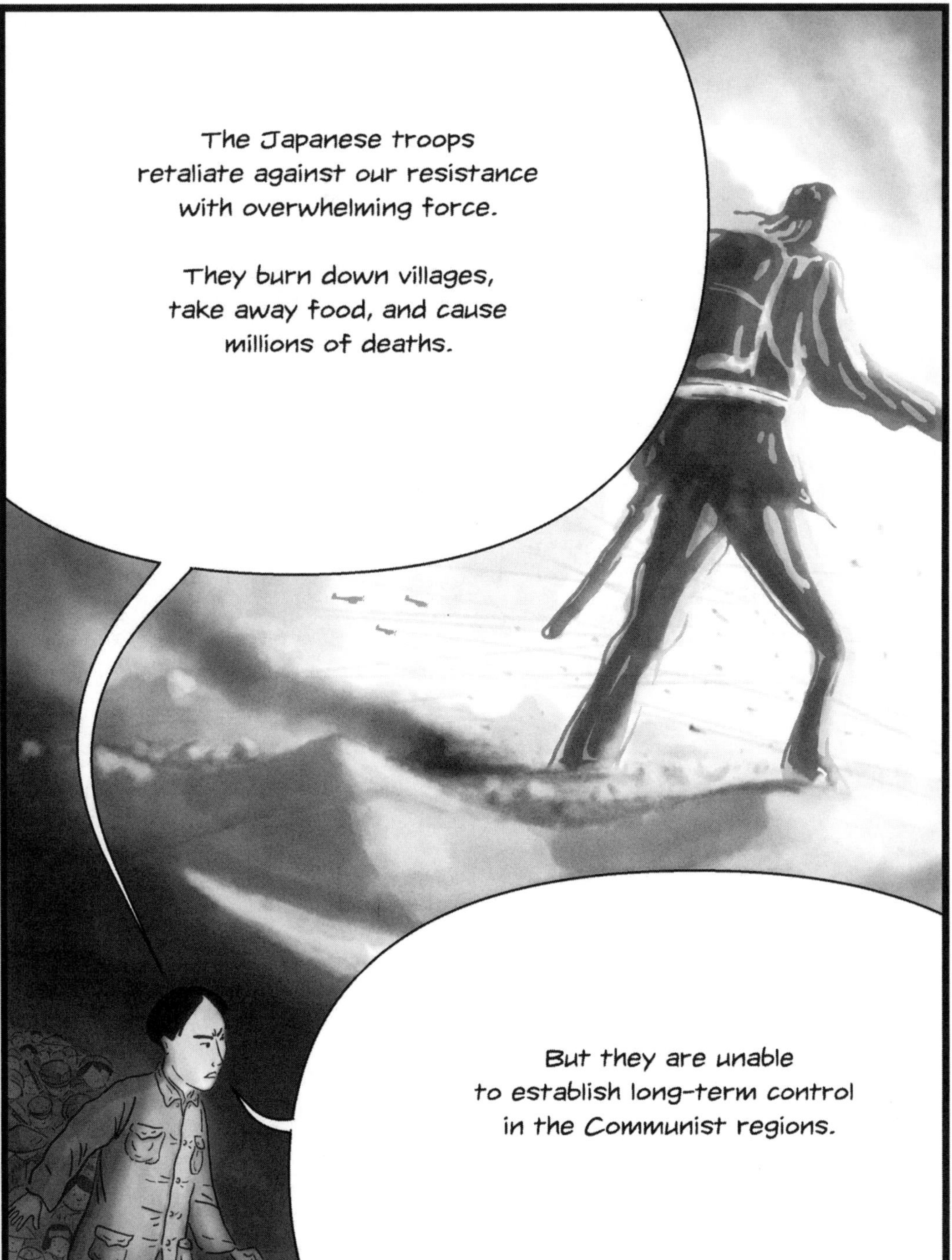
The Japanese troops retaliate against our resistance with overwhelming force.
They burn down villages, take away food, and cause millions of deaths.
But they are unable to establish long-term control in the Communist regions.

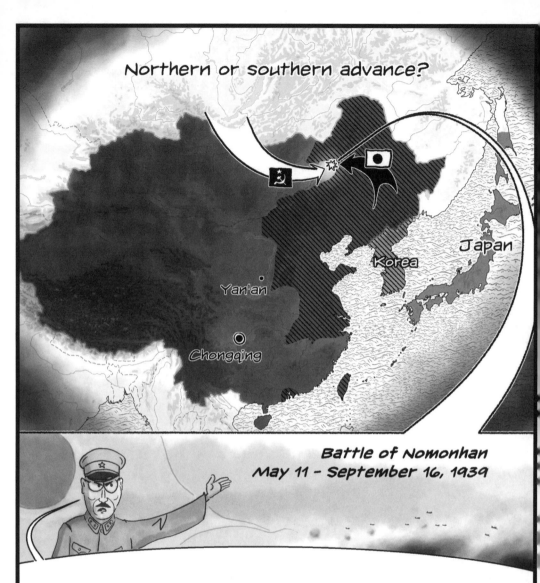

Northern or southern advance?

Yan'an

Chongqing

Korea

Japan

**Battle of Nomonhan
May 11 - September 16, 1939**

The Soviet troops are moving into
Outer Mongolia while we are preoccupied with
the Chinese resistance.

Border clashes with the Soviets escalate into a war
involving more than 100,000 men.

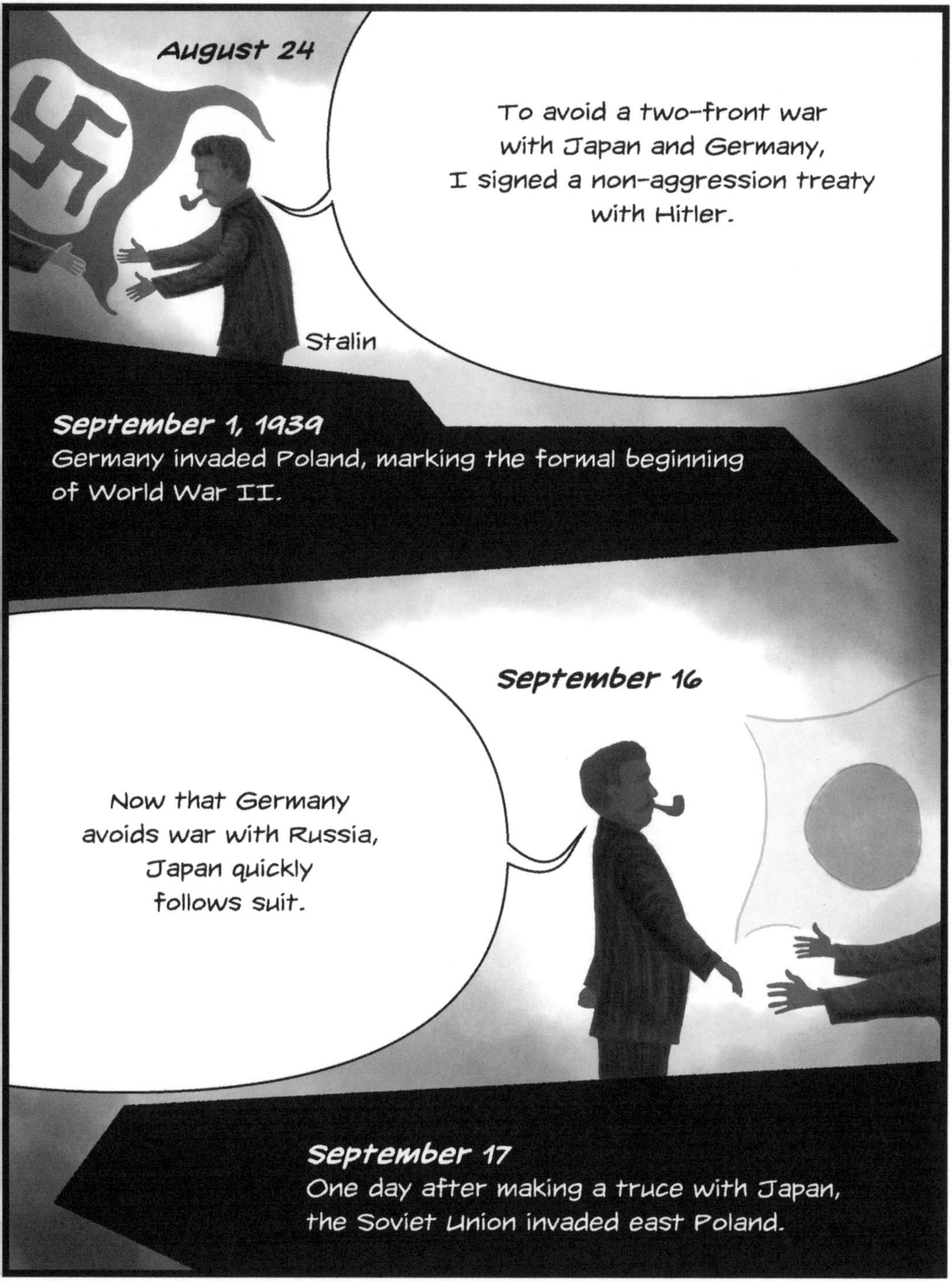
August 24
To avoid a two-front war with Japan and Germany, I signed a non-aggression treaty with Hitler.
Stalin
September 1, 1939
Germany invaded Poland, marking the formal beginning of World War II.
September 16
Now that Germany avoids war with Russia, Japan quickly follows suit.
September 17
One day after making a truce with Japan, the Soviet Union invaded east Poland.

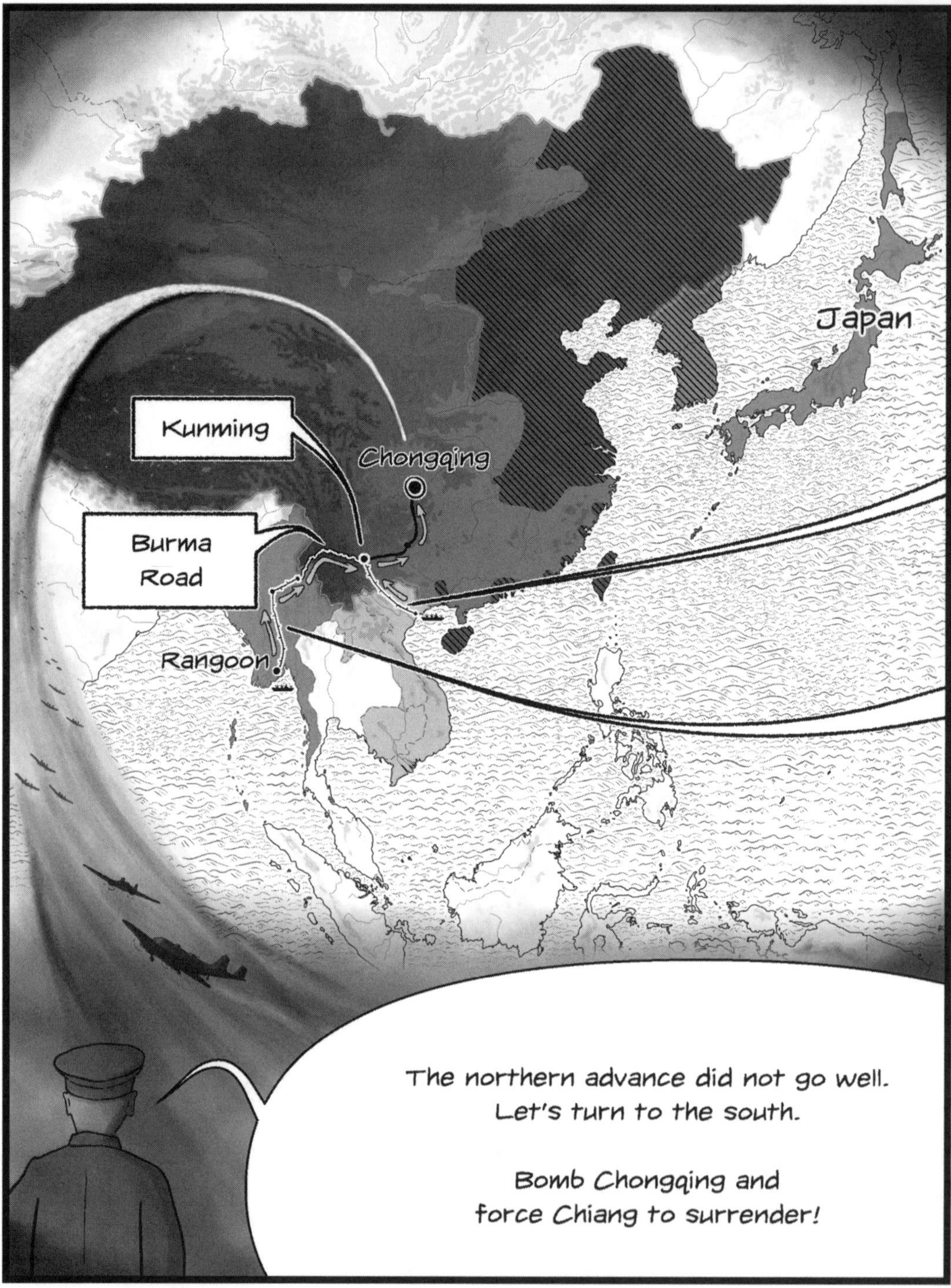
Japan
Kunming
Chongqing
Burma
Road
Rangoon
The northern advance did not go well.
Let's turn to the south.
Bomb Chongqing and
force Chiang to surrender!

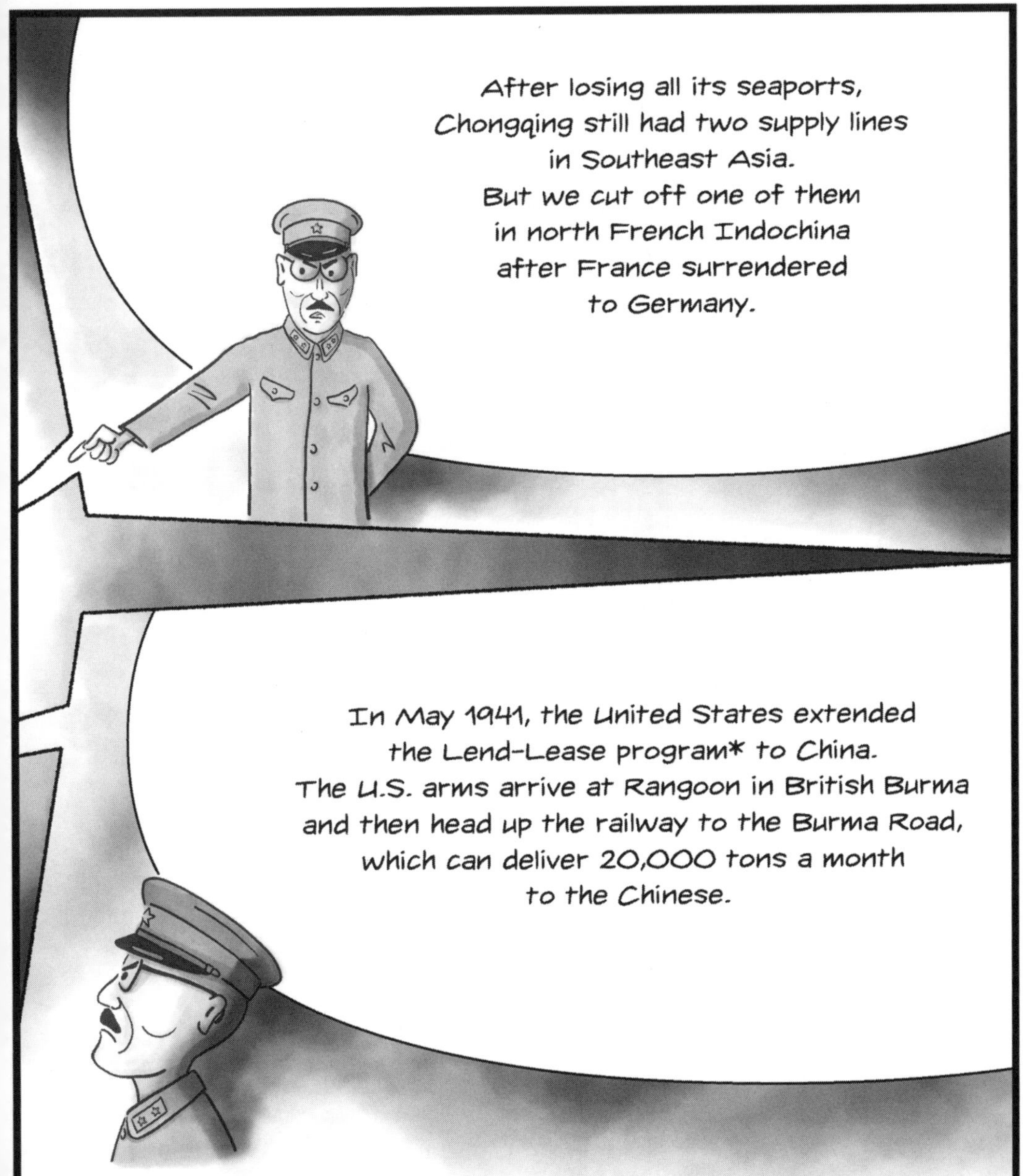
After losing all its seaports, Chongqing still had two supply lines in Southeast Asia. But we cut off one of them in north French Indochina after France surrendered to Germany.
In May 1941, the United States extended the Lend-Lease program* to China. The U.S. arms arrive at Rangoon in British Burma and then head up the railway to the Burma Road, which can deliver 20,000 tons a month to the Chinese.

* With the Lend-Lease program, the United States provided supplies to the United Kingdom, Free France, China, and the Soviet Union, between 1941 and 1945.

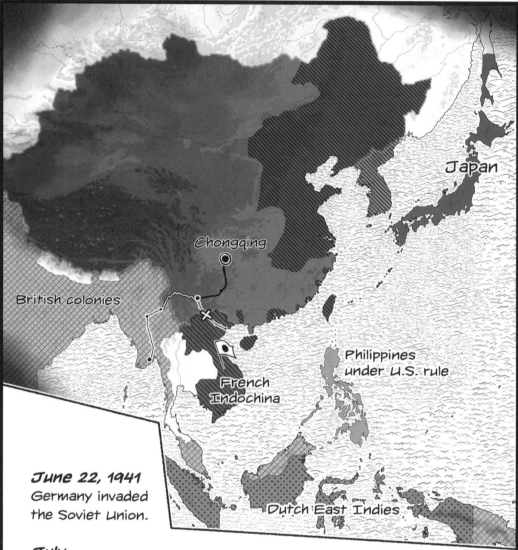

Japan

Chongqing

British colonies

French Indochina

Philippines under U.S. rule

Dutch East Indies

June 22, 1941
Germany invaded the Soviet Union.

July
Encouraged by the German success, Japan took all of French Indochina, threatening other Western colonies in Southeast Asia.

August
The United States stopped oil exports to Japan.
Britain and the Netherlands joined the oil embargo.

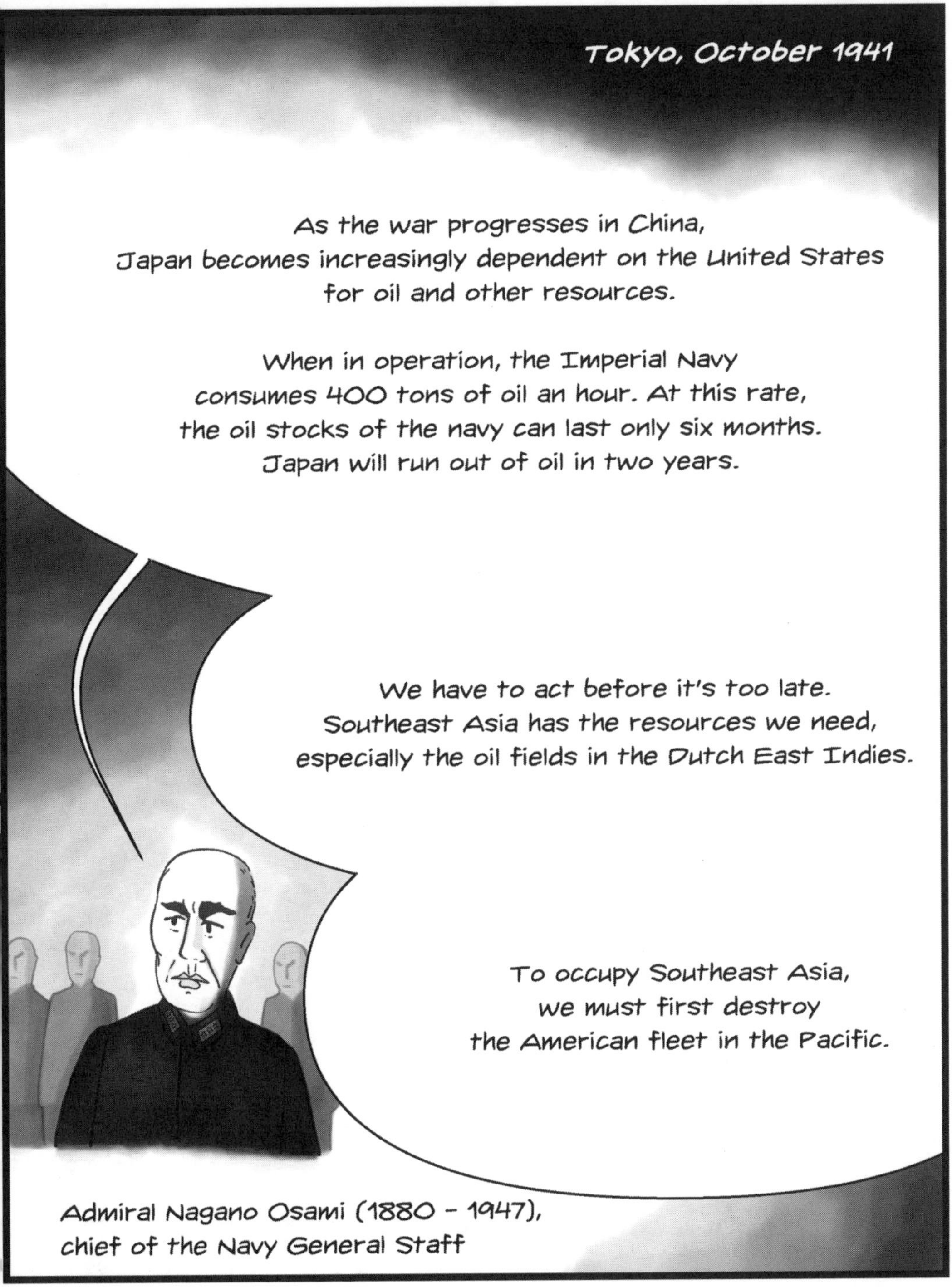
Tokyo, October 1941
As the war progresses in China, Japan becomes increasingly dependent on the United States for oil and other resources.
When in operation, the Imperial Navy consumes 400 tons of oil an hour. At this rate, the oil stocks of the navy can last only six months. Japan will run out of oil in two years.
We have to act before it's too late. Southeast Asia has the resources we need, especially the oil fields in the Dutch East Indies.
To occupy Southeast Asia, we must first destroy the American fleet in the Pacific.
Admiral Nagano Osami (1880 – 1947), chief of the Navy General Staff

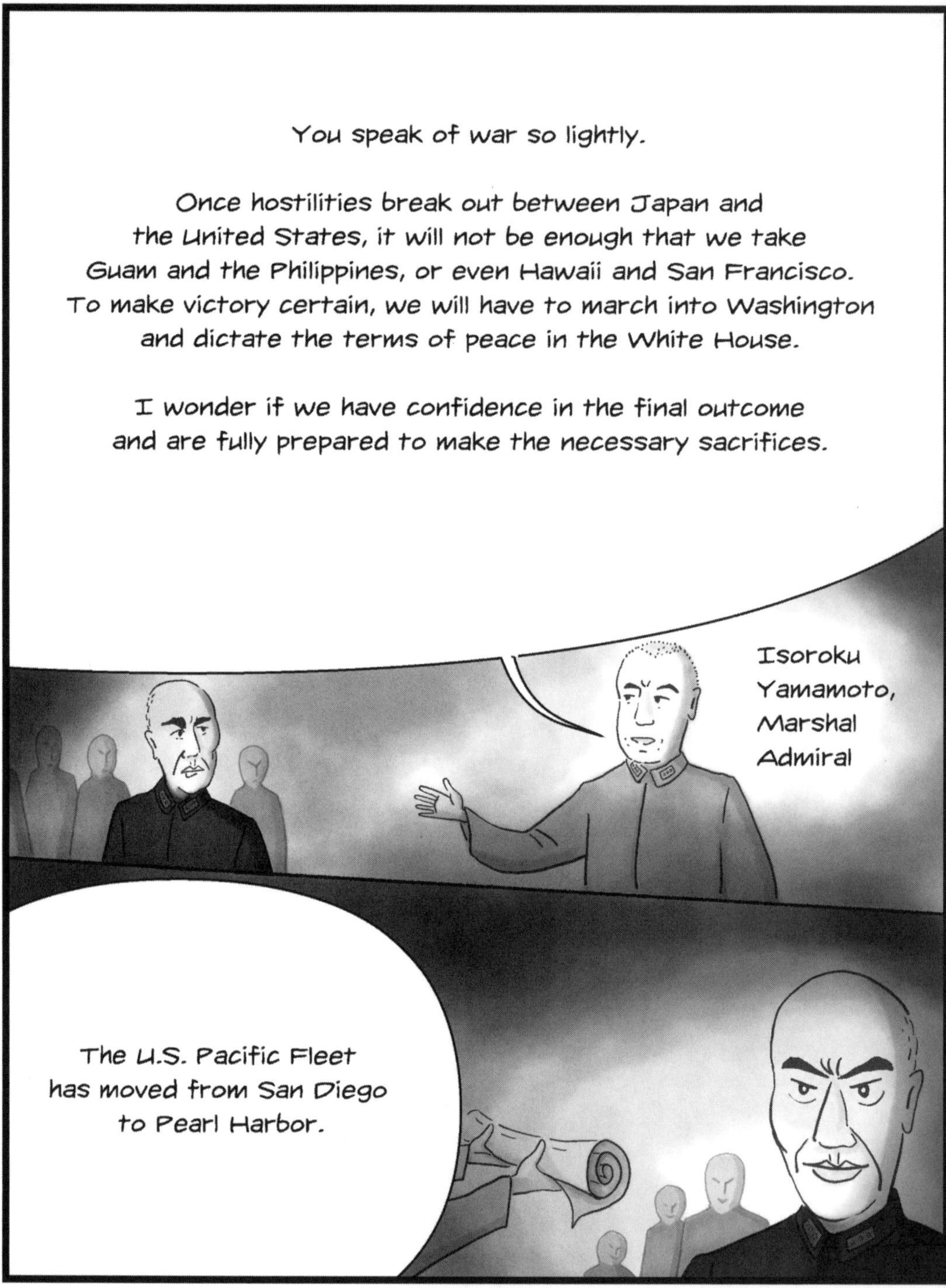

You speak of war so lightly.
Once hostilities break out between Japan and the United States, it will not be enough that we take Guam and the Philippines, or even Hawaii and San Francisco. To make victory certain, we will have to march into Washington and dictate the terms of peace in the White House.
I wonder if we have confidence in the final outcome and are fully prepared to make the necessary sacrifices.
Isoroku Yamamoto, Marshal Admiral
The U.S. Pacific Fleet has moved from San Diego to Pearl Harbor.

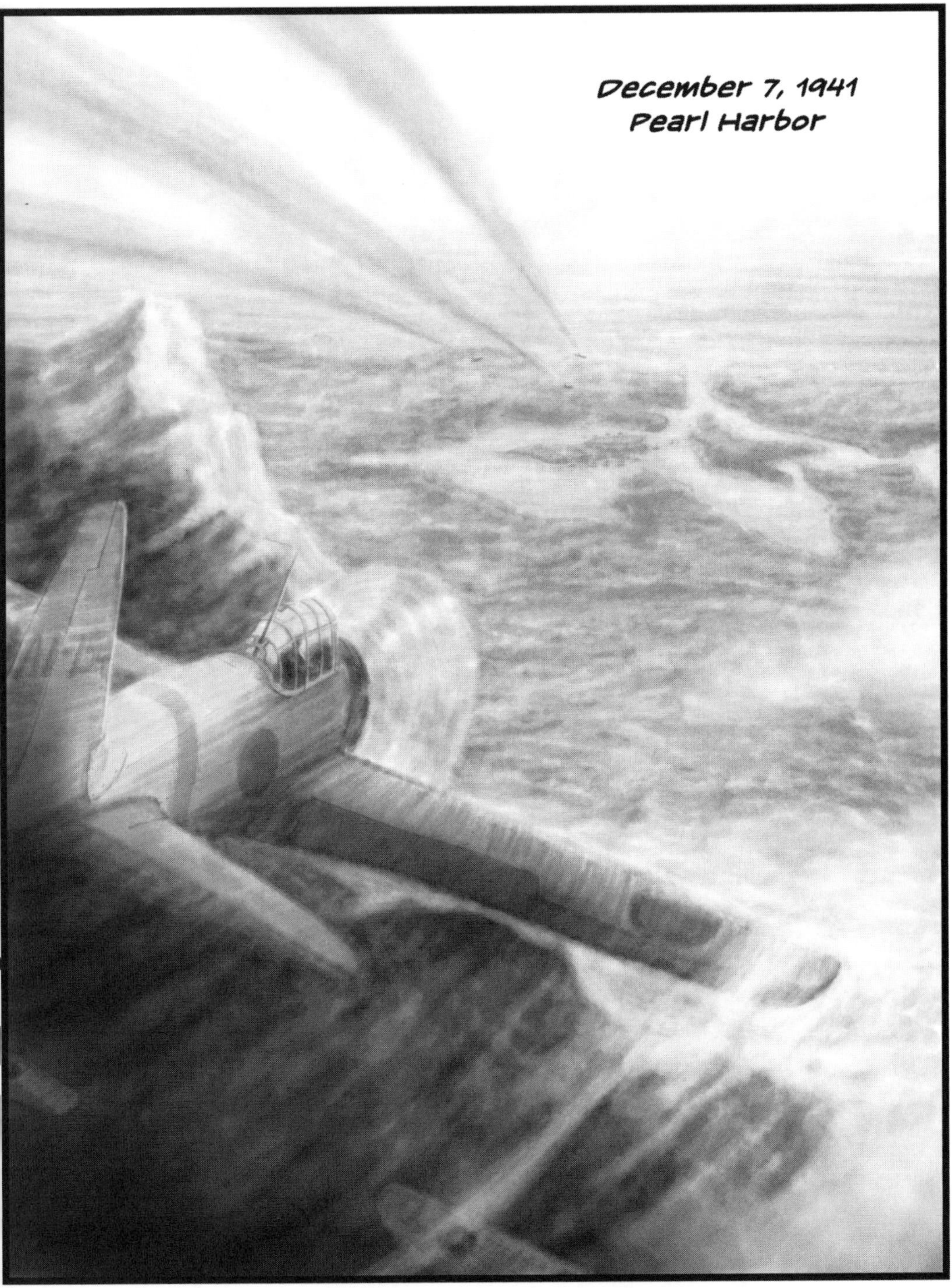
December 7, 1941
Pearl Harbor

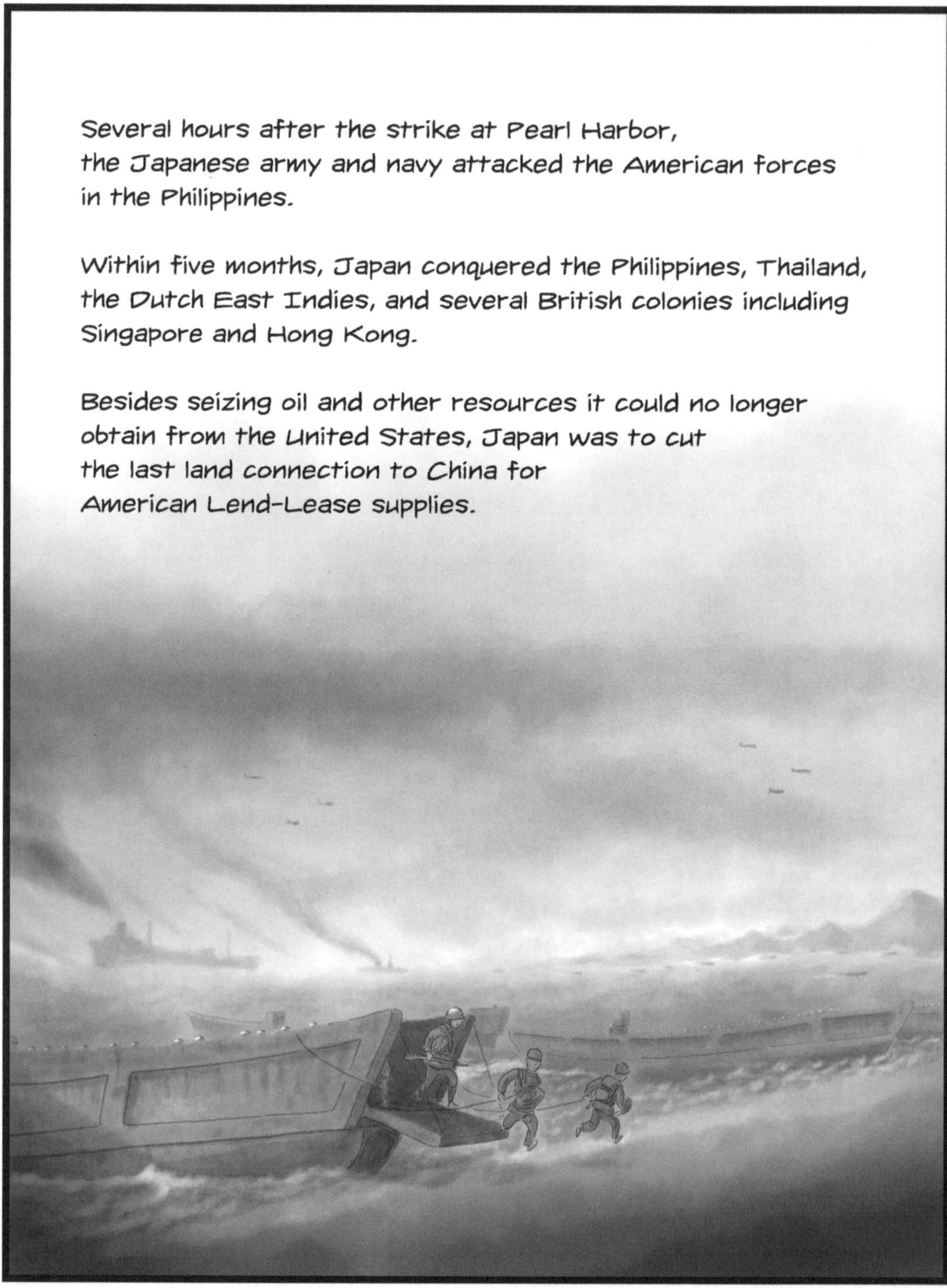
Several hours after the strike at Pearl Harbor, the Japanese army and navy attacked the American forces in the Philippines.
Within five months, Japan conquered the Philippines, Thailand, the Dutch East Indies, and several British colonies including Singapore and Hong Kong.
Besides seizing oil and other resources it could no longer obtain from the United States, Japan was to cut the last land connection to China for American Lend-Lease supplies.

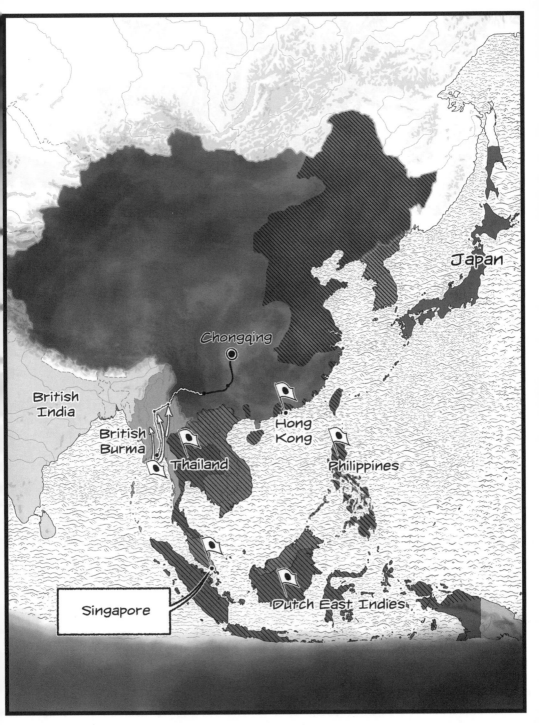

British India

British Burma

Thailand

Chongqing

Hong Kong

Japan

Philippines

Singapore

Dutch East Indies

Second Sino-Japanese War, 1937 – 1945 | 135

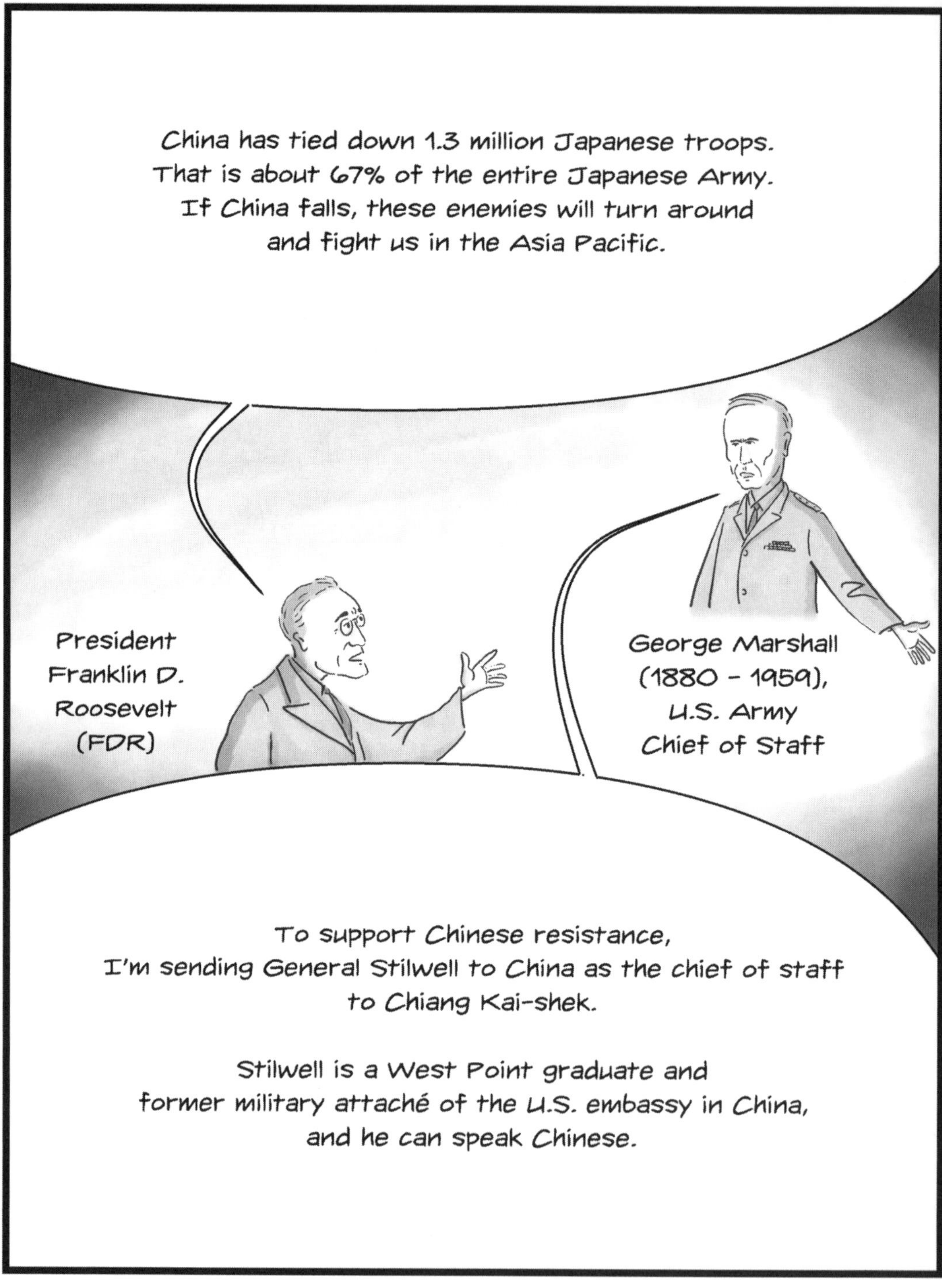
China has tied down 1.3 million Japanese troops. That is about 67% of the entire Japanese Army. If China falls, these enemies will turn around and fight us in the Asia Pacific.
President Franklin D. Roosevelt (FDR)
George Marshall (1880 - 1959), U.S. Army Chief of Staff
To support Chinese resistance, I'm sending General Stilwell to China as the chief of staff to Chiang Kai-shek.
Stilwell is a West Point graduate and former military attaché of the U.S. embassy in China, and he can speak Chinese.

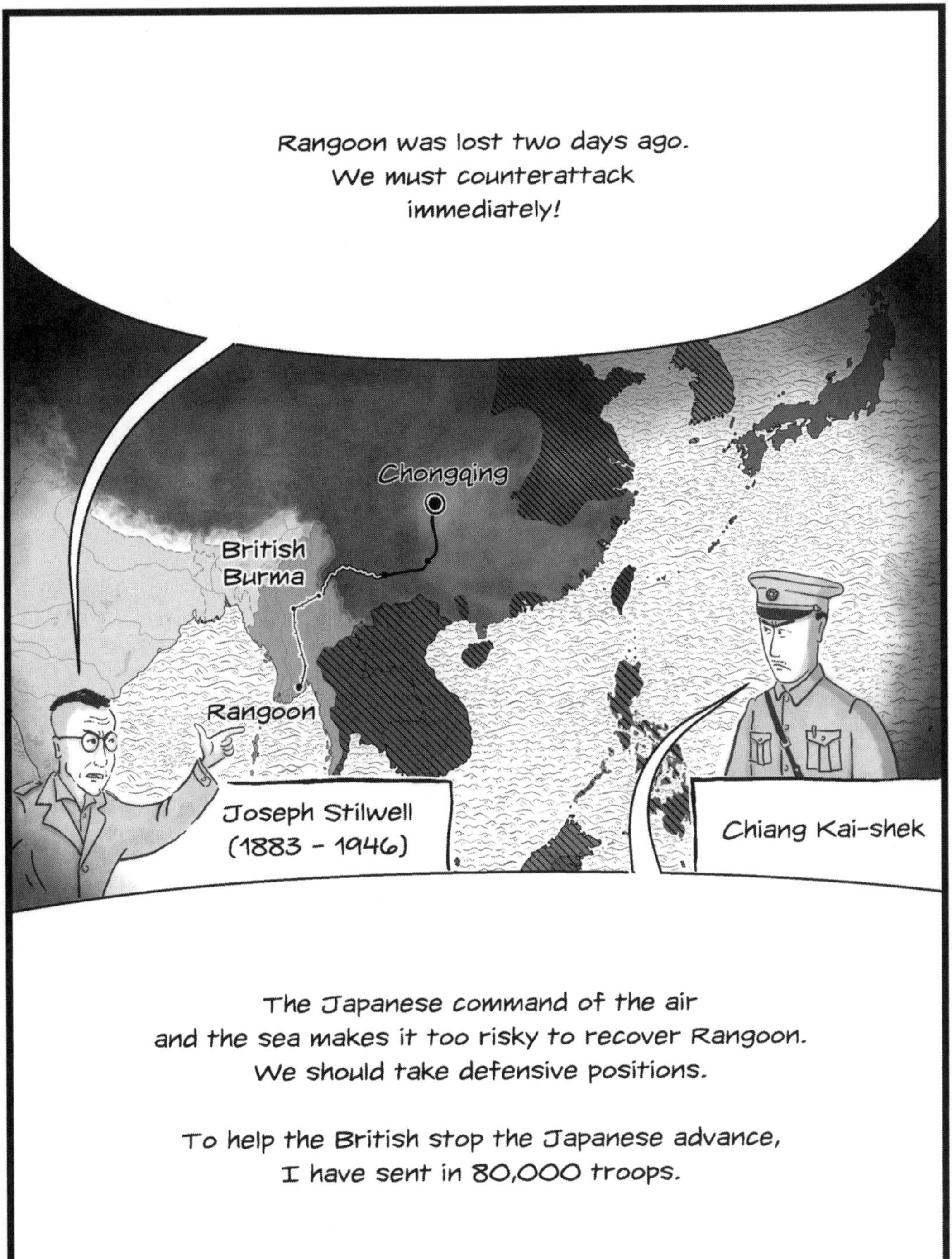

Rangoon was lost two days ago. We must counterattack immediately!
Chongqing
British Burma
Rangoon
Joseph Stilwell (1883 - 1946)
Chiang Kai-shek
The Japanese command of the air and the sea makes it too risky to recover Rangoon. We should take defensive positions.
To help the British stop the Japanese advance, I have sent in 80,000 troops.

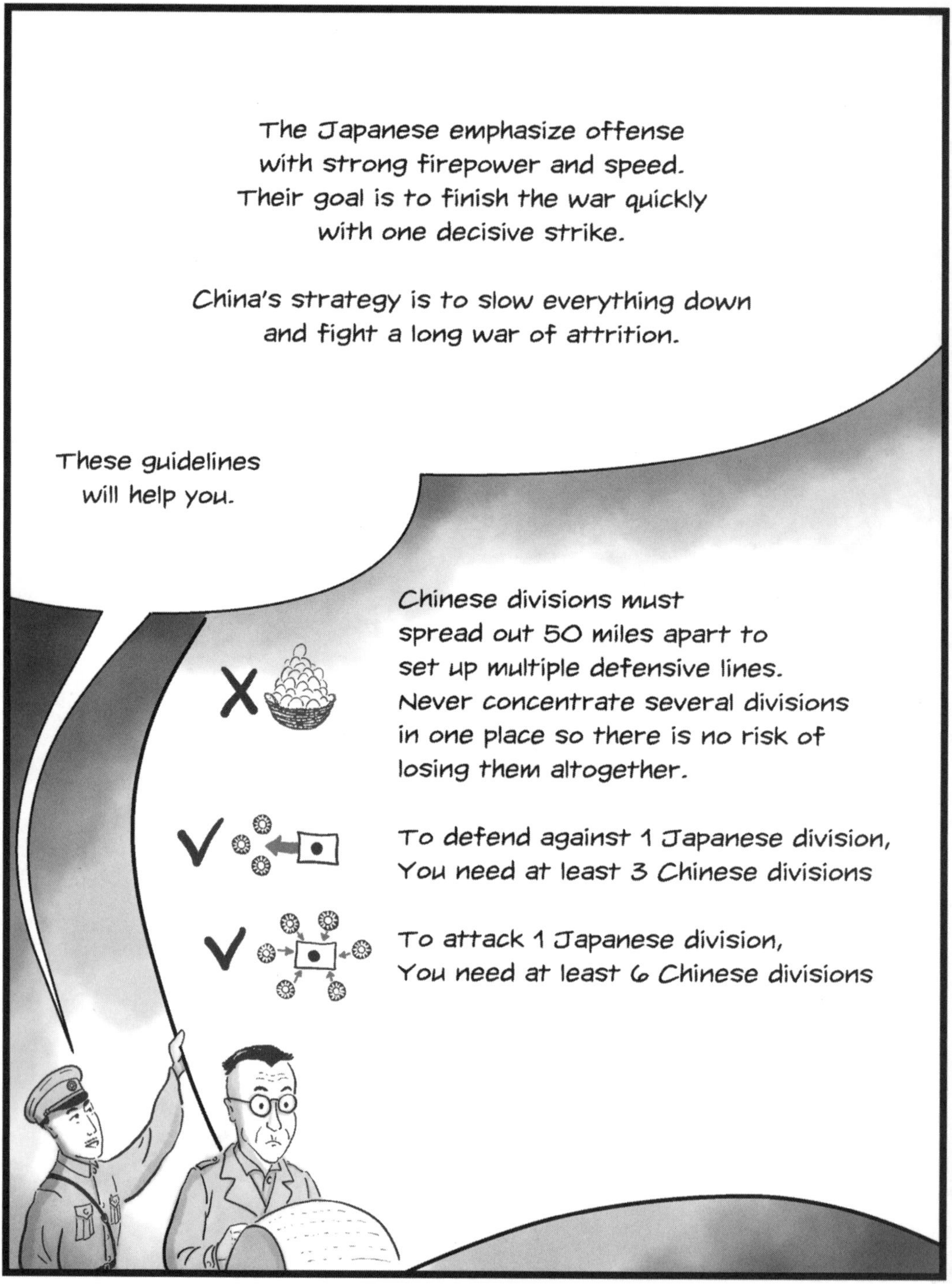

The Japanese emphasize offense
with strong firepower and speed.
Their goal is to finish the war quickly
with one decisive strike.

China's strategy is to slow everything down
and fight a long war of attrition.

These guidelines
will help you.

Chinese divisions must
spread out 50 miles apart to
set up multiple defensive lines.
Never concentrate several divisions
in one place so there is no risk of
losing them altogether.

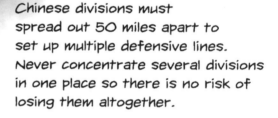

To defend against 1 Japanese division,
You need at least 3 Chinese divisions

To attack 1 Japanese division,
You need at least 6 Chinese divisions

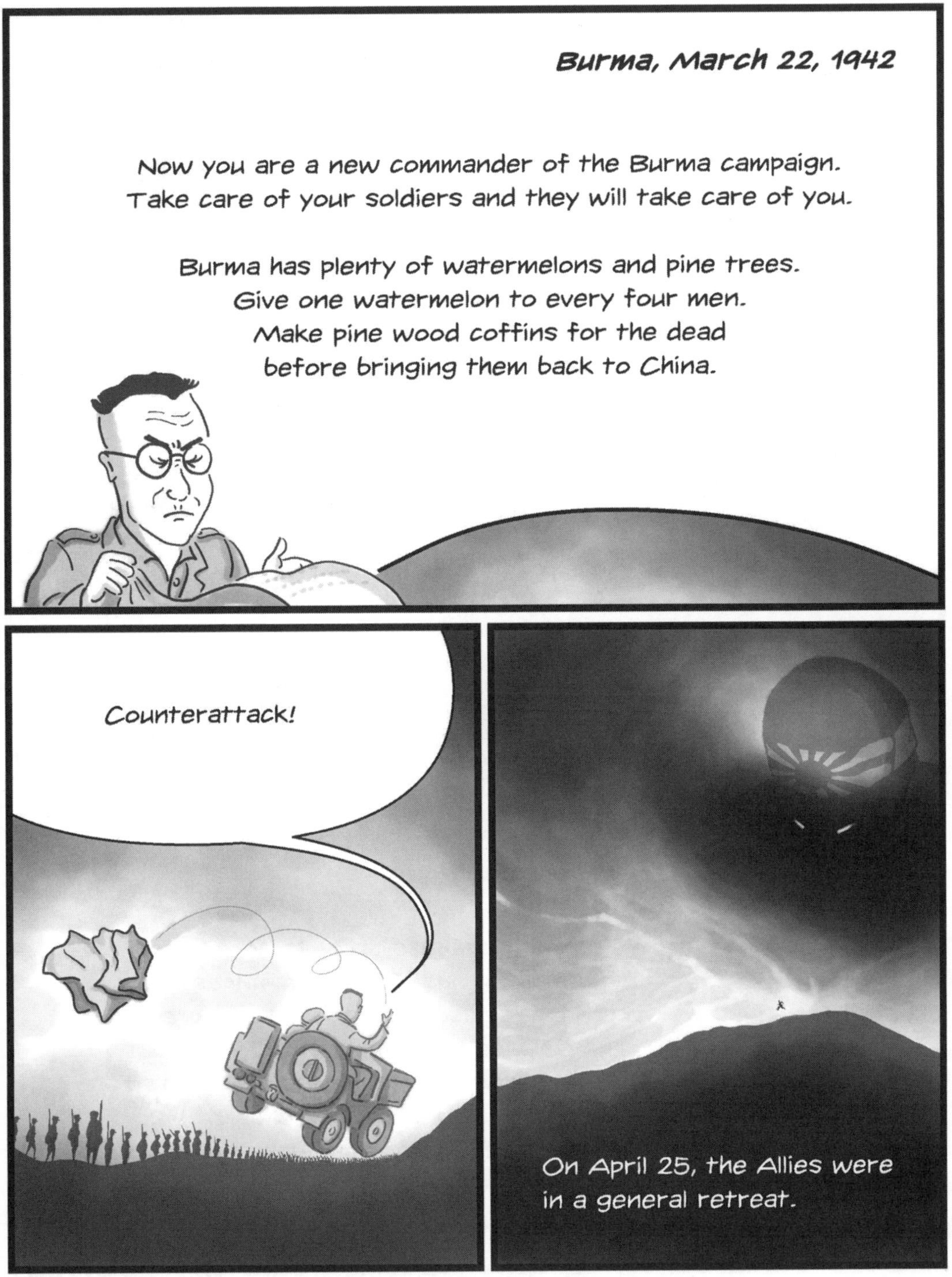
Burma, March 22, 1942
Now you are a new commander of the Burma campaign. Take care of your soldiers and they will take care of you.
Burma has plenty of watermelons and pine trees. Give one watermelon to every four men. Make pine wood coffins for the dead before bringing them back to China.
Counterattack!
On April 25, the Allies were in a general retreat.

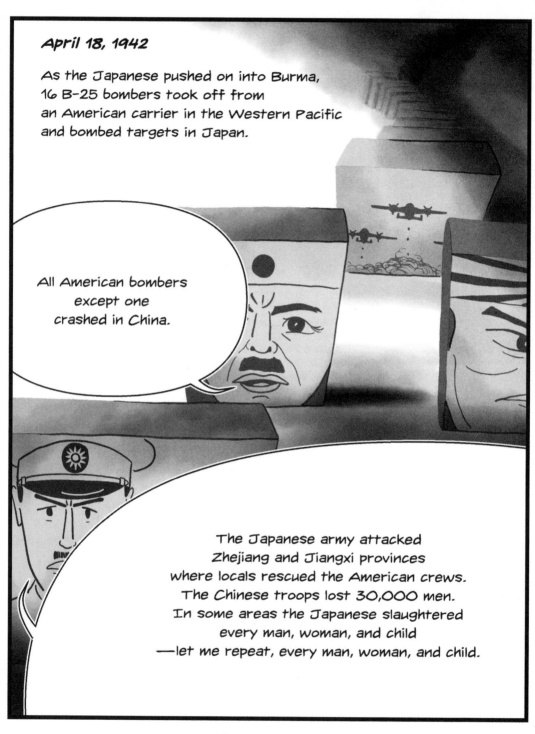

April 18, 1942

As the Japanese pushed on into Burma, 16 B-25 bombers took off from an American carrier in the Western Pacific and bombed targets in Japan.

All American bombers except one crashed in China.

The Japanese army attacked Zhejiang and Jiangxi provinces where locals rescued the American crews. The Chinese troops lost 30,000 men. In some areas the Japanese slaughtered every man, woman, and child —let me repeat, every man, woman, and child.

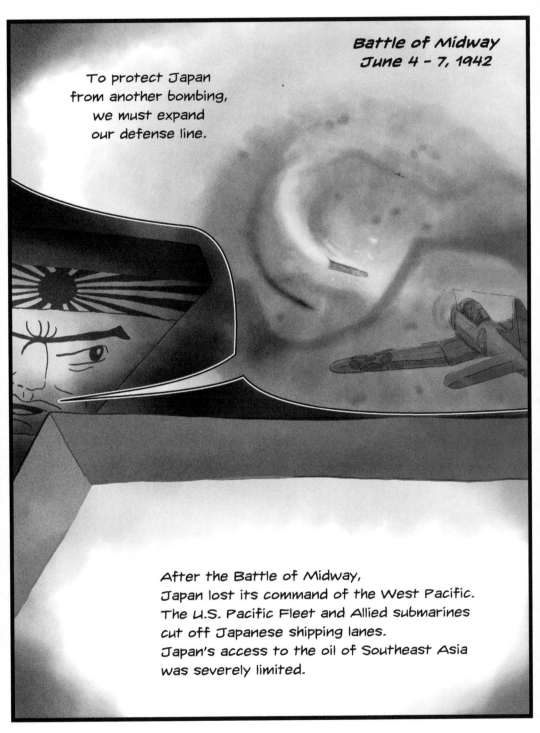

Battle of Midway
June 4 – 7, 1942

To protect Japan from another bombing, we must expand our defense line.

After the Battle of Midway,
Japan lost its command of the West Pacific.
The U.S. Pacific Fleet and Allied submarines
cut off Japanese shipping lanes.
Japan's access to the oil of Southeast Asia
was severely limited.

The Hump

After both land routes were lost, the only option to supply China was through Air Transport Command (ATC) coordinated by Stilwell.

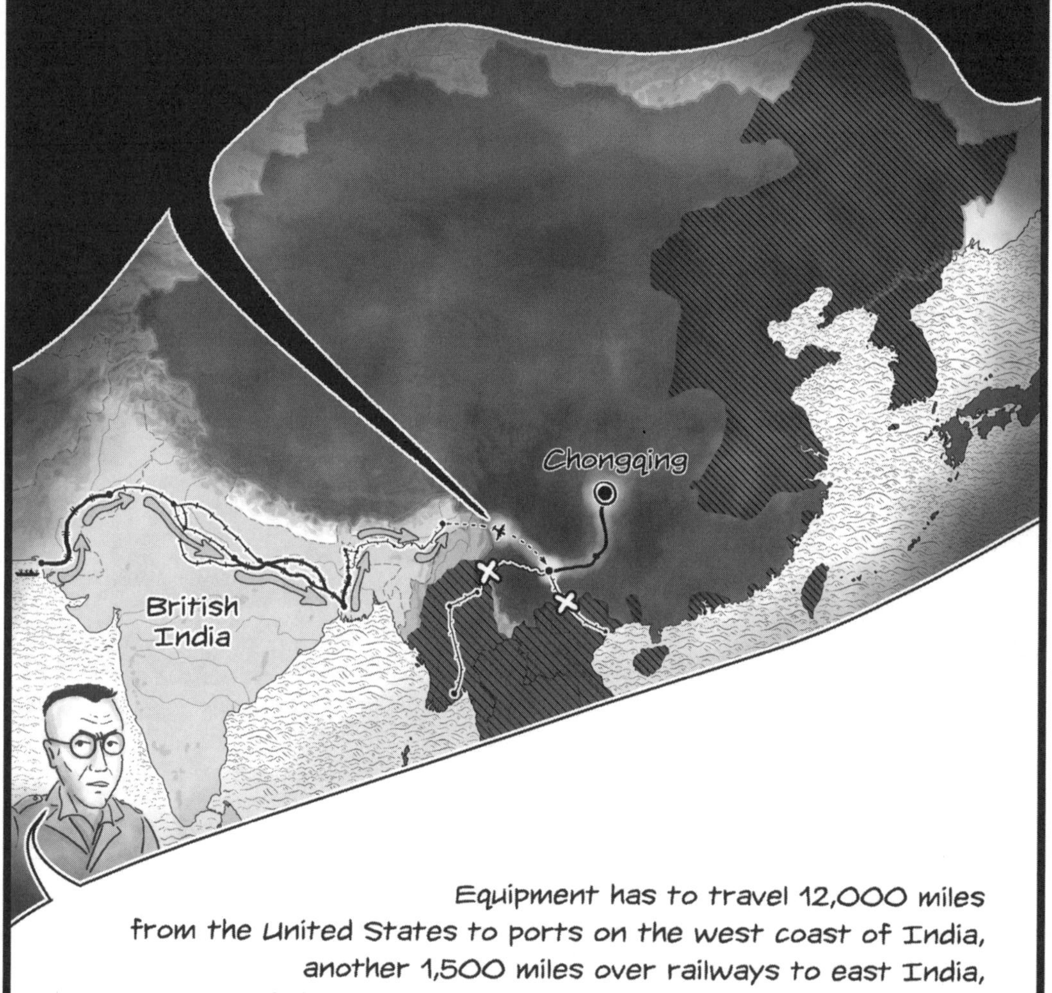
Chongqing
British India

Equipment has to travel 12,000 miles from the United States to ports on the west coast of India, another 1,500 miles over railways to east India, and then over a narrow-gauge railway to the airfields.

The Hump portion of the air route is over
the 15,000-foot Himalayan mountain region.
An airplane has to fly around 20,000 feet,
where sudden turbulence can break up the plane.

We started with 57 cargo planes.
Each plane can carry approximately 4 to 5 tons.
Because air crews and equipment are short,
maintenance poor, airfields inadequate,
and the weather treacherous, each plane can only
manage two round trips every month.

Under these conditions, the initial air cargo capacity
is no more than 500 tons a month. By comparison,
the Burma Road used to transport 20,000 tons a month.

Around 90% of the Hump tonnage is distributed to
the air force commanded by General Chennault.*
The rest goes to the Chinese Expeditionary Force.**
Lend-Lease arms to the regular Chinese troops
are practically zero.

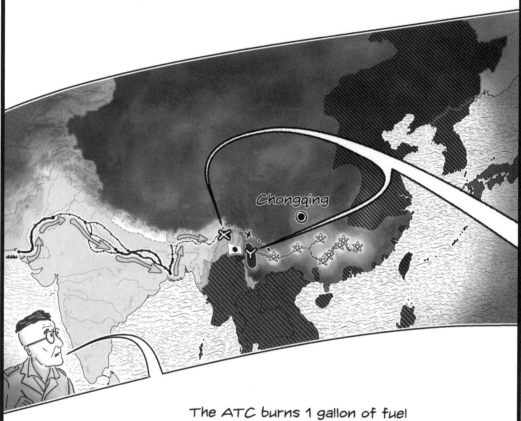

The ATC burns 1 gallon of fuel
for every gallon it delivers in China
and has to deliver 18 tons of supplies
to enable the air force to
drop 1 ton of bombs
on the Japanese.

✳ Chiang Kai-shek appointed
Claire Lee Chennault (1893 – 1958)
as his Chief Air Adviser to set up
the American Volunteer Group (AVG)
of the Chinese Air Force, known as the Flying Tigers.
In July 1942, the AVG became part of
the U.S. Army Air Force (USAAF).

 USAAF major airfields in China

✳✳ The Chinese Expeditionary Force,
or the Y force, had 20 divisions in Yunnan.

The Chinese Army in India (CAI),
or the X force, had 5 divisions
that retreated to India from Burma.
The X force could access the Lend-Lease
supplies stockpiled in India.

Both the X and Y forces were
trained and armed with the intent
of retaking Burma.

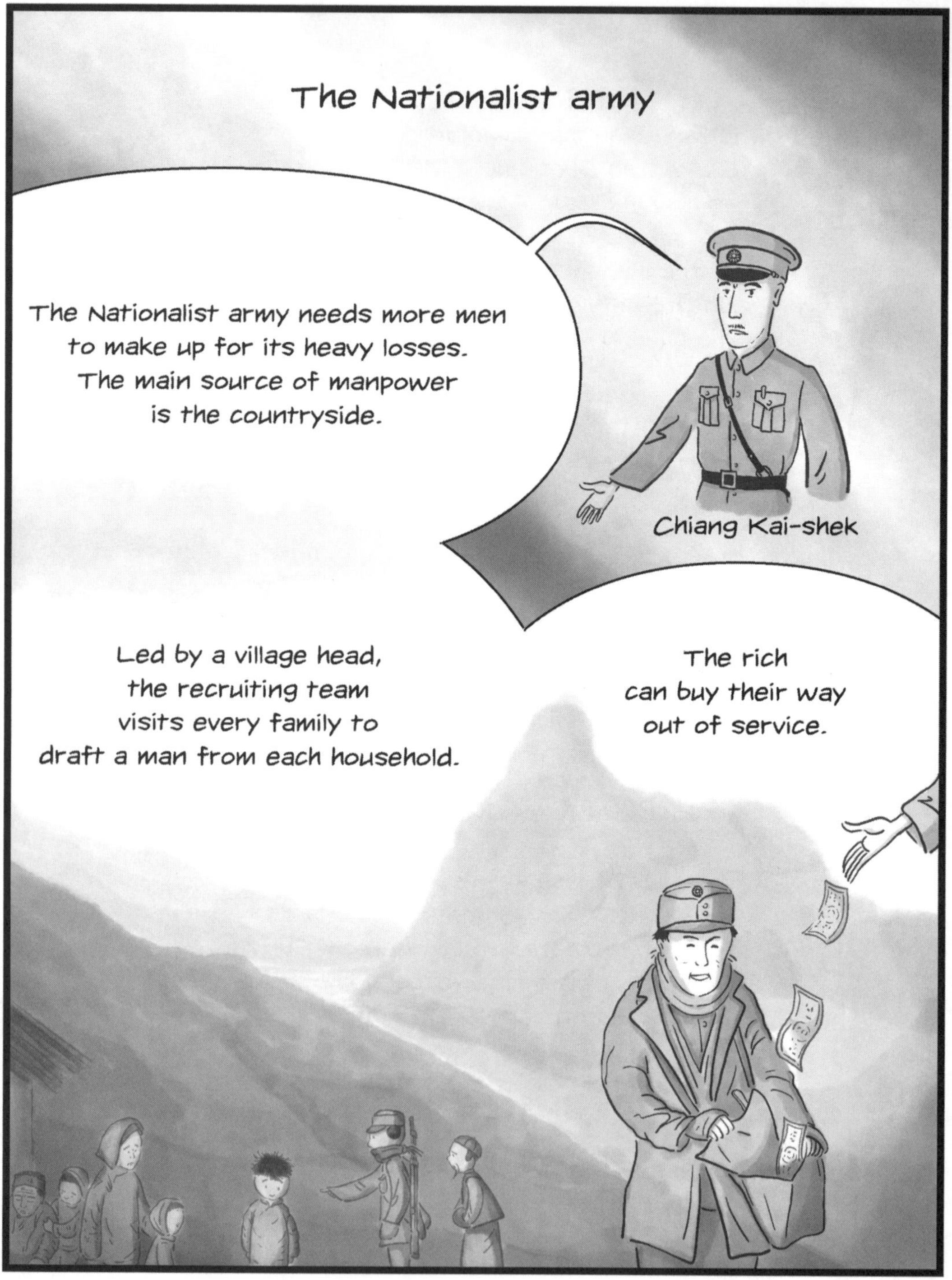
The Nationalist army
The Nationalist army needs more men to make up for its heavy losses. The main source of manpower is the countryside.
Chiang Kai-shek
Led by a village head, the recruiting team visits every family to draft a man from each household.
The rich can buy their way out of service.

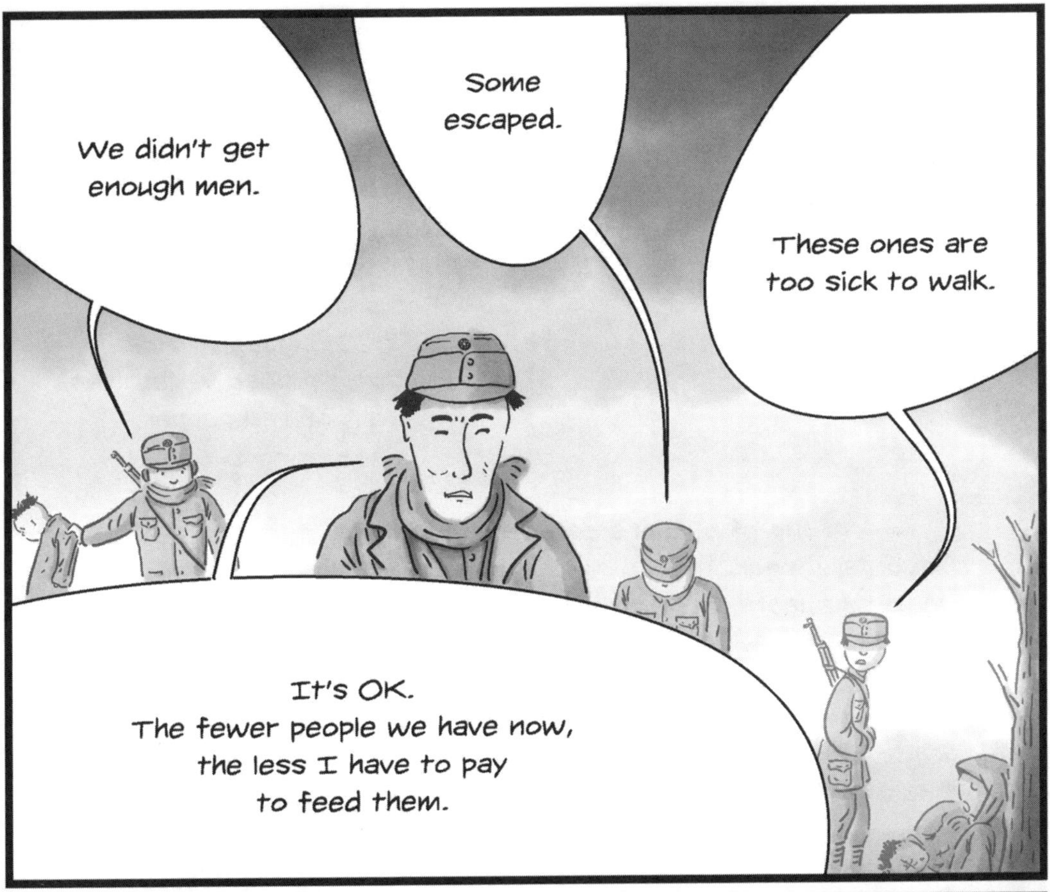
We didn't get enough men.
Some escaped.
These ones are too sick to walk.
It's OK. The fewer people we have now, the less I have to pay to feed them.

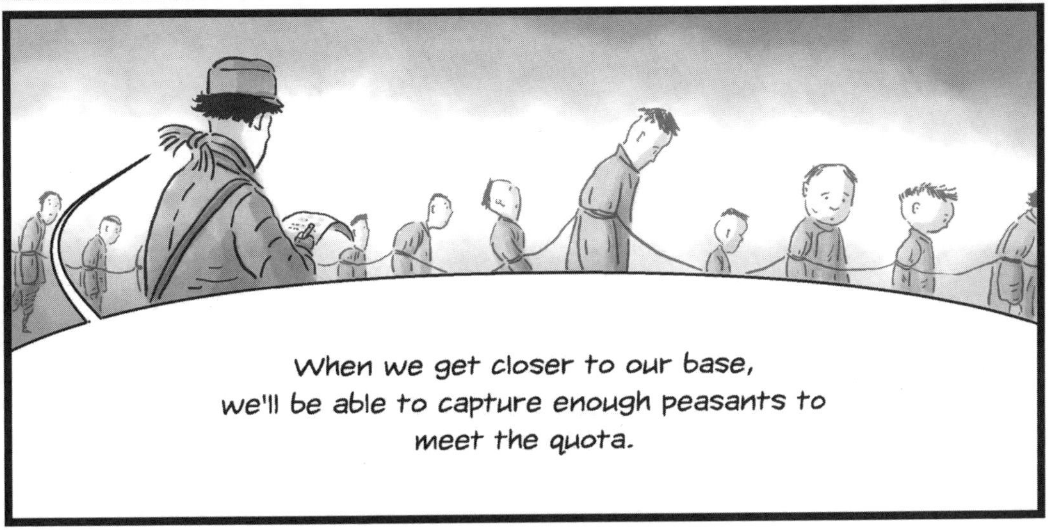
When we get closer to our base, we'll be able to capture enough peasants to meet the quota.

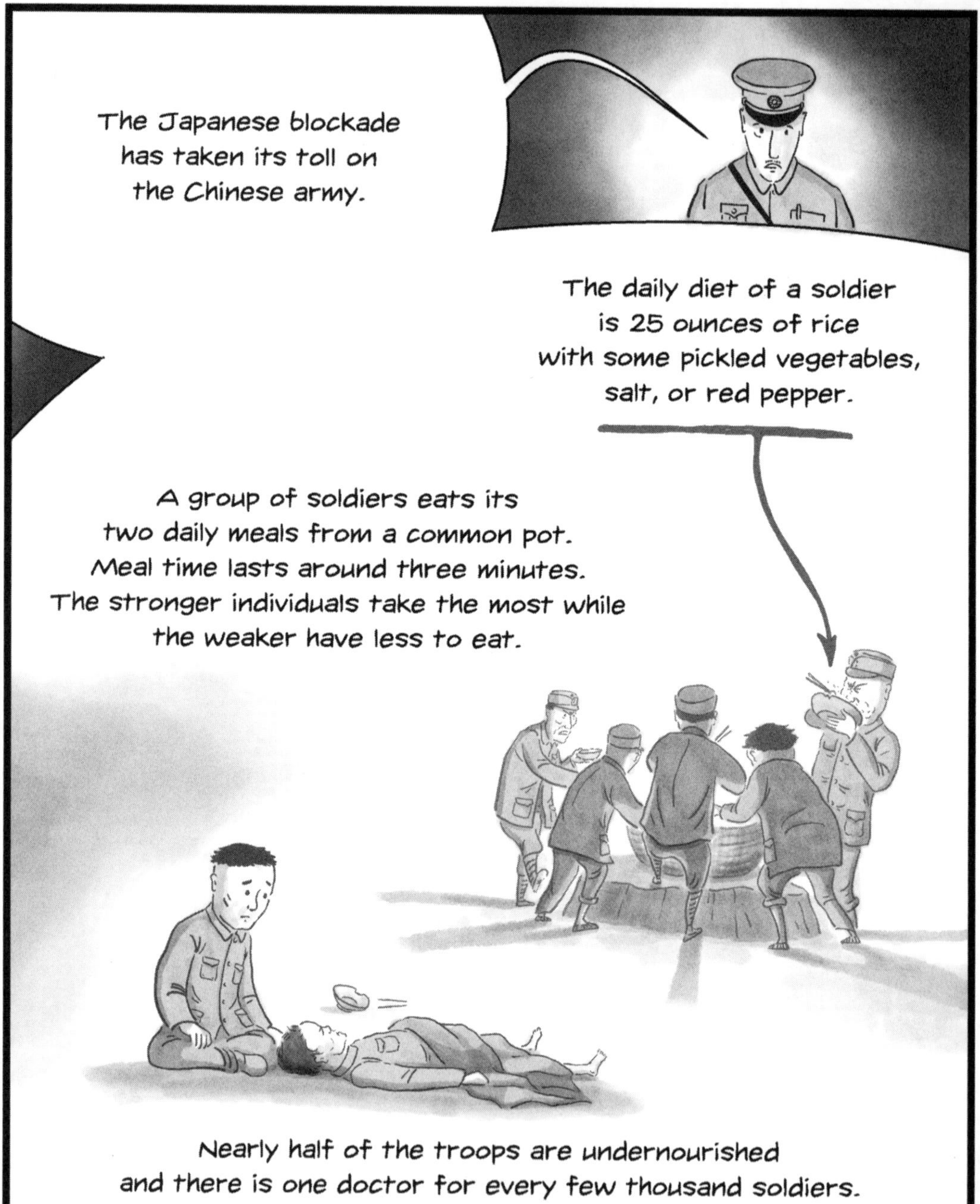
The Japanese blockade has taken its toll on the Chinese army.
The daily diet of a soldier is 25 ounces of rice with some pickled vegetables, salt, or red pepper.
A group of soldiers eats its two daily meals from a common pot. Meal time lasts around three minutes. The stronger individuals take the most while the weaker have less to eat.
Nearly half of the troops are undernourished and there is one doctor for every few thousand soldiers. Losses due to malnutrition and disease sometimes reach more than 40% of one division in a year.

Uniforms are often in short supply. Some soldiers wear the same clothes for three years.

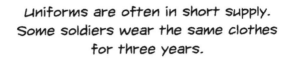

The army cannot provide shoes and socks. Soldiers have to make their own straw sandals.

There is one blanket for every five men.

In my platoon, the soldiers have no toothbrushes, no soap, no towels, and no toilet paper.

The whole platoon shares one coarse cloth for wiping faces. If one man has an eye infection, almost everyone else will get it.

A division commander is financially
responsible for all the expenses of his troops.
His funding is always tight and does not cover costs
like equipment repair, change of clothes,
or his subordinates' family emergencies.

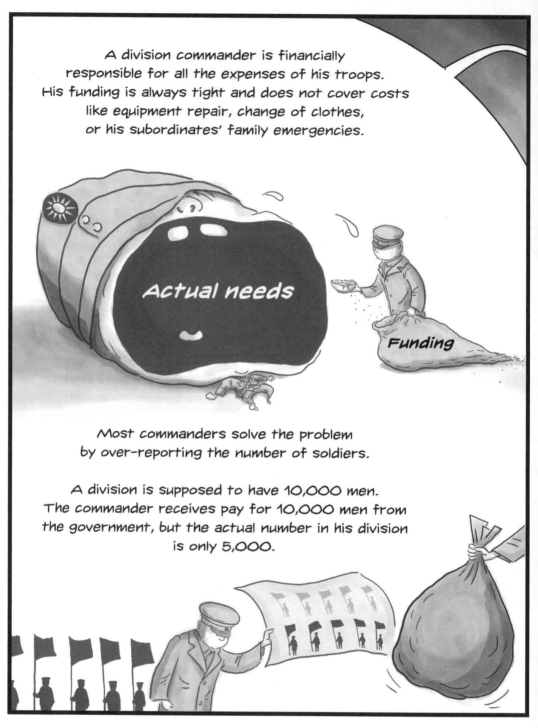

Most commanders solve the problem
by over-reporting the number of soldiers.

A division is supposed to have 10,000 men.
The commander receives pay for 10,000 men from
the government, but the actual number in his division
is only 5,000.

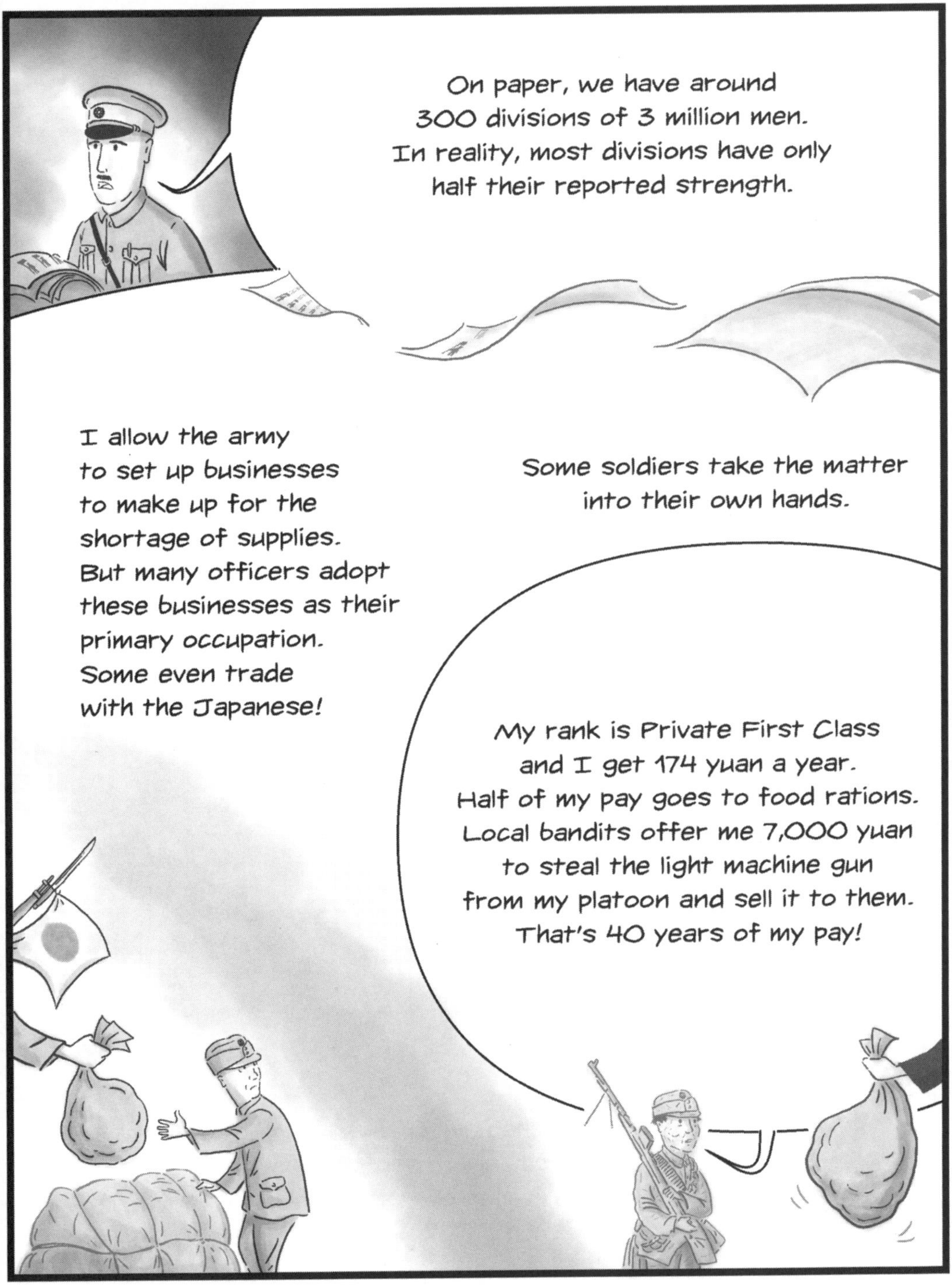
On paper, we have around 300 divisions of 3 million men. In reality, most divisions have only half their reported strength.
I allow the army to set up businesses to make up for the shortage of supplies. But many officers adopt these businesses as their primary occupation. Some even trade with the Japanese!
Some soldiers take the matter into their own hands.
My rank is Private First Class and I get 174 yuan a year. Half of my pay goes to food rations. Local bandits offer me 7,000 yuan to steal the light machine gun from my platoon and sell it to them. That's 40 years of my pay!

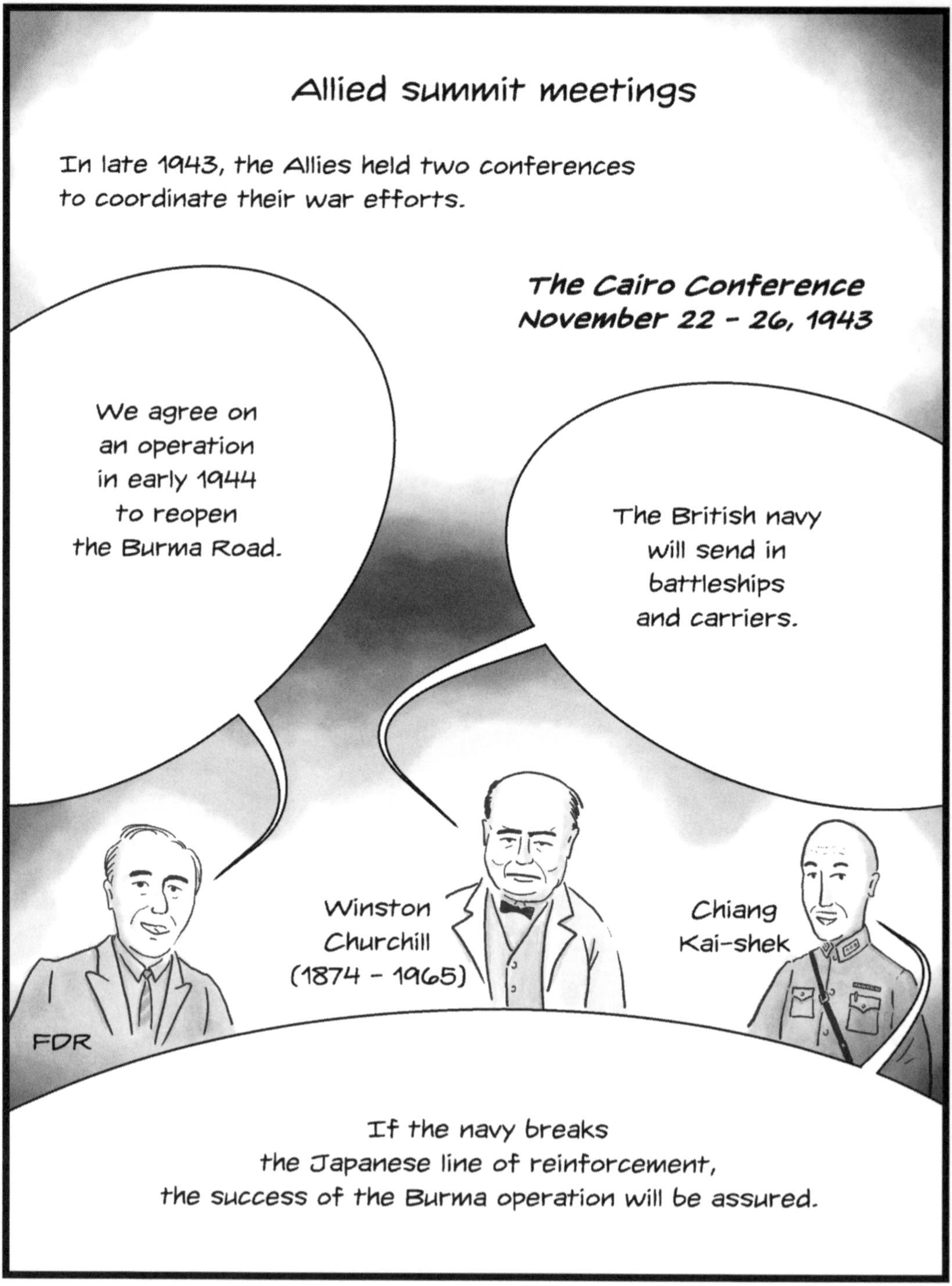
Allied summit meetings
In late 1943, the Allies held two conferences to coordinate their war efforts.
The Cairo Conference November 22 - 26, 1943
We agree on an operation in early 1944 to reopen the Burma Road.
The British navy will send in battleships and carriers.
FDR
Winston Churchill (1874 - 1965)
Chiang Kai-shek
If the navy breaks the Japanese line of reinforcement, the success of the Burma operation will be assured.

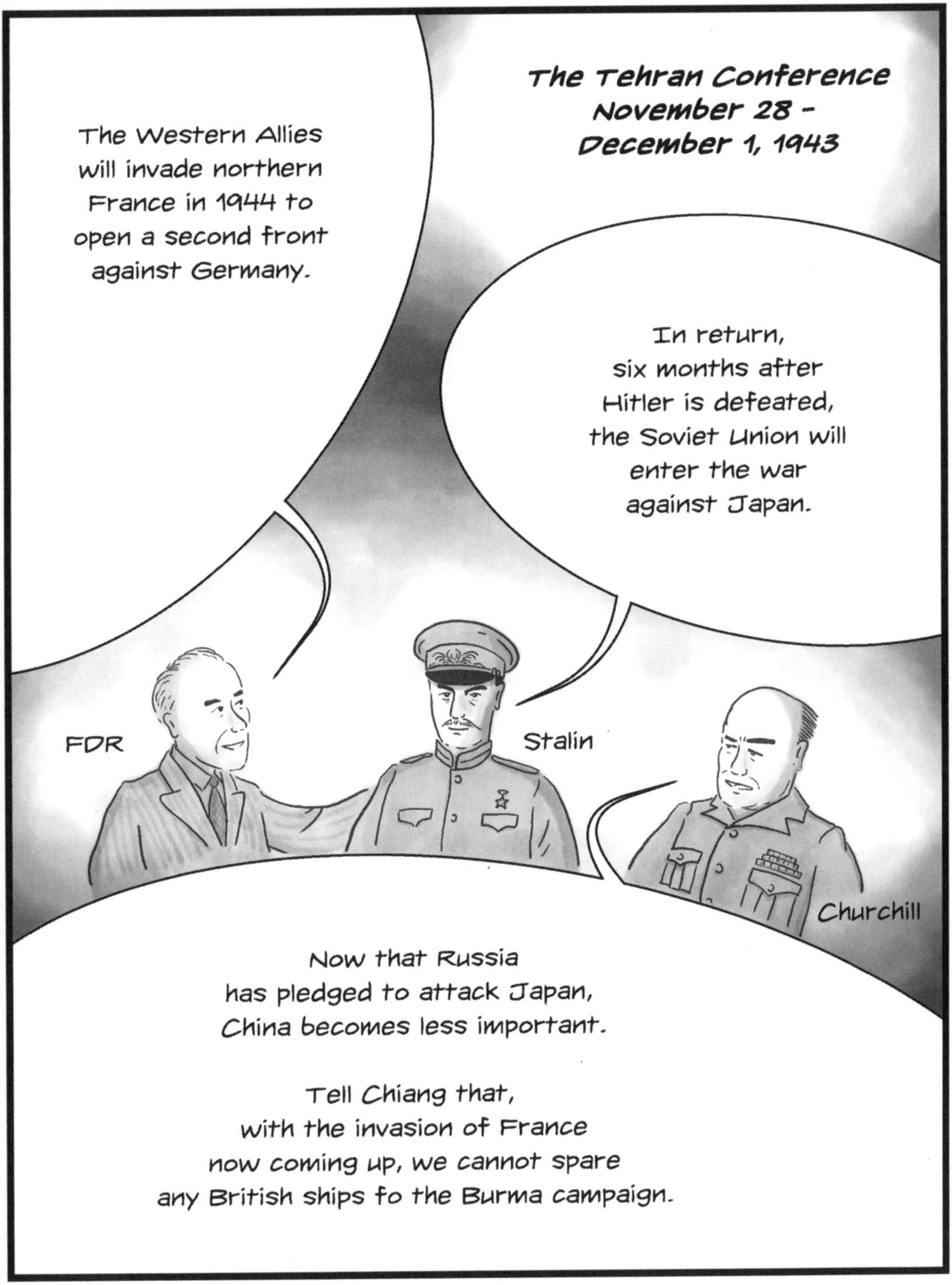
The Tehran Conference November 28 - December 1, 1943
The Western Allies will invade northern France in 1944 to open a second front against Germany.
In return, six months after Hitler is defeated, the Soviet Union will enter the war against Japan.
FDR
Stalin
Churchill
Now that Russia has pledged to attack Japan, China becomes less important.
Tell Chiang that, with the invasion of France now coming up, we cannot spare any British ships to the Burma campaign.

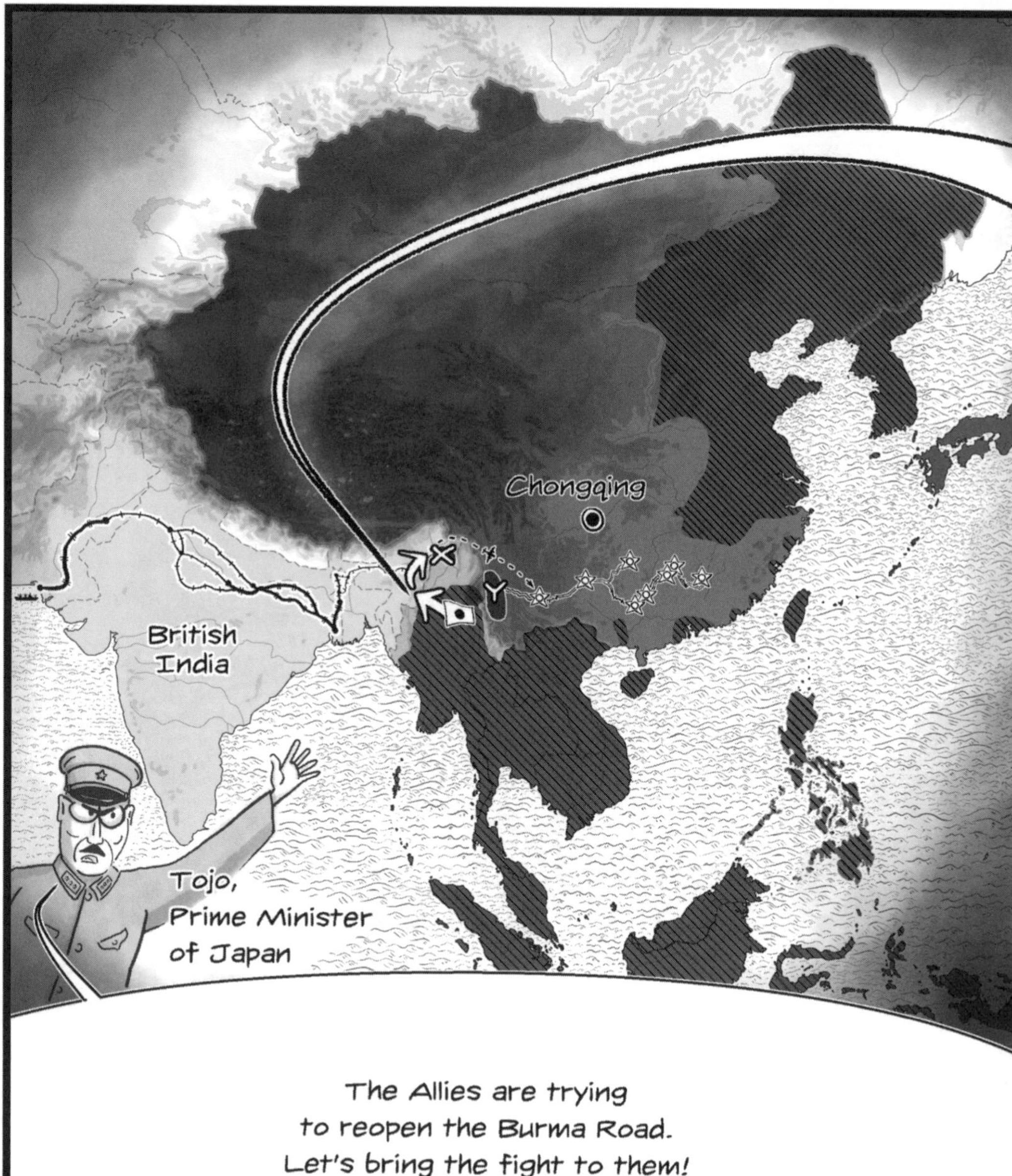
Chongqing
British India
Tojo, Prime Minister of Japan
The Allies are trying to reopen the Burma Road. Let's bring the fight to them! Launch a surprise attack to seize the Allied supply bases in India and cut off the Hump route to China.

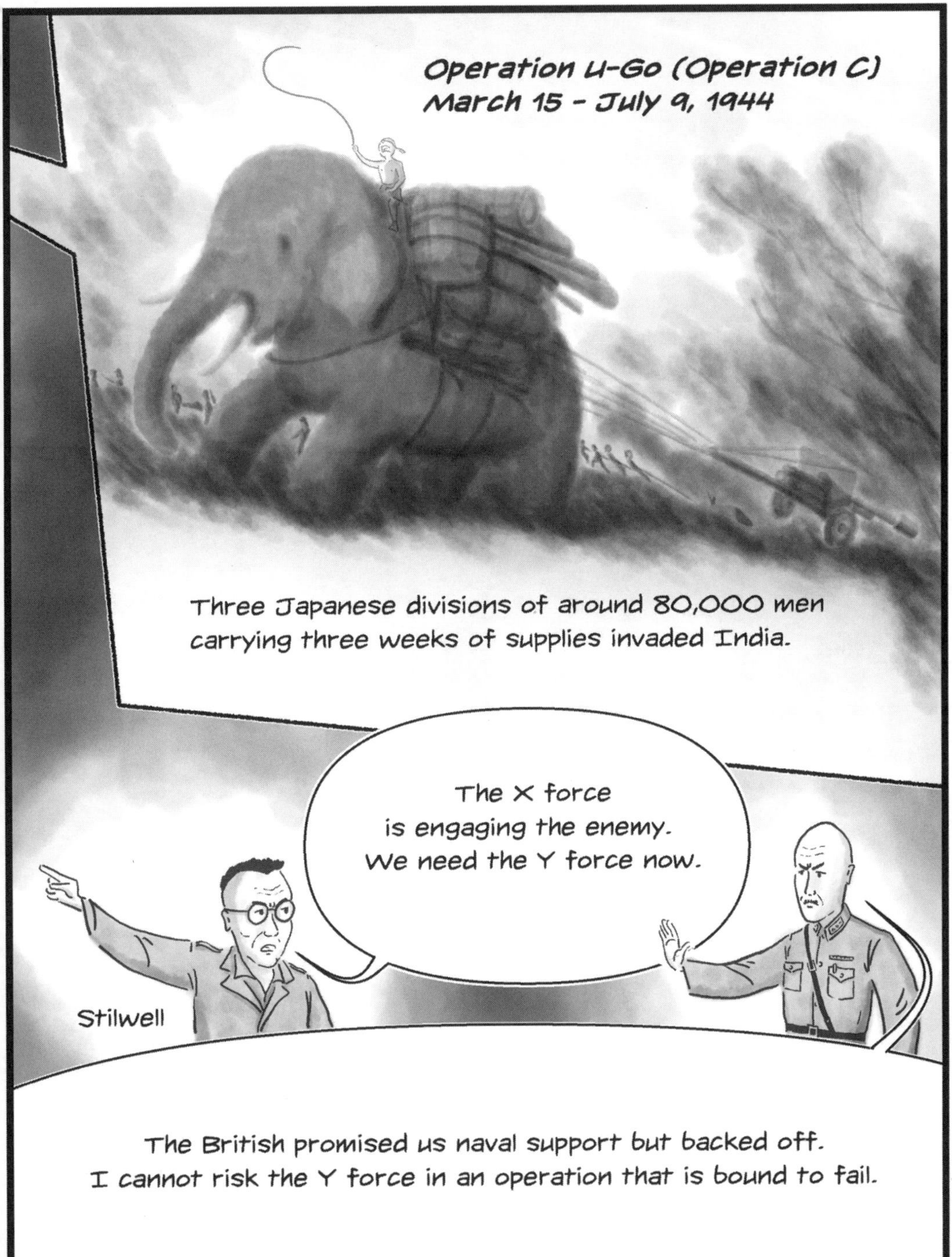
Operation U-Go (Operation C)
March 15 - July 9, 1944
Three Japanese divisions of around 80,000 men carrying three weeks of supplies invaded India.
The X force is engaging the enemy. We need the Y force now.
Stilwell
The British promised us naval support but backed off. I cannot risk the Y force in an operation that is bound to fail.

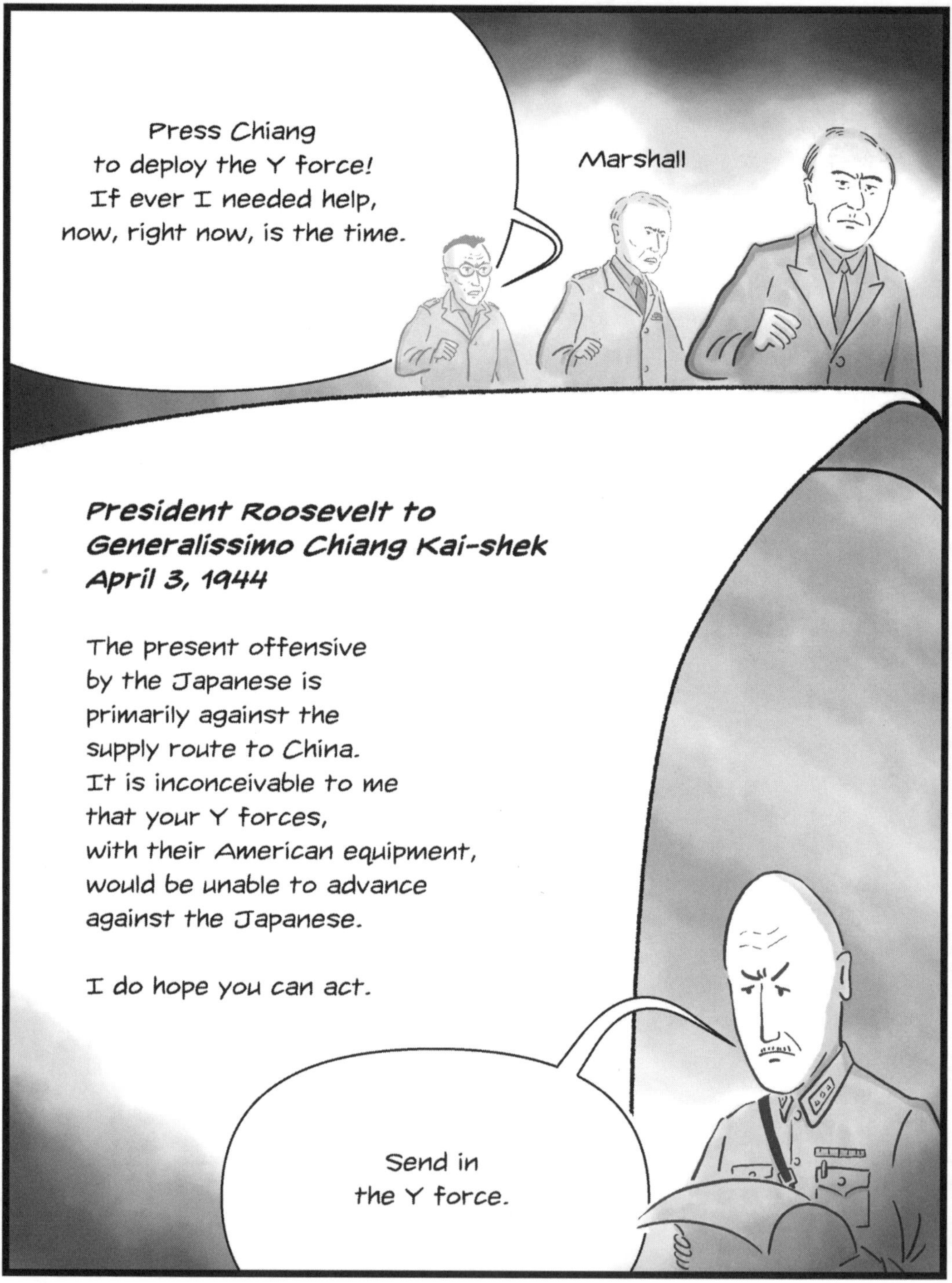

Press Chiang to deploy the Y force! If ever I needed help, now, right now, is the time.
Marshall
President Roosevelt to Generalissimo Chiang Kai-shek April 3, 1944
The present offensive by the Japanese is primarily against the supply route to China. It is inconceivable to me that your Y forces, with their American equipment, would be unable to advance against the Japanese.
I do hope you can act.
Send in the Y force.

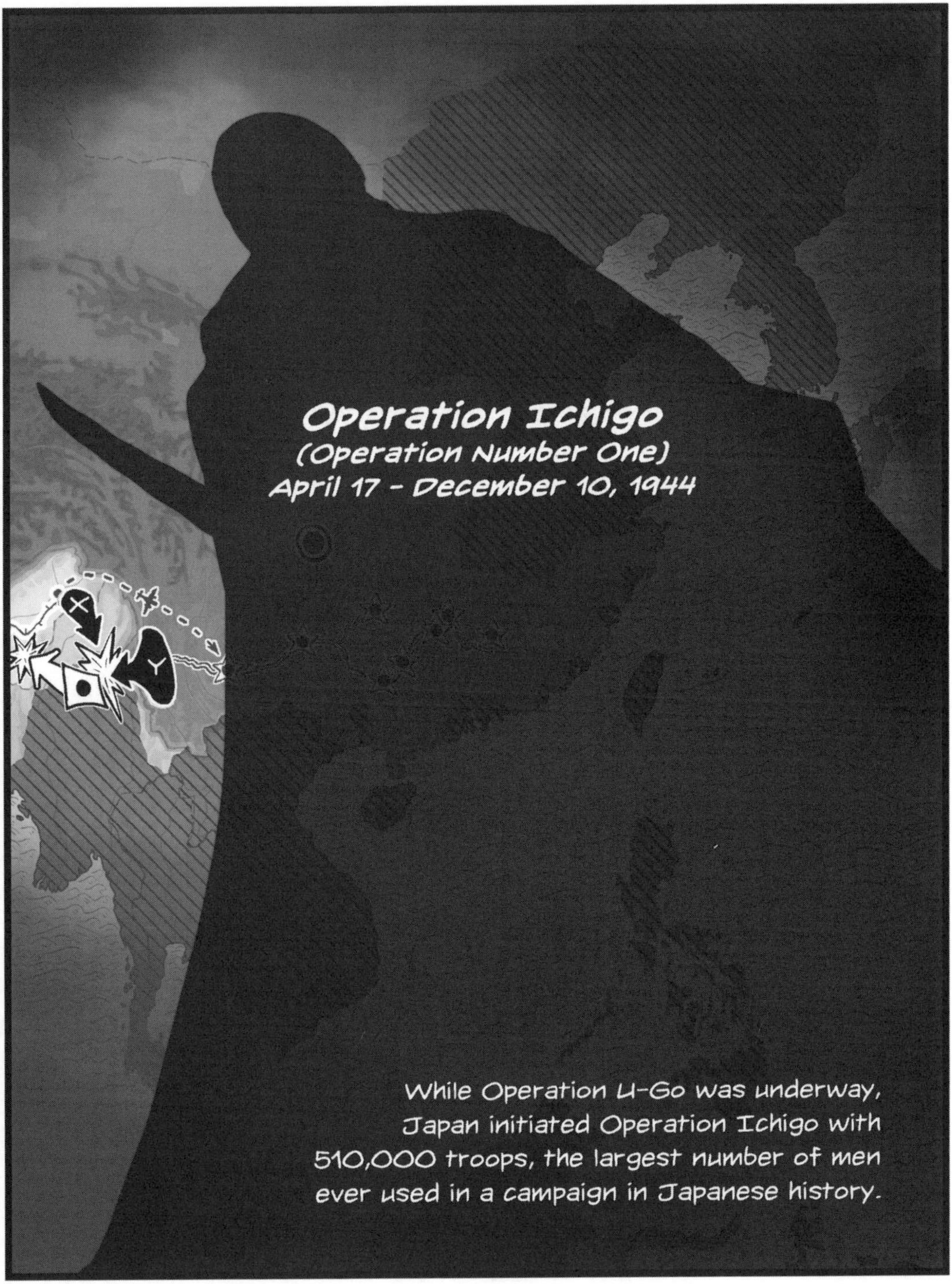
Operation Ichigo
(Operation Number One)
April 17 - December 10, 1944
While Operation U-Go was underway, Japan initiated Operation Ichigo with 510,000 troops, the largest number of men ever used in a campaign in Japanese history.

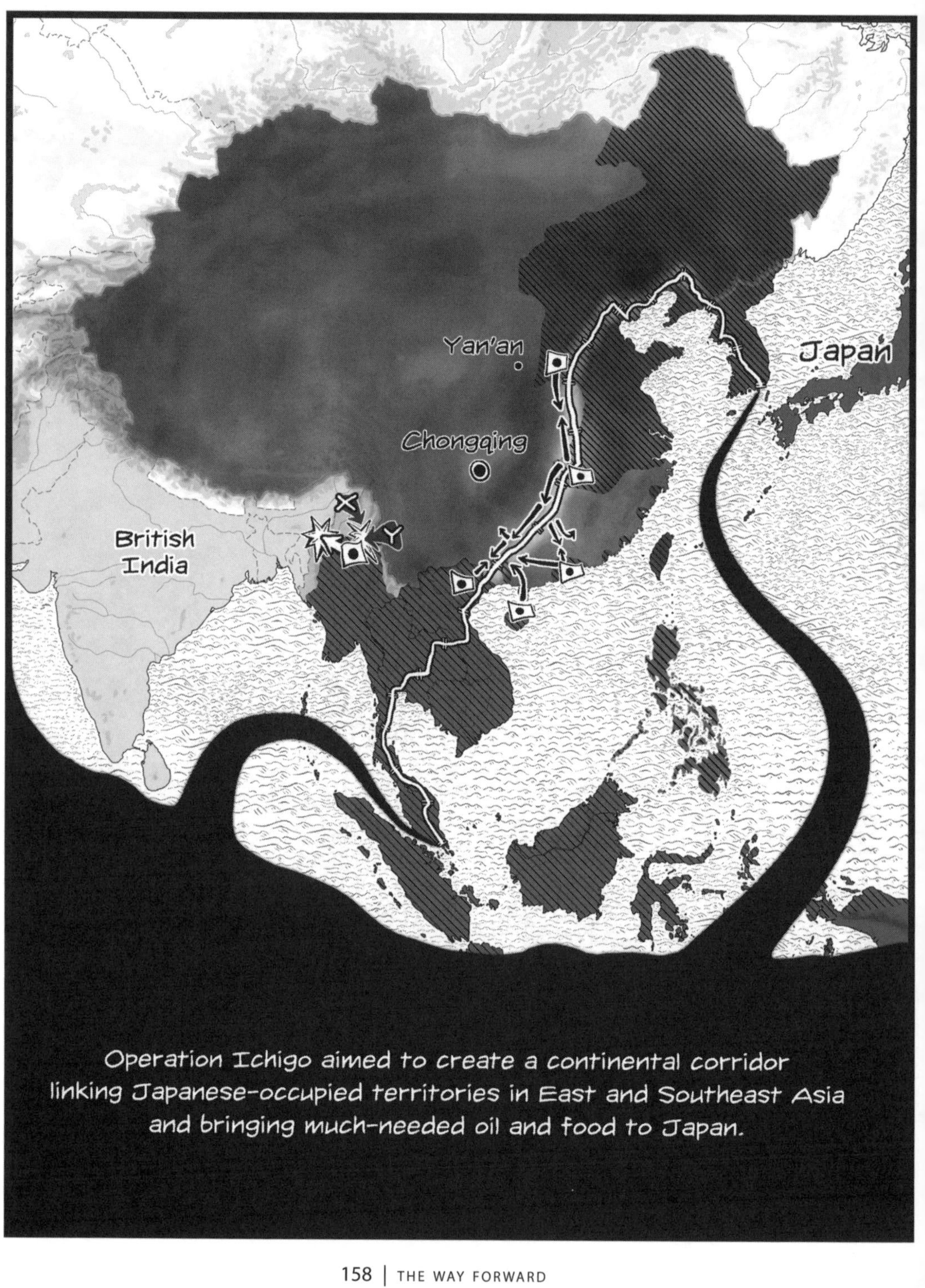
Yan'an
Chongqing
Japan
British
India
X
Y
Operation Ichigo aimed to create a continental corridor linking Japanese-occupied territories in East and Southeast Asia and bringing much-needed oil and food to Japan.

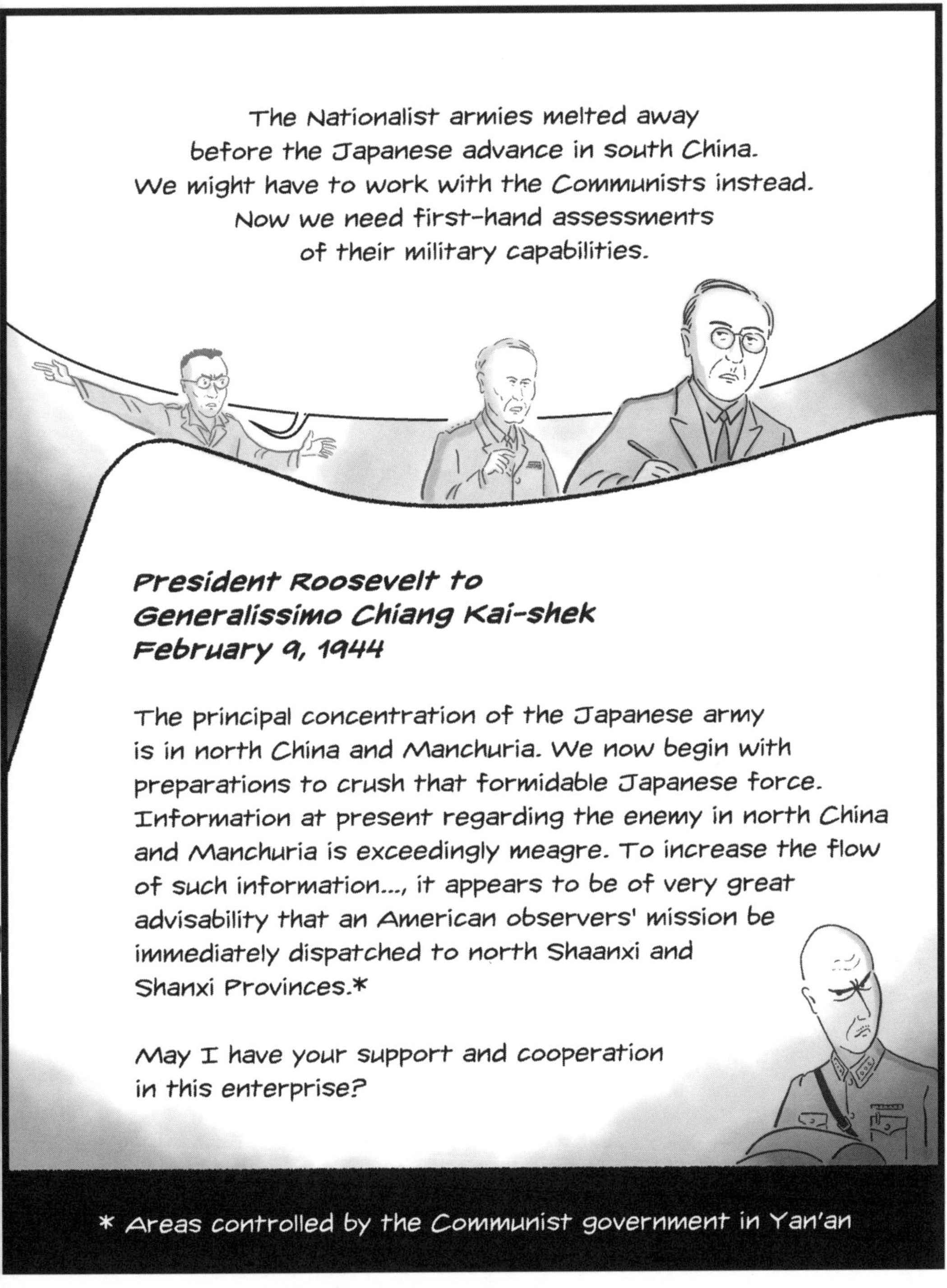
The Nationalist armies melted away before the Japanese advance in south China. We might have to work with the Communists instead. Now we need first-hand assessments of their military capabilities.
President Roosevelt to Generalissimo Chiang Kai-shek February 9, 1944
The principal concentration of the Japanese army is in north China and Manchuria. We now begin with preparations to crush that formidable Japanese force. Information at present regarding the enemy in north China and Manchuria is exceedingly meagre. To increase the flow of such information..., it appears to be of very great advisability that an American observers' mission be immediately dispatched to north Shaanxi and Shanxi Provinces.*
May I have your support and cooperation in this enterprise?
* Areas controlled by the Communist government in Yan'an

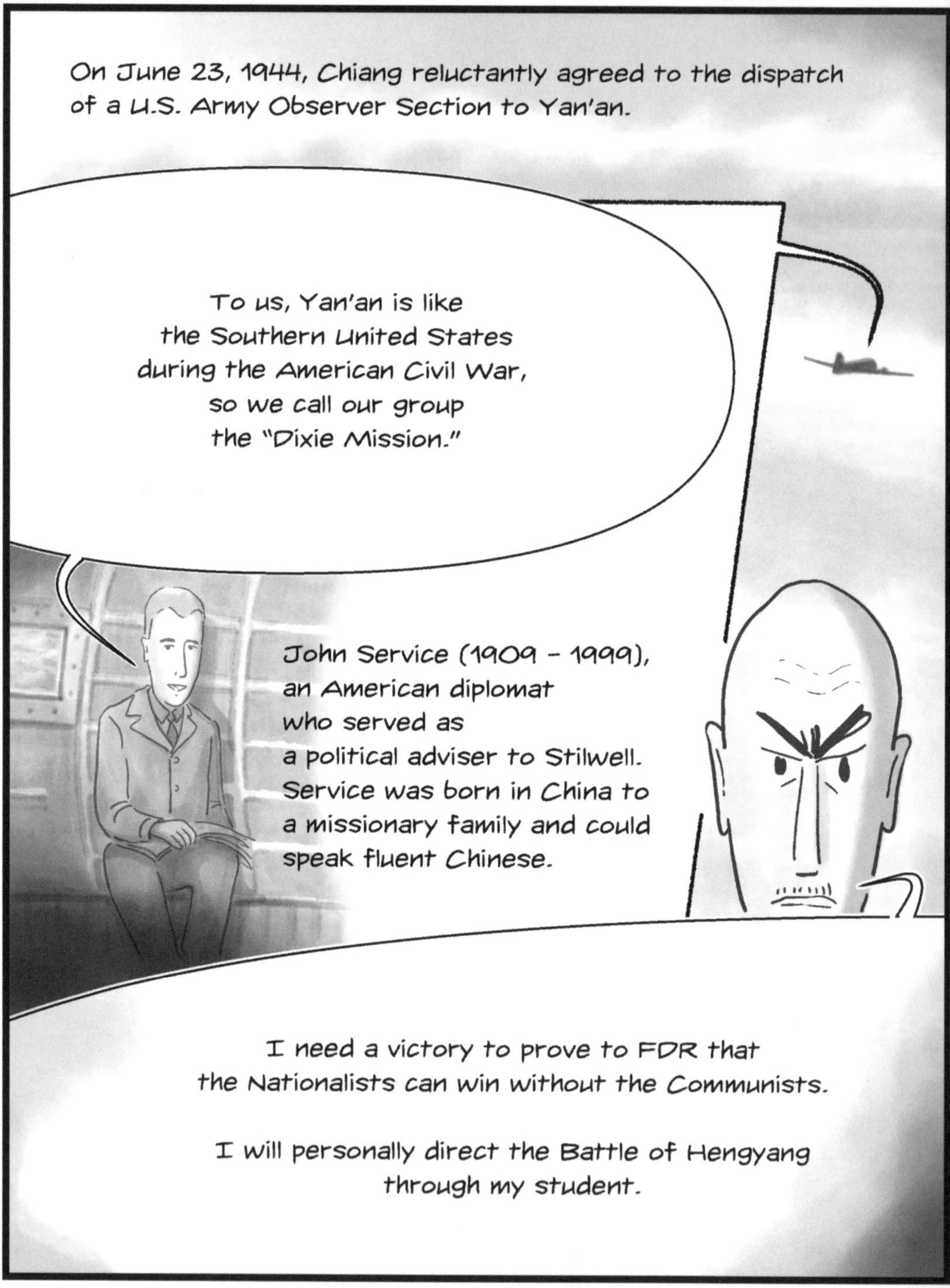
On June 23, 1944, Chiang reluctantly agreed to the dispatch of a U.S. Army Observer Section to Yan'an.
To us, Yan'an is like the Southern United States during the American Civil War, so we call our group the "Dixie Mission."
John Service (1909 – 1999), an American diplomat who served as a political adviser to Stilwell. Service was born in China to a missionary family and could speak fluent Chinese.
I need a victory to prove to FDR that the Nationalists can win without the Communists.
I will personally direct the Battle of Hengyang through my student.

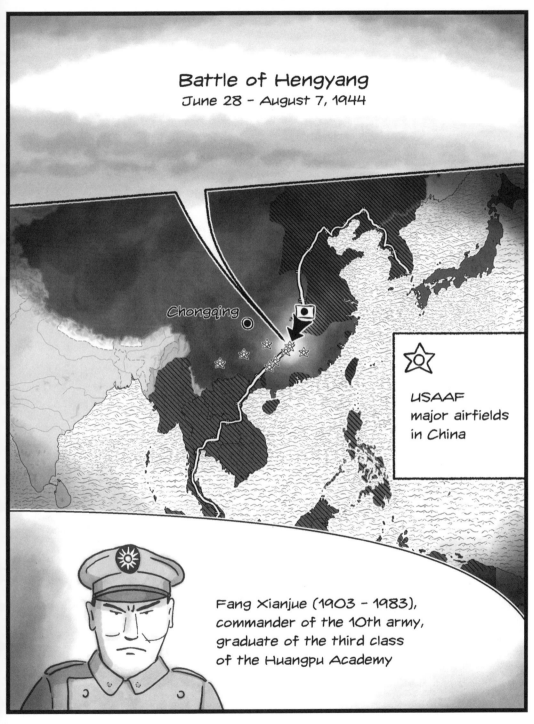

Battle of Hengyang
June 28 – August 7, 1944

Chongqing

USAAF
major airfields
in China

Fang Xianjue (1903 – 1983),
commander of the 10th army,
graduate of the third class
of the Huangpu Academy

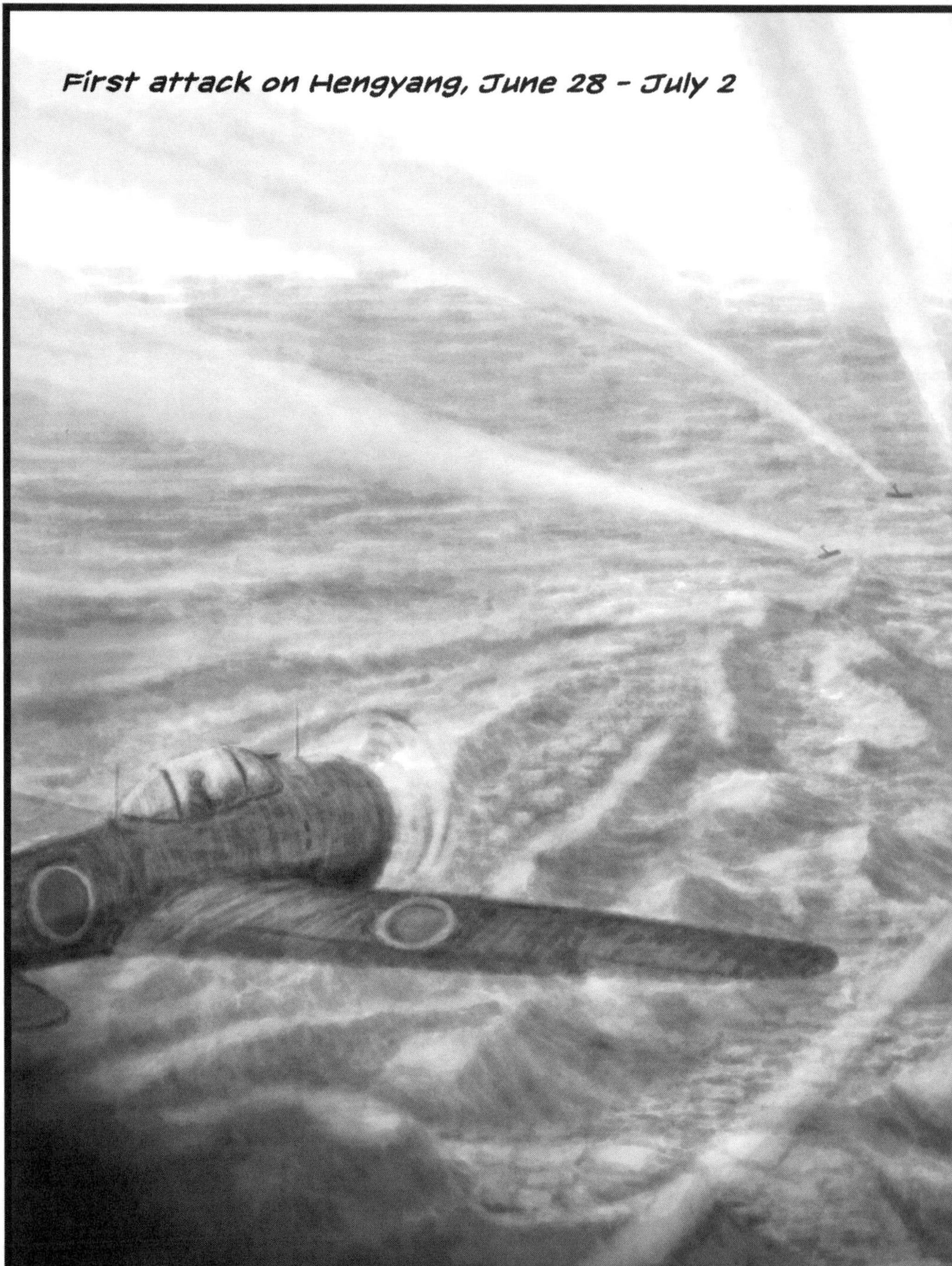
First attack on Hengyang, June 28 - July 2

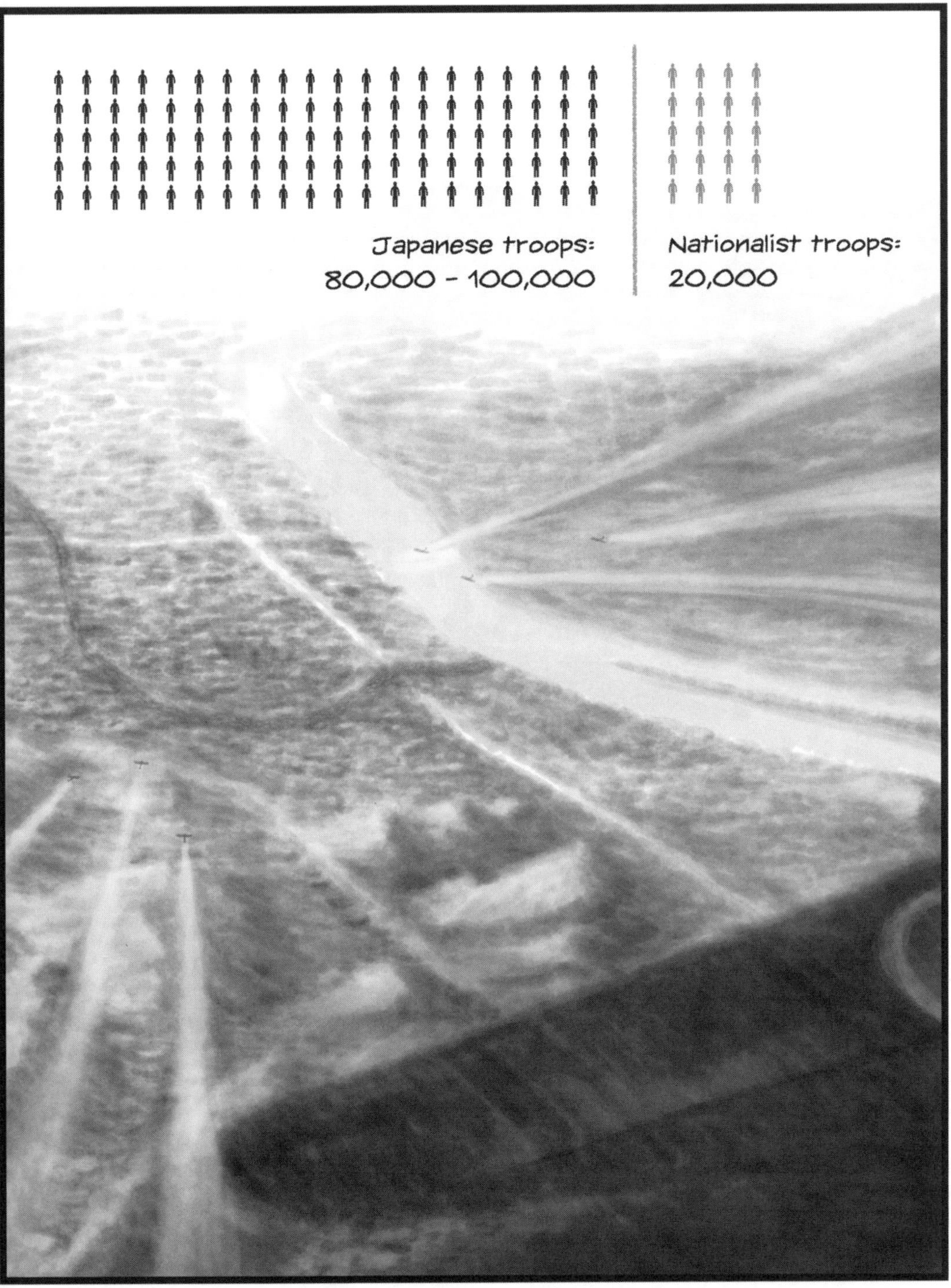
Japanese troops:
80,000 - 100,000
Nationalist troops:
20,000

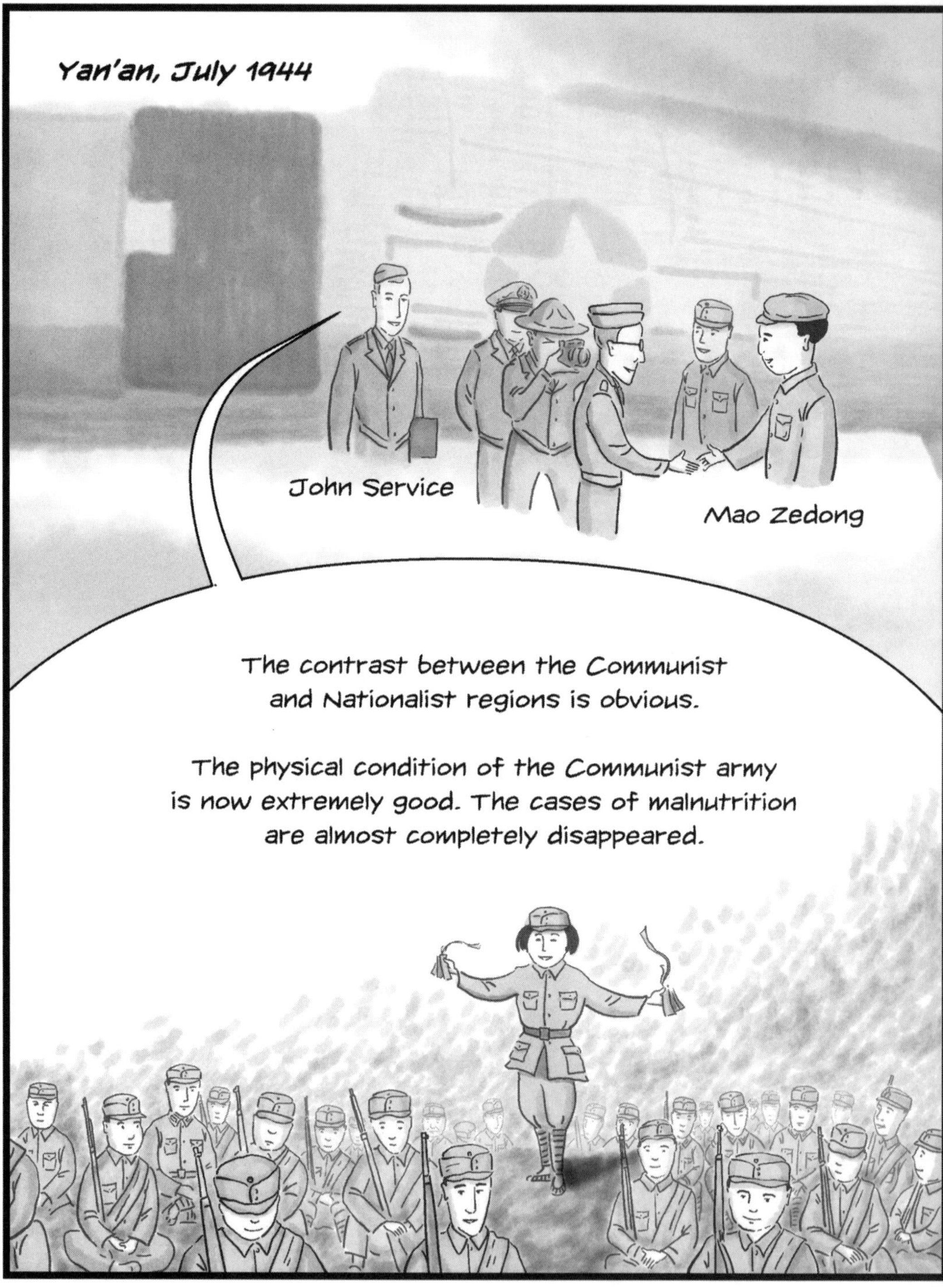
Yan'an, July 1944
John Service
Mao Zedong
The contrast between the Communist and Nationalist regions is obvious.
The physical condition of the Communist army is now extremely good. The cases of malnutrition are almost completely disappeared.

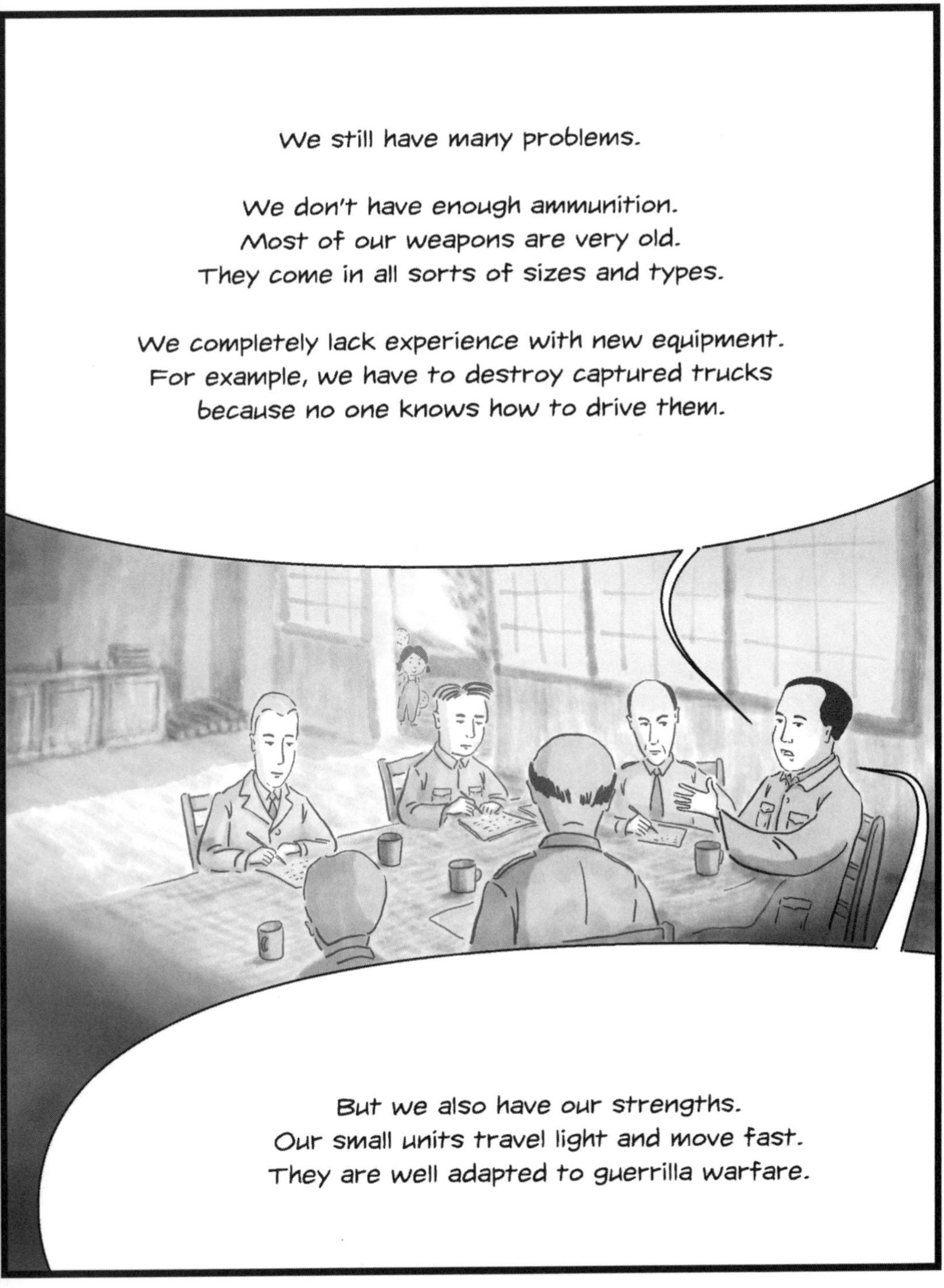
We still have many problems.
We don't have enough ammunition.
Most of our weapons are very old.
They come in all sorts of sizes and types.
We completely lack experience with new equipment.
For example, we have to destroy captured trucks
because no one knows how to drive them.
But we also have our strengths.
Our small units travel light and move fast.
They are well adapted to guerrilla warfare.

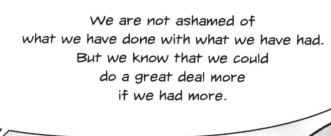

We are not ashamed of
what we have done with what we have had.
But we know that we could
do a great deal more
if we had more.

President Roosevelt to Generalissimo Chiang Kai-shek
July 6, 1944

The critical situation in China calls for the delegation
to one individual of the power to coordinate
all the military resources in China,
including the Communist forces.

I recommend for your most urgent consideration
that you place Stilwell directly under you in command
of all Chinese and American forces.

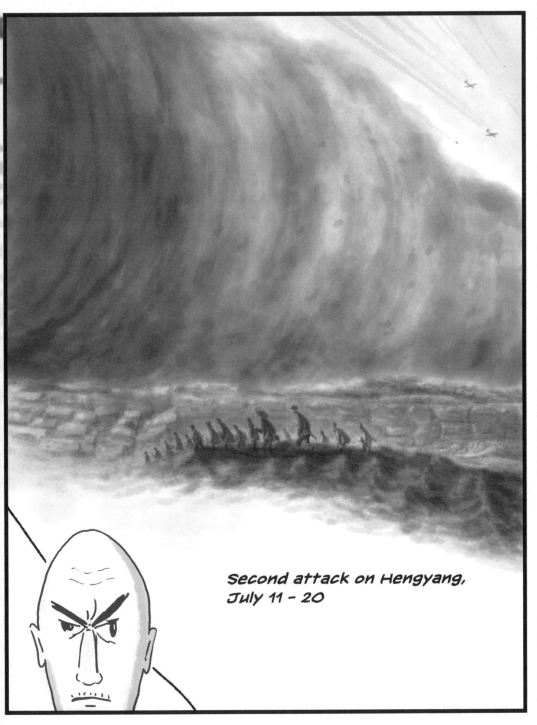

Second attack on Hengyang,
July 11 – 20

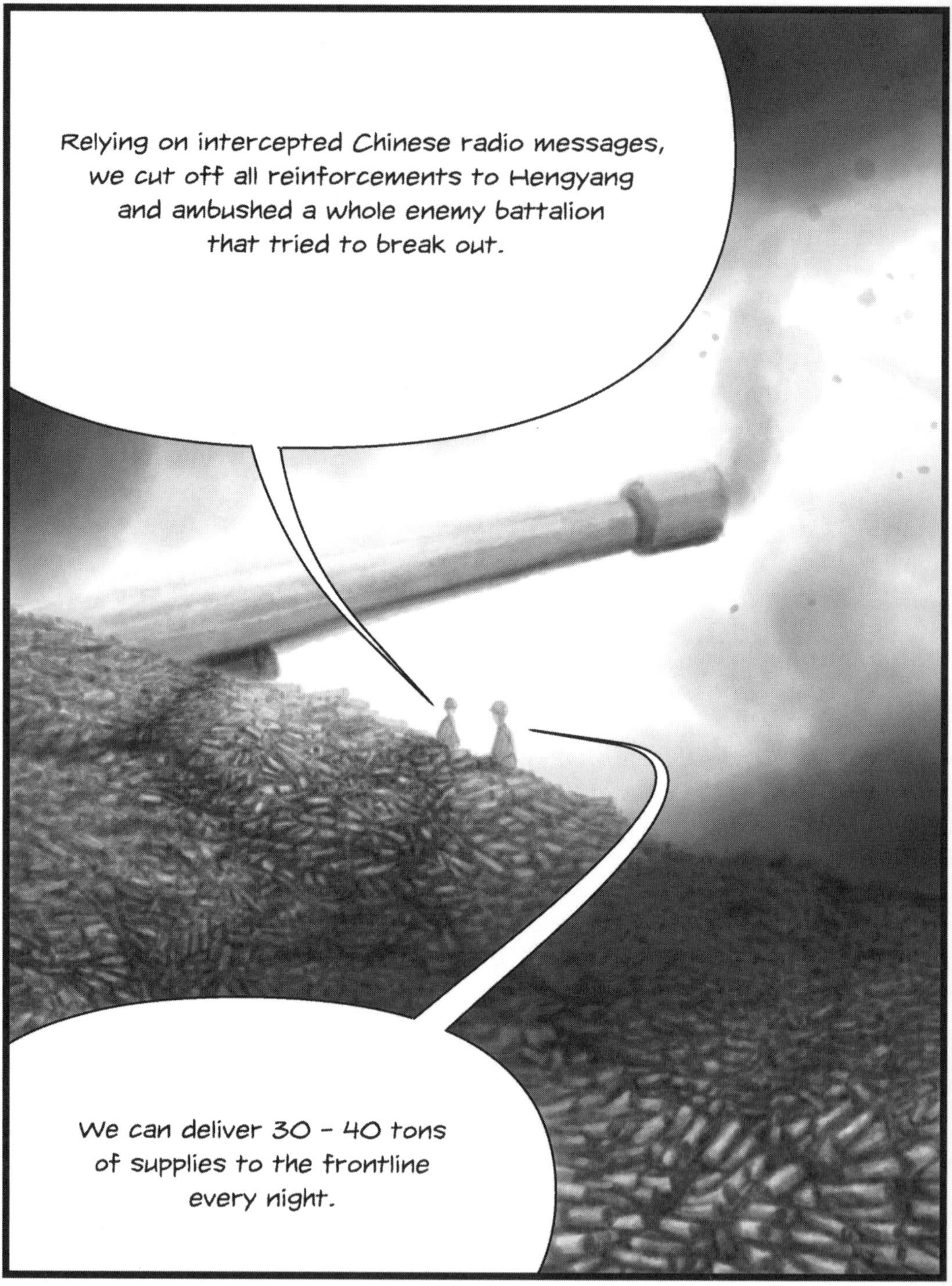
Relying on intercepted Chinese radio messages, we cut off all reinforcements to Hengyang and ambushed a whole enemy battalion that tried to break out.
We can deliver 30 - 40 tons of supplies to the frontline every night.

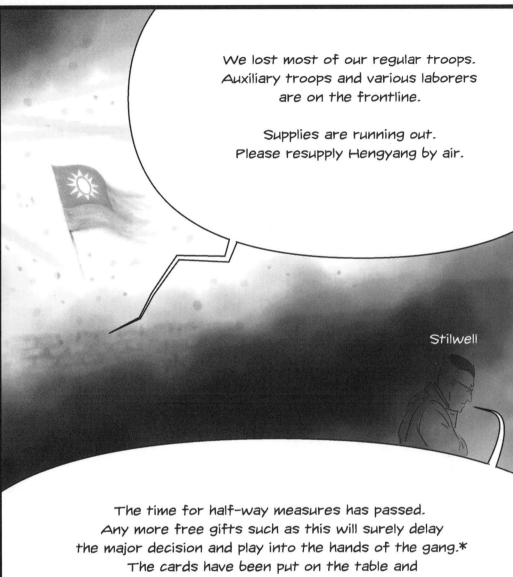

We lost most of our regular troops.
Auxiliary troops and various laborers
are on the frontline.

Supplies are running out.
Please resupply Hengyang by air.

Stilwell

The time for half-way measures has passed.
Any more free gifts such as this will surely delay
the major decision and play into the hands of the gang.*
The cards have been put on the table and
the answer has not been given.
Until it is given, let them stew.

* Chiang Kai-shek and other Nationalist leaders
who oppose the appointment of Stilwell

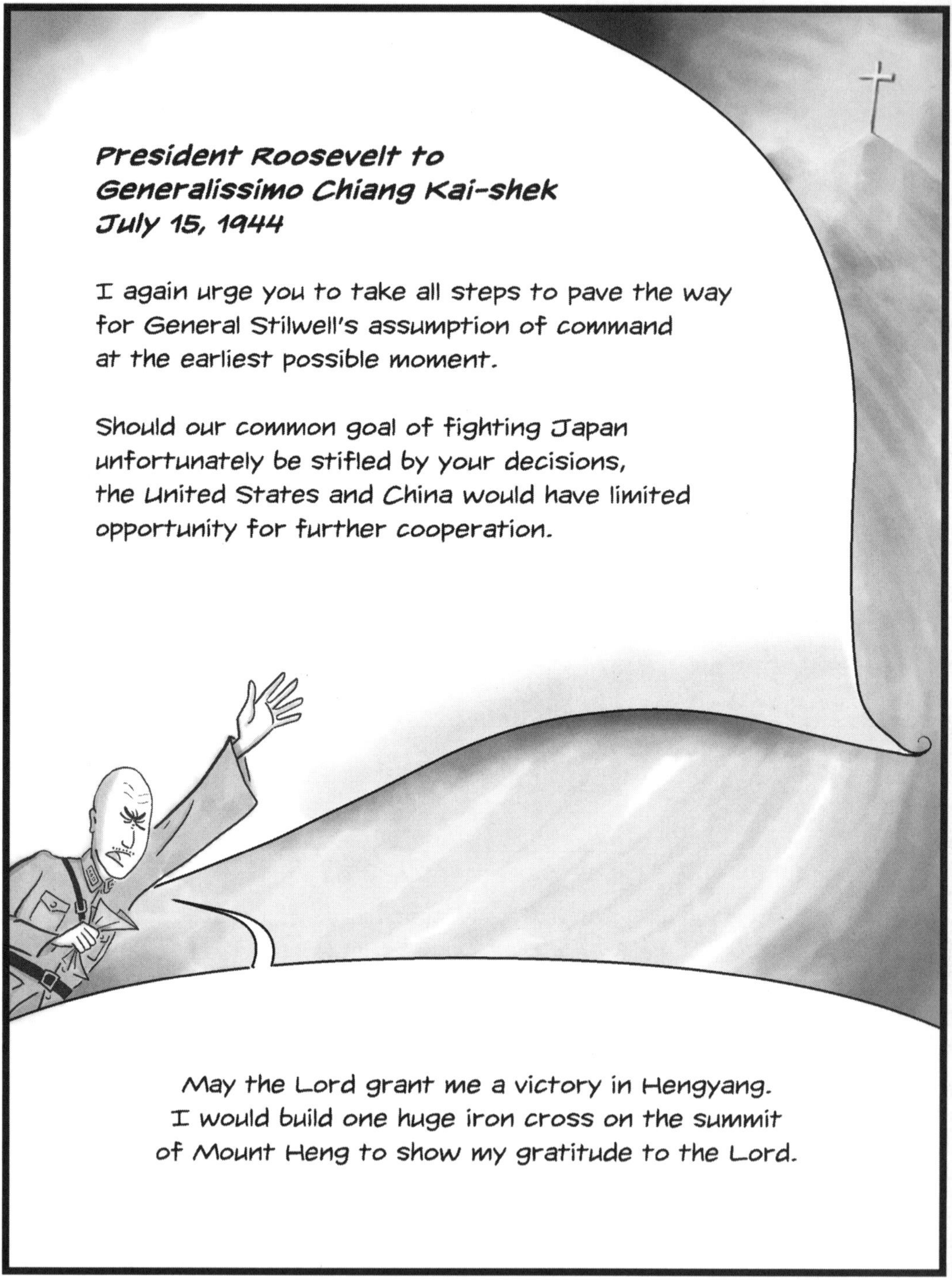
President Roosevelt to
Generalissimo Chiang Kai-shek
July 15, 1944
I again urge you to take all steps to pave the way for General Stilwell's assumption of command at the earliest possible moment.
Should our common goal of fighting Japan unfortunately be stifled by your decisions, the United States and China would have limited opportunity for further cooperation.
May the Lord grant me a victory in Hengyang. I would build one huge iron cross on the summit of Mount Heng to show my gratitude to the Lord.

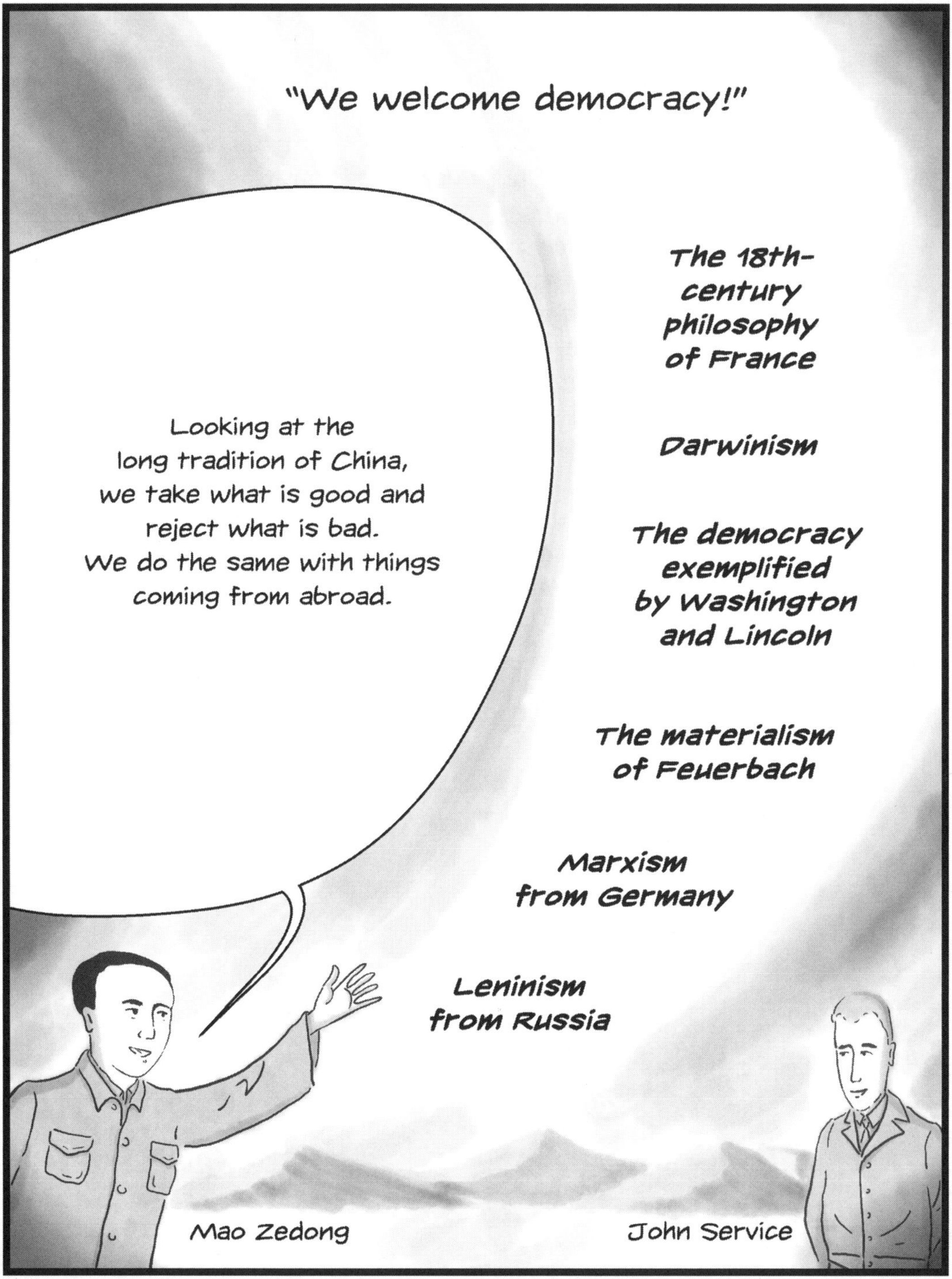
"We welcome democracy!"
Looking at the long tradition of China, we take what is good and reject what is bad. We do the same with things coming from abroad.
The 18th-century philosophy of France
Darwinism
The democracy exemplified by Washington and Lincoln
The materialism of Feuerbach
Marxism from Germany
Leninism from Russia
Mao Zedong
John Service

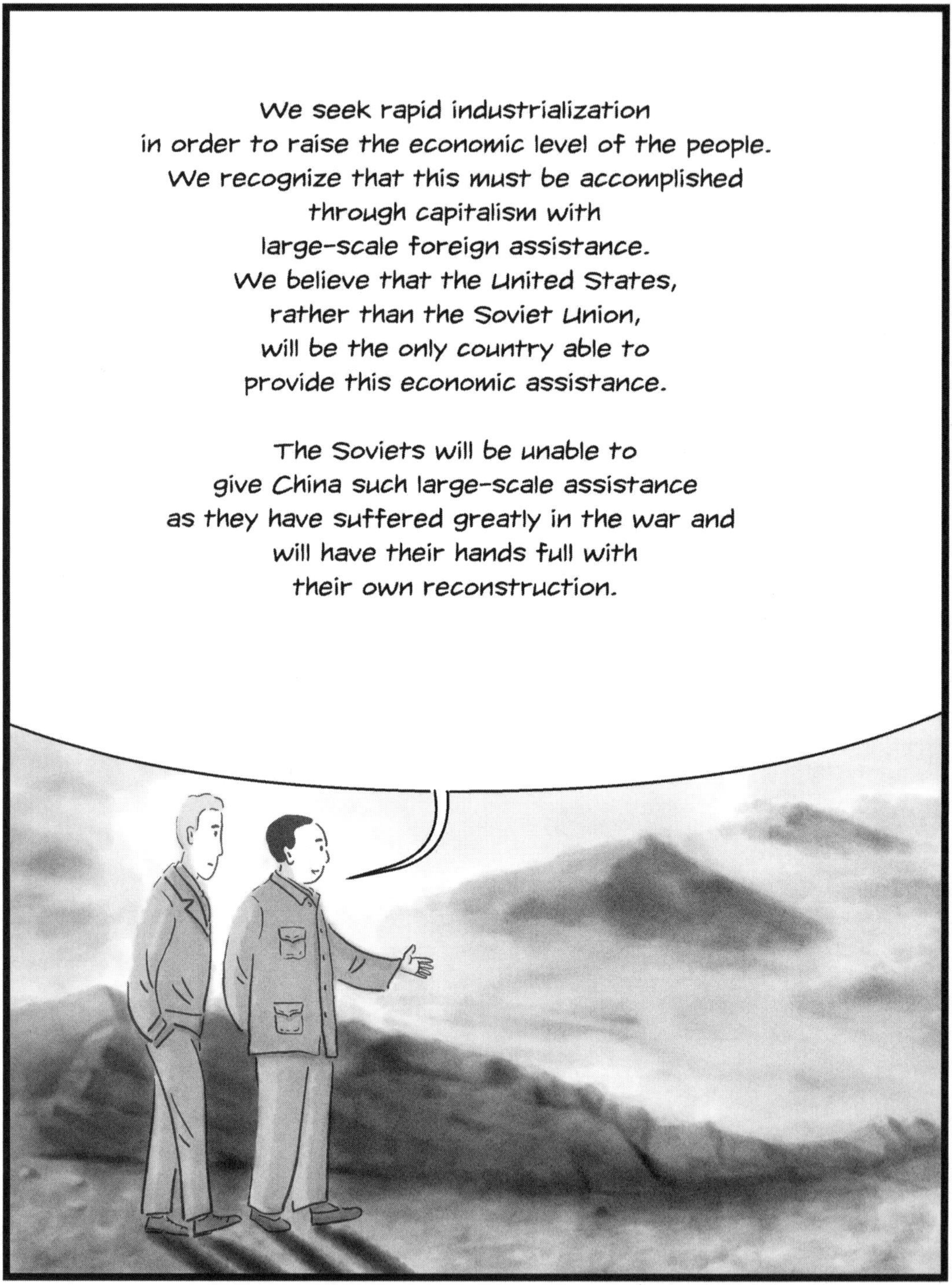
We seek rapid industrialization
in order to raise the economic level of the people.
We recognize that this must be accomplished
through capitalism with
large-scale foreign assistance.
We believe that the United States,
rather than the Soviet Union,
will be the only country able to
provide this economic assistance.

The Soviets will be unable to
give China such large-scale assistance
as they have suffered greatly in the war and
will have their hands full with
their own reconstruction.

The United States, with its tremendous resources,
is logically the best country to turn to for help.

The United States will find us
more cooperative than the Nationalists.
We will not be afraid of democratic American influence.
We welcome it.

China and the United States
can and must work together.*

* The conversation is based on
"Interview with Mao Tse-tung, August 23, 1944"
written by John Service for the U.S. Department of State.

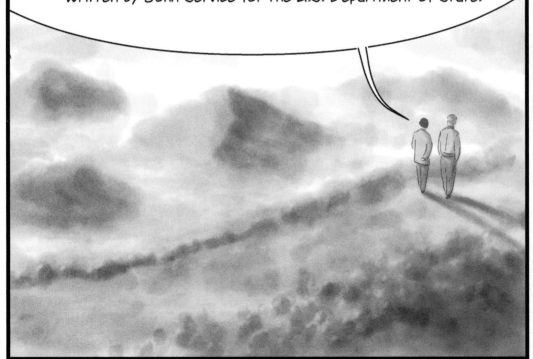

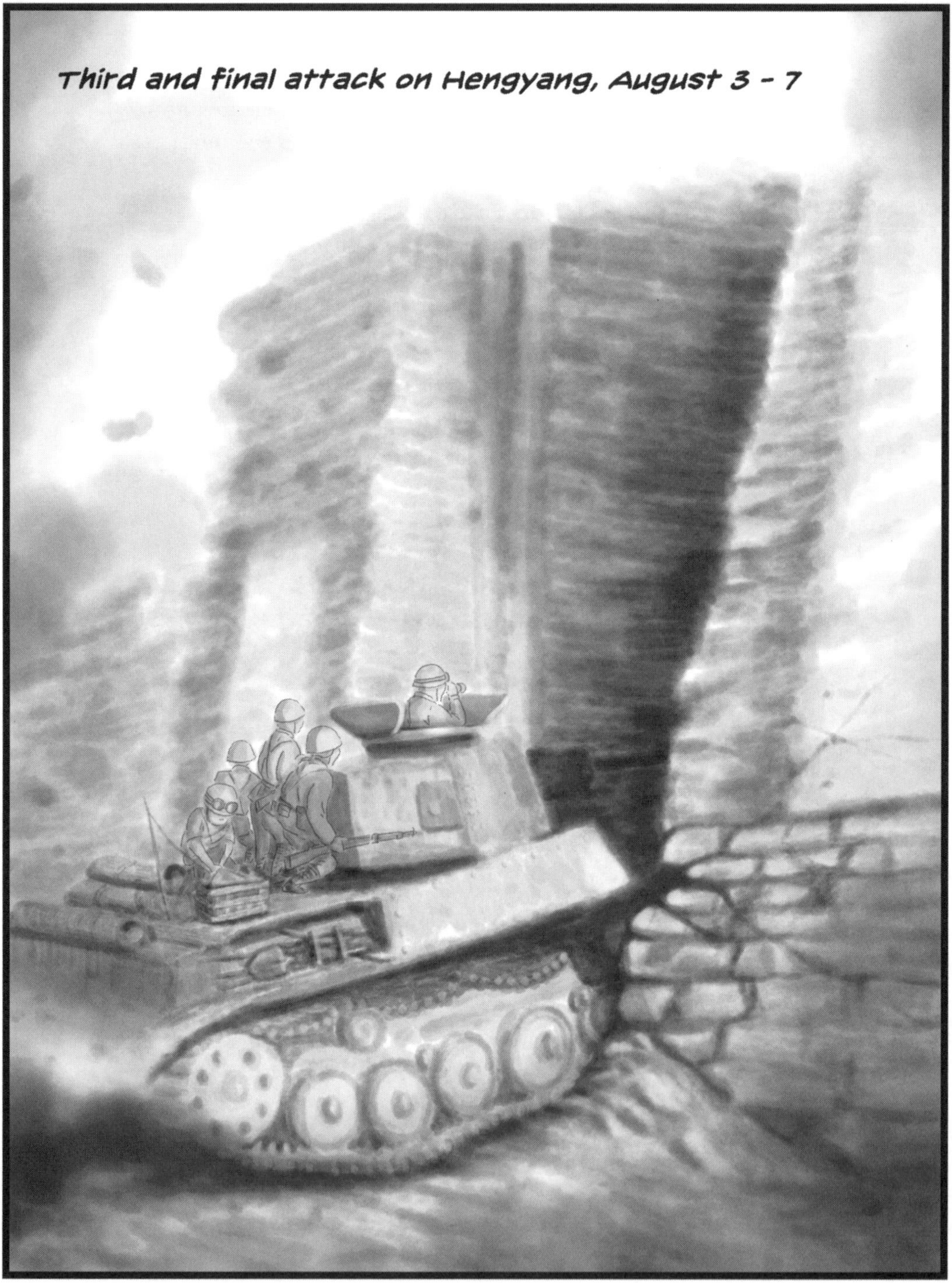
Third and final attack on Hengyang, August 3 - 7

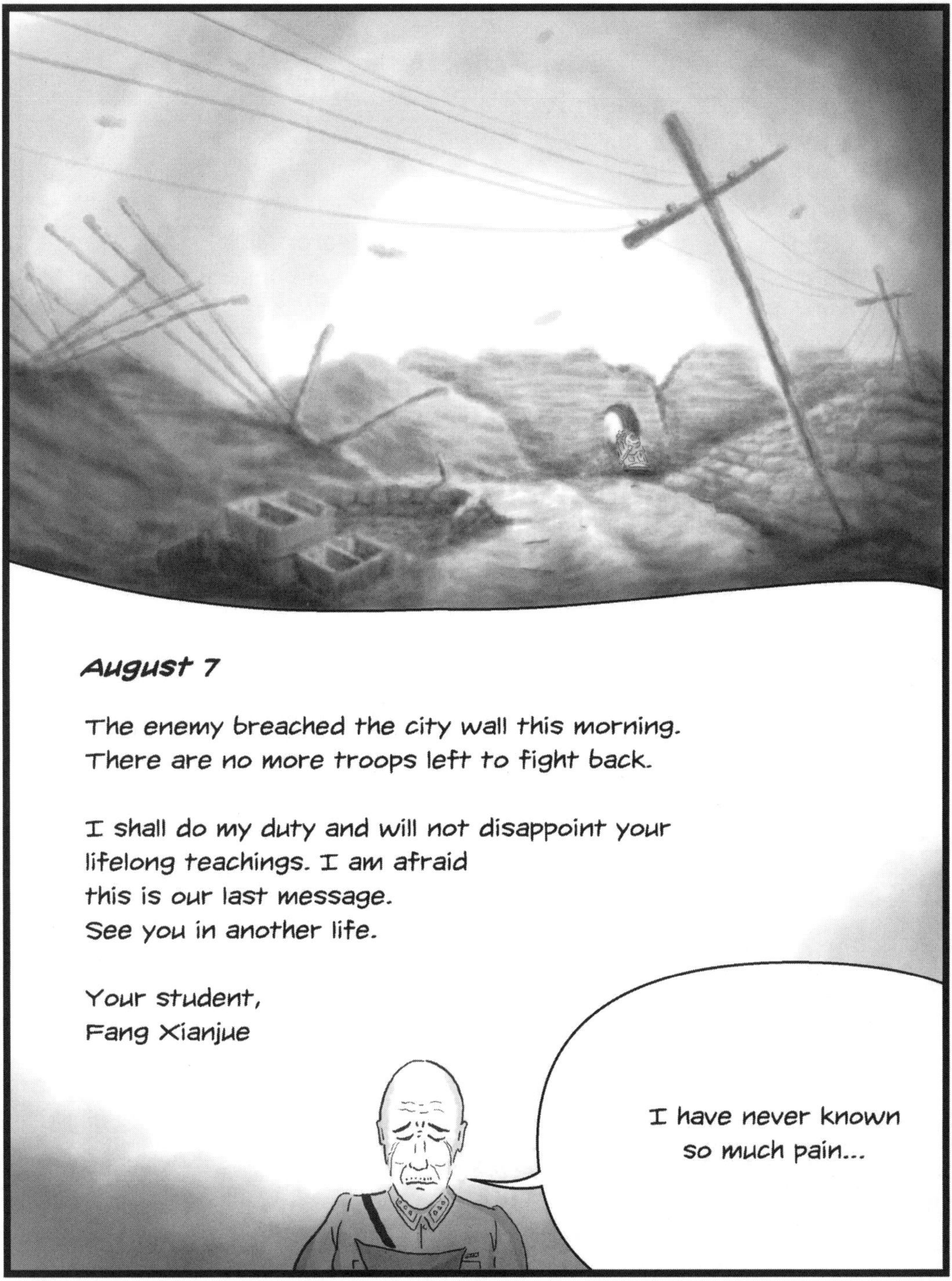
August 7
The enemy breached the city wall this morning.
There are no more troops left to fight back.
I shall do my duty and will not disappoint your lifelong teachings. I am afraid this is our last message.
See you in another life.
Your student,
Fang Xianjue
I have never known so much pain...

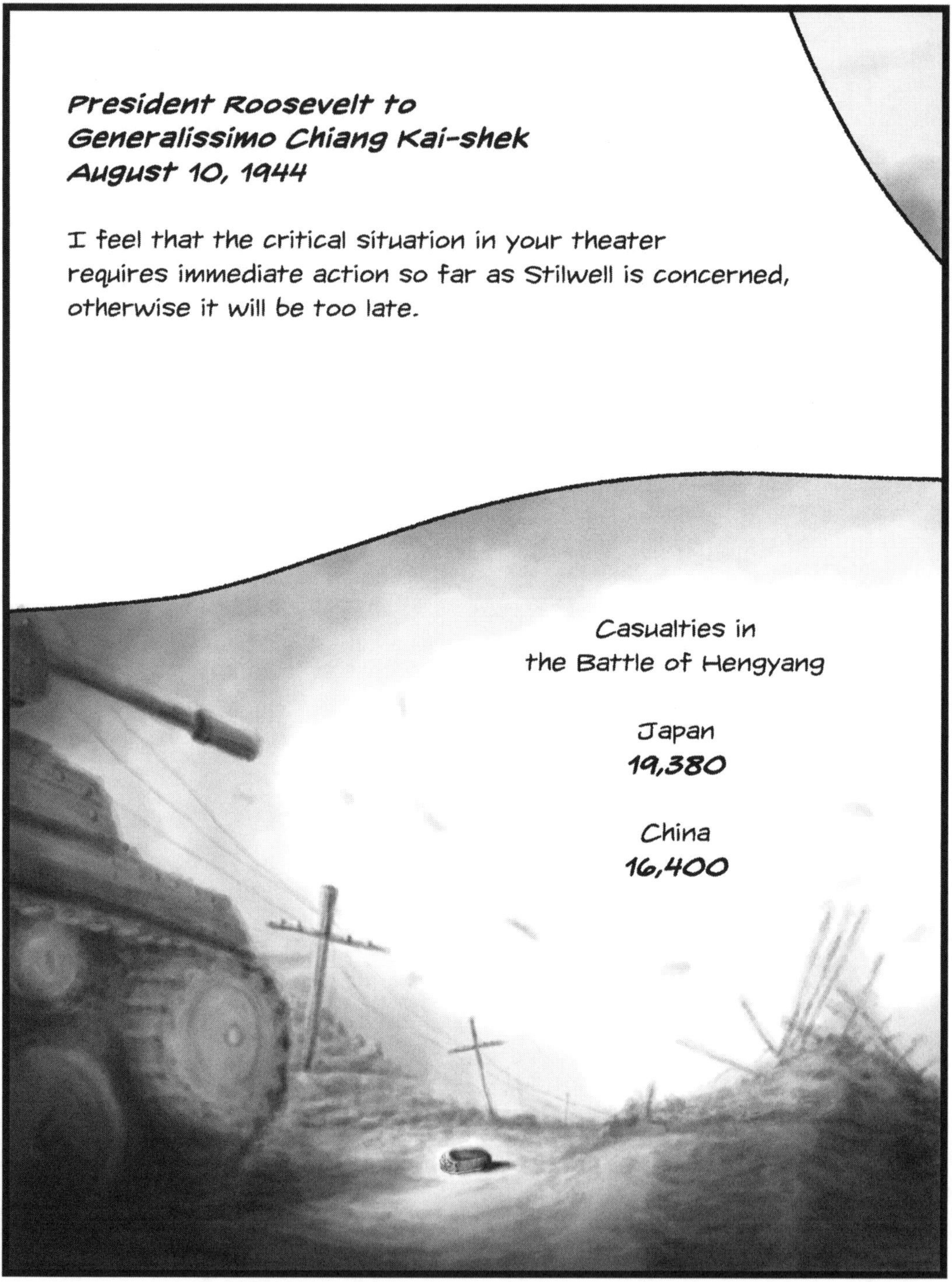
President Roosevelt to
Generalissimo Chiang Kai-shek
August 10, 1944
I feel that the critical situation in your theater requires immediate action so far as Stilwell is concerned, otherwise it will be too late.
Casualties in the Battle of Hengyang
Japan
19,380
China
16,400

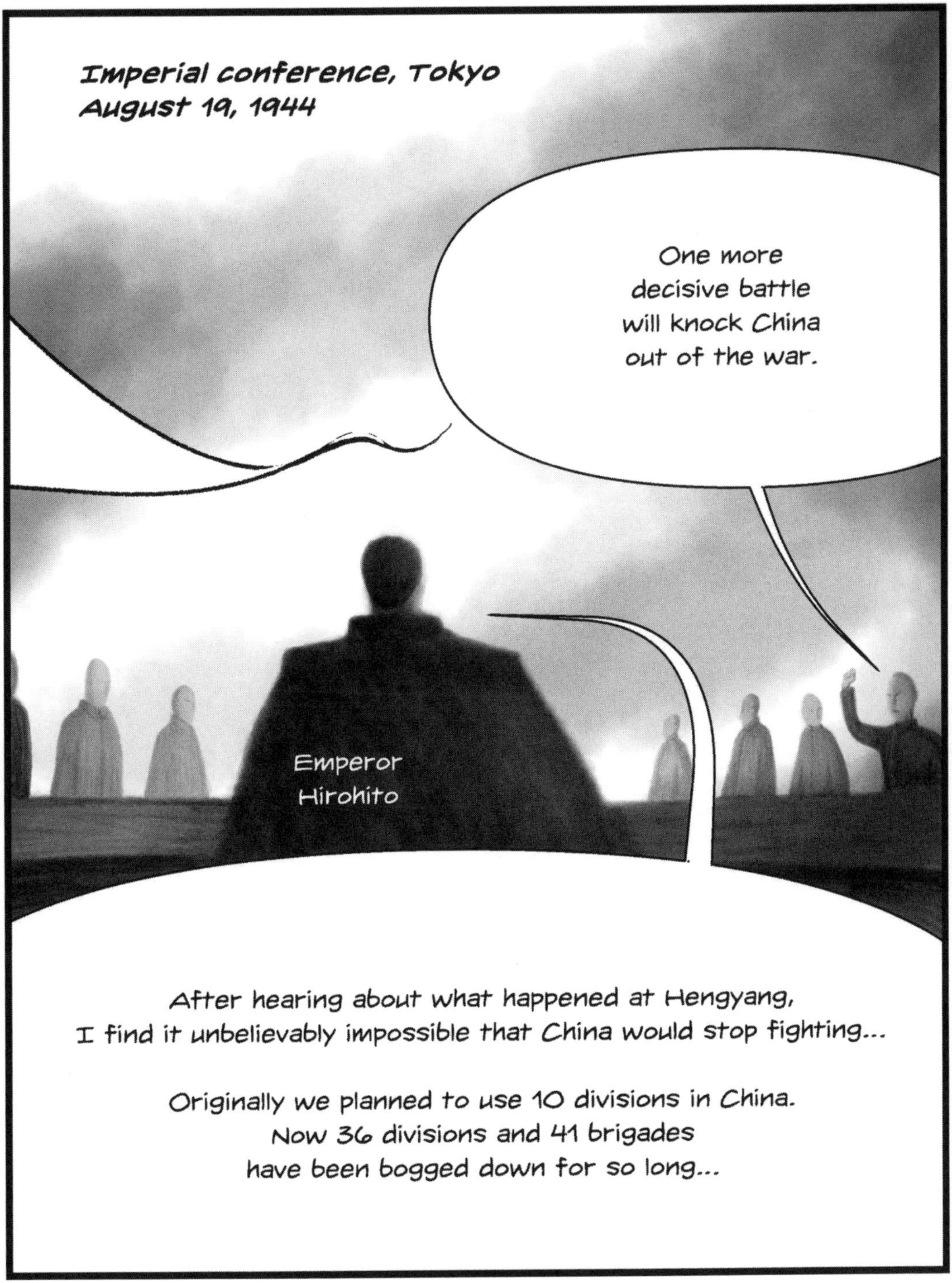
Imperial conference, Tokyo
August 19, 1944
One more decisive battle will knock China out of the war.
Emperor Hirohito
After hearing about what happened at Hengyang, I find it unbelievably impossible that China would stop fighting...
Originally we planned to use 10 divisions in China. Now 36 divisions and 41 brigades have been bogged down for so long...

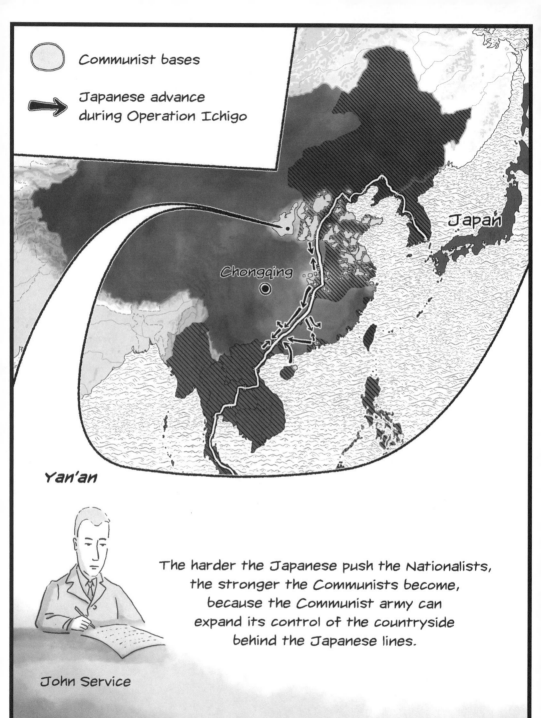

Communist bases

Japanese advance during Operation Ichigo

Chongqing

Japan

Yan'an

The harder the Japanese push the Nationalists, the stronger the Communists become, because the Communist army can expand its control of the countryside behind the Japanese lines.

John Service

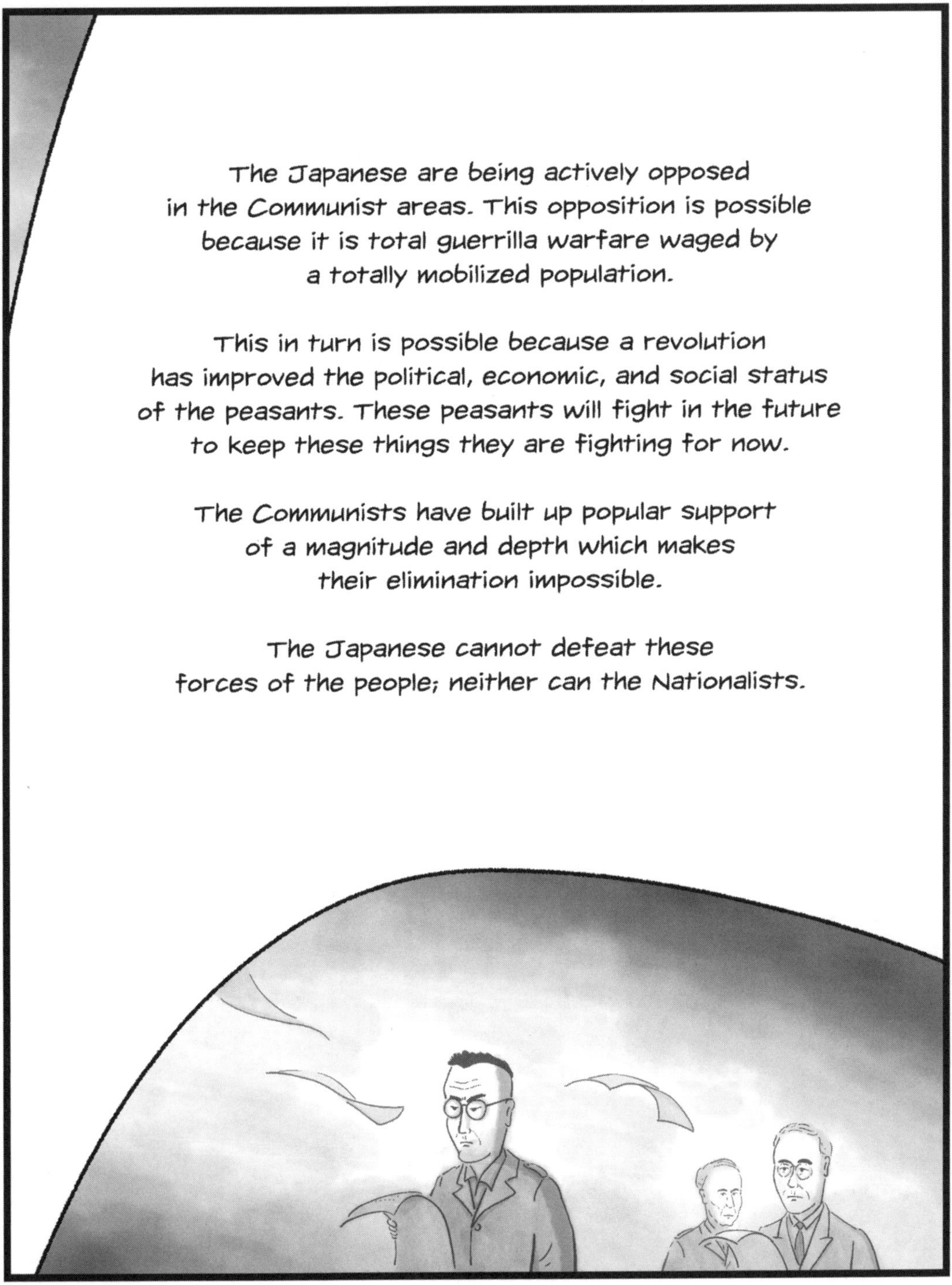
The Japanese are being actively opposed in the Communist areas. This opposition is possible because it is total guerrilla warfare waged by a totally mobilized population.
This in turn is possible because a revolution has improved the political, economic, and social status of the peasants. These peasants will fight in the future to keep these things they are fighting for now.
The Communists have built up popular support of a magnitude and depth which makes their elimination impossible.
The Japanese cannot defeat these forces of the people; neither can the Nationalists.

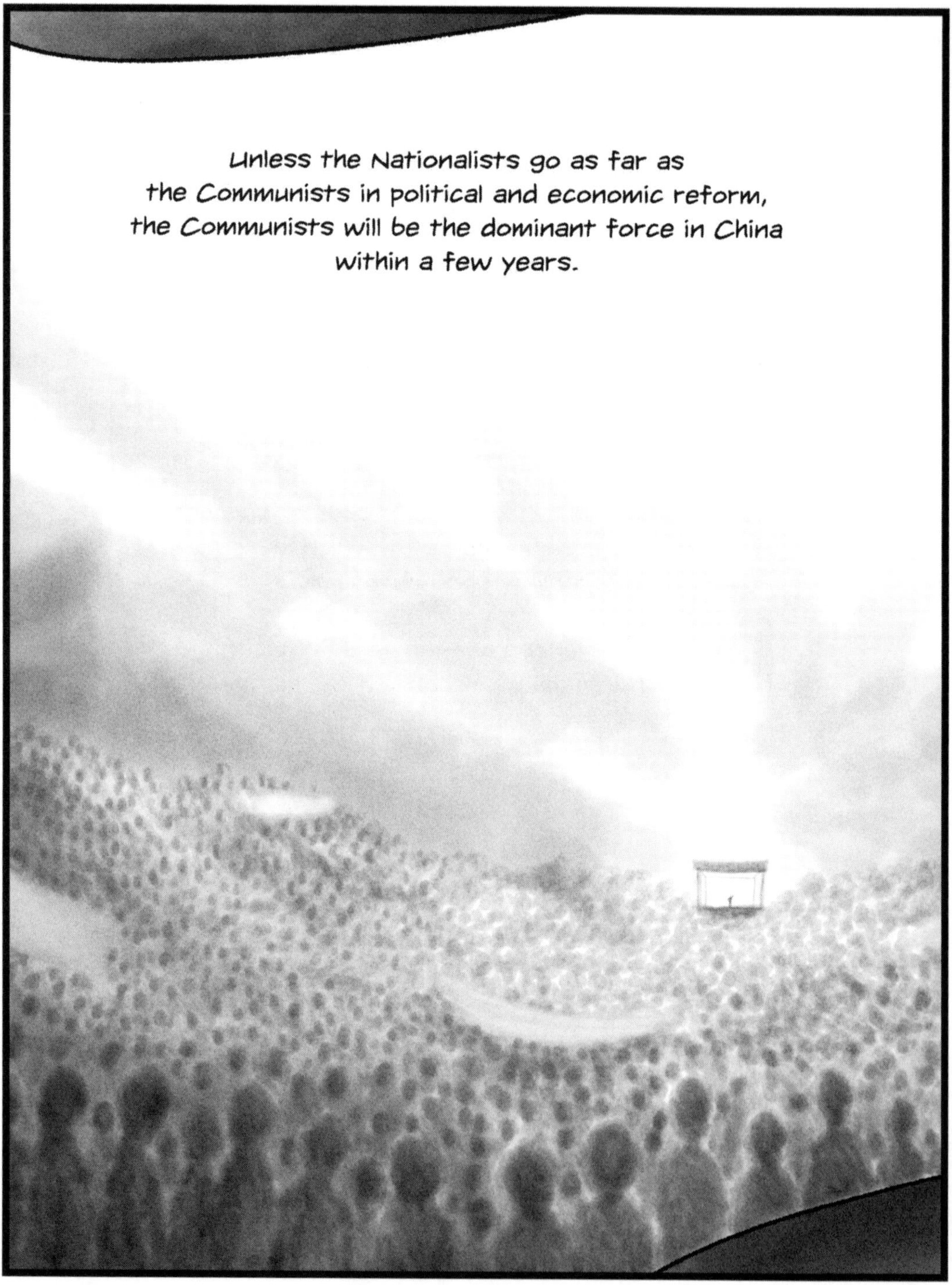
Unless the Nationalists go as far as the Communists in political and economic reform, the Communists will be the dominant force in China within a few years.

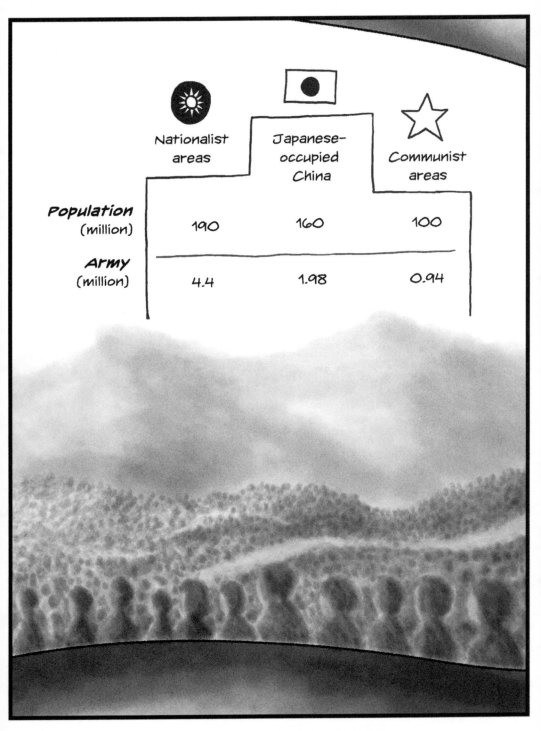

	Nationalist areas	Japanese-occupied China	Communist areas
Population (million)	190	160	100
Army (million)	4.4	1.98	0.94

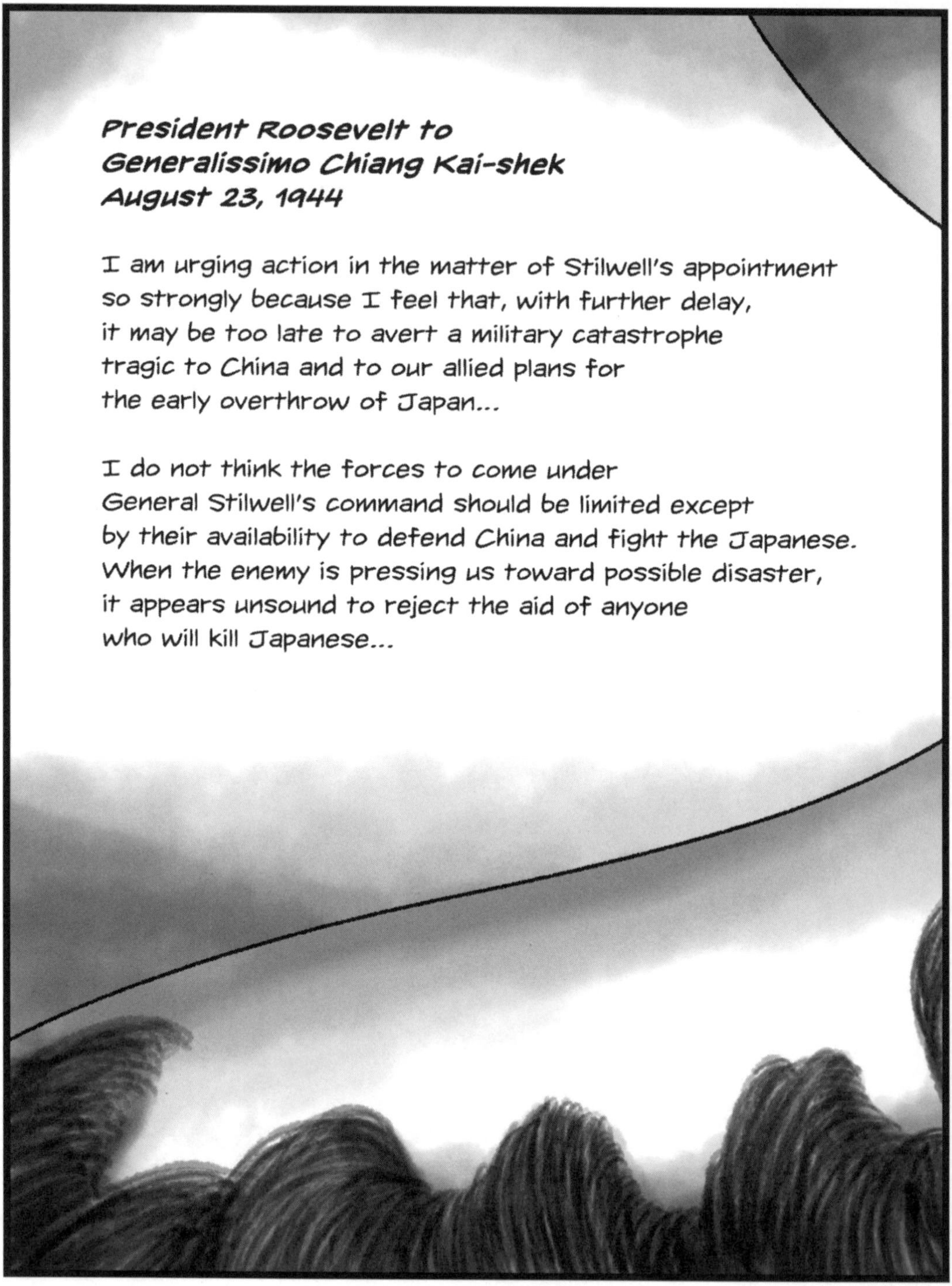
President Roosevelt to
Generalissimo Chiang Kai-shek
August 23, 1944
I am urging action in the matter of Stilwell's appointment so strongly because I feel that, with further delay, it may be too late to avert a military catastrophe tragic to China and to our allied plans for the early overthrow of Japan...
I do not think the forces to come under General Stilwell's command should be limited except by their availability to defend China and fight the Japanese. When the enemy is pressing us toward possible disaster, it appears unsound to reject the aid of anyone who will kill Japanese...

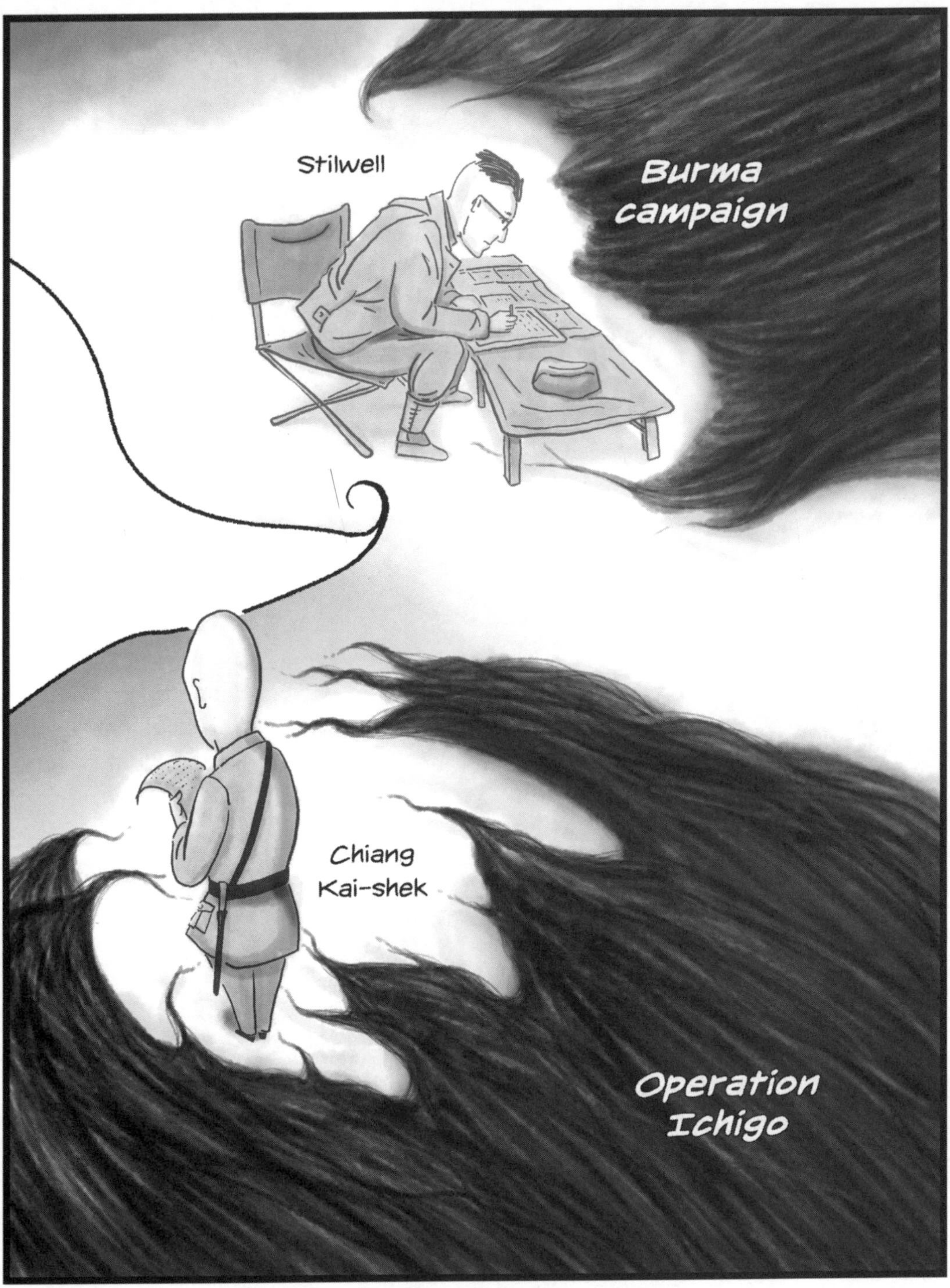
Stilwell
Burma campaign
Chiang Kai-shek
Operation Ichigo

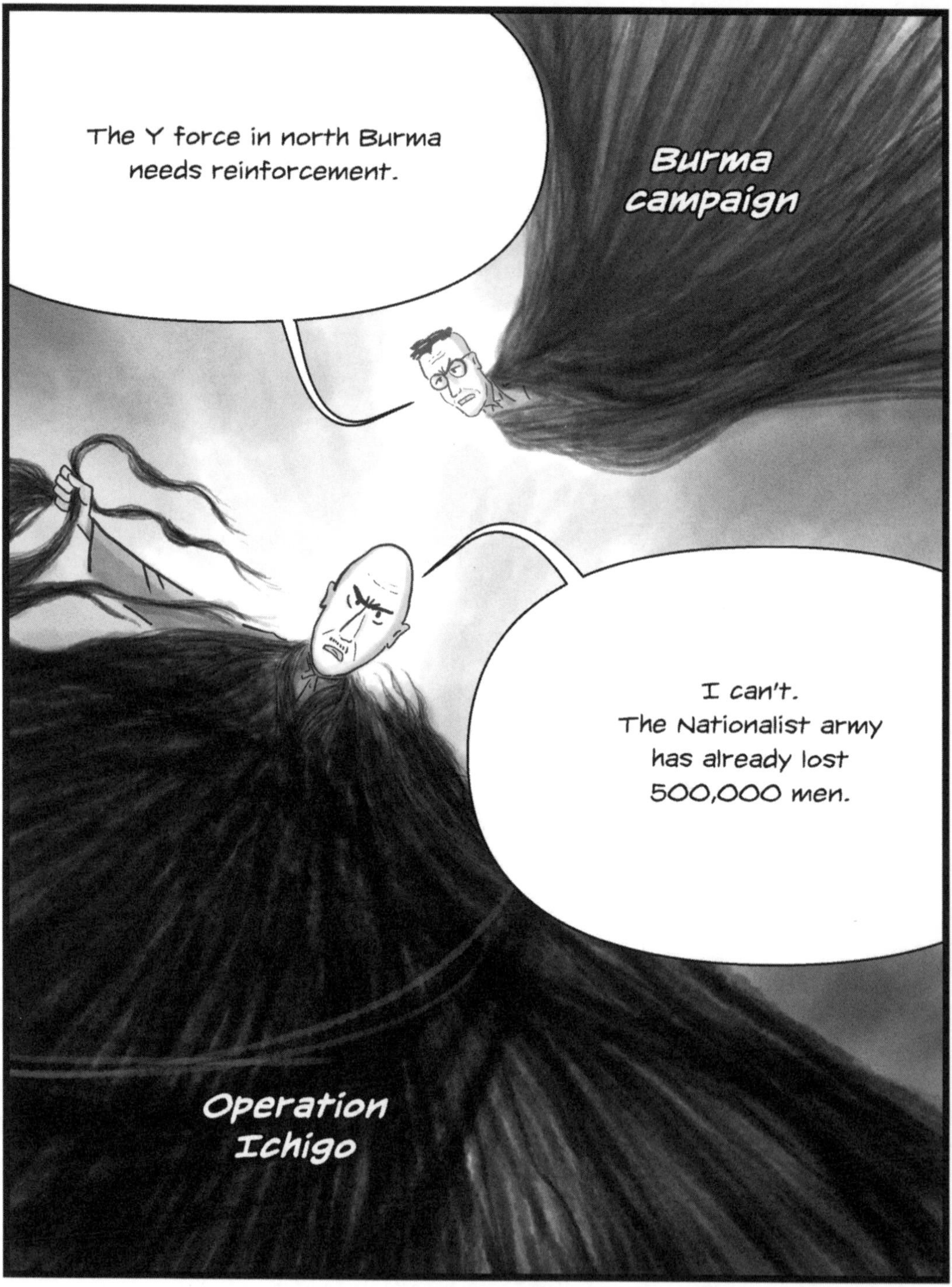
The Y force in north Burma needs reinforcement.
Burma campaign
I can't. The Nationalist army has already lost 500,000 men.
Operation Ichigo

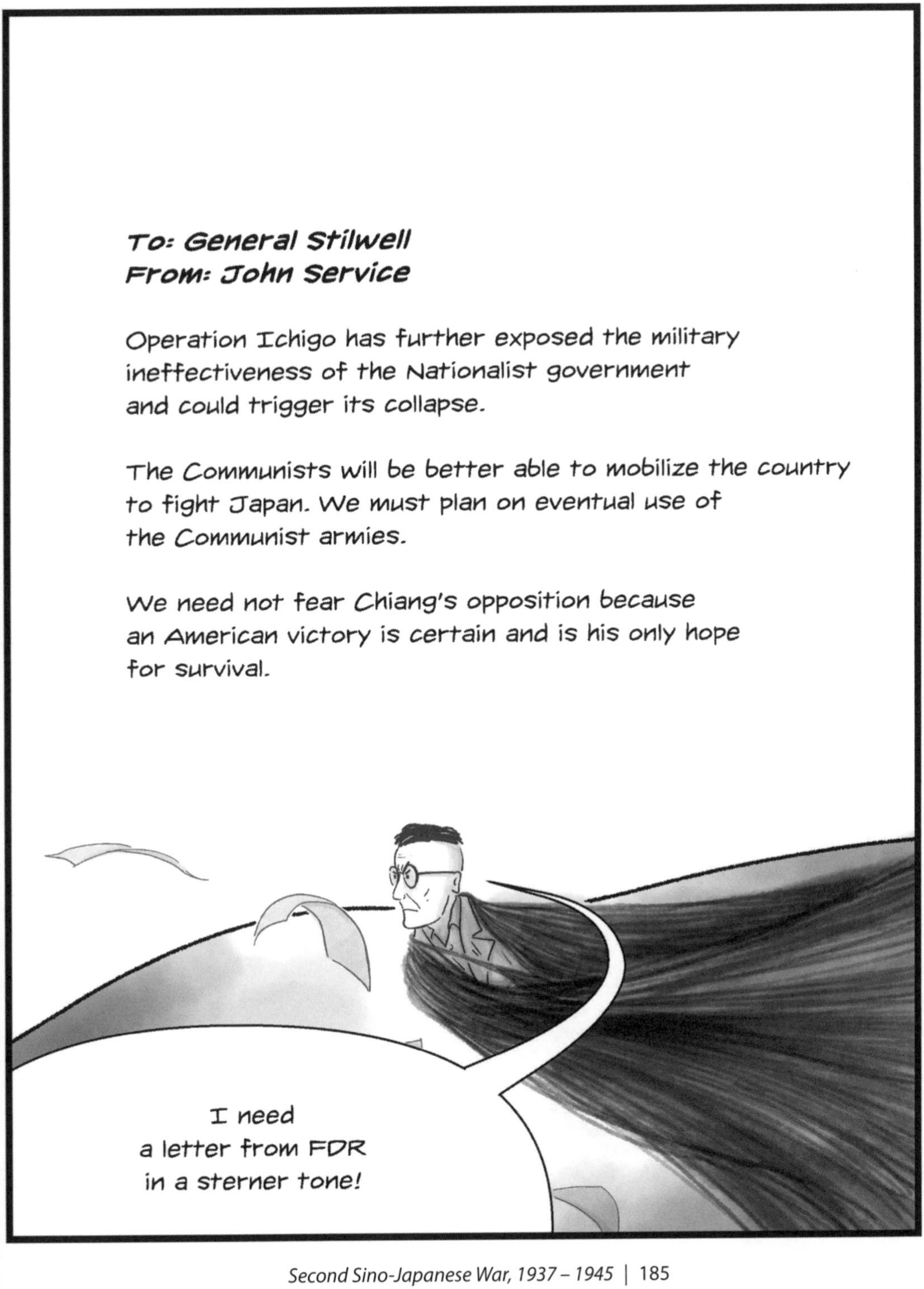
To: General Stilwell
From: John Service
Operation Ichigo has further exposed the military ineffectiveness of the Nationalist government and could trigger its collapse.
The Communists will be better able to mobilize the country to fight Japan. We must plan on eventual use of the Communist armies.
We need not fear Chiang's opposition because an American victory is certain and is his only hope for survival.
I need a letter from FDR in a sterner tone!

President Roosevelt to Generalissimo Chiang Kai-shek September 18, 1944

If you do not provide manpower for your divisions in north Burma and, if you fail to send reinforcements to the Y force, we will lose all chance of opening land communications with China and immediately jeopardize the air route over the Hump. For this you must yourself be prepared to accept the consequences and assume the personal responsibility.

I have urged time and again in recent months that you take drastic action to resist the disaster which has been moving closer to China and to you. Now, when you have not yet placed General Stilwell in command of all forces in China, we are faced with the loss of a critical area in south China with possible catastrophic consequences...

It appears plainly evident to all of us here that all your and our efforts to save China are to be lost by further delays.

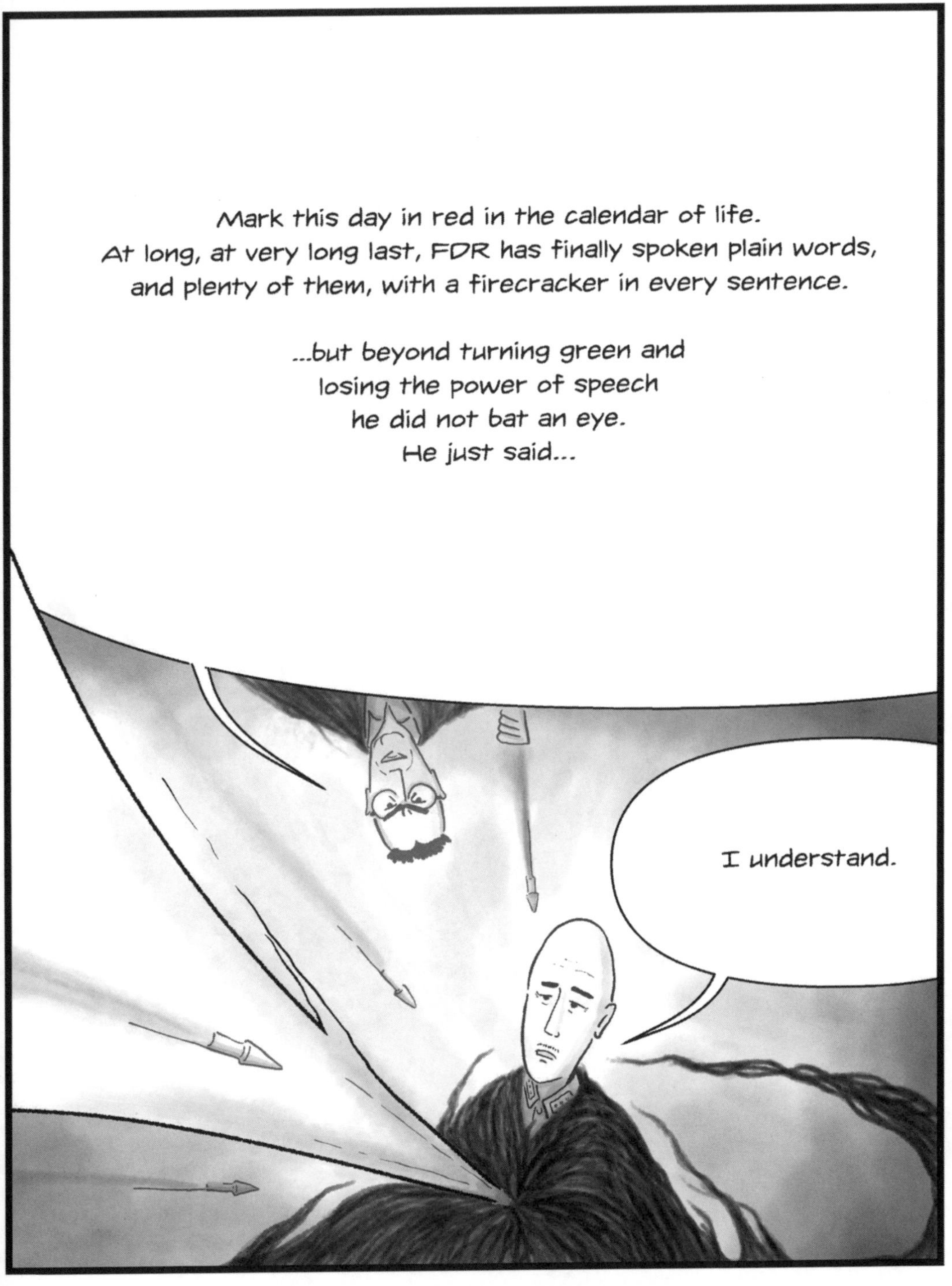
Mark this day in red in the calendar of life.
At long, at very long last, FDR has finally spoken plain words, and plenty of them, with a firecracker in every sentence.
...but beyond turning green and losing the power of speech he did not bat an eye. He just said...
I understand.

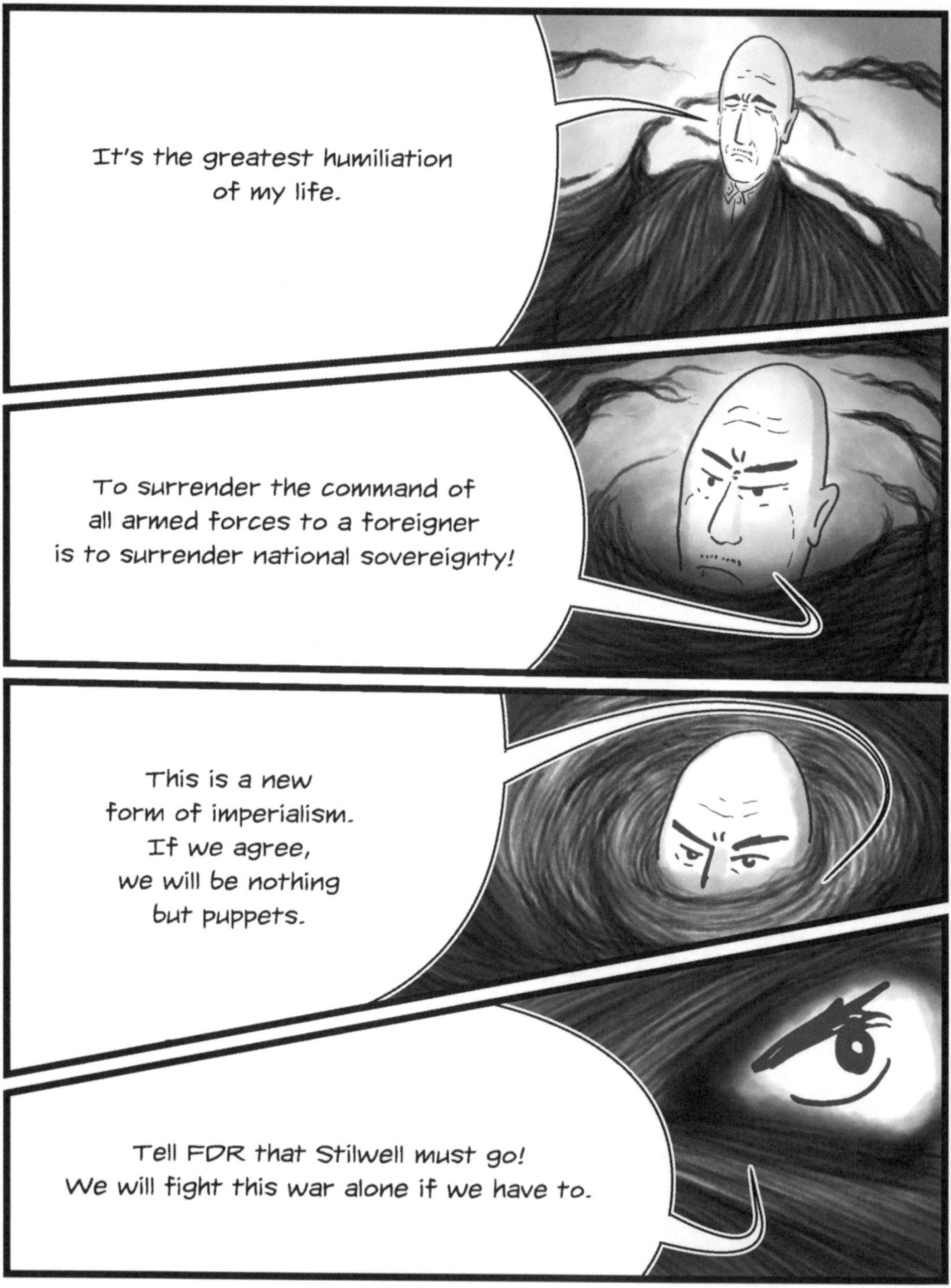
It's the greatest humiliation of my life.
To surrender the command of all armed forces to a foreigner is to surrender national sovereignty!
This is a new form of imperialism. If we agree, we will be nothing but puppets.
Tell FDR that Stilwell must go! We will fight this war alone if we have to.

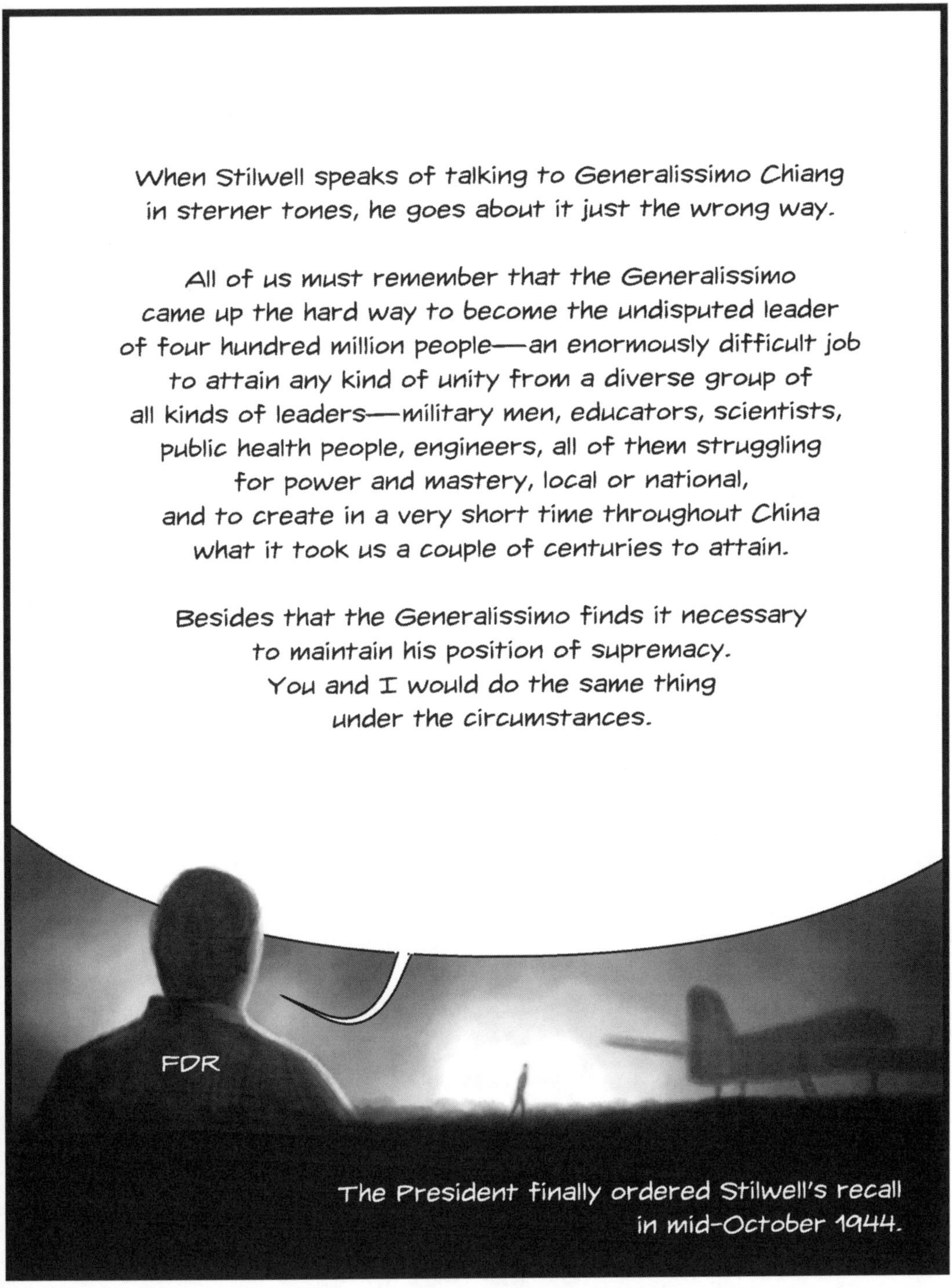
When Stilwell speaks of talking to Generalissimo Chiang in sterner tones, he goes about it just the wrong way.
All of us must remember that the Generalissimo came up the hard way to become the undisputed leader of four hundred million people—an enormously difficult job to attain any kind of unity from a diverse group of all kinds of leaders—military men, educators, scientists, public health people, engineers, all of them struggling for power and mastery, local or national, and to create in a very short time throughout China what it took us a couple of centuries to attain.
Besides that the Generalissimo finds it necessary to maintain his position of supremacy. You and I would do the same thing under the circumstances.
FDR
The President finally ordered Stilwell's recall in mid-October 1944.

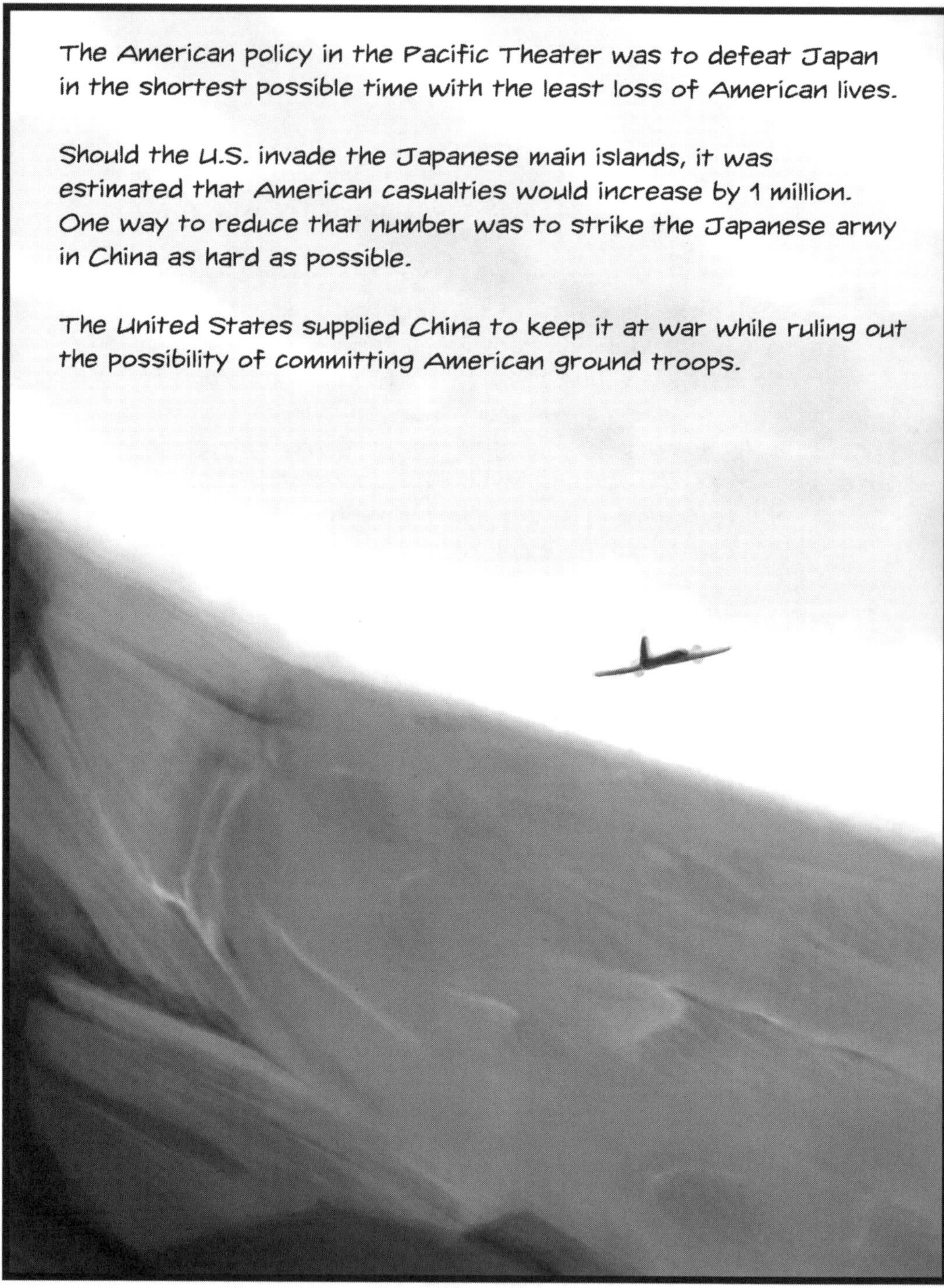
The American policy in the Pacific Theater was to defeat Japan in the shortest possible time with the least loss of American lives.
Should the U.S. invade the Japanese main islands, it was estimated that American casualties would increase by 1 million. One way to reduce that number was to strike the Japanese army in China as hard as possible.
The United States supplied China to keep it at war while ruling out the possibility of committing American ground troops.

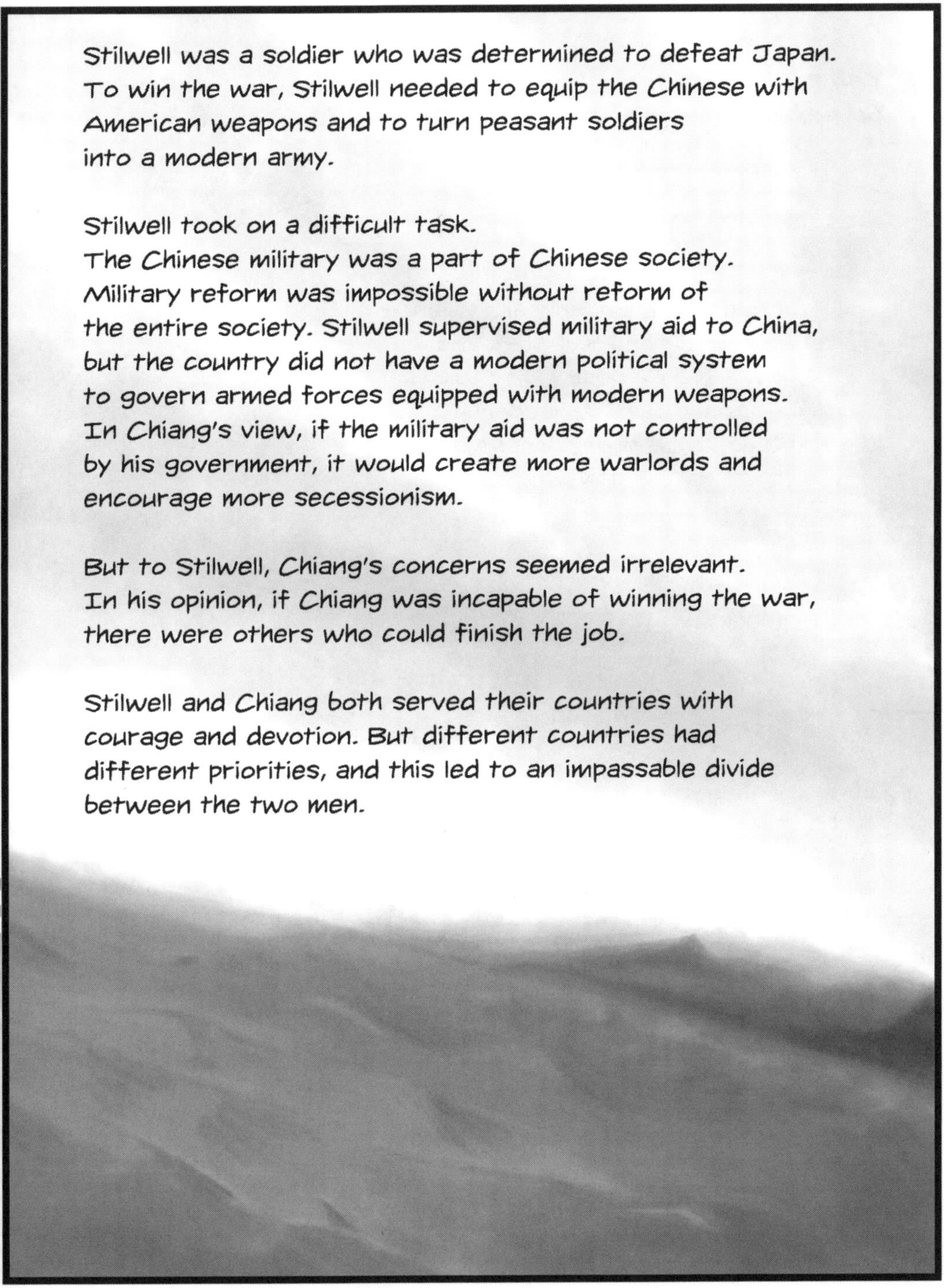
Stilwell was a soldier who was determined to defeat Japan. To win the war, Stilwell needed to equip the Chinese with American weapons and to turn peasant soldiers into a modern army.
Stilwell took on a difficult task. The Chinese military was a part of Chinese society. Military reform was impossible without reform of the entire society. Stilwell supervised military aid to China, but the country did not have a modern political system to govern armed forces equipped with modern weapons. In Chiang's view, if the military aid was not controlled by his government, it would create more warlords and encourage more secessionism.
But to Stilwell, Chiang's concerns seemed irrelevant. In his opinion, if Chiang was incapable of winning the war, there were others who could finish the job.
Stilwell and Chiang both served their countries with courage and devotion. But different countries had different priorities, and this led to an impassable divide between the two men.

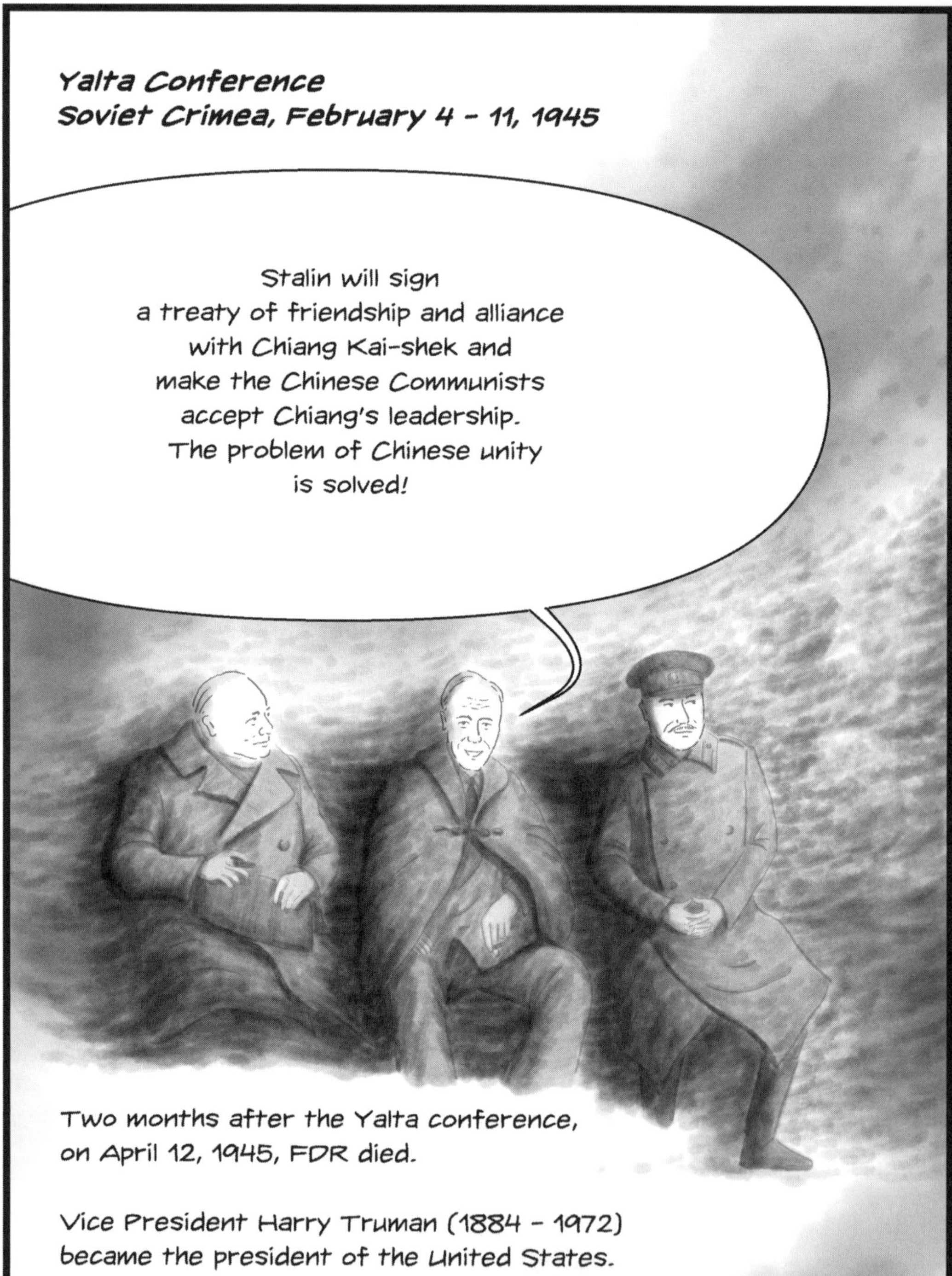
Yalta Conference
Soviet Crimea, February 4 - 11, 1945
Stalin will sign a treaty of friendship and alliance with Chiang Kai-shek and make the Chinese Communists accept Chiang's leadership. The problem of Chinese unity is solved!
Two months after the Yalta conference, on April 12, 1945, FDR died.
Vice President Harry Truman (1884 - 1972) became the president of the United States.

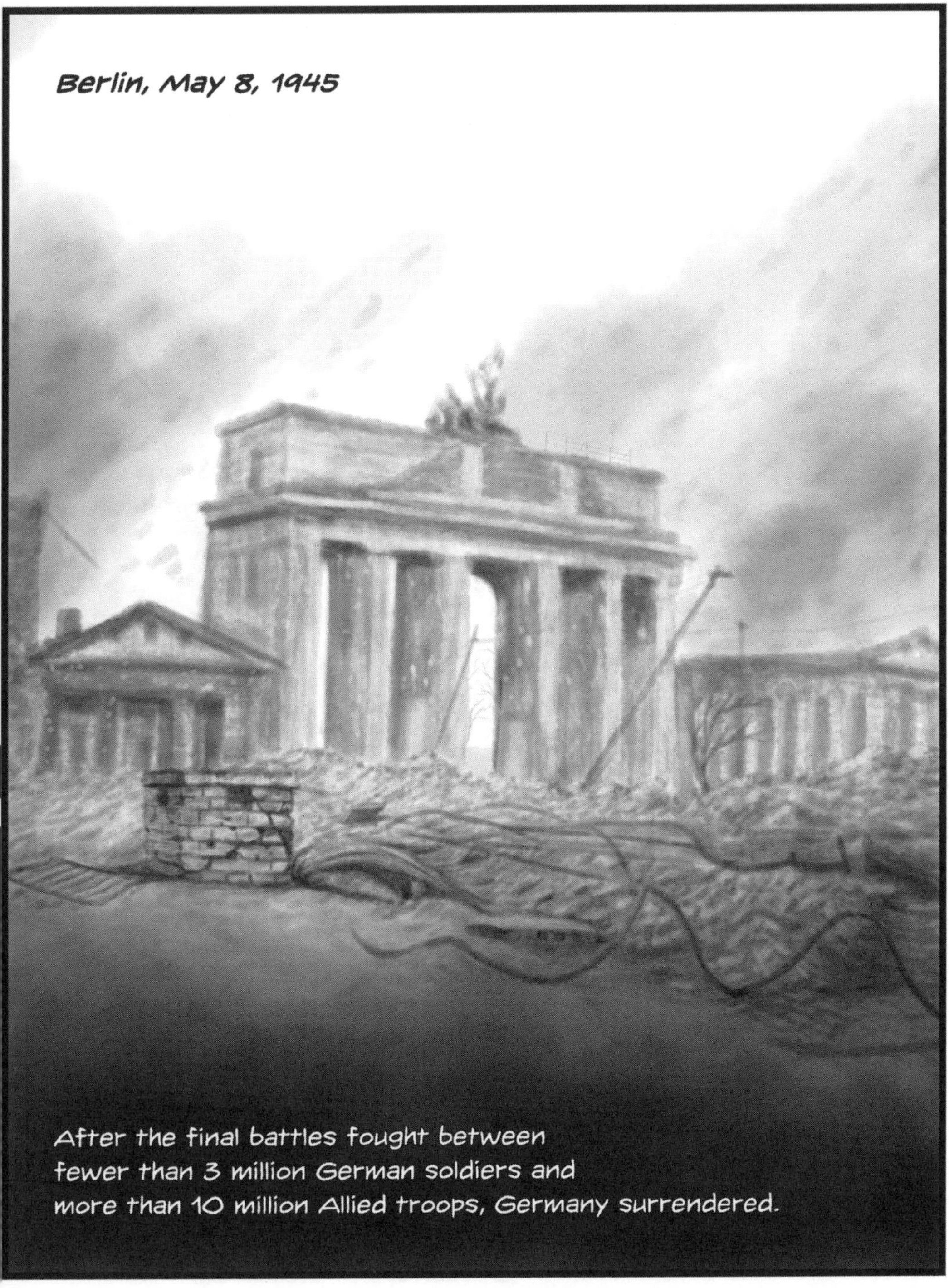
Berlin, May 8, 1945
After the final battles fought between fewer than 3 million German soldiers and more than 10 million Allied troops, Germany surrendered.

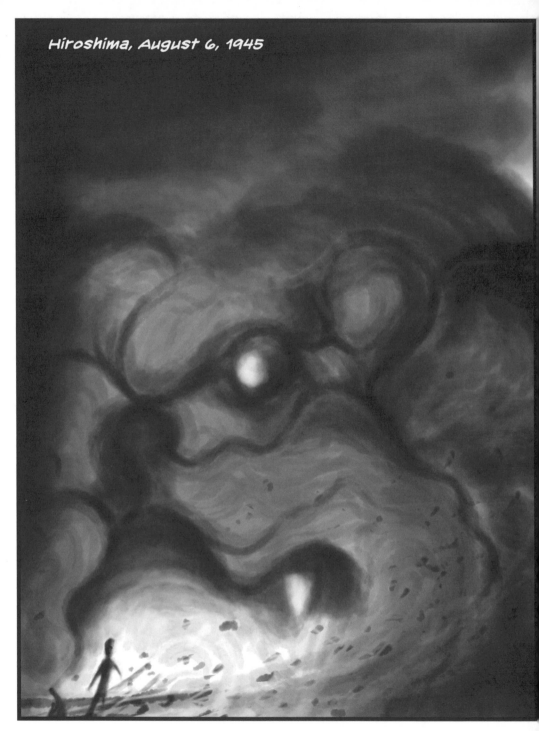

Hiroshima, August 6, 1945

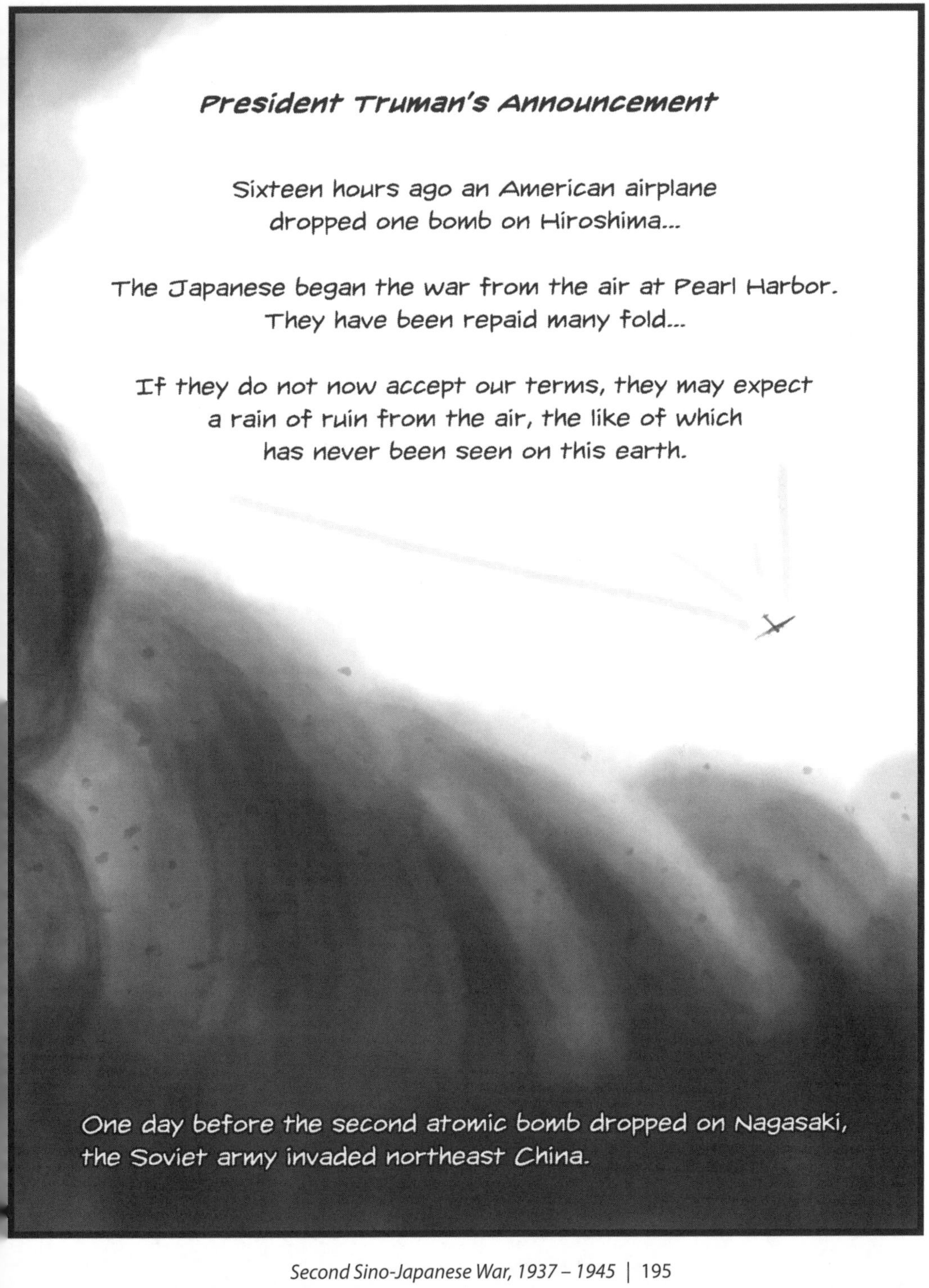
President Truman's Announcement
Sixteen hours ago an American airplane dropped one bomb on Hiroshima...
The Japanese began the war from the air at Pearl Harbor. They have been repaid many fold...
If they do not now accept our terms, they may expect a rain of ruin from the air, the like of which has never been seen on this earth.
One day before the second atomic bomb dropped on Nagasaki, the Soviet army invaded northeast China.

Tokyo, August 15, 1945
Emperor Hirohito's Radio Announcement

To our good and loyal subjects:

We have ordered our government to communicate
to the governments of the United States, Great Britain,
China, and the Soviet Union that our empire accepts
the provisions of their Joint Declaration*...

Indeed, we declared war on America and Britain
out of our sincere desire to ensure Japan's self-preservation
and the stabilization of East Asia...

Despite the best that has been done by everyone,
the war situation has developed not necessarily to
Japan's advantage, while the general trends of the world
have all turned against her interest.

* The Proclamation Defining Terms for Japanese Surrender
  was issued at Potsdam, Germany on July 26, 1945.

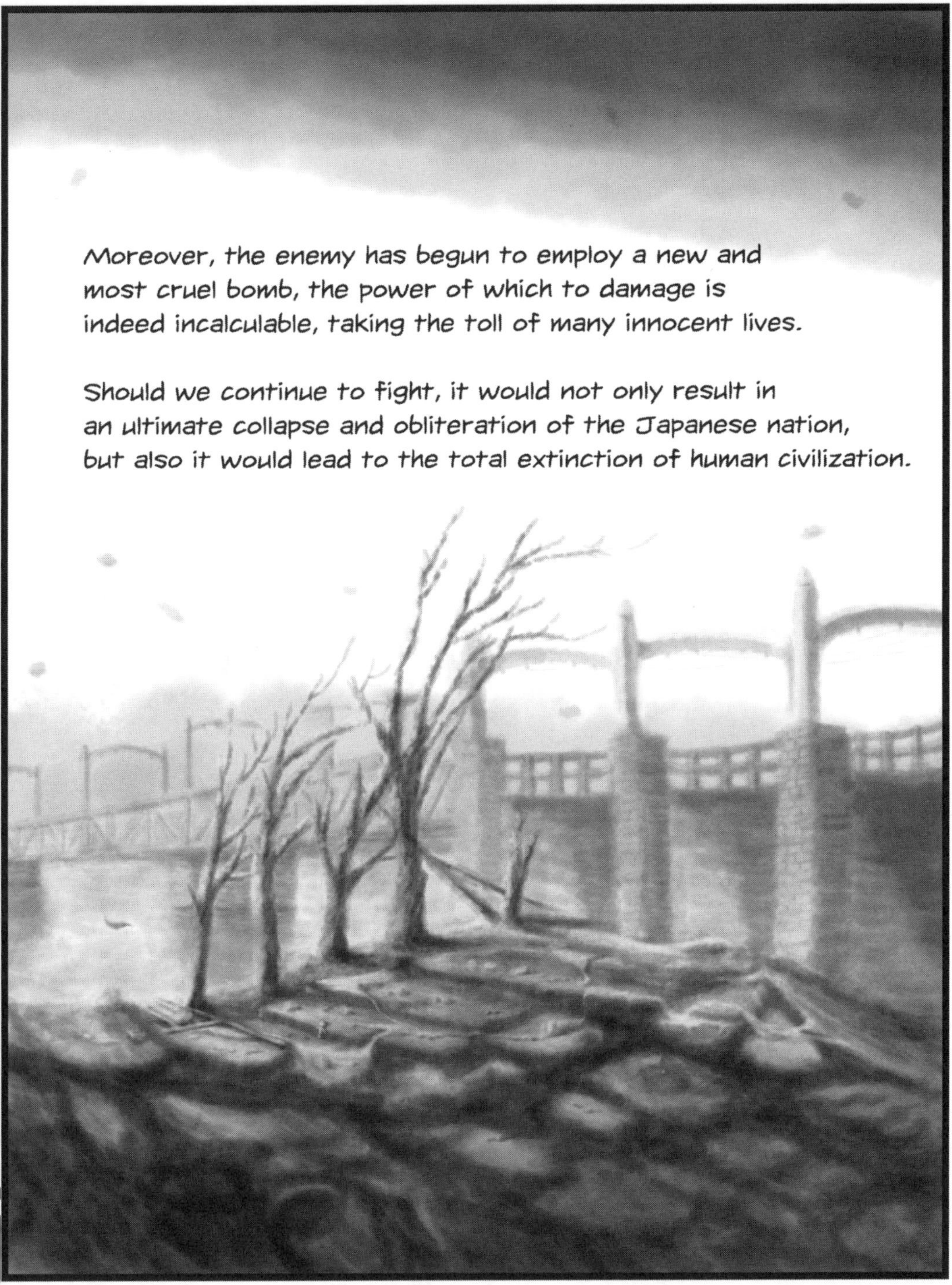
Moreover, the enemy has begun to employ a new and most cruel bomb, the power of which to damage is indeed incalculable, taking the toll of many innocent lives.
Should we continue to fight, it would not only result in an ultimate collapse and obliteration of the Japanese nation, but also it would lead to the total extinction of human civilization.

Chongqing, August 15, 1945

Generalissimo Chiang Kai-shek's Victory Broadcast

Today victory is won in our war of resistance.
Right will triumph over might—this great truth
has been finally spoken!

For the peace that lies before us
we are grateful to our soldiers and civilians
who so bravely sacrificed their lives.
We are grateful to our Allies
who fought by our side for freedom.
Christians all over the world are grateful
to our righteous and merciful God.

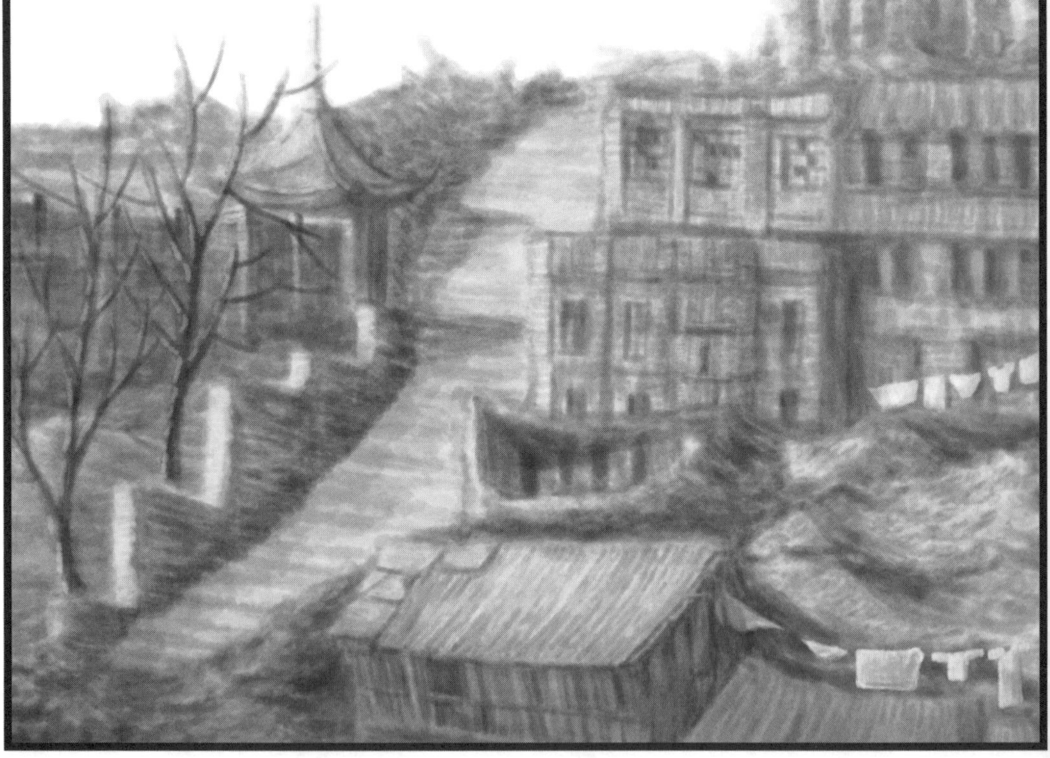

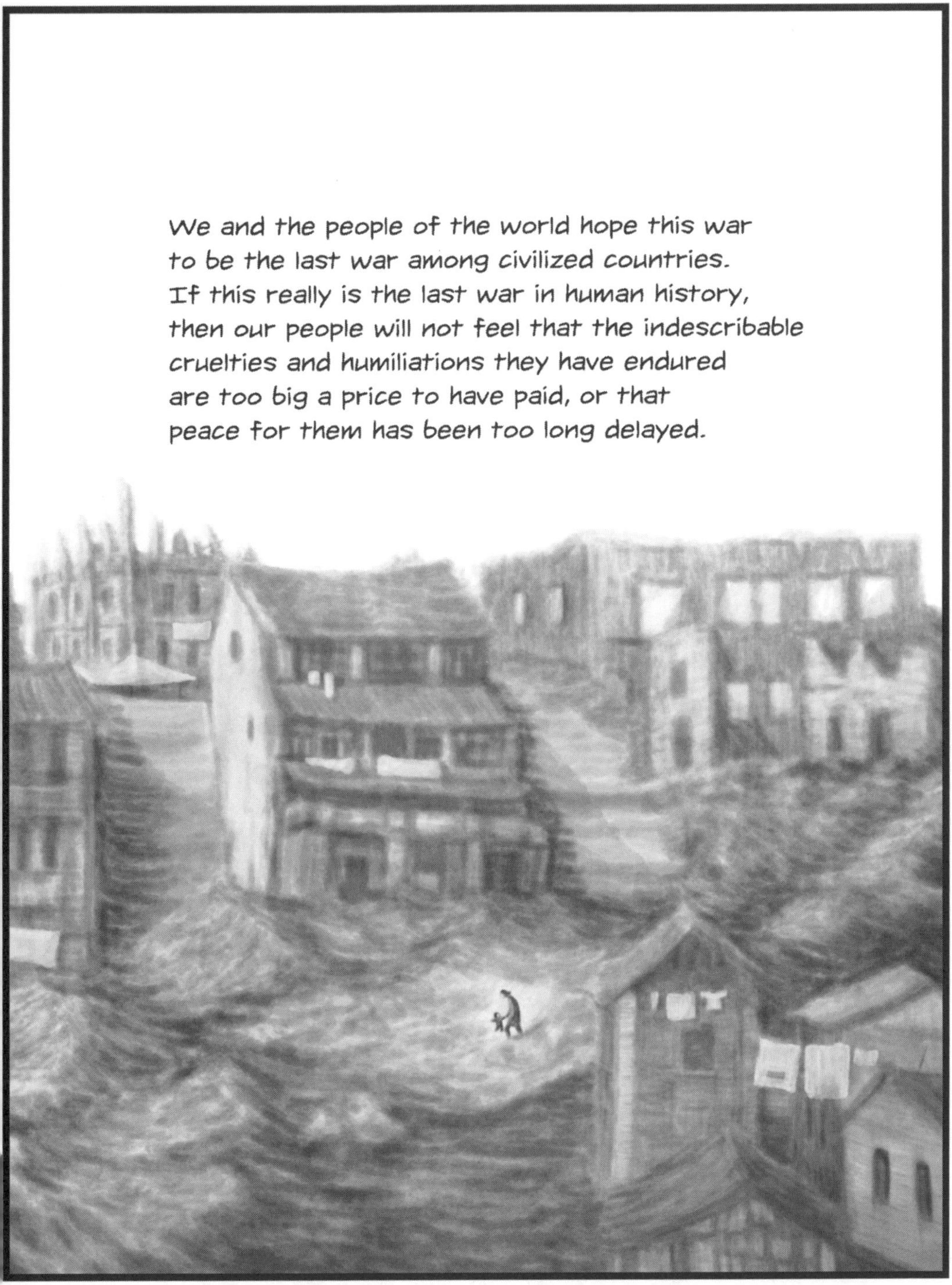
We and the people of the world hope this war
to be the last war among civilized countries.
If this really is the last war in human history,
then our people will not feel that the indescribable
cruelties and humiliations they have endured
are too big a price to have paid, or that
peace for them has been too long delayed.

September 2, 1945
Japan signs the unconditional surrender.
WWII ended.

Around 75 million people, or 3% of the world's population
at the time, died in World War II.

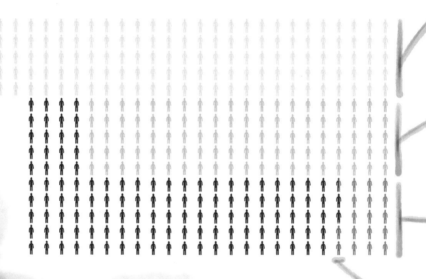

🧍 = 200,000 people

Civilian and military deaths
(million)

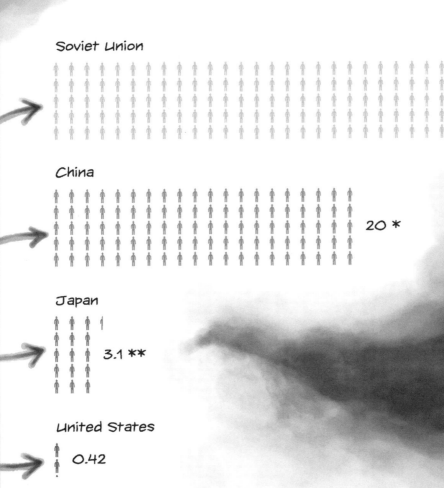

Soviet Union

27

China

20 *

Japan

3.1 **

United States

0.42

* Including more than 3 million military deaths

** Including 2.12 million military deaths,
of which 0.54 million were in China

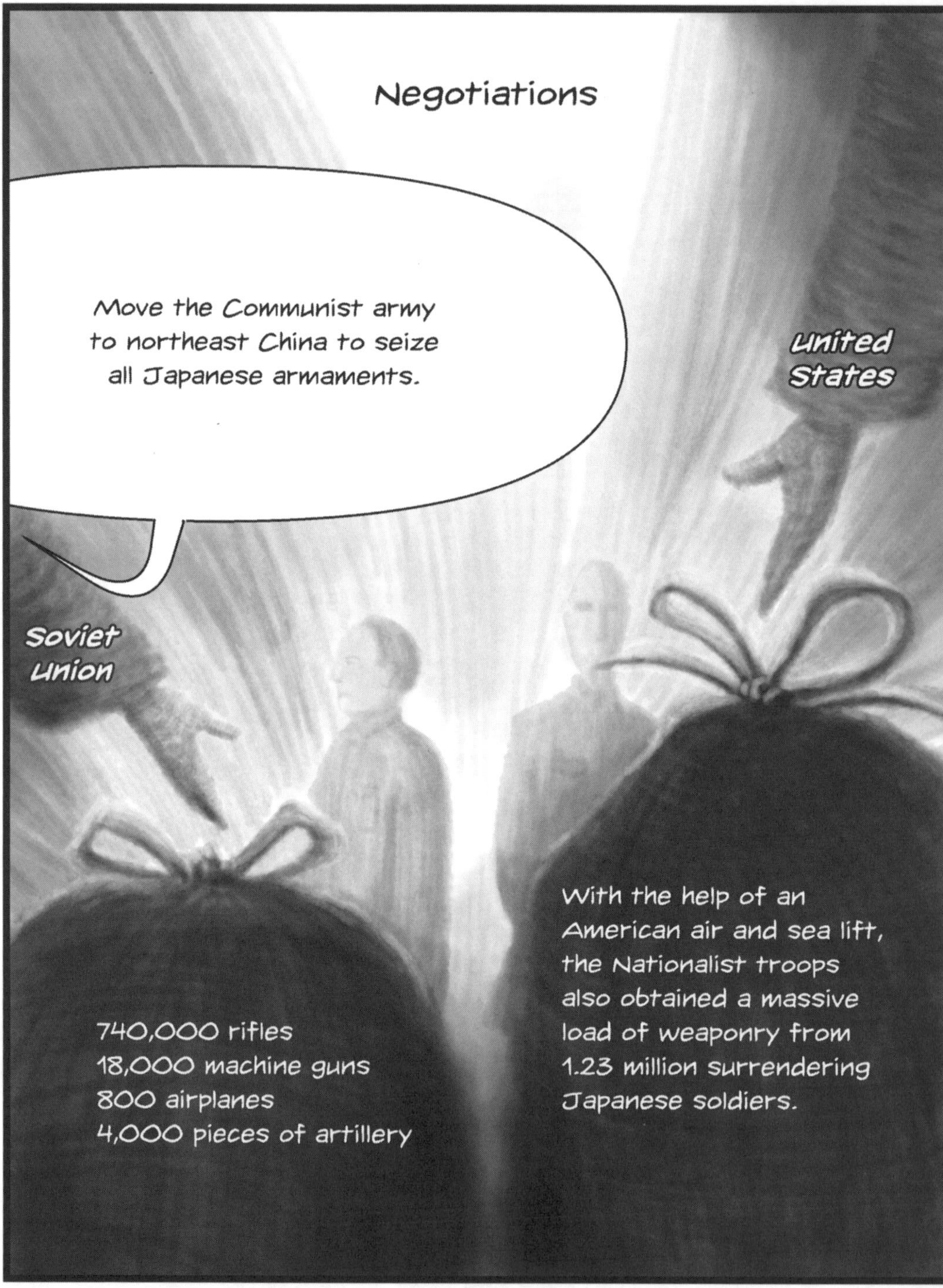
Negotiations
Move the Communist army to northeast China to seize all Japanese armaments.
United States
Soviet Union
740,000 rifles
18,000 machine guns
800 airplanes
4,000 pieces of artillery
With the help of an American air and sea lift, the Nationalist troops also obtained a massive load of weaponry from 1.23 million surrendering Japanese soldiers.

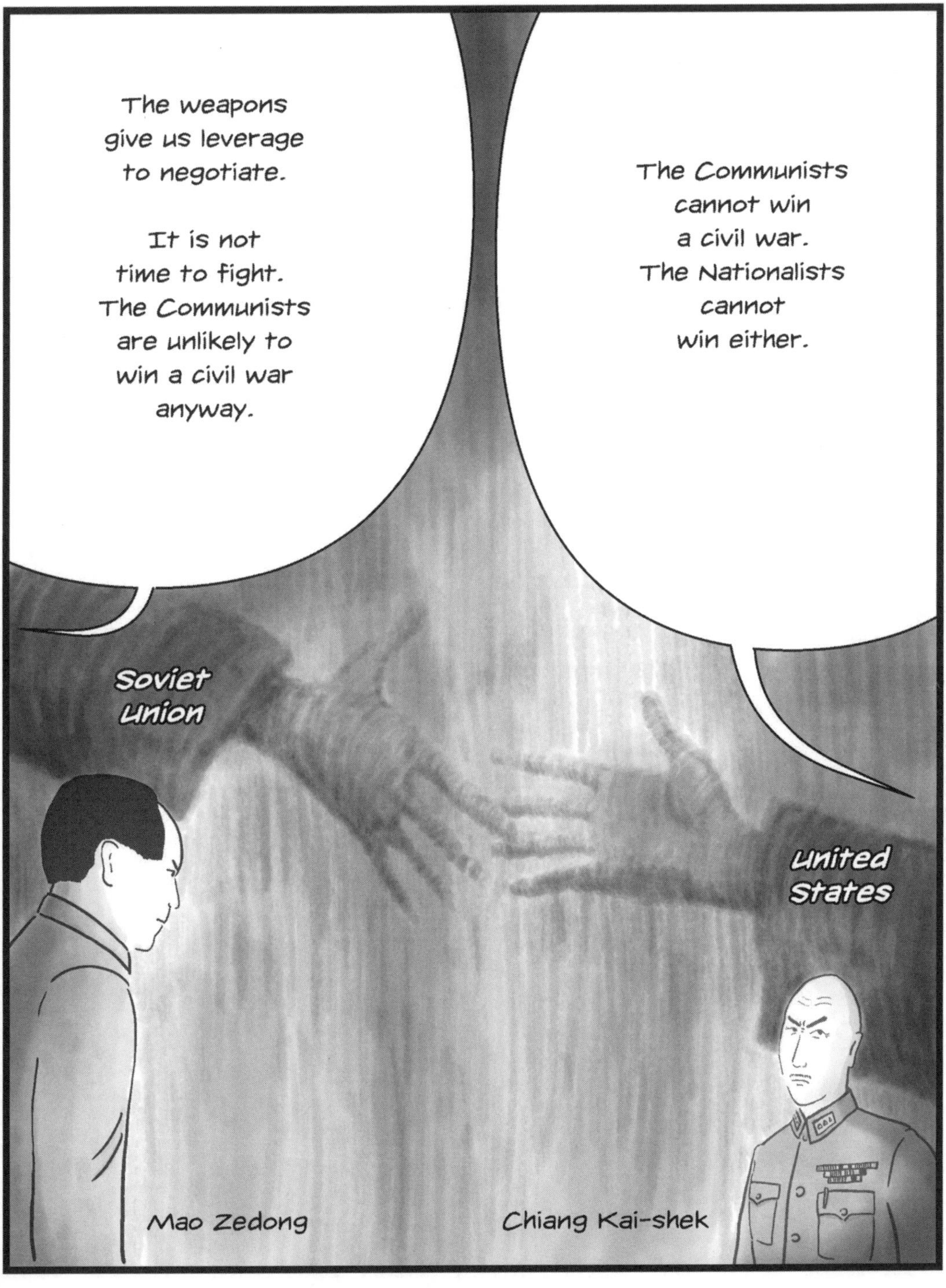
The weapons give us leverage to negotiate.
It is not time to fight. The Communists are unlikely to win a civil war anyway.
The Communists cannot win a civil war. The Nationalists cannot win either.
Soviet Union
United States
Mao Zedong
Chiang Kai-shek

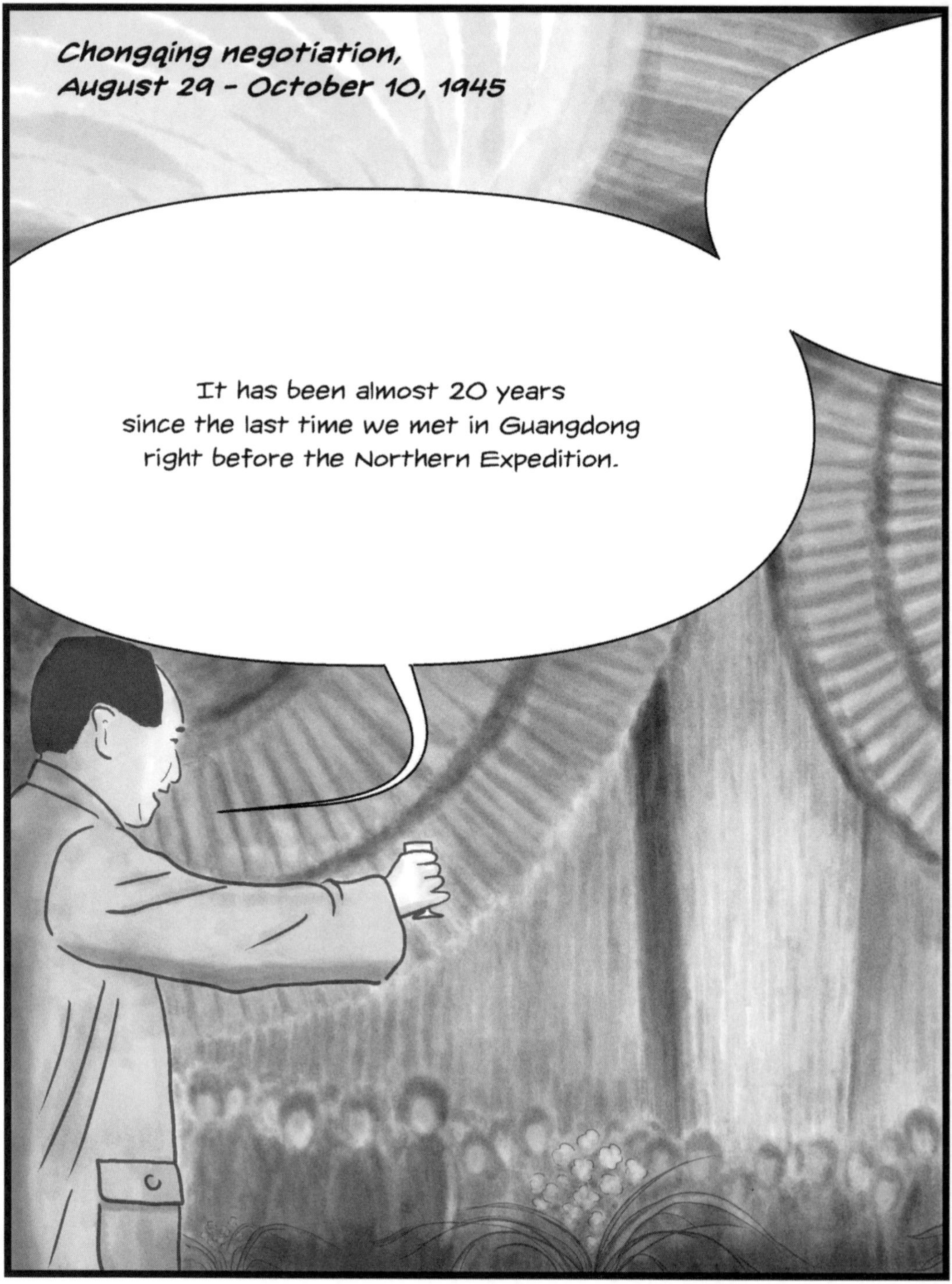
Chongqing negotiation,
August 29 - October 10, 1945
It has been almost 20 years since the last time we met in Guangdong right before the Northern Expedition.

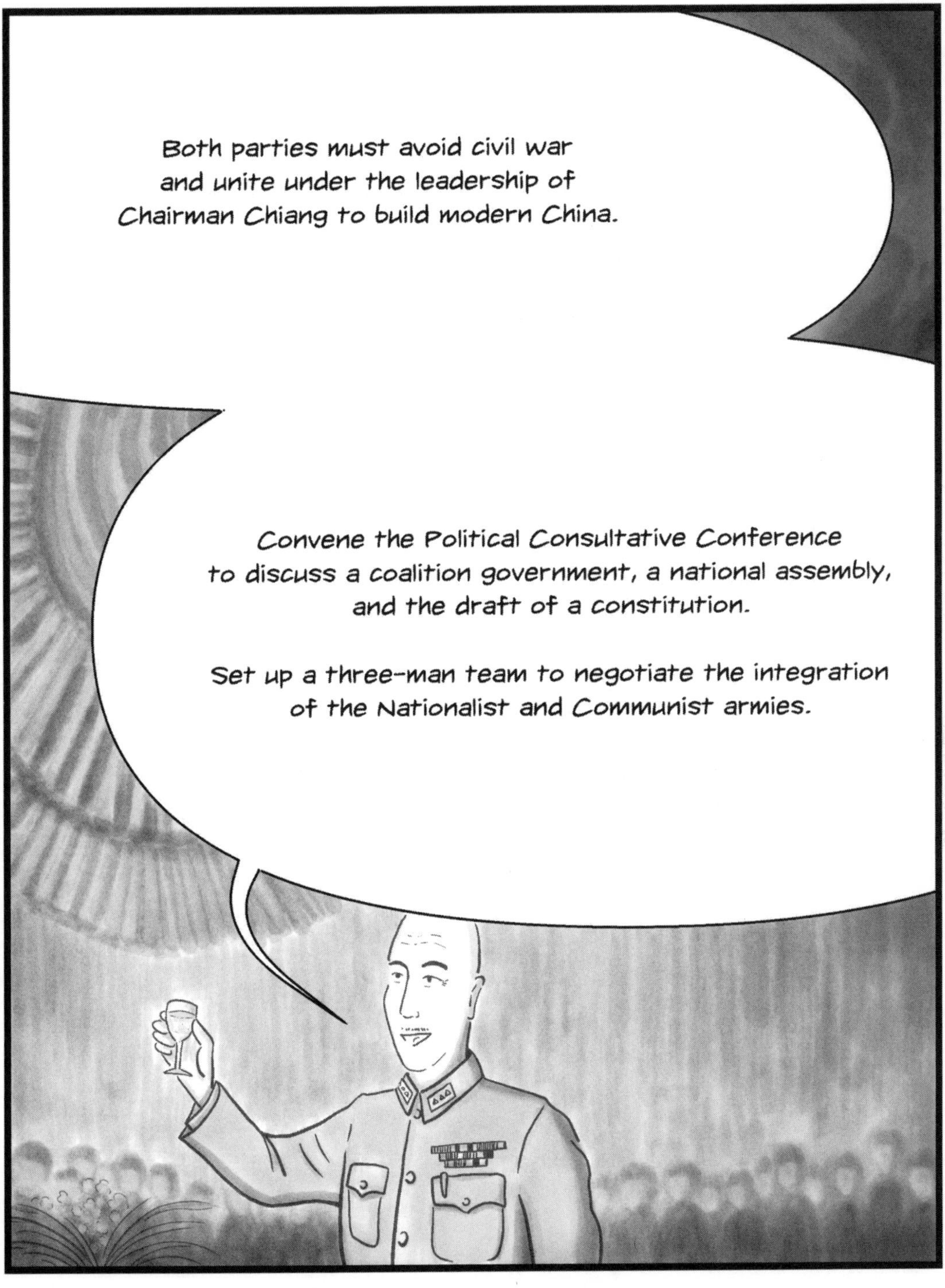
Both parties must avoid civil war and unite under the leadership of Chairman Chiang to build modern China.
Convene the Political Consultative Conference to discuss a coalition government, a national assembly, and the draft of a constitution.
Set up a three-man team to negotiate the integration of the Nationalist and Communist armies.

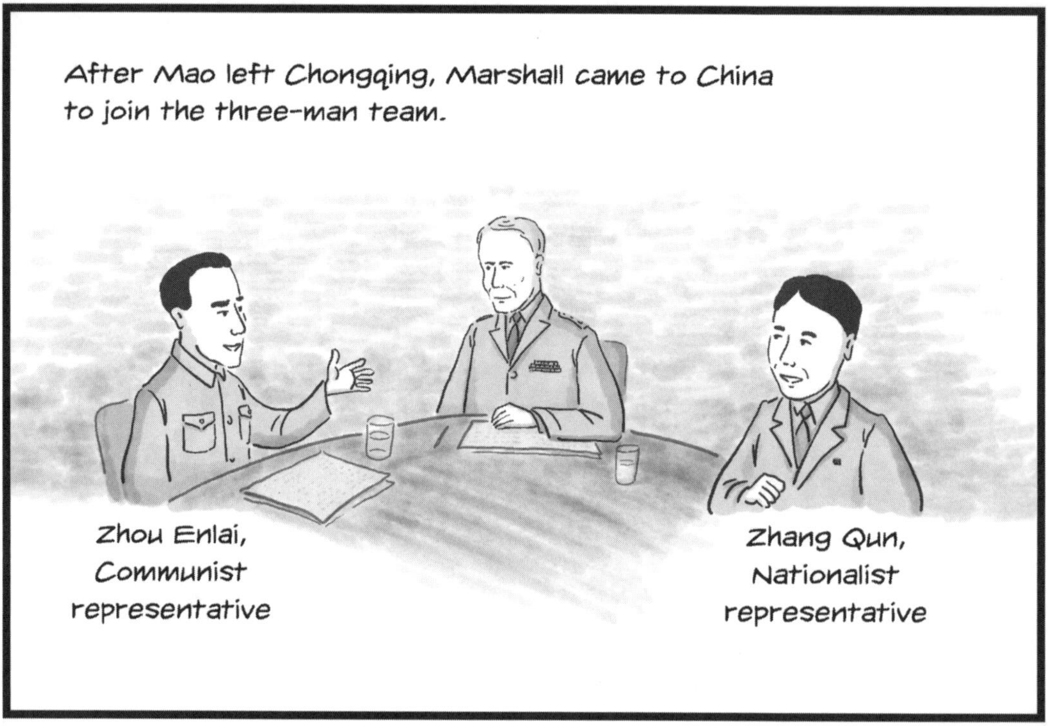
After Mao left Chongqing, Marshall came to China to join the three-man team.
Zhou Enlai, Communist representative
Zhang Qun, Nationalist representative

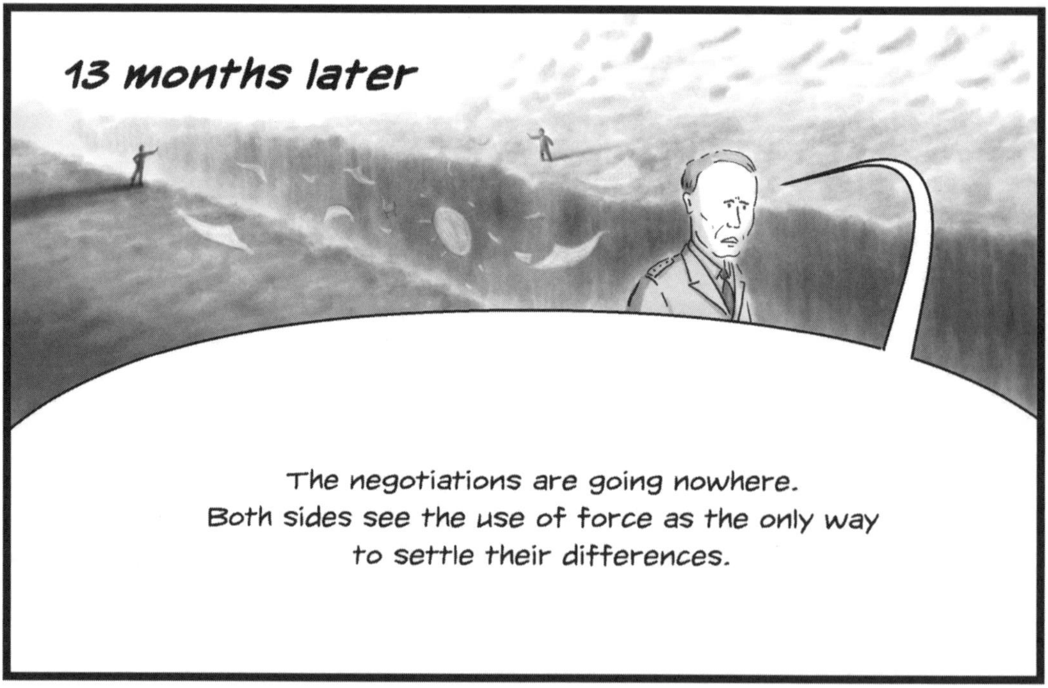
13 months later
The negotiations are going nowhere. Both sides see the use of force as the only way to settle their differences.

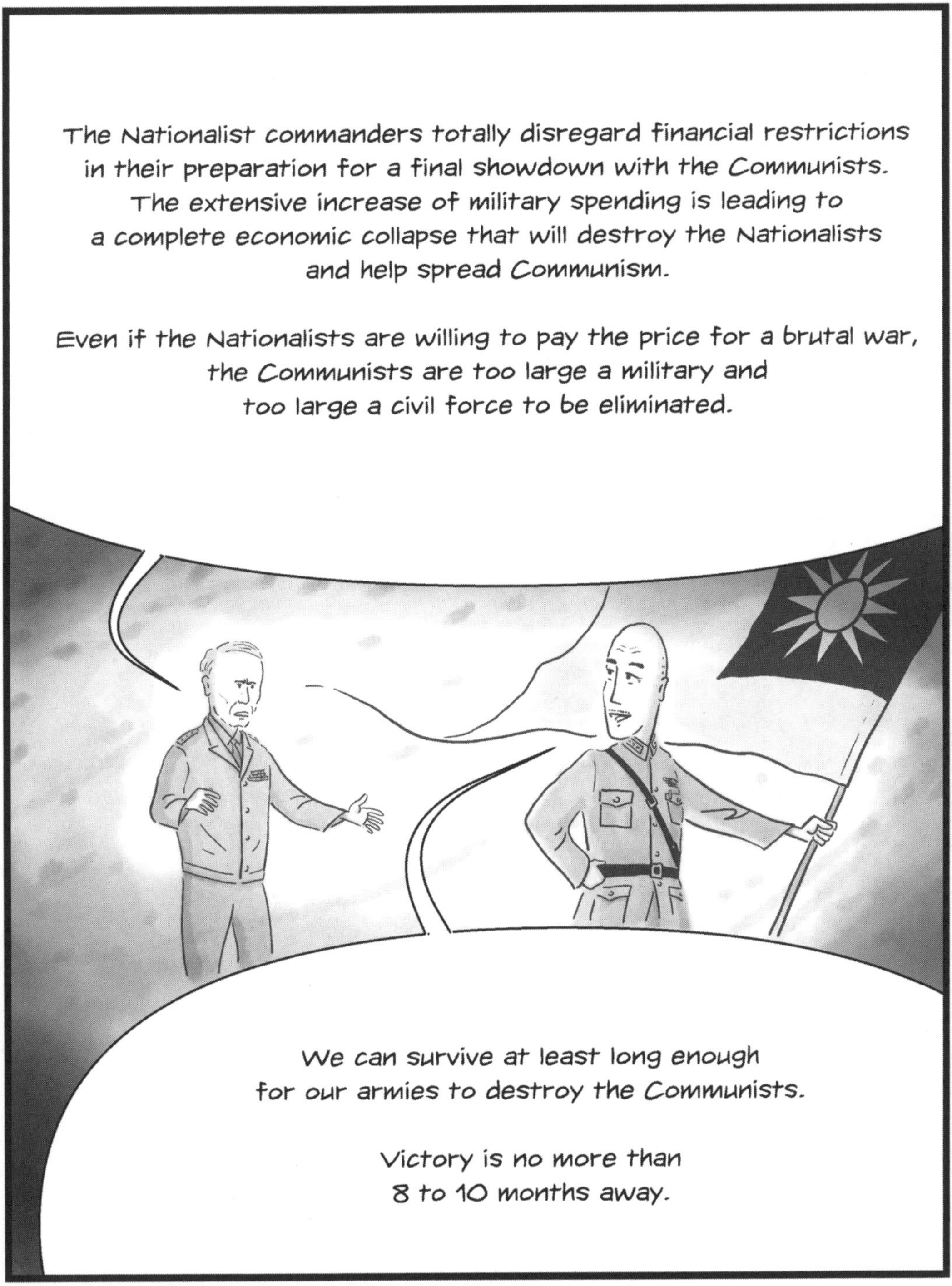
The Nationalist commanders totally disregard financial restrictions in their preparation for a final showdown with the Communists. The extensive increase of military spending is leading to a complete economic collapse that will destroy the Nationalists and help spread Communism.
Even if the Nationalists are willing to pay the price for a brutal war, the Communists are too large a military and too large a civil force to be eliminated.
We can survive at least long enough for our armies to destroy the Communists.
Victory is no more than 8 to 10 months away.

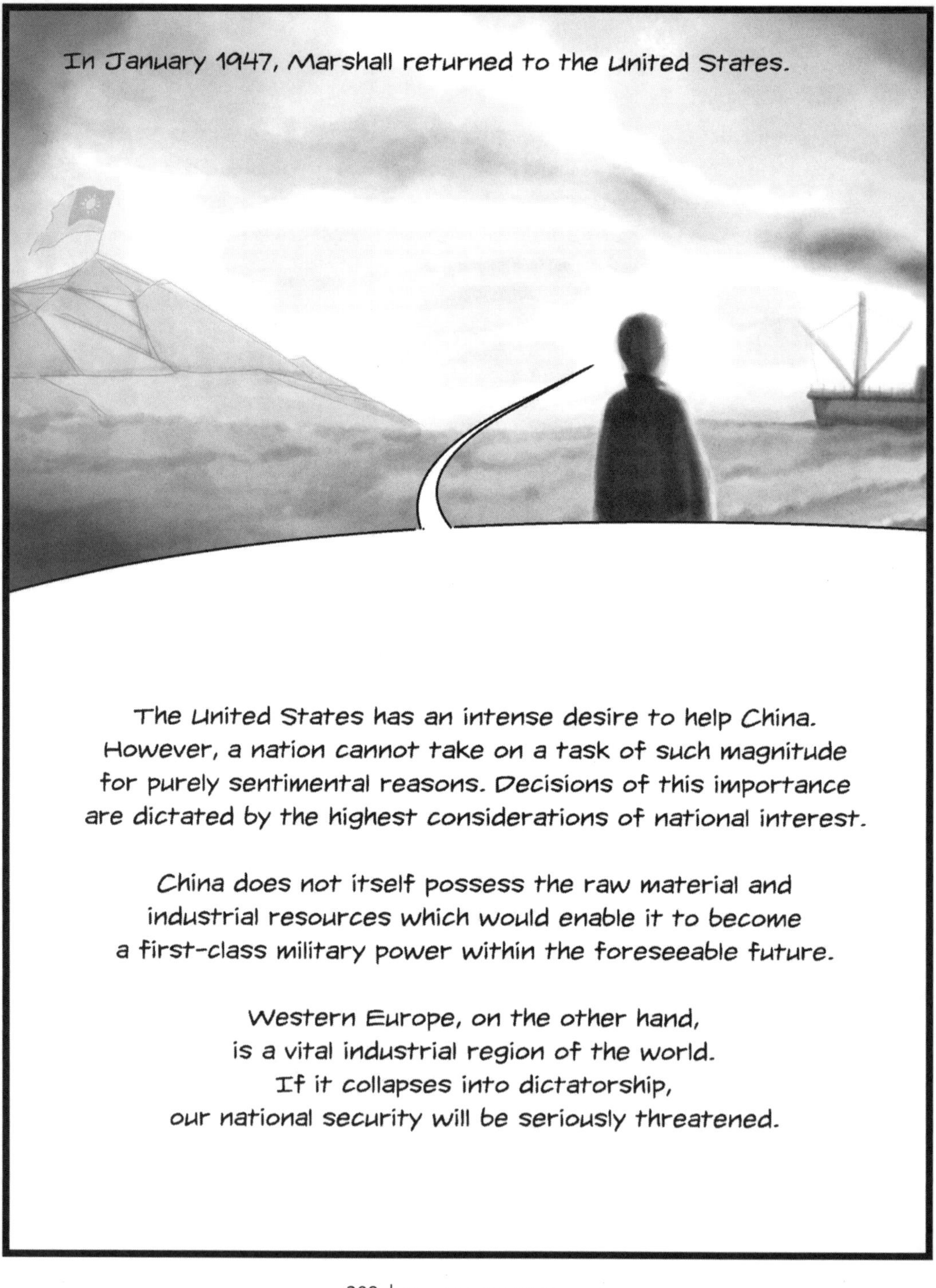
In January 1947, Marshall returned to the United States.
The United States has an intense desire to help China. However, a nation cannot take on a task of such magnitude for purely sentimental reasons. Decisions of this importance are dictated by the highest considerations of national interest.
China does not itself possess the raw material and industrial resources which would enable it to become a first-class military power within the foreseeable future.
Western Europe, on the other hand, is a vital industrial region of the world. If it collapses into dictatorship, our national security will be seriously threatened.

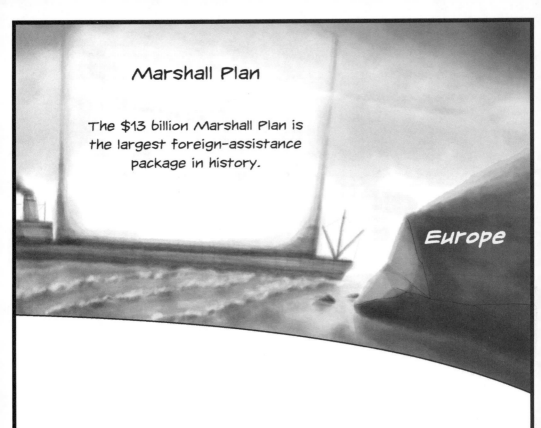

Marshall Plan

The $13 billion Marshall Plan is
the largest foreign-assistance
package in history.

Europe

Furthermore, we cannot afford, economically or militarily,
to make the Nationalist government capable of reestablishing
its control throughout all of China.

The United States should focus on European economic recovery.
The effort will cost our country billions of dollars.
It will impose a burden on the American taxpayer.
It will require sacrifices today in order that
we may enjoy security and peace tomorrow.

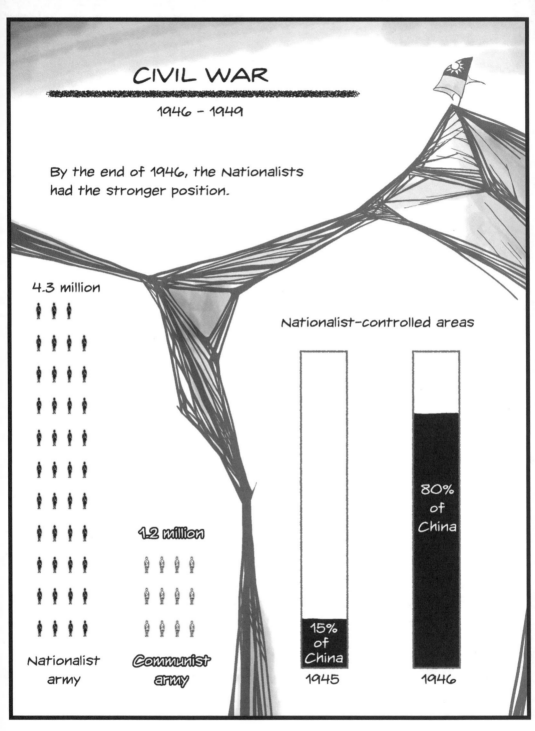

CIVIL WAR

1946 – 1949

By the end of 1946, the Nationalists had the stronger position.

4.3 million

1.2 million

Nationalist army

Communist army

Nationalist-controlled areas

15% of China

1945

80% of China

1946

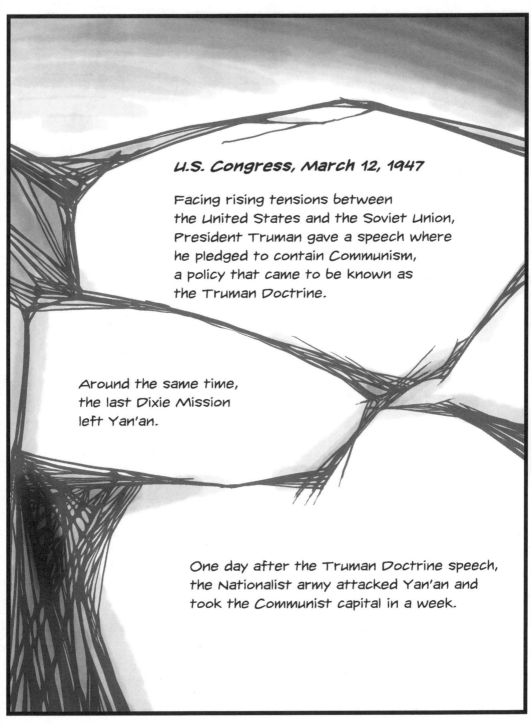

U.S. Congress, March 12, 1947

Facing rising tensions between
the United States and the Soviet Union,
President Truman gave a speech where
he pledged to contain Communism,
a policy that came to be known as
the Truman Doctrine.

Around the same time,
the last Dixie Mission
left Yan'an.

One day after the Truman Doctrine speech,
the Nationalist army attacked Yan'an and
took the Communist capital in a week.

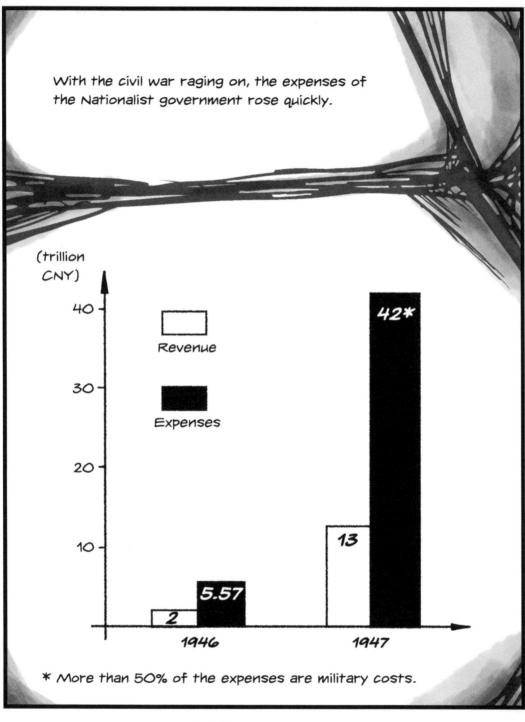

With the civil war raging on, the expenses of the Nationalist government rose quickly.

(trillion CNY)

Revenue

Expenses

40

30

20

10

2 | 5.57

1946

13 | 42*

1947

* More than 50% of the expenses are military costs.

The Nationalist government printed more money to cover the deficit. In 1947, hyperinflation kicked in and riots started in cities.

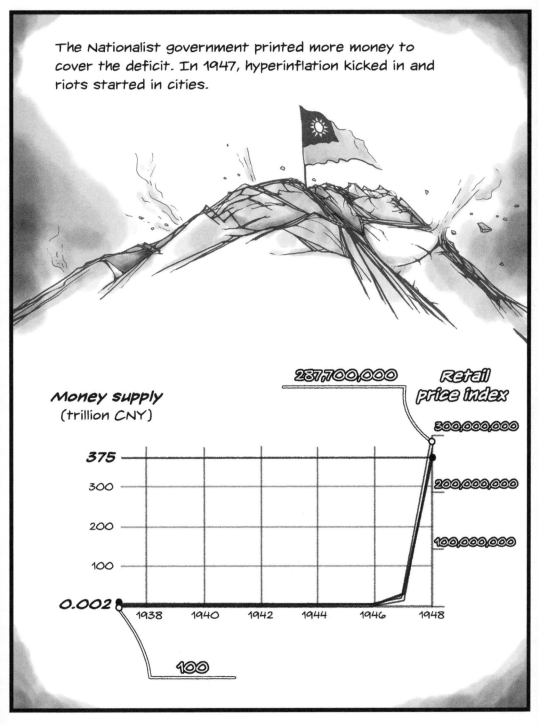

Money supply
(trillion CNY)

287,700,000

Retail
price index

300,000,000

375

300

200,000,000

200

100

100,000,000

0.002

1938   1940   1942   1944   1946   1948

100

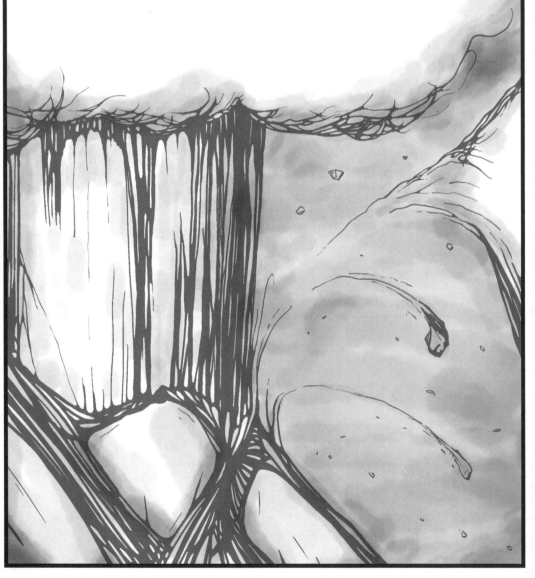

September 1947

While the Nationalists were being overwhelmed
by the economic and social crisis,
the Communists attacked.

Millions of Nationalist troops ended up switching sides, making up around 70% of the 4 million Communist army.

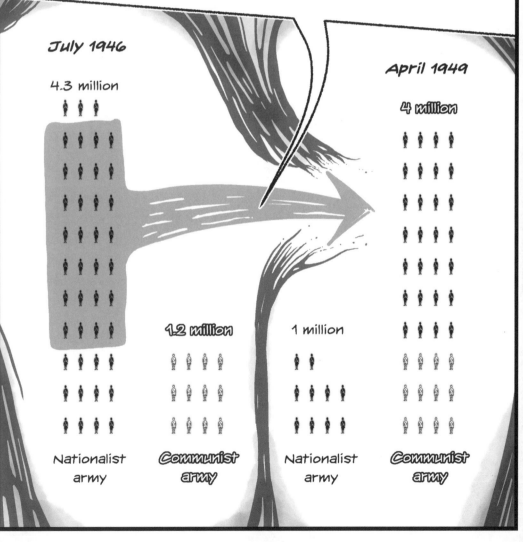

July 1946

4.3 million

1.2 million

Nationalist army

Communist army

April 1949

4 million

1 million

Nationalist army

Communist army

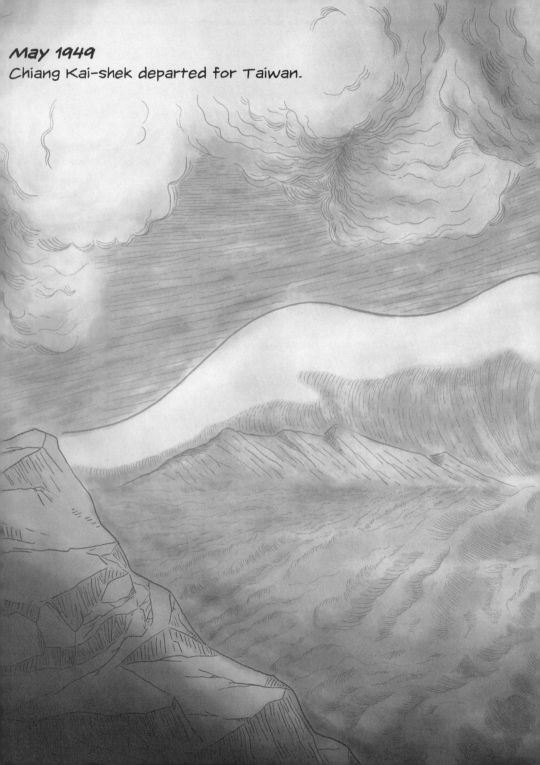

May 1949
Chiang Kai-shek departed for Taiwan.

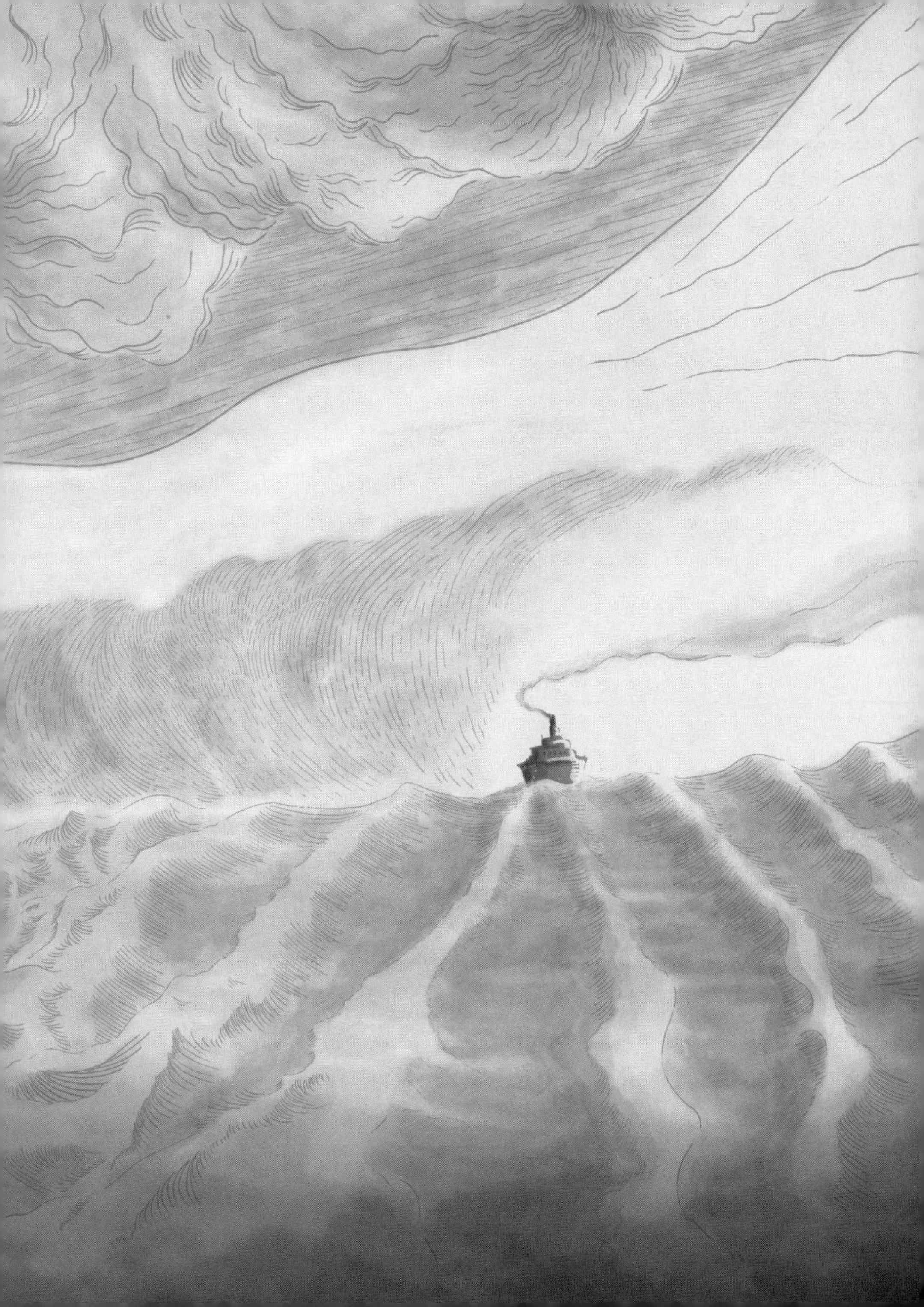

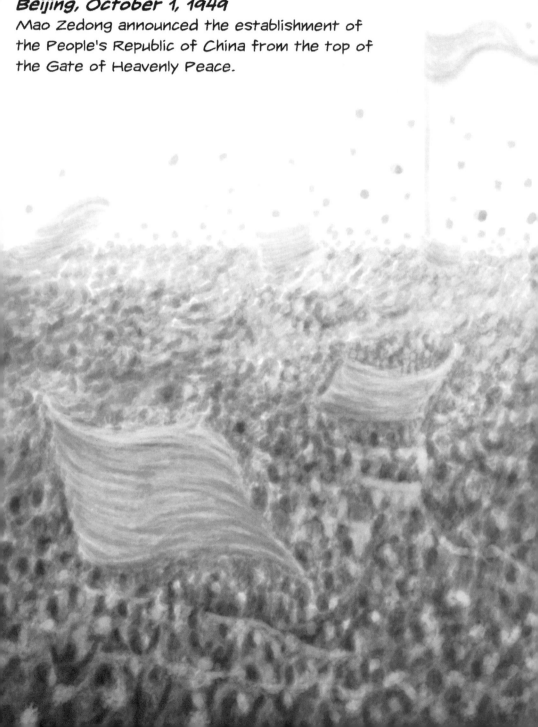

Beijing, October 1, 1949
Mao Zedong announced the establishment of the People's Republic of China from the top of the Gate of Heavenly Peace.

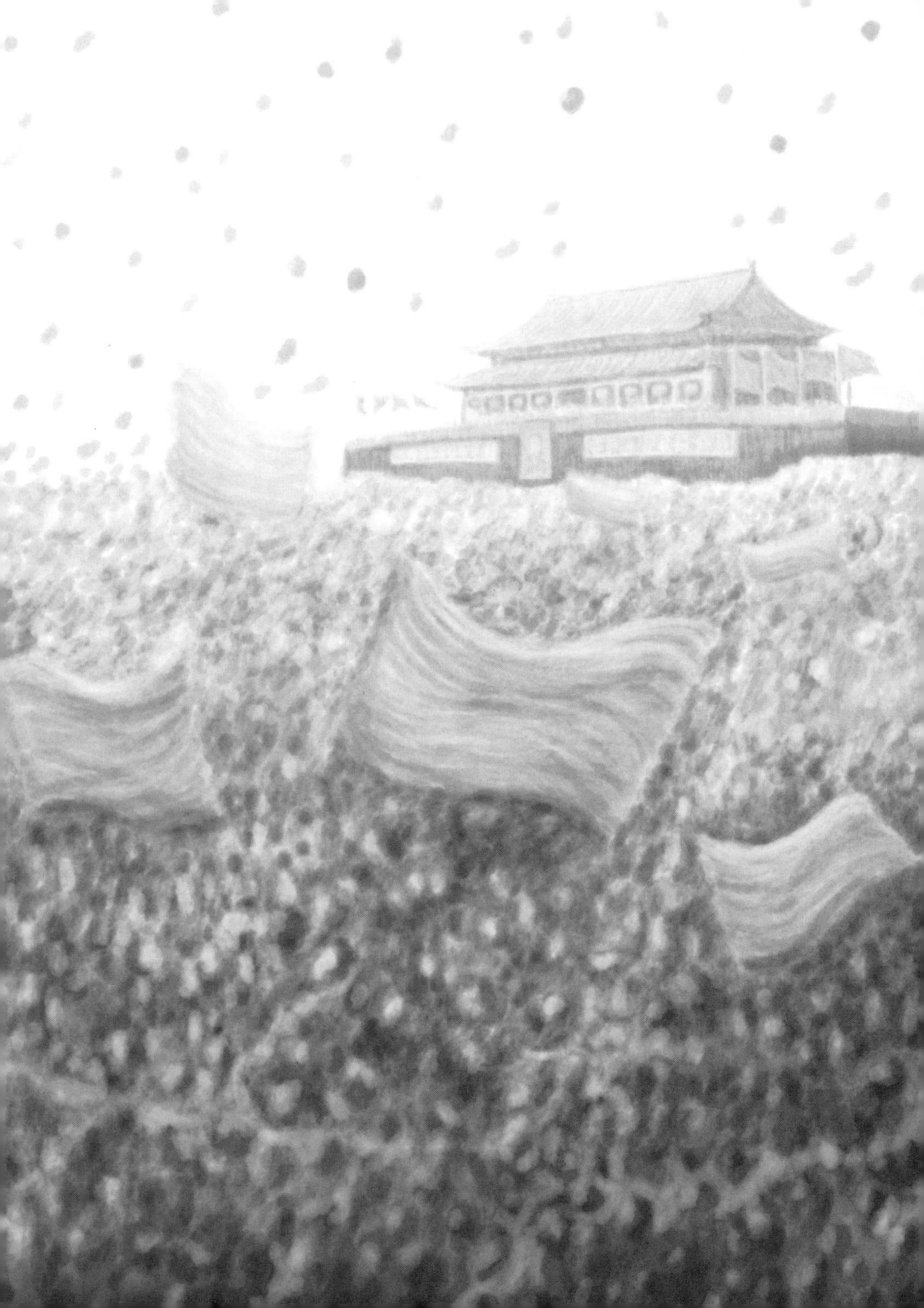

Shortly after the Chinese Communist victory, U.S. Senator Joseph McCarthy charged that George Marshall and John Service were directly responsible for the loss of China to Communism.

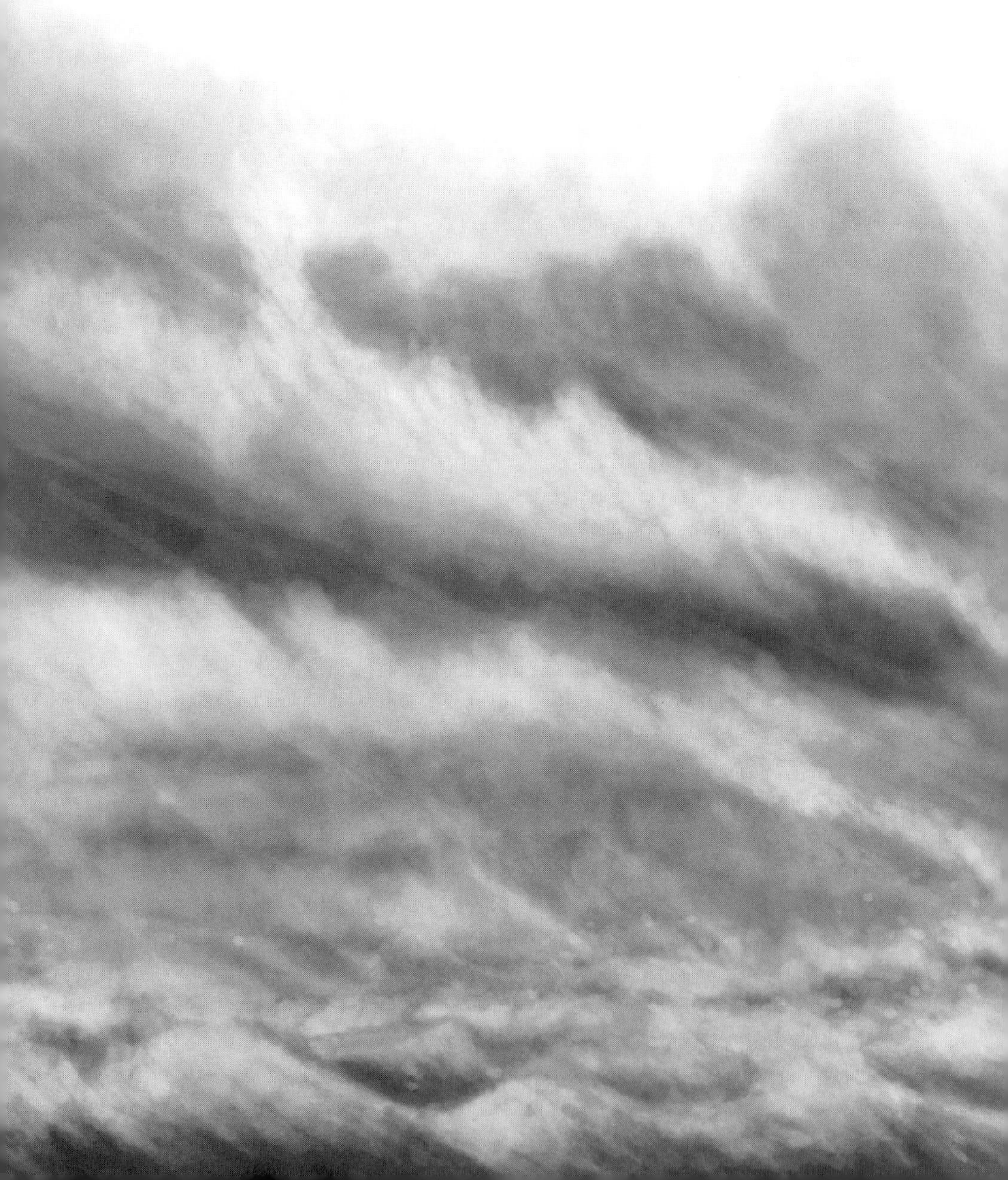

Fearing another Communist takeover in Asia, President Truman committed armed forces to the Korean War (1950 – 1953).

Sensing the danger of another invasion of northeast China through Korea, like the one conducted by the Japanese, Mao sent the People's Volunteer Army into North Korea.

Less than a year after the Korean War, the United States stepped in to aid South Vietnam and continue its policy of trying to contain Communism.

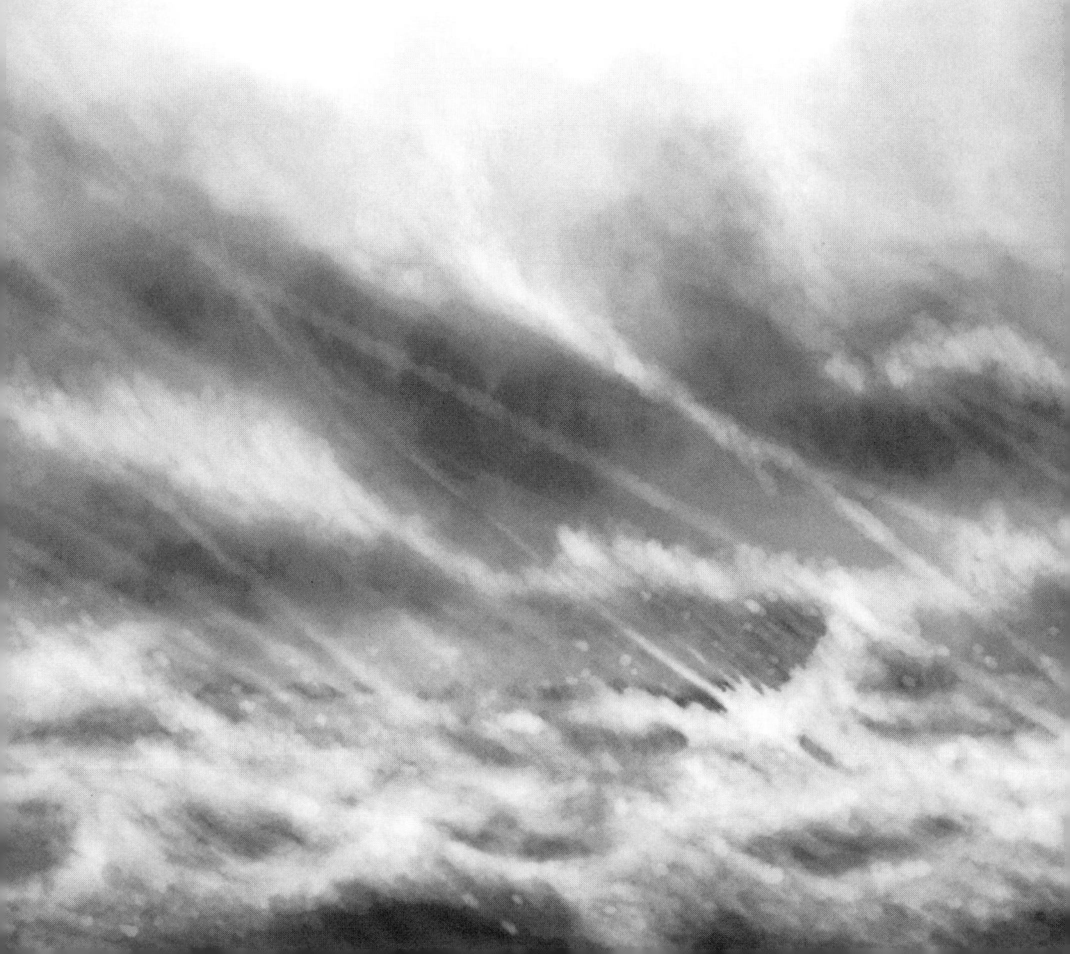

NOTES AND SUGGESTED READING

Pronouncing Chinese names can be difficult. To keep things as simple as possible I've kept all Chinese names in pinyin, the standard phonetic method for transcribing Chinese words.

The only exceptions are names previously romanized according to different standards that are now very common. An example is the name of Chinese Nationalist leader Chiang Kai-shek. If I were to write it in Mandarin pinyin it would be spelled "Jiang Jieshi." Instead, I use "Chiang Kai-shek," a well-known romanization based on the Cantonese pronunciation of his name.

If you want to check your pinyin pronunciation, there are a number of useful online resources available to you. An excellent web dictionary with audio capabilities can be found at www.mdbg.net. The Pleco app for iOS and Android phones allows you to check proper pronunciation.

In writing *The Way Forward* I relied on a number of sources. These include:

The Cambridge History of China by John K. Fairbank

The China Mission: George Marshall's Unfinished War by Daniel Kurtz-Phelan

The Generalissimo: Chiang Kai-shek and the Struggle for Modern China by Jay Taylor

Global Economic History: A Very Short Introduction by Robert C. Allen

Historical documents from the Office of the Historian, U.S. Department of State

Lost Chance in China by John S. Service and Joseph W. Esherick

Mao Zedong and The Search for Modern China by Jonathan D. Spence

Read Chiang's Diary from Macro History Perspective by Ray Huang Renyu

Red Star Over China by Edgar Snow

Stilwell and the American Experience in China by Barbara W. Tuchman

United States Relations with China: With Special Reference to the Period 1944–1949 by the United States Department of State

ACKNOWLEDGMENTS

To Sara, Elizabeth, Malcolm, Connor, Katelyn, Jackson, Yifu, and many, many more children who have been born with a connection to China.

BOOKS IN THIS SERIES

Volume 1

Foundations of Chinese Civilization:
The Yellow Emperor to the Han Dynasty
(2697 BCE – 220 CE)

Volume 2

Division to Unification in Imperial
China: The Three Kingdoms to the Tang
Dynasty (220 – 907)

Volume 3

Barbarians and the Birth of Chinese
Identity: The Five Dynasties and
Ten Kingdoms to the Yuan Dynasty
(907 – 1368)

Volume 4

The Making of Modern China: The
Ming Dynasty to the Qing Dynasty
(1368 – 1912)